WESLEY: THE PI

and

NEWTON: THE LIBERATOR

By the same author:

Two Timeless Books in One

Wesley
The Preacher

JOHN POLLOCK

KINGSWAY PUBLICATIONS
EASTBOURNE

Cover design: PinnacleCreative.co.uk
Front cover photo © Marty141 | Dreamstime.com

ISBN 978 1 84291 387 1

Published by
KINGSWAY COMMUNICATIONS LTD
26-28 Lottbridge Drove, Eastbourne BN23 6NT, UK
books@kingsway.co.uk

Printed in Great Britain

Contents

Preface

The Edge of the Sea

Peter Martin, the hostler of the London Inn at Redruth, Cornwall, was harnessing two post-horses to a small carriage which had driven in from the East one day in the late 1770s.

He had already washed down the carriage and polished it extra bright, for it belonged to the Reverend John Wesley, still traveling despite his great age. Dusting the inside, Peter had admired the ingenious desk and book rack; Mr. Wesley must work all the time, despite the swaying and shaking on the rough roads of England.

Peter had heard him preach some years earlier to a big crowd near the marketplace in Helston. He had also heard the old folk tell stories of the riots and stonings which had greeted the Wesley brothers when they had first preached in Cornwall, and of their courage, and how they spoke so plainly that all could understand. By now there were thousands in Cornwall who followed their teaching, went to church, met in societies and classes, and sang those stirring hymns.

Mr. Wesley was in the inn eating his dinner at the round table with the other wayfarers, and to judge by a roar of laughter, he must have been telling one of his innumerable anecdotes. Then there was silence, and Peter Martin guessed that Mr. Wesley was speaking of the things of God.

His thoughts were interrupted by Wesley's servant, who looked worried. He did not know the road beyond Redruth, he said, and had heard that the ford across the Hayle estuary could be dangerous: would the hostler drive if his master gave him leave? Mr. Wesley had promised to preach at St. Ives that evening.

The neat little parson in black left the inn and entered the carriage with a smile to Peter, who then put the horses in the shafts and mounted the right-hand animal. With Wesley reading or writing inside, the hostler drove the twelve miles to Hayle against a freshening wind. Beyond Hayle, at that time, the main road ran down the right bank of the Hayle River toward the sea. It then disappeared into the sands. Peter Martin and every local knew the ford exactly, and at low tide the wheels of a carriage hardly got wet. But the tide was coming in now, and the wind was rising. The broad sands along the shore were narrowing every minute, and the estuary was filling with rough water. Peter could see St. Ives on its low cliff to the northwest and the steep rise from the sand where the road began again, but a deepening channel of choppy sea cut them off. He stopped the carriage. He recalled in old age: "I advised Mr. Wesley of the danger of the crossing." The captain of a vessel awaiting the tide saw them stop and came up "to dissuade us from an undertaking so full of peril."

Wesley listened politely but said he must keep his appointment to preach: "Looking out the carriage window, he called loudly to me, 'Take the sea! Take the sea!'"

Peter Martin spurred the horses, and the carriage entered the ford with a splash: "The horses were now swimming," his story continued, "and the carriage became nearly overwhelmed with the tide, as its hinder wheels not infrequently merged into the deep pits and hollows in the sands. I struggled hard to maintain my seat in the saddle, while the poor affrighted animals were snorting and rearing in the most terrific manner and furiously plunging through the opposing waves. I expected every moment to be swept into eternity, and the only hope of escape I then cherished was on account of my driving so holy a man."

He heard Wesley call to him. Turning with difficulty in the saddle, he saw Wesley's "long white locks dripping the salt sea down the rugged furrows of his venerable countenance. He was looking calmly forth from the windows, undisturbed by the tumultuous war of the surrounding waters or by the danger of his perilous situation."

Wesley called, quite loudly, "What is thy name, driver?"

"Peter."

"Peter, fear not; thou shalt not sink!"

Wesley put back his head and Peter urged on the horses. They got safely over, but, as Peter recalled, "It was a miracle, as I shall always say."

They arrived at St. Ives, both wet. "Mr. Wesley's first care was to see me confortably lodged at the tavern: he procured me warm clothes, a good fire, and excellent refreshments. Nor were the horses forgotten by him.

"Totally unmindful of himself, he proceeded, wet as he was, to the chapel, and preached according to his appointment."

A biographer of Wesley may well feel like Peter, in danger of being drowned—in the sea of material: the millions of words that

Wesley wrote, in diary and journal, sermons and letters and books; and the millions of words written about him, whether in full-length biographies running to three and even to six volumes, or in studies and articles on every aspect of his life and thought. Since his death two centuries ago, biographies have been written from every angle: the admiring and hostile, the social, psychological, and technological. Writers have sought to interpret or even to reconstruct him according to their own preconceptions, or to place him on a slab and dissect him.

As I looked at the literature, reread the journals, and recalled how often Wesley had influenced, directly or posthumously, the subjects of my previous biographies, I realized that there was a need for a straightforward book. It must have more substance than the excellent brief biographies and be true to the man, his times, and his faith, yet not drown the reader by attempting to describe and discuss every aspect and activity. Moreover, research on John Wesley has advanced rapidly in the last quarter of the twentieth century, putting out of date many earlier conclusions, even demolishing some of the stories.

By the 250th anniversary of his conversion, May 1988, nine volumes had appeared of the magisterial Bicentennial (formerly Oxford) Edition of *The Works of John Wesley*. By March 2, 1991, when we marked the 200th anniversary of his death, many more were in various stages of preparation. The project is long term, but when all thirty-five volumes have appeared, most of his vast output, public or private, will be in print.

Brilliantly edited, with wide-ranging introductions, the Bicentennial *Works* gives Wesley to the world in a depth and accuracy never before attained. When it is complete, an able historical biographer who can spare several years will be able to produce a more definitive life. Until then, I hope that readers will catch something of Wesley's humanity, his faith, and his achievement as they come with me. I confess that I feel I have been paddling on the edge of the ocean. I can only hope that many readers will wish to put out to sea, as it were, embarking on a fresh study of his letters or the journal with its reflections and hundreds of anecdotes. (A biographer must not fall into Wesley's own fault in his old age—too many anecdotes.) Readers may also be spurred by my book to study closely some of the aspects which I can only show briefly as the story moves.

I should add that I refer to John Wesley usually as "Wesley," once past his youth. To call him just "John" in the modern manner seems distasteful, although in some instances John is used for clarity. He was scarcely ever addressed as John: to his mother, brothers, and sisters, he was Jacky or Jack; to his father, Jack or "son John"; most of his contemporaries referred to him as Mr. Wesley or Brother Wesley; possibly only Molly, the partner in his unfortunate marriage, called him John.

John Wesley, in a real sense, belongs to the whole world and to every age and church. He is particularly relevant to his own country because his revival was a primary factor in changing national attitudes and character, although the change was not widely evident for two or more generations. Victorian values (in the true sense of the phrase) are really Wesley's values, which are Christian values.

Wesley saw what Britain needed: a strong Christian message and morality. He had the courage to endure hostility and unpopularity for what he believed to be right. He succeeded, and thus gives a resounding message of hope.

Part One

WALKING TO GLORY

1703–1737

1

Plucked from the Burning

The room seemed light already, yet the bed curtains were closed, and the nursemaid had not got him up. Jacky lay puzzled for a moment, then put out his head from the four-poster. He saw streaks of fire on the ceiling.

In the lurid glow he noticed that Molly and Anne, two of his sisters who slept in the same great bed with him, were gone, and the other bed, where the nurse slept with Patty and baby Charles, was empty. Five-year-old Jacky ran to the open door. The floor outside was ablaze. He ran back and climbed onto a chest of drawers near the window and pulled at the latch.

Above him the thatched roof of the rectory crackled and burned in the strong northeast wind. Below, a crowd of neighbors were gathered in the yard and were trying to douse the flames. Jacky edged onto the windowsill as far as he dared. He saw a man point up, then call out that he would fetch a ladder.

Another cried, "There will not be time!" This tall, burly neighbor leaned against the wall while eager hands helped a lighter man to climb onto his shoulders. As the heat behind Jacky grew intense, the fellow stood upright, stretched his arms, and plucked the boy out of the window. At that moment the roof fell in, "but it fell inward, or we had all been crushed at once."

They carried Jacky to the house where the family had taken refuge. Apparently Hetty, who was eleven, had been woken by a piece of burning thatch and had given the alarm. Their father, the rector of Epworth, had run to the room where his wife slept apart because she was ill and pregnant. She woke their eldest daughter, and they dashed through the flames to safety.

Then the rector rushed upstairs to the nursery. The maid seized baby Charles and ordered the others to follow, but no one noticed that Jacky lay fast asleep through the uproar. When the rector realized the child was missing, he tried to get up the stairs again, but they were on fire and would not bear his weight. In agony of mind he knelt in the hall and commended John Wesley's soul to God.

But here was Jacky safe and sound, "a brand plucked out of the burning." The Reverend Samuel Wesley, his house in ashes, his books and writings gone, cried out in joy: "Come, neighbors! Let us kneel down! Let us give thanks to God! He has given me all eight children. Let the house go. I am rich enough!"

The family found shelter in the homes of neighbors or relatives, except for the eldest child, Samuel, who was away at Westminster School. Soon the rectory was being rebuilt in red brick with a tiled roof, and long before it was finished the children were together again, and their mother, who was exceptionally well-read for a woman of the reign of Queen Anne, had resumed their lessons.

Jacky Wesley[1] grew up in an extraordinary household. Both parents had distant connections with the peerage and with landed gentry. Each came from Dissenting families but had rejoined the Church of England. Wesley's grandfather and great-grandfather, both as diminutive as his father, had been rectors of parishes in Dorset until ejected for refusing to accept the new *Book of Common Prayer* in 1662. His grandfather, John Wesley, an ardent young Puritan preacher, had suffered imprisonment after the Restoration Settlement, like John Bunyan, and had died when Wesley's father, Samuel, was four.

Samuel went to a Dissenting academy, then he conformed—an act of conscience which opened the way to Oxford University. Having no money, he walked there and entered Exeter College as a servitor, the lowest rank of undergraduate, and survived much poverty to take his degree and to be ordained. He then eked out his small stipend as a curate in London by writing witty essays and poor verse for a magazine and married his editor's sister-in-law.

Samuel's bride, Susanna ("Sukey"), was the youngest of numerous children born to the respected and scholarly leader of London's Dissenters, Dr. Samuel Annesley. She was beautiful, scholarly, and serious. Like her husband, she had read herself out of her father's nonconformity into an adherence to the high church party in the Church of England.

Samuel secured a small country living at South Ormsby in Lincolnshire through the influence of John Sheffield, Earl of Mulgrave, but in 1696 he offended a local nobleman by refusing to receive his mistress. Anxious to move, he obtained the parish of Epworth, which was in the gift of the Crown, and settled in that small struggling town in a remote part of north Lincolnshire. He believed that he had received it at the dying wish of Queen Mary II, to whom he had dedicated a "Life of Christ" in heroic verse and who had refused him an Irish bishopric. Since she had died two years before he obtained the living, he is more likely to have owed the preferment to the influence of his patron John Sheffield, now Marquess of Normanby, the principal landowner of the district.

At Epworth, Susanna continued to bear a child a year, five of whom died. By early 1702 the Wesleys had one surviving son, Samuel, and five daughters, including the latest baby, Anne. She might have been the last—for the rector left his wife.

Both Samuel and Susanna were strong willed with violent loyalties. They were Tories, but he supported William III while she sympathized with the non-jurors, those bishops and clergy who had refused the oath of allegiance to William and had lost their dioceses and livings. Her heart was with the exiled James II. Each day at evening household prayers the rector prayed for "our sovereign Lord, King William." His wife said "Amen" but seems to have silently switched the petition to "the King over the water." When the news trickled down to Epworth that James II had died in exile, she stopped saying "Amen," "upon which," she wrote to Lady Yarborough, a kindly neighbor fourteen miles away, "he retired to his study, and calling me to him asked me the reason of my not saying 'Amen' to the prayer.

"I was a little surprised at the question and don't well remember what I answered, but too well I remember what followed. He immediately kneeled down and imprecated the divine Vengeance upon himself and all his posterity if ever he touched me more or came into a bed with me before I had begged God's pardon and his, for not saying 'Amen' to the prayer for the King."

Samuel moved to another room. Susanna refused to recant, despite "my extreme affliction" that "he will not live with me." After Easter he went to London for convocation, muttering that he would never return; he would go to sea again as a naval chaplain, such as he had been briefly before they were married.

King William had died in March. Queen Anne, an undoubted Stuart, had ascended the throne. Yet the rector would not forgive his wife, and though he returned from London, he kept away from her body. Then, in July, their thatched rectory caught fire and was three-quarters burned. This first fire brought him to his senses.

In August 1702 the Wesleys slept together again, and on June 17, 1703 John Wesley was born.

In a sense he owed his existence to Queen Anne's accession and to a fire. Five years and eight months later, in February 1709, his life was saved by that stalwart neighbor in that second fire.

In later years John Wesley would often apply to his life the Old Testament text "A brand plucked out of the burning," yet he did not think of himself as a child of destiny nor did his parents. Though Susanna pledged herself to take particular care of Jacky's soul, they loved all their children. Jacky was their fifteenth, including the two sets of twins whose tiny graves were their only memorial. He was the seventh to survive, to be followed by Martha, Charles, and finally Kezia (Kezzy) born soon after the second fire.

In the years of Jacky's early childhood, his father was in his late forties, and his mother, though eight years younger, seemed already middle-aged through much childbearing and ill health. Samuel Wesley was a hard-working, rather disorganized clergyman. When he was not out among his parishioners as they weaved their flax or worked their hemp or cut the peat which lay all around, he would be scribbling his heroic verse or compiling a parallel Bible in Hebrew, Greek, and "Chaldee" (Aramaic) or preparing his monumental commentary (in Latin) on the Book of Job. A stout upholder of the orthodox doctrines of the Church of England, he was also one of the small band of church people, scattered across the land, who wanted to spread Christianity throughout the world. Were it not for his large family, he would willingly have sailed to distant parts.

As a rector, he held glebe lands which he tried to farm. His soil was fertile, since the Isle of Axenholme, on which Epworth stood, had once been mainly a marsh, drained in the previous century. But his efforts had little success and only increased his debts, especially when his barn fell down and his flax caught fire.

Nor was he popular with the morose and inbred inhabitants of Axenholme, then one of the most isolated parts of eastern England, so low-lying that in winter or spring the flooding of three rivers would frequently cut off Epworth from the Lincolnshire wolds except by boat. Even the roads, passable in dry weather, were merely cart tracks across the fields.

Despite his wit and his laugh, Samuel Wesley's high moral teaching annoyed many of his people. Once he had to stand up to a mob, and when his Tory convictions and loyalty to the Church, which the Whigs seemed to threaten, thrust him into the thick of a general election, his enemies turned on him. In London they canceled his military chaplaincy, and at Epworth they maimed his cows, which ran dry, so that his debts increased yet more.

One Friday morning, when he came out of church after a baptism, he was confronted by a bailiff who demanded immediate repayment of a debt. Samuel Wesley asked for a few hours' grace. This was refused. He was arrested in his own churchyard and carted off to the debtors prison in Lincoln Castle, where he promptly began services, distributed books, and quipped that he was "getting acquainted with my brother jailbirds as fast as I can."

Susanna was left to find bread for the children and the servants until wealthy friends could send donations which cleared the debt and allowed the rector to return home. John Wesley once commented that his mother "did not *feel* for others near so much as my father did; but she *did* ten times more than he did," both among the poor and needy and in her own home. Susanna always managed the household. She regarded her husband as her master, though she argued with him frequently. But he left the details of kitchen, nursery, and schoolroom to her.

She had strong views on the upbringing of their children: "The first thing to be done is to break their wills and bring them to an obedient temper." She taught them to fear the rod—the universal sanction of the day for children of both sexes—and never to cry when beaten but to "murmur softly." She held that to spoil a child was a worse cruelty than the rod, yet she never stinted praise and encouragement. She also laid down a law that if a child confessed a naughtiness, he or she would not be beaten; but to her disgust, the children could often get round their father and be let off without acknowledging a wrong, even when caught red-handed.

She was a brilliant teacher. Jacky, like the others before him, was not allowed to read until he was five, with the result that he developed a good memory by ear, especially for the stories in the Bible. On the day after his fifth birthday he was taught the letters of the alphabet and told to read the first verses of Genesis. Since he almost knew the creation of the world by heart, he learned quickly, and like his elder brother and sisters, he could read within two days.

The children sat together in class, each doing a lesson appropriate to age. Since Samuel had gone to Westminster School and then to Oxford, and Charles was too young, Jacky was virtually being educated in a girls' school. Discipline was strict during the daily six hours of lessons—no running into the garden or playing around until school was out. Each weekday evening Susanna taught one child individually; Jacky's turn came on Thursdays.

He was also taught from infancy to say the Lord's Prayer, night and morning, and other prayers and Bible passages as he grew older. Whatever his little mischiefs, he regarded piety as a part of life. Epworth might have its tumults and his parents their eccentricities and arguments, but they gave Jacky sound learning, a sensitive conscience, and good manners. They grounded him in classics and divinity and never discouraged his inquisitive mind.

He was happy and no rebel, though perhaps, surrounded by sisters, he was a little fastidious. Looking back on his childhood, John Wesley considered that by the age of ten he had not lost his innocence, "having been strictly educated, and carefully taught that I could only be saved 'by universal obedience, by keeping all the commandments of God,' in the meaning of which I was diligently instructed." He gladly received and often thought about the duties he must perform and the sins he must shun.

But it was all on the surface of his soul.

2

Slippery Paths of Youth

Lord Normanby, Samuel Wesley's patron, had received yet another step in the peerage and was now Duke of Buckingham. He had married King James II's illegitimate daughter immediately upon the death of her estranged husband, Lord Anglesey (an Annesley relative of Susanna) and had built Buckingham House in St. James' Park, the future royal palace, to keep her in style.

The duchess was regarded as the haughtiest woman in England, but she showed kindness to the Wesleys. The Buckinghams became aware that Jack's parents had no money for the next stage of his education.

The duke, Lord President of the Council, second only in the Cabinet to Robert Harley, Earl of Oxford, had been for many years a governor of Sutton's Hospital in Charterhouse, founded in 1611 by a soldier who had made a great fortune in coal. Thomas Sutton had provided free education for eighty pensioner brothers, such as former sea captains, military officers who had been captives of the infidels, or merchants who had fallen on evil times; and for forty boys of similar class, to be called "gownboys," from the scholar's gown which they wore in class and chapel. He had bought the Charterhouse, the former Carthusian monastery which had been made into a great Tudor mansion after the Dissolution. It lay just beyond the walls of the city of London to the northwest, a few hundred yards from Smithfield, the open space where Protestant martyrs had been burned at the stake and which now was used as a market for the herds of cattle which came on the hoof from the provinces.

When a gownboy left school, each governor of Charterhouse had the right in rotation to nominate a replacement. The Duke of Buckingham nominated John Wesley, aged ten, "in the place of Thomas Tipping."

In January 1714, therefore, eight months before the death of Queen Anne, Jack made the long winter journey on rough roads from northern Lincolnshire to London, probably in the care of his elder brother since Samuel was now an usher at Westminster School. Despite the twelve-year gap in age, they were close friends. Jack's respect for Samuel never wavered, even when theology divided them.

On January 28, dressed as a gownboy in black breeches and jerkin (short coat) with white collar under a long black coat, John Wesley entered the Charterhouse with its wide courts and stone buildings. Only one other new boy had come that quarter, and Wesley was the youngest gownboy, by nearly a year, until one William Camell arrived six months later, only to die of smallpox within weeks.

The whole school numbered about 100 Carthusians. Detailed evidence for the early eighteenth-century Charterhouse is scarce, but apparently it now included fee-paying Oppidans. They were day boys or lodgers in nearby private houses, while the lives of the gownboys centered on the Duke of Norfolk's former indoor tennis court (for the "royal" or "real" game) which had been redesigned internally with two floors. Upstairs were the bitterly cold dormitories where gownboys slept two to a bed—no hardship for a Wesley from Epworth rectory. Downstairs, the Writing School ran the former tennis court's full seventy feet. The splendidly paneled ceiling, one of the finest in Europe, was decorated with the armorial bearings of the first governors, which were blackened by a hundred years of London fogs and the smoke of sea coals burning in the great fireplace. Under this ceiling, between the square-cut oak columns, the classes sat all in one room. Wesley learned more Greek and Latin classics than his parents could teach, and presumably he felt the usher's cane or the schoolmaster's birch rod for wrong translations or petty misdeeds.

The schoolmaster was the elderly Dr. Thomas Walker. His chief assistant, the usher, who later succeeded him, was the learned Andrew Tooke, professor of geometry and author of a celebrated schoolbook on Greek mythology—Wesley would have had to learn it by heart. He also learned much of the *Greek Anthology*. Two centuries later, when the school had moved to Surrey, a headmaster, whose hobby was to rummage among uncataloged books in the small hours of the night, discovered a copy of the *Anthology* in which Tooke (or perhaps an assistant usher) had listed the boys in his class. Among them came the name: Wesley. It was later found in other textbooks of the period.

Few of Wesley's contemporaries were outstanding. James Hotchkis, son of a canon of St. Paul's, and Eberhard Crusius, son of another London clergyman, grew up to follow one another as schoolmasters of Charterhouse, Crusius having acquired some celebrity for his *Lives of Roman Poets*. Another boy, William Yorke, became chief justice of Ireland and was buried at Charterhouse. One of his class, the son of a Baltic baron, wrote a biography of Charles II's doctor. Eleven of the boys who sat with Wesley became clergymen.

The young scholars did not spend all day long in the Writing School. Games were not yet organized, but Charterhouse had converted the Great Cloister into a field called Green, where in summer they probably played a primitive form of cricket. The Carthusian version of football, in which a ball was dribbled up and down the cloisters by the feet of competing hordes of boys, was one of the ancestors of soccer, but Wesley made no mention of it. Nor does he mention the wild and dangerous primitive ball game played traditionally on Good Friday on Green, as in many parts of Europe, in which a boy as small as Wesley would have emerged bruised and muddy. His father had told him to run around Green three times every day before breakfast, and this he did, claiming that he owed his good health to the exercise.

It would have made him hungry. The main meal of the day was at noon. Wesley afterward claimed that the older boys ("the upper boys seemed to me to be very big and tall") bullied the younger by seizing their meat, so that for the most of his time he existed on bread, the explanation of his small stature. This explanation seems unlikely, because all the Wesleys were small.

If Wesley got plenty of knocks, this was normal. The school was well-disciplined for the times, but Carthusians were lively. Nine boys immediately junior to Wesley were involved (soon after he had left) in such "great misdemeanors and disorders" that they were degraded from their rank as monitors and reported to the governors, who ordered them to be punished "with due correction of the school," which was never administered publicly.

Every day the boys attended chapel. The gownboys sat on
the north side in front of the fine tomb of the founder, with its
recumbent effigy and coats of arms. The monitors sat at right angles
to the boys, and they were also under the eyes of the schoolmaster
and the usher in their stalls on either side of the communion rail
on the opposite sides of the chapel. Thus, while Dr. King, the
preacher, droned the liturgy or Dr. Burnet, the ancient master,
delivered long sermons, the boys could not doze, nudge each
other, or make faces at the elderly brothers in their black and gold
gowns.

Young Wesley reckoned that this regular chapel-going would
help earn his eternal salvation. He continued to say his prayers
morning and evening, and to read the Bible. But he was no
longer subject to his mother's strict spiritual discipline: "Outward
restraints being removed, I was much more negligent than before,
even of outward duties, and almost continually guilty of outward
sins, which I knew to be such, though they were not scandalous
in the eyes of the world." If there was sexual impurity in the
dormitories, he had no part in it, but the sensitive conscience
which Epworth had bred would nag him whenever he was angry
or greedy, when he swore, laughed at smut, or thought or did
whatever might have distressed his parents.

The Victorian biographer who asserted that "John Wesley
entered Charterhouse a saint, and left it a sinner" was wrong in his
facts and hazy in theology. The truth lies closer to the couplet of a
celebrated Old Carthusian of the day, Joseph Addison:

> When in the slippery paths of Youth
>   With heedless steps I ran,
> Thine arm, unseen, conveyed me safe
>   And led me up to man.

At Charterhouse, Wesley was a trifle smug. He was not "so bad as other people," he reckoned, and would get through at the Day of Judgment.

One day the elderly schoolmaster was crossing Green out of school hours when he noticed that the smaller boys, including Wesley, were not playing their various games. Dr. Walker could hear no sound from the cloisters and therefore assumed they were up to mischief. He turned back and entered the gownboys' writing room.

He found Crusius, Yorke, Widdowson, and all the junior gownboys gathered around. As the story was told many years later by Charles Wesley's daughter, they were "assembled in the schoolroom round my uncle, who was amusing them with instructive tales, to which they attentively listened rather than follow their accustomed sports." Walker expressed approval and told Wesley that "he wished him to repeat this entertainment as often as he could obtain auditors, and so well employ his time."

The incident was later garbled by a hostile writer. He portrayed Wesley as a monitor who harangued younger students and when rebuked by the master, exclaimed, "Better rule in hell than serve in heaven." But Sally Wesley confuted this and said that her version "was thus related to me by my father," who may have heard John Wesley tell it among his anecdotes.

Old Dr. Walker encouraged Wesley in many other ways as he rose in the school, finding him a hard worker, proficient in Greek and Latin verse. Walker did not need to provide hospitality during the shorter holidays, despite the distance to Epworth, because Wesley had an uncle nearby, his father's elder brother Matthew, a wealthy physician of somewhat crabbed character, whose only son became a rake and a drunkard. Uncle Matthew disapproved of his brother's bad management but was generous to nephews and nieces.

In 1716, when John Wesley was in his second year at Charterhouse, his older brother, Samuel, married, and his younger brother Charles, aged nine, entered Westminster School at Samuel's expense until Charles was elected King's Scholar. Samuel's wife Ursula ("Nutty") was somewhat shrewish and not always kind to Charles, but Jack told their mother, "She has always been particularly civil to me." He often walked the mere two and a half miles from the Charterhouse, past Newgate Prison, down Fleet Street, the Strand, and Whitehall, to the home of Samuel and Nutty in Westminster. He was there when Samuel read aloud a letter from Epworth describing the extraordinary disruption caused at the rectory by a ghost. Years later John Wesley made a thorough enquiry into "Old Jeffrey," as the family called the ghost, but the matter remains unresolved.

Brother Samuel (they had all been taught to address each other as "Brother" or "Sister," not by Christian name alone) was already a poet. He lacked genius but moved among poets and essayists: Jack and Charles would have seen Pope, Swift, and Prior at the Westminster home. Samuel was counted a Jacobite (but he denied it) and was devoted to Bishop Atterbury, the dean of Westminster and bishop of Rochester who later was exiled for sedition.

Jack, though following the statesmen who put Church and Crown before Parliament (now called Tories), supported the new dynasty. Yet this loyalty could open no doors to the future. His own patron, the Tory Duke of Buckingham, had fallen from power, and so had Brother Samuel's patron, the Earl of Oxford. Both remained governors of the Charterhouse and no doubt tipped

Wesley handsomely when the gownboys formed a guard of honor at the arrival of the great ones, in their full-bottomed wigs, before the Governors' Assemblies.

Though Buckingham could not help, the late founder of Charterhouse had made provision for every gownboy's next step if funds were otherwise unprovided. The slower students were apprenticed to trades, like Wesley's classmate John Spencer, who was bound to a periwig maker. The brighter students received grants to Oxford or Cambridge, especially to Christ Church, Oxford. The schoolmaster had no hesitation in nominating John Wesley for a grant, and he was entered at Christ Church as a Commoner on June 24, 1720, a week after his seventeenth birthday; the first time his name appears in the battel book, charging him for provisions on July 13, 1720, it was written *John Westley*.

The rector of Epworth was delighted at his son's success. Thinking to forward Jack's career, he had told him before he left Charterhouse to call on Dr. Henry Sacheverell. The celebrated Tory cleric lived a short walk away at St. Andrew's, Holborn, the rich rectory which Queen Anne had given him after his inflammatory sermons and notorious trial for sedition had led to the fall of the Whig government, which she hated. Samuel Wesley had helped Sacheverell by writing his defense to read at the trial and now felt entitled to expect a return. Sacheverell had been an Oxford don, though his scholarship was not highly regarded, and his letters of introduction could open many doors.

Jack duly presented himself. "I was a very little fellow when I was introduced to him," Wesley would afterward recall with amusement. "I found him alone, as tall as a Maypole and as fine as an Archbishop. After I had made known to him the object of my visit, he said: 'You are too young to go to the University. You cannot know Greek and Latin yet. Go back to school.'" This was cool treatment for a boy whose father had befriended the pompous doctor in his hour of need. Little Wesley was outraged. Well-bred in the classics at Charterhouse, even learning Hebrew with Sam at Westminster, he felt himself a giant of knowledge beside such a Maypole. "I looked at him as Goliath looked at David, and despised him in my heart. I thought, *if I do not know Greek and Latin better than you I ought to go back to school indeed.* I left him, and neither entreaties nor commands could have brought me back to him."

3

The Red Notebook

Early in September 1723 John Wesley, twenty years of age and in his third year at Christ Church, was walking one evening a mile or two from Oxford.

Smallpox raged among town and gown, but he had survived a mild attack in childhood and therefore was immune; neither had he caught the prevalent fever which had carried off "a very ingenious young gentleman of our college." Wesley wrote home that he was "seldom troubled with anything but bleeding at the nose, which I have frequently"—a condition which would not necessarily imply a serious physical defect or high blood pressure.

As he walked through water meadows, his nose began to bleed again. He tried to stop it. Every method proved useless. Then "I stripped myself and leapt into the river, which happened luckily not to be far off." The shock contracted the muscles and stopped the flow of blood.

Wesley loved bathing and exercise. He swam and boated; he played "real" tennis; he rode and occasionally went hunting.

Sometimes he was given a gun at a shoot. But all his activities were hemmed in by lack of money and drove him into debt from time to time.

As a commoner, he had to pay all his board, room rent, and college expenses out of the Charterhouse grant and what his family could scrape together, whereas Sam, the riper scholar, had been a student on the Foundation, living free. Sam retained his studentship until 1723, passing the compensation to Jack as a loan.

John Wesley worked hard at the classics and at logic. He fulfilled his tutor's requirements with ease despite a tendency to spend hours in wide reading, which did little except feed his intellectual curiosity, though he would generally make a synopsis ("collecting," he called it) of each book. He was sociable, though neither his parentage nor his pocket took him into the company of the aristocrats of The House, as Christ Church was always known at Oxford. To save money he wore his own hair instead of a fashionable wig.

Still small in physique, he was neat in dress and appearance. According to a tradition passed down in his brother Samuel's family, he had a gaiety and sprightliness about him in his early twenties "with a turn for wit and humor, a young fellow of the finest classical taste, of the most liberal and manly sentiments." He also had a relish for ghost stories and enjoyed card playing.

None of this would ensure him a livelihood. The Duke of Buckingham was dead, and Wesley lacked a patron to open the way to the law, politics, or literary pursuits. The sword had no attraction, even if he had possessed the means to purchase a commission. He had already begun a lifelong interest in medical matters but showed no desire to follow Uncle Matthew.

The obvious career, especially for a Wesley, was that of clergyman. Many of his Oxford contemporaries would slip casually into Holy Orders to be tutors or schoolmasters or country curates; some had family livings waiting. Susanna Wesley hoped that Jack would help his father, who had lately accepted the additional parish of Wroot, a gloomy village seven miles from Epworth with a less expensive rectory where they now lived. "I heartily wish you were in Orders," she wrote to Jack in September 1724, shortly after he had taken his degree as Bachelor of Arts.

But her own teaching and example had made his conscience too sensitive to allow him to seek Holy Orders without a true inward calling. He seemed a clean-living young man to his friends, and if rather fond of the ladies, his behavior toward them was correct. He did not forget to say his prayers, "both in public and in private." He read several commentaries on the New Testament as well as his Bible regularly, yet he reckoned afterward that he was "continually sinning against that little light I had [despite] transient fits of what many divines taught me to call repentance."

He hesitated when old Mr. Wesley began to press him to prepare properly and be ordained: "You don't admire a callow clergyman any more than I do." Jack would prefer to be an Oxford don, though it would oblige him to be in Orders. He loved Oxford, and his father had already mentioned him for a fellowship to Dr. Morley, a Lincolnshire man who was rector of Lincoln, the small college across the High.

At last, soon after Christmas 1724, Wesley wrote to both his parents that he had decided to seek Holy Orders, partly to ensure himself a livelihood and partly to help toward a stricter life.

The letters arrived at Wroot and started an argument. His father was against "your going over hastily into Orders." He suggested, alarmingly, that Jack spend a year collating the Hebrew, Greek, Syrian, and Latin texts of Old Testament books to assist the polyglot Bible, which the rector had been preparing, and added: "You ask me which is the best commentary on the Bible. I answer, the Bible."

Susanna disliked delay. After more discussion, she retired to bed, "very ill and confined to my chamber." In February she complained to Jack that "'tis an unhappiness almost peculiar to our family, that your father and I seldom think alike. I approve the disposition of your mind ... and I think the sooner you are a deacon the better." She particularly liked the idea because it would set him to study practical divinity.

Three weeks later on March 17, the rector wrote again: "I've changed my mind since my last, and now incline to your going this summer into Orders." He promised to scrape together the money for the fees.

This letter must have reached Oxford at the beginning of Holy Week 1725. Wesley began to prepare. A remark in his mother's recent letter had struck him forcibly: she had urged him to "enter now upon a serious examination of yourself, that you may know whether you have a reasonable hope of salvation by Jesus Christ, that is, whether you are in a state of faith and repentance or not." To stay always in this state of mind and soul, she urged, was the essential condition of salvation.

An old red notebook which had belonged to his grandfather, the Puritan preacher, lay ready to hand. Wesley knew a shorthand code which would enable him to write fast and protect his more intimate jottings from prying eyes. He adapted and developed the code so cleverly that it was not fully and accurately deciphered until 1972, nearly 250 years later.

Early in the morning of Good Friday, he went to the college service in the Latin chapel of Christ Church Cathedral. The prayers were in Latin, which was familiar enough to John Wesley, but they were generally read in a perfunctory manner by a bored canon in the cold, half-lit cathedral. Wesley's attention wandered, and he found "a great many unclean thoughts arising in chapel."

Back in his rooms he opened the red notebook. "Friday, March 26," he wrote in longhand at the top of the first right-hand page. Examining himself as his mother had suggested, he put down in shorthand code a list of his temptations:

a. Too much addicting myself to light behavior at all times;
b. Listening too much to idle talk, and reading vain plays and books;
c. Idleness; and lastly
d. Want of due consideration in whose presence I am.

From which I perceive it is necessary

a. To labor for a grave and modest carriage;
b. To avoid vain and light company; and
c. To entertain awful apprehensions of the presence of God;
d. To avoid idleness, freedom with women, and high-seasoned meats [possibly because he believed they stimulated his virility]

He determined "to resist the very beginnings of lust, not by arguing with, but by thinking no more of it or by immediately going into company." He had plenty of friends in different colleges.

For ten days he wrote no more in the red notebook. His good resolutions hardly affected his usual manner or activities. Then he began a daily diary to check how he spent his time, writing a single line for each morning and afternoon for a fortnight until he "went out of town." A friend who was a little younger than Wesley, Robin Griffiths of Merton, had invited him home.

They rode through the springtime Cotswold hills to Broadway, the lovely village of sandstone houses where the Cotswolds meet the vale of Evesham, some forty miles from Oxford. Griffiths' father had the parish and thus the Elizabethan rectory. Wesley found himself accepted into a circle of intellectual, charming, and devout people of about his age. Robin often took him to Stanton rectory, a mile or two away on the hillside, where the Reverend Lionel Kirkham and his wife lived with a son and three daughters, Sally, Betty, and Damaris.

Wesley fell a little in love with Sally, but he hoped to be a college fellow, who must be unmarried. And only that month his eldest sister, Emily, miserable from an unhappy love affair, had warned him to avoid "engaging his affections" before he could marry speedily.

The next village to Stanton was Buckland. Here lived the Tookers in the fifteenth-century rectory with its moot hall. Behind the church at "the Farm" were the romantic Granvilles, political exiles from London, whose aristocratic connections did not make them proud. Mrs. Granville's late husband, a descendant of the famous Sir Richard Grenville of the *Revenge*, had been implicated in the recent Jacobite rising, and his brother, Lord Lansdowne, had been exiled to France, where the old Pretender gave him the empty title of duke. Lansdowne later made his peace with the Hanoverians.

Only one of Mrs. Granville's daughters, Ann, was at home. Wesley had not yet met her brilliant sister Mary, Mrs. Alexander Pendarves, recently widowed of an elderly husband whom she had been forced to marry. It may have been Mary who later suggested the use of literary code names. As "Varanese,"[1] the unmarried Sally Kirkham might correspond in the third person with the bachelor John Wesley as "Cyrus"; Mary Pendarves began to write to him too, taking the name "Aspasia."

While Wesley was in the Cotswolds this spring of 1725, two months short of his twenty-second birthday, one of the group of friends urged him to read a book "which I had frequently seen but never much looked into before." *The Christian's Pattern* was a paraphrase by George Stanhope, the incumbent dean of Canterbury, of the medieval classic *The Imitation of Christ* by Thomas à Kempis.

Some of *The Imitation's* strictness made Wesley angry: "I can't think that when God sent us into the world," he complained to his mother, "he had irreversibly decreed that we should be perpetually miserable in it ... that all mirth is vain and useless, if not sinful. But why then does the Psalmist so often exhort us to rejoice in the Lord?"

The more that he read à Kempis, however, the more "I began to see that true religion was seated in the heart, and that God's law extended to all our thoughts as well as words and actions." Reading à Kempis was comforting, especially in the flowing English of the dean of Canterbury: "So all-sufficient, so delightful, so heavenly sweet is the Friendship and Company of Jesus." But à Kempis could give him no assurance that Jesus was always present in his heart. Wesley determined to make himself worthy of so great a Guest, then to watch and work carefully lest Jesus depart again. As à Kempis taught: "While Jesus is present by his Grace and Comfort, nothing is too hard to do, nothing grievous to suffer; but Happiness and perfect Peace dwell and reign in my breast. But the moment he withdraws his cheering face, all my Supports are lost and gone."[2]

Back in Oxford, Wesley took a step which was unusual and frowned upon. He began to attend Holy Communion in the cathedral every Sunday. Students and Commoners were required to communicate once a quarter, but to go more frequently was considered indecent, possibly Popish. The congregations at the weekly celebrations were tiny. It was not easy to be outwardly religious at Christ Church. As Charles Wesley was to describe it four years later, "Christ Church is certainly the worst place in the world to begin a reformation; a man stands a very fair chance of being laughed out of his religion at his first setting out, in a place where 'tis scandalous to have any at all.'"

Susanna urged "Dear Jacky" not to mind. In the course of a long and theological letter, discussing the subject with zeal, she stiffened his resolution: "If it be a weak virtue that can't bear being laughed at, I am very sure 'tis a strong and well confirmed virtue that can stand the test of a brisk buffoonery."

Wesley did not mind buffoonery, but he longed for a companion. One evening in July 1725, he and Robin Griffiths were at a party but were due later at the funeral of a tradesman's daughter who had died of consumption (tuberculosis) at the age of fifteen. They slipped out of the party and walked the short distance to St. Mary's, the university church. They were early and took a turn up and down the aisle, lit by the evening sun through the stained glass.

Wesley asked Robin: "Do you really think yourself my friend? If so, why will you not do me all the good you can?"

Robin began to protest. Wesley cut him short. "Please oblige me in something which you can't deny is in your power. Let me have the pleasure of making you a whole Christian! I know you are at least half persuaded already." Robin, Wesley went on, could do him no greater kindness, and both of them would need to be whole Christians when it was their turn "to follow that young woman."

Robin turned "exceedingly serious." Wesley may not have realized that Griffiths was already a consumptive.

They became fellow pilgrims: Wesley pressing ahead, Robin following the more lamely. Into the first page of his diary Wesley inserted a list of rules "collected" from the devotional book *Rules for Holy Living* by Bishop Jeremy Taylor. Sally Kirkham (Varanese) had called some of Taylor's rules "altogether impracticable," and Wesley soon found that she was right.

Early in September he received the bishop of Lincoln's Letters Dimissory, giving authority for his ordination on the title of a curacy to his father at Epworth and Wroot, and presented them to the bishop of Oxford's registrar. Wesley hardly thought himself worthy to be made deacon. On the night before the service, he confessed in cipher in his diary: "Boasting, greedy of praise, intemperate sleep, detraction, lying—Lord have mercy—heat in arguing."

Thus abashed and anxious, he was ordained in Christ Church Cathedral on the morning of Sunday, September 19, 1725 by Bishop of Oxford John Potter, a future archbishop of Canterbury.

The new Reverend John Wesley could not leave Oxford while working for a fellowship; therefore, he rode out to little country churches in Oxfordshire and Buckinghamshire where he donned his canonicals and preached his carefully written sermons. Back in his rooms he labored at Homer or Horace or divinity, composed verses, and wrote letters. He went for walks, played tennis (two hours on the second day after his ordination), and sat at the coffee house.

One evening he "disputed warmly on a trifle." When he opened his diary, he repented. His friends might regard him as an upright and delightful man when not in an argument; but if he draws a true self-portrait in his secret diary, rather than over-etching the warts, it would seem that he was proud, both of his intellectual powers and of his holiness, and inclined to be peevish. He admits to being idle—by which he probably meant that he read light books and plays such as *The Ambitious Stepmother*, *The Fair Penitent*, and other tragedies by the late Poet Laureate Nicholas Rowe, of which he was especially fond. Wesley confessed to himself that he broke his word, dissembled, and was quick to condemn or censure, especially the canons of Christ Church.

Meanwhile, in Lincoln College and far away in Lincolnshire, intense lobbying was propelling him toward the vacant fellowship, which would provide a home and income until death or marriage. In March he sat in the lodge of the rector of Lincoln to write a theme, then a few days later was examined in Homer and Horace. The rector and fellows judged that he was not a scholar of the first water, but they liked him and approved of him as a High Churchman and a Tory.

On March 17, 1726 the twelve fellows elected John Wesley unanimously. When the news reached Epworth and Wroot, his father rejoiced. Debts and an uncertain future meant nothing: "Wherever I am, my Jacky is Fellow of Lincoln!"

4

"You Cannot Serve Him Alone"

The new Fellow of Lincoln spent the summer of 1726 helping his father. Visiting the cottagers at Wroot or Epworth, or wandering through the market, Wesley kept an ear for the dialect and the curious Lincolnshire phrases: "You muck spout"; "You clarhkettle, I'll tan your bonecart!" "As rough as a hackle." Many of the words were unknown beyond the county.

Wesley had an insatiable curiosity; he even attended an archaelogical dig. Meanwhile, he tried to keep his rules and to regulate his days and was leaning toward self-denial. One July day he discussed this with his mother. She offered the opinion that "one act of self-denial is more grateful to your Master than the performance of many duties, as it is an undeniable instance of the love we bear him."

But all was not well at home. During the previous year Jack's beautiful and clever sister Hetty had eloped with a lawyer. The rector thought the man a scoundrel and opposed their match. His instinct was sure: Hetty returned home after one night. Her father refused to forgive her. To efface the scandal, she married the first man to ask the rector for her hand: a rough, lazy, poorly educated glazier and plumber called Wright from the nearby town of Louth. Wright's love soon cooled. He took to drink and made Hetty's life miserable.

Jack found his father "inconceivably exasperated against her." He had disowned her and "never spoke of her in my hearing but with the utmost detestation." Jack visited her in Louth and was sure she had repented of her misdeeds and craved her parents' love, yet their mother took the rector's part as did several of the sisters and nineteen-year-old Charles, who had left Westminster and was about to go up to Christ Church. Only crippled Molly supported Jack in his concern for Hetty.

One evening at dinner in Wroot rectory, Jack deliberately launched a disputation on the theology of forgiveness, affecting not to notice his father's irritation. Jack, who had long considered preparing a sermon on universal charity, or so he said, now retired to write it. When he showed his mother the script, she saw through him at once: "You wrote this sermon for Hetty. The rest was brought in for the sake of the last paragraph." But she asked for only one change.

He preached it on the last Sunday in August in Wroot parish church. His father said nothing afterward. Next day Jack rode to Epworth, returning later that week. While he was away, the rector and Charles visited sister Suky and her worthless husband, Richard Ellison, a farmer who had come down in the world. As they returned, the rector exploded against Jack.

When they were all back at Wroot, young Charles asked Jack to take a walk in the garden after supper and informed him, "My father last night was telling me of your disrespect to him. He said you had him at open defiance."

Jack was genuinely surprised. Not for the last time he had failed to see that he might give offense by his stand on a principle. He asked how or when.

"Every day," replied Charles and repeated their father's words: "'You hear how he contradicts me, and takes your sister's part before my face. Nay, he disputes with me, preach—' and then he stopped short," said Charles, "as if he wanted to recall his word, and talked of other things."

Jack ran into the house. He found the rector by himself in the hall and burst into tears, saying he had learned from his brother that he had offended by often contradicting him and not offering to write for him, "but now I promise to do whatever you please."

His father kissed him and cried a little too. "I always believed you were good at bottom," he said, "and I will employ you next day."

John Wesley therefore spent hours, when he would rather have studied Xenophon and Horace or relaxed with *Half Pay Officers* or another play, writing sermons for his father and transcribing long Latin quotations for the *magnum opus* on Job until the time came to ride off to Oxford.

"I never knew a college besides ours whereof the members were so perfectly satisfied with one another"—so Wesley described Lincoln's six or eight fellows in residence. He found them "well-natured and well-bred," and peaceable and neighborly among themselves and toward their acquaintances outside. The fellows liked their new colleague too.

He worshiped with them in the chapel, which seemed small after Christ Cathedral and was lit at the east end by unusual seventeenth-century stained glass, from Lincolnshire, which told the story of the Faith. He dined at high table and played cards or conversed in the intimate common room with its oak paneling. And every Saturday night, after he had mounted the steep staircase in Chapel Quad to his rather cramped set of rooms overlooking the Turl, he would open his diary and examine himself. He seldom liked what he saw as he searched his soul and would jot down in code his frequent failures to keep resolutions.

Wesley's college duties were light. He loved, therefore, to walk out on the Woodstock road, hire a horse from a hostler at Yarnton, and ride into the Cotswolds.

Sally Kirkham had married the local schoolmaster, John Chapone, in December 1725, to Wesley's sorrow, if one of his sisters is to be believed. He was present at the wedding, and "Cyrus" Wesley and "Varanese" Chapone remained devoted friends. They corresponded, and this alarmed Susanna Wesley: "The more I think of it, the less I approve it." They kept the friendship on a strictly moral and pious level, however much their hearts might flutter, and as Sally said as she sat with Wesley and her sister, "I can't think it expedient, nor indeed lawful, to break off that acquaintance which is one of the strongest incentives I have to virtue." One Sunday after Wesley had read the prayers and preached at Stanton, he walked up Horrell Hill with the sisters. Sally said she loved him "more than all mankind except her father and her husband." Betty felt the same, "though a maid must not say much." Wesley asked for "just the same freedom with her as with my sisters," and when she went off to bed that night, Betty said, "Good night, brother."

He returned to Stanton for a Christmas visit, getting up late despite his rule for early rising. Sometimes they talked or danced or had company; one evening he read aloud from Dean Swift's new satire, *Gulliver's Travels*, which had taken England by storm that year. He also read to them Congreve's play *The Way of the World* and Shakespeare, or they might bring out the cards and the circular revolving tray, extract the eight of diamonds, and play "Pope Joan," a popular card game of the day.

Wesley's blend of social ability and seriousness made him, at twenty-three, an interesting mixture. His open face, with full lips, a nose which was a little too long, and rather large eyes, was framed by luxuriant silky hair which fell to his shoulders in defiance of current fashion; it had an unusual color, a dark brown which looked auburn in certain lights. His clerical dress was always spotless, in contrast to the rough coat of the Buckland parson, Trewythn Tooker, who generally appeared more like a grazier than a clergyman.

The Kirkham family's fondness for their young don was well put a year later by Bob, the lazy and amusing young brother of Sally and Betty, then in his first year at Oxford. He wrote in a jocular letter to Wesley from Stanton that they had spent pleasant hours reminiscing about "your most deserving, queer character—your worthy personal accomplishments—your noble endowments of mind—your little and handsome person—and your obliging and desirable conversation." The Tookers, the Granvilles, and the Griffiths would have said the same that Christmas and new year of 1726–1727.

Then came tragedy. Robin Griffiths' consumption had steadily gained on him. When Wesley had stayed at Broadway rectory, he and Robin shared much religious talk, but they would also spend a morning foxhunting with the local squire's hounds (his son was another Oxford contemporary). Robin was now weaker but looked forward to marrying one of the Tooker girls from Buckland Rectory. Early in January 1727 Wesley walked over to see him. Three days later a message came that Robin Griffiths was dead.

Wesley preached the funeral sermon in the twelfth-century church dedicated to the royal princess of Wessex, Saint Eadburgha, and rode sadly back to Oxford.

That March he submitted to the university his Latin theme on *Reason in Brutes and How Flies and Fishes Respire*. The examiners awarded him the degree of Master of Arts: Oxford and Cambridge had not yet turned the award of M.A. into a formality to be claimed by any B.A. of two years' standing who kept his name on the books.

Wesley marked the occasion by starting in his diary an hourly introspection of his behavior. This he kept up for four days, then abandoned the first notebook with twenty pages to fill. He began another, reverting to twice-daily reports and a Saturday night appraisal. When he described his system to his mother, she commented: "There's nothing like a clear method to save both time and labor in anything."

He continued his wide reading in history, divinity, literature, and plays, for the Bodleian Library was only a few steps from Lincoln; but as no tutorship fell vacant, he had only one pupil and sorely felt the loss of Robin, his fellow pilgrim on the steep ascent to heaven. Brother Charles had come up, as a student on the foundation of Christ Church, but brotherly affection brought little affinity. Charles was high-spirited and clever and already a skilled versifier, but he envied the Christ Church noblemen who had money to spend and costly clothes. In chapel, he was "utterly inattentive" by his own later admission. John Wesley saw much good in him, noting that he "merits emulation—in meekness, tenderness and learning." But "if I spoke to him about religion he would warmly answer, 'What, would you have me be a saint all at once?' and would hear no more."

In August 1727, when the summer floods had subsided between Wroot and Epworth, Wesley went back to serve as his father's curate. The college renewed his leave of absence every six months. His father was aging, and his mother had nearly died in June. The rector had written in July: "Though she has now and then some very sick fits, yet I hope the sight of you will revive her." It did, for she lived to be seventy-three.

For the next two years John Wesley was a country curate. He studied in the mornings, visited cottages in the afternoon, and kept his health by exercise—swimming in the river in summer, shooting with his dog, Tony, in autumn, and playing tennis when opportunity offered. (Shooting and tennis were his favorite sports.) In the evenings he would often dance a little with his sisters and their friend Kitty Hargreaves, who much attracted him. Dancing was the only exercise permitted a woman except for walking or riding, and Wesley had bought a flute to play as they danced.

Sometimes he left Epworth for a round of visits to married sisters and to the unmarried Kezzy, the youngest, who was a teacher in Lincoln. Once he visited Wentworth Woodhouse, the great house in south Yorkshire belonging to the descendants of Strafford, Charles I's executed statesman, and was allowed to spend days in their library. In September 1728 he went up to London with Charles to stay with Brother Sam at Westminster and attend a play. Charles was somewhat smitten with an actress, whereas Jack felt less sure that he should continue to enjoy the stage or the reading of plays.

The two brothers rode on to Oxford, and Bishop Potter ordained John into priest's orders. Some words given to the candidates by the bishop's examining chaplain sank into his mind. "Do you know what you are about?" asked Dr. Hayward. "You are bidding defiance to all mankind. He that would live a Christian priest ought to know that, whether his hand be against every man or not, he must expect every man's hand should be against him." Wesley was ready for the world's contempt, which would help work out his own salvation.

He was increasingly serious in his manner, seeking to refine and renew his nature by keeping to his method, yet longing for assurances that he pleased God. He was still "constrained to travel alone, having no man to guide or help." He knew the need for a companion, for an elderly Lincolnshire clergyman, Joseph Hoole of Haxey, had impressed upon him some words which Wesley quoted so often in later life that he was generally credited as their source: "The Bible knows nothing of a solitary religion." "Sir," Hoole had said, "you wish to serve God and go to heaven. Remember, you cannot serve Him alone. You must therefore *find* companions or *make* them."

In effect, he did both. During their journey to London and on to Oxford, Wesley had argued long and hard with his brother. By January he knew that Charles had renounced his frivolity, perhaps scared by his flirtation with the actress, "though I can't tell myself," he wrote to John, "how or when I first awoke out of my lethargy—only that 'twas not long after you went away." He was sure he would be established in faith by John's help and their mother's prayers and would never quarrel with her again "till I do [quarrel] with my religion." He relied on his brother's prayers that such a quarrel would never occur.

Brother Sam noticed the difference at Christmas vacation. He told John—and thereby gave a profile of Wesley in late

1728—that Charles was "so entirely infected with your gravity that every motion and look made me almost suspect it was you; nay, I begin now to think he will hardly ever lay aside the present solemnity of his person and behavior."

Charles had wasted his time on "diversions." Now he set out to redeem it. In the early weeks of 1729 he started reading seriously and began to keep a diary on John's system, leaning heavily on his advice. Wesley gladly paid the postal fees for the long and vivid letters which arrived from Oxford at Gainsborough post office, to be collected when one of the family took the boat up the Trent.

Charles had persuaded Bob Kirkham, amusing and still rather idle, to join him in keeping the rules which John had formulated. Charles had rescued William Morgan, a "modest, humble, well-disposed youth" in the next set of rooms, from "vile hands." Morgan wanted to be guided in things temporal and eternal though he dared not "receive the sacrament but at the usual times for fear of being laughed at." Charles managed to persuade Bob "to neglect censure on a religious account and thereby encouraged myself to do so." Soon Charles, Morgan, and Bob were all defying ridicule by going to the Eucharist once a week.

Charles was about to ride into the Cotswolds, though he feared that without his brother the delights of Stanton might trip him. He told gaily how the Kirkhams "have had the good fortune there to have a couple of aunts die and leave the three girls £200 a piece. There's news for you, you rogue!"

Wesley also heard from Charles that the vice-chancellor was taking measures to stem the tide of Deism in Oxford, for if few men openly rejected the Divinity of Christ, a growing crowd of dons and undergraduates were indifferent to Christian doctrine and practice. Charles, in contrast, having looked at the University

Statutes, which were grounded firmly in Christianity, was trying to observe the methods of study and worship laid down for Oxford many centuries before.

Fifty-six years later in 1785, Charles Wesley claimed that it was for this reason, and in that year of 1729, that an undergraduate of Christ Church first mocked him, Kirkham, and Morgan with the "harmless name of 'Methodist.'" The term had been used occasionally in the previous century to describe medical men of a certain sort, and occasionally in religion.

Charles' memory, however, was at fault, perhaps misled by an unconscious desire to strengthen his authority in the Methodist movement. His claim to be "the first Methodist" was accepted, for no one was alive to contradict him except his brother John, who did not choose to do so. It became part of Methodist tradition. But it cannot be sustained against contemporary documentary evidence. The nickname *Methodist* was not used at Oxford for another three years; it first appears in letters, diaries and publications, all within a few weeks, in late summer of 1732. Charles had not organized his two friends into any religious club; Bob Kirkham was still more interested in the company of his drinking friends, although he did brave mockery to attend the Eucharist weekly with Morgan and Charles.

Christ Church men, this spring of 1729, joked about "the whimsical Mr. Wesley, his preciseness, and pious extravagancies." Charles was now convinced that eternal salvation depended on what they could do to prepare themselves for heaven, and he needed John. "I earnestly long for and desire," he wrote, "the blessing God is about to send me in you. I am sensible *this* is my day of grace." He also assumed that his destination in eternity would largely depend on how well he employed his time. John came from Epworth in the summer. He encouraged Charles and Morgan, then returned by way of Westminster, where he, Charles, and Sam visited the playhouse.

Back in Lincolnshire, relations with his father were becoming tense. Wesley longed to be back in Oxford for good. The opportunity came when the new rector of Lincoln, Dr. Euseby Isham, wrote that the college required his presence to take up a tutorship.

Wesley made a leisurely journey, visiting relations and friends in the cities of Lincoln, London, and Westminster. On the evening of November 22, 1729, when the towers and spires of Oxford were silhouetted in the early winter sunset, he rode down Headington Hill and over Magdalen Bridge. He went straight to visit Charles at Christ Church—the beginning of eight formative years which would end very differently from what John Wesley expected.

5

"Our Little Society"

One summer evening in August 1730, William Morgan, whom Charles had befriended, knocked on the door of John Wesley's rooms in Chapel Quad, Lincoln, with exciting news.

He had regularly been visiting a man who lay shackled in Oxford Castle under sentence of death for murdering his wife. Among the other prisoners were several debtors. These were free to walk about the prison. Morgan had talked with one of them that afternoon and was convinced, he told Wesley, that "it would do much good if anyone would be at the pains of now and then speaking with them."

Wesley replied cautiously that dons and undergraduates did not visit prisons. Morgan raised the subject again at their regular readings, which Wesley had organized for Charles, Bob Kirkham, and Morgan. Four evenings a week they would meet in each others' rooms in rotation. Wesley read prayers; they had supper; then he read to them from the classics on weekdays and a book of divinity on Sundays. They would tell each other how they had spent the day and examine their spiritual progress.

At each session that week, Morgan urged upon them the good they might do the prisoners and their own souls. He brought along another undergraduate, John Boyce, who, as the son of a former mayor of Oxford, was sure that the civic authorities would not object.

On August 24 the two Wesleys walked down with Morgan to the Castle at the edge of the city and were "so well satisfied with our conversation there that we agreed to go thither once or twice a week." Morgan next took Wesley to a cottage in the town where a woman in extreme poverty, Mrs. Vesey, lay sick.

Morgan's suggestion that the four friends and Boyce help the prisoners and the poor seemed a true imitation of Christ, and when Wesley wrote to Epworth, his father sent back strong encouragement. He was pleased that Morgan was "breaking the ice for you" and revealed that he too, in his Oxford days, had visited prisoners. But Jack must seek the approval of the local clergyman and of the bishop.

Bishop Potter promptly sent a message that he "was greatly pleased with the undertaking."

Wesley therefore preached once a month at the Castle and at Bocardo, the prison where most of the debtors lay (and where Cranmer, Ridley, and Latimer had lain before they were burned at the stake.) Wesley and the laymen took turns visiting the prisons daily; twice a week they read prayers. They raised a little fund to buy medicine and books and sometimes to help a debtor gain discharge. They also adopted three or four poor families in the town, visiting them regularly and reading to the sick and aged.

In the spring of 1731 Wesley started a small school for poor children, paying a woman to teach. The friends took turns to hear the children read or say their prayers, and to inspect their knitting and weaving. When necessary, Wesley would buy a child clothes.

The numbers of "our little society" grew slightly. John Gambold of Christ Church who joined them wrote shortly afterward that "Mr. John Wesley was always the chief manager, for which he was very fit. For he had not only more learning and experience than the rest, but he was blest with such activity as to be always gaining ground, and such steadiness that he lost none." His proposals "were sure to charm them," wrote Gambold, because Wesley was in earnest and was "always the same. To this I may add that he had, I think, something of authority in his countenance; though ... he could soften his manner and point it as occasion required."

Wesley strongly urged "method and order" on all his disciples so that every hour of the day had its proper use, whether study, devotion, exercise, or charity. He urged them to "keep in their minds an awful sense of God's presence." He put together and published *A Collection of Forms of Prayer*, "which, lying by them as they stood at their studies, they at intervals snatched a short petition out of it." Wesley liked to shoot up a prayer on the first second of every hour. He "thought prayer to be more his business than anything else," wrote Gambold, "and I have seen him come out of his closet with a serenity of countenancy that was next to shining."

When John Wesley told his father about the charitable work they had begun, the old rector declared that "none but such as are out of their senses would be prejudiced against your acting in this manner." He was wrong. Soon after they began to visit the prisons, Bob Kirkham reported that he had been ridiculed at Merton for being a member of "the Holy Club." He had never heard of such a club nor known the strange customs assigned to it by rumor, yet he learned that it had "become a common topic of mirth." And his college thought that nothing was so ridiculous as visiting prisoners and the poor: Oxford had forgotten her great medieval and Tudor traditions of charity.

As the rumors spread, most undergraduates and many dons looked on the Wesleys with a mixture of amusement and anger. To receive the Sacrament weekly was bad enough and smacked of Popish or of Jacobite sympathies (the professor of New Testament Greek, a canon of Christ Church, threatened to turn his nephew out of doors for joining the Wesleys in this), "yet nothing," as Gambold recalled a few years later, "was so much disliked as these charitable employments." Wesley heard that several seniors of Christ Church had consulted on "the speediest way to stop the progress of enthusiasm" in the college and that the university censors "were going to blow up the Godly Club (this was now our common title, though we were sometimes dignified with that of the Enthusiasts, or the Reforming Club)."

Wesley prepared a careful paper to place before serious critics, but he taught his disciples to ignore the jeering or to glory in it as helping to make them more worthy of God's favor, more certain that he would accept them when they died, and more like Christ while they lived. Wesley worked hard to imitate Christ. Since the return to Oxford, he had resolved to "make the Scripture my study." The Bible now shaped his wide and unremitting reading in divinity as he struggled to understand it.

To give himself more time and inclination he shook off his "trifling acquaintances" and kept a sharp eye on the use he made of each hour. He offered prayers at intervals throughout the day, including prayer when the college clock struck the hour, and he trained himself to rise at 5 o'clock or even at 4. Early rising became a hallmark of the Methodists; across Oxford the handful of disciples struggled and groaned to obey Wesley's insistence on this self-denial, and nothing seemed more absurd to the university.

To save on coals or logs and sometimes to inflict a penance on himself, Wesley sat in a fireless room unless he had company. To deepen humility and to save the hire of horses, the Wesley brothers took to walking all the way on their visits to Epworth, some 150 miles. This fad worried their father. "I should be so pleased to see ye here this spring," he wrote in 1731, "if it was not upon the hard conditions of your walking hither, but that always terrifies me, and I am commonly so uneasy for fear ye should kill yourselves with coming so far on foot that it destroys much of the pleasure I should otherwise have in conversing with you."

After that visit, walking each way, they assured him when they were safe back in Oxford that twenty-five miles a day for six days improved their health. They had walked through the Lincolnshire wolds and through the shires, under the shadow of Warwick Castle, and down by Stratford-on-Avon so that they could visit their Cotswolds friends. Farmers on their hacks or ponies trotting to market or drovers behind their herds would have thought nothing of young men on foot. To walk or ride could be more comfortable and sometimes faster than riding in a wagon or coach.[1] But these two, a parson and a layman, looked odd, for as they walked they read, despite the fact that even main roads were rough and broken and often hilly; they were deep in learned books, redeeming the time. Wesley reported that reading for ten of twenty-five daily miles had brought no harm.

In 1732 they learned a new way of self-denial. The celebrated London bookseller Rivington had told Wesley about a young

Oxford man named John Clayton. The two soon met in an Oxford street and became friends. Clayton, the son of a Manchester bookseller, was a tutor of Brasenose College, intending to take Holy Orders. He was a high churchman of the kind going out of fashion as the Hanoverian age wore on, and an ardent Jacobite. He approved the Wesleys' religious method, but he urged them to keep the fasts of the primitive church, which were enjoined in the *Book of Common Prayer* yet had lapsed from general use.

The Wesleys accepted Clayton's advice and brought him into their "little society." They began to fast every Wednesday and Friday. On the next visit to Epworth they refused even to breakfast with their parents on a Wednesday or a Friday, to the rector's indignation, and on the way home they refrained from eating until evening. Their mother wrote in disgust: "I must tell ye, Mr. John Wesley, Fellow of Lincoln, and Mr. Charles Wesley, Student of Christ Church, that ye are two scrubby travelers, and sink your characters strangely by eating nothing on the road ...[2] to save charges. I wonder ye are not ashamed of yourselves." She was sure that a little thought would return them to a better mind.

John Clayton was two years younger than Charles and would be close to the brothers for only six months before he was ordained and left Oxford, yet he had great influence. He tightened their system. The Godly Club never met all together, as was supposed by an imaginative painting of the next century, but in small groups in different colleges. Some of them hardly knew each other, but Clayton urged them to fill every hour with prayer or action to promote God's glory and their soul's health. He reorganized the visiting of the back streets and secured permission for regular readings in the bleak Workhouse, where broken old men and women were kept at labor for much of the day.

He also introduced Wesley to the writings of the Early Fathers. Wesley would walk round to the Bodleian Library and spend hours discovering new strands of Christian thought. In beautifully printed Tudor and Stuart editions of Greek and Latin texts, he studied afresh the great Christian doctrines. He bought two huge volumes of texts culled from the Fathers by William Beveridge, a learned bishop who had died some twenty years before. Wesley learned about the asceticism of the Desert Fathers and began to glimpse ideas of Christian perfection. His conviction was strengthened: that true Christianity could not be fully experienced by simple souls though all must start on the path.

Wesley had maintained his Cotswold connections. His chief correspondents now were Mrs. Mary Pendarves ("Aspasia") in London and her sister Ann ("Selima"), who had moved with their mother, Mrs. Granville, from Stanton to Gloucester. Wesley and the ladies wrote elaborate letters to each other. Romance was excluded. Wesley's heart dwelt tenderly on the affection of these cultured women. Once the two brothers rode to Gloucester and came back in a coach with the sisters, on their way to London, and were charmed by their pious conversation. Mrs. Pendarves teased Wesley a little by calling him "Primitive Christianity."

It was Mrs. Pendarves (as the evidence tentatively suggests) who showed him a new book which became a powerful influence, *A Serious Call to a Devout and Holy Life* by William Law.

Law was a non-juring, celibate clergyman in his forties who was living near London as tutor to young Edward Gibbon, future father of the great historian. Law had already written *Christian Perfection*, which Wesley does not seem to have noticed. *A Serious Call*, published in 1729, went into numerous editions and became famous in upper-class circles and clerical households for its gentle wit and wise advice conveyed by a cast of curious characters whose behavior displayed Law's lofty view of a truly devout and holy life.

Wesley disliked parts of the book, but *A Serious Call*, together with *Christian Perfection*, which he then read, "convinced me more than ever of the exceeding height and breadth and depth of the law of God. The light flowed in so mightily upon my soul, that everything appeared in a new view. I cried to God for help, and resolved not to prolong the time of obeying him as I had never done before. And by my continued endeavor to keep his whole law, inward and outward, to the utmost of my power, I was persuaded that I should be accepted of him, and that I was even then in a state of salvation."

To reach Christian perfection became the driving force of his life; nearly six years with many adventures would pass before he realized that he was driving in the wrong direction.

6

Sons of Sorrow

On the night of July 25, 1732 Wesley took two hours' sleep, then set off from Oxford after 11 o'clock to walk to London.

Unless he boarded a coach or a swift boat on the Thames for part of the fifty-four mile journey, he must have walked hard all night and day, for by the evening of July 26 he was at Rivington's shop in the city. The next morning he met a wealthy patron of the Society for the Promotion of Christian Knowledge (SPCK), who gave him a substantial donation for use among the prisoners and poor children of Oxford.

Brother Sam had obtained an invitation for Jack to preach at St. Margaret's, Westminster, the parish church in the shadow of the Abbey. After the service Sam introduced him—without either realizing what would eventually flow from the introduction—to young Colonel Oglethorpe, who had received a royal charter to found the colony of Georgia as a buffer between Spanish Florida and the British provinces in America. Georgia was intended to be a haven for English debtors, persecuted Continental Christians, and others in distress. Oglethorpe was about to sail with the first colonists.

Meanwhile, Sam was somewhat worried by Jack, who seemed to be weaving himself into a cocoon of stiff regulations and becoming even more grave; the Wesley sense of humor was being buried. Sam suspected that Jack now thought all laughter to be wrong, but Jack assured him it was permissible at the right times.

Wesley visited other relations and inspected Guy's Hospital, the new charitable foundation on the south bank of the Thames, to gather ideas for his own more humble philanthropies. He also walked out to Putney to sit at the feet of William Law; they discussed the attainment of a devout and holy life, not dreaming that in a few years they would reject each other's views. Wesley returned to Westminster by river, reading Law's gift of a German mystic text.

While in London, Wesley received a letter written on August 6, 1732 from Clayton in Oxford, which mentioned a new nickname. A Christ Church man named Bingham had derided Wesley as a "Methodist." Possibly Bingham had been reading about a small group of divines in the last ten years of the seventeenth century who had been known as "New Methodists." John Wesley's sermons and Charles Wesley's precise and particular practices had smacked of this approach to religion. The name caught on more widely than "Holy Club" and "Godly Club" and was soon used in letters and diaries, but when Wesley left London that August, he was still hardly aware of it.

On the walk back he talked with other wayfarers as they trudged the highway or sat outside taverns. He inquired how they worked out their salvation, and he urged them to seek God. Their confused replies emphasized his own uncertainties, although he was sure that his earnestness must please God; and in Oxford, where few scholars and dons remained in high summer and the grass grew in the High, he continued his reading and his good works, aiming always to improve his soul.

Then early in September 1732 he received bad news: William Morgan had died in Ireland and had died insane.

Morgan had been a youth of "sweetness and simplicity," whose greatest love was to encourage others to live a good life; but an unspecified (and possibly undiagnosed) disease had caused him to retire to a country village in Wiltshire where he spent much of his time teaching cottage children. His illness had slowly disordered his mind as Wesley noticed when they met. Wesley did not therefore enjoin him to keep the church fasts like the others: Morgan had once been severely abstemious but had reverted to a normal diet.

Morgan returned to Ireland. On a journey to the South, he became raging mad. The family servant brought him home to Dublin, where he died in delirium, calling out the names of the Wesleys.

Morgan's father, who had fumed to his son about "the ridiculous society you are engaged in," was won over by the manner of his death and showed gratitude to the Wesleys for their kindness to William. Oxford gossip, however, accused them of killing the youth by insisting that he fast. When the university filled up again for the new term, they found themselves the objects of hatred.

Worse than gossip followed at the end of term. On December 11 Wesley entered the common room at Lincoln to find the dons talking about him and "this sect called Methodists"—a quotation from the latest edition of *Fog's Weekly Journal*, freshly arrived from London. In the *Journal* was a long anonymous letter to the editor complaining that "the university at present is not a little pestered with those sons of sorrow, whose number daily receives addition" and who designed to "make the whole place nothing but a monastery."

The letter writer complained of their "absurd and perpetual melancholy," of their early rising, and of their time spent in prayer. He attacked them for believing that every conceivable action, however trivial, was of religious importance and for shedding social entertainments and diversions. The anonymous author's criticisms fell thick: "Gloomy and disconsolate way of life.... Weighed down by a habitual sorrow.... Some suppose them to use religion only as a veil to vice.... Enthusiastic madness and superstitious scruples...." The writer ended with a suggestion on how to clear their heads and expel "this gloomy stupidity."

Wesley made no answer, for he was due to preach before the university—his second university sermon—three weeks later on Monday, January 1. It would be the Feast of the Circumcision of Christ and the traditional New Year's Day, though not the legal start of the year, which still fell on March 25.

He was already preparing his sermon. He worked on it for a total of twenty-seven hours, writing and revising. Then he read all forty minutes of it aloud to different friends and discussed their suggestions. On the final Saturday he did not play cards in the common room, for his mind was on the sermon.

At 10 o'clock on Monday morning, January 1, 1733, the vice-chancellor of Oxford and the heads of houses and the customary officials processed to St. Mary's church, which had a larger congregation than usual for a weekday sermon since so many wished to hear the controversial Mr. Wesley. The feast being that of the Circumcision of Christ, Wesley chose as his text Romans 2:29, the words of St. Paul: "Circumcision is that of the heart, in the spirit, and not in the letter" and explained this circumcision of the heart as being "that habitual disposition of soul which in the sacred writings is termed 'holiness.'"

In a long, closely reasoned argument which he read carefully, he preached that Christians were to be so endued with the virtues of Christ, so "renewed in the image of our mind" as to be (in Christ's words) "'perfect, as your Father in heaven is perfect.'" He spoke of the Christian's love of God and neighbor which arose from faith in Christ. He concluded with a reasoned plea that "in every motion of our heart, every word of our tongue, in every work of our minds ... whatever we do, we do all to the glory of God."

His sermon won approval from the vice-chancellor and the rector of Lincoln and increased Wesley's standing as a theologian. It left him elated.

He was further vindicated by an anonymous pamphlet with the title "The Oxford Methodists," replying to the attack in *Fog's Weekly*. He never discovered the author, but it helped to stem "the torrent rolling down from all sides upon me." Nevertheless, several undergraduates and young dons were "frightened away from a falling house." One day in March he was even confronted by a hostile mob at the gate of Lincoln College.

John Wesley faced "the ill consequences of my singularity": loss of earnings as pupils deserted him, loss of friends, and loss of reputation. He concluded that nothing mattered but "a clean heart, a single eye, a soul full of God! A fair exchange, if by loss of reputation we can purchase the lowest degree of purity of heart!"

7

Oxford Deserted

By the winter of 1734–1735, when Wesley had been a tutor of Lincoln for five years, some three dozen Oxford men had been with the Holy or Godly Club. Most had gone down; Wesley now counted only four or five in his "little society." The Holy Club had never had formal structure, membership, or leader: Wesley's authority derived from his prestige and experience.

His zeal in inducing undergraduates "to mix more devotion into their study," especially the many who were reading for Holy Orders, met varying success. The Yorkshireman Benjamin Ingham, the gentle studious James Hervey, and a servitor of Pembroke called George Whitefield, with deep blue eyes and a squint, were ardent among the later disciples. But Richard Morgan, the late William Morgan's younger brother, was not. His father had placed him at Lincoln under Wesley as a mark of trust. Richard arrived in Oxford with a greyhound, against university regulations. After two months of Wesley's tutorship, he scrawled a long letter to his father, which caught Wesley's eye when he happened to enter Richard's room while he was out. Wesley ("contrary to my custom") read a line or two. He was so astonished that he read the rest—a mixture of fact and hearsay about "a society of gentlemen ... whom the world calls Methodists, of which my tutor is president. They imagine they cannot be saved if they do not spend every hour, nay every minute of their lives in the service of God."

Bemoaning Wesley's strictness, Richard went on to write his father: "By being his pupil I am stigmatized with the name of Methodist, the misfortune of which I cannot describe. For what they reckon the greatest happiness, namely of being laughed at, is to me the greatest misery.... If I am continued under Mr. Wesley I shall be ruined."

Wesley hurriedly wrote a rebuttal to old Mr. Morgan, who replied tactfully that he had never received the letter of complaint. He then wrote to his son, praising Wesley and ordering Richard to banish the greyhound, not to squander the mornings "in tea and chat," and to be careful of criticizing others. But Mr. Morgan did not want Richard to be drawn into "that society," nor did Wesley, though Richard became a disciple later.

Wesley continued his ministry, by evil report and good report, like the Apostle Paul. The future looked settled: employment as a controversial tutor with unusual influence on a restricted circle in each Oxford generation, earning perhaps a brief footnote to English church history.

In 1735, however, his world was turned upside down by two unrelated events: the death of his father and the conversion of George Whitefield.[1] Whitefield had come up from his native Gloucester with religion and good works. He had admired the Wesleys from afar before he came to know Charles, who brought him into their activities. Among the books which Charles lent him was a late seventeenth-century work of devotion, Scougal's *The Life of God in the Soul of Man.*

George eventually discovered in Scougal a phrase which set him afire: "True religion is a union of the soul with God ... or, in the Apostle's phrase, it is *Christ formed within us.*" He saw in a flash that he must be born again. He began to wrestle spiritually and believed he needed to strive to renounce evil and cultivate virtue, to subordinate all his moments to make himself good enough for Christ to enter his soul. The Wesleys believed that they had been born again at baptism and needed a lifetime to reach Christian perfection. George Whitefield saw instinctively that their attitude lacked logic. If union with Christ was essential for salvation, it must be acquired by the earliest possible day, whatever the cost. Whitefield was too much in awe of John Wesley to argue, and neither of them realized that winter of 1734–1735 that Whitefield would soon discover the key to evangelical revival.

In October 1734 Wesley hurried home. His father's health had worsened. Samuel rallied, but he was now seventy-two, and he urged his son to succeed him as rector. Brother Sam was now headmaster of Blundell's School at Tiverton in Devon and had already refused to consider the parish of Epworth, but the Crown might be influenced to offer it to John. Father and son had discussed it as far back as 1732, but in October 1734, as Wesley walked to Epworth, he was undecided. On his return to Oxford, however, he reached an "unalterable resolution" not to accept. His reason was bleak: "The question is not whether I could do more good to others *there* or here, but whether I could do more good to myself." He believed he could best promote holiness in others in a place where he himself could be most holy, and Oxford was the place.

When the rector protested, Wesley spent days preparing a letter of 5,000 words, which he dated December 10, 1734 and finished finally eight days later, to explain in great detail why, as a tutor in Oxford, he "could be holier myself here than anywhere else."

Thus he would do good to others, not least because "being despised is absolutely necessary to our doing good in the world." A parish would only "crush my own soul, and so make me useless to others."

Brother Sam shot down the arguments even before he had seen a full copy of Jack's letter. "I judge every proposition flatly false.... I see your love to yourself, but your love to your neighbor I do not see." He contended that Jack's Holy Orders as a priest had solemnly engaged him to take a parish.

This argument alarmed Wesley and "almost convinced me," until the bishop of Oxford agreed that ordination did not engage him to a parish if he could serve God better in "your present or some other station."

Family discussion continued into March 1735 when a letter reached Oxford from Sister Emily, saying that the brothers must come at once if they wished to see their father alive. On Palm Sunday, after taking the Sacrament, they set out through the mud on foot. They took with them Westley Hall, one of Wesley's pupils at Lincoln, an Oxford Methodist who had not yet showed that he was a ruffian, though he could not decide whether to marry Patty or Kezzy and had virtually pledged his troth to both. Hall was sick and therefore rode while they walked, but he could hardly keep his balance on the horse. They reached Epworth on Good Friday, April 4.

The dying rector laid his hands on Charles' head: "Be steady," he murmured. "The Christian faith will surely revive in this kingdom. You shall see it, though I shall not."

John Wesley took charge of the family, the parish, and the final arrangements for completing the printing of the *magnum opus* on the Book of Job. To help their father "end his days in peace," he abandoned his unalterable resolution and wrote to intermediaries in London who could influence Sir Robert Walpole, the Prime Minister, to present him to Epworth. The reply was discouraging, and the old rector died on April 25, 1735 without knowing who would succeed him.

Charles told Sam that his brother had "laid aside all hopes (or fears, for I cannot certainly say which) of succeeding." The living went to the Reverend Samuel Hirst.

As rector of Epworth, Wesley might have been lost to history. Perhaps he would have married Betty or Damaris Kirkham or Kitty Hargreaves, for "Aspasia" Pendarves had cooled toward him.

While the Wesleys were at Epworth attending to their dying father, George Whitefield lay sick and gloomy in Pembroke College. His excesses, such as praying for hours in the rain in Christ Church meadows, had alarmed the Wesleys. Before they left Oxford, Charles had brought John to advise George spiritually and medically (for as Gambold said, "His knowledge of the world and his insight into physic were often of use to us"), but Whitefield had worsened.

He wrote frequently. Wesley sent ministrations by return post. Unknown to him, at about the time the rector died, Whitefield was transformed.

One day in his misery, he picked up a book which someone had lent him, *Contemplations on the New Testament* by Joseph Hall, a seventeenth-century bishop. Writing on the Crucifixion,

Hall suddenly made Whitefield aware that the new birth was not a reward but a gift. Because Christ had paid the price of sin, no method of prayers and good works or self-denial could earn forgiveness. Whitefield threw himself on his bed and prayed a prayer of utter helplessness.

Joy flooded his soul. He had discovered that grace was free, received by faith alone.

Whitefield wrote another long letter to Wesley on May 5. Awe of his spiritual master prevented him saying openly what had happened. One phrase, however, might have saved John Wesley nearly three more years of struggle: "Into his all gracious arms," wrote Whitefield, "I blindly throw myself."

W esley stayed at Epworth as acting rector for two months. Then he went up to London in late June to see *Dissertationes in Librum Jobi* through the press and to attempt to resolve the triangular love affair of Westley Hall, Patty, and Kezzy.

Epworth rectory ceased to be the Wesley home. Their mother would go to Tiverton to live with Sam and Ursula. The unmarried and married sisters were scattered in Lincolnshire and London. John Wesley expected to return to Oxford. During the last months of his father's life, however, there had been much talk of Georgia, for Oglethorpe was home and seeking clergy. The old rector had exclaimed that he would have gone himself were he younger.

In November, when the crippled Molly died giving birth to a child, he recommended to the Georgia trustees his bereaved son-in-law, Johnny Whitelamb, now vicar of Wroot. Whitelamb was a local boy from a poor home who had assisted the old rector with his papers, then had been helped through Lincoln College by the

Wesleys, though they kept him short of money. Molly had fallen in love with him while he worked at the rectory. She had married him despite his involvement with a prostitute near Oxford, and they became a devoted couple, the only love match of all the sisters.

The trustees rejected Whitelamb, who remained at Wroot, a disconsolate, gloomy man who in later years seemed to become a deist.

At this time John Wesley had no close interest in Georgia. Nine months earlier, when he had been at a meeting of the SPCK in Barlett's Buildings, Holborn, as a corresponding member, some Protestant Salzburgers had arrived at Gravesend, and he helped to plan their departure to Georgia on the *Prince of Wales*. But it had not crossed his mind to serve there. On August 28, 1735, however, he was walking down Ludgate Street near St. Paul's when he met, by accident, a theologian and a Georgia trustee named John Burton, a fellow of Eton. Burton urged upon Wesley the opportunity which Georgia presented to himself, Charles, and the other Oxford Methodists to fulfill their exalted religious aims. Wesley was attracted. To go among the Indians would help him to be more ascetic, to withdraw more from the world in his pursuit of Christian perfection. And he would be less tempted by women, he thought, if they were "of a different species from me."

He talked with Colonel Oglethorpe. He consulted William Law. He went north to Manchester to consult John Clayton, then back by Epworth, which his mother had not yet left. She declared that had she twenty sons, she would rejoice if all went as missionaries to Georgia.

Charles agreed to come as Oglethorpe's secretary for Indian affairs. The bishop of London hastily made him a deacon; a week later the bishop of Oxford ordained him a priest. The brothers persuaded Benjamin Ingham to accompany them to Georgia. Meantime, Westley Hall, having given a ring to Kezzy in the country, married Patty in London "in spite of her poor astonished parent, of her brothers, of all your vows and promises." He left Kezzy a brokenhearted old maid for life. Hall offered to go to Georgia, and the trustees accepted him and Patty.

At John's insistence the two Wesleys would be volunteer missionaries; only their passage and book supplies would be paid for by the SPCK, which announced that Messrs. John Wesley and Ingham designed "after a short stay at Savannah, to go among the Indian nations bordering upon that Settlement, in order to bring them to the knowledge of Christianity."

Westley Hall withdrew at the last moment; therefore, Patty could not come.

One last duty remained. Queen Caroline, George II's consort, had accepted the dedication of *Job*. On Sunday morning, October 12, 1735, Wesley went to Kensington Palace with Colonel Oglethorpe and a Christ Church friend, a bishop's son who was angling (successfully) for a good living. Sir Robert Walpole introduced them to the royal presence. Wesley reported to Sam that the Queen gave him "many good words and smiles." Later in his life she became one of his anecdotes: The Queen was romping with her ladies when he made his bow, he would say. She received him graciously. He presented his father's book on bended knee. She said: "It is prettily bound," and laid it unopened on a window ledge though she could read Latin easily. After kind words to Wesley and the two other gentlemen introduced by Walpole, she smiled a dismissal and returned to her romp.[2]

Two days later, barely six weeks after Georgia was first suggested to him, Wesley embarked at Gravesend with Brother Charles, Benjamin Ingham, and Charles Delamotte, a twenty-year-old Londoner of the Wesleys' acquaintance.

John Wesley had no doubt why he wanted to be a missionary. "My chief motive, to which all the rest are subordinate, is the hope of saving my own soul. I hope to learn the true sense of the Gospel of Christ by preaching it to the heathens."

8

Sophy of Savannah

On the evening of Saturday, January 17, 1736, John and Charles Wesley were sitting with Colonel Oglethorpe and others in the state cabin of the *Simmonds* far out in the Atlantic. The sea had been rough, and the clouds had been thickening all day. Now the pitching of the ship became more alarming every minute.

Suddenly a huge wave "burst into the cabin ... with a noise and shock almost like that of a cannon." A bureau had sheltered Wesley, but he was shocked to discover himself "afraid to die." At midnight he added a note to his diary: "Stormy still and afraid!"

The Wesleys and their fellow passengers had been three months on board already, for the *Simmonds*, held off the Isle of Wight by contrary winds, had only cleared the English Channel in the second week of December. Wesley, as chaplain, had been much impressed by a group of twenty-six German emigrants. They were members of the Church of the United Brethren, colloquially known as the Moravian Church, which descended directly from the pre-Reformation martyr John Hus, but had been revived from a moribund state by young Count Zinzendorf, who was only three years older than Wesley.

An English locksmith named Ambrose Tackner knew German and was willing to teach Wesley, who soon conversed with Moravian Bishop David Nitschman and his flock. The Wesleys would not invite them to Holy Communion but admired their serenity and unselfishness. The Germans were always cheerful. They undertook servile tasks which the English emigrants were too proud or lazy to consider, and when crewmen or passengers abused, vilified, or even knocked them down, they turned the other cheek. At their services they sang hymns of great beauty. The Church of England's metrical psalms sounded tawdry and stilted in contrast.

The Wesleys, Benjamin Ingham, and young Charles Delamotte had signed an agreement to consult each other on every move, abiding by the majority decision. If they divided equally, they would draw lots. They had pledged themselves to continue their introspective diaries and the rigorous Oxford Methodist system of prayers, readings, fasts, and good works.

The Moravians were not impressed, for they detected that Wesley's tight routine was chiefly intended to acquire merit. They offered him, in contrast, the great Reformation doctrine of justification by faith. As Wesley wrote some two years later, they "endeavored to show me 'a more excellent way.' But I understood it not at first. I was too learned and too wise. So that it seemed foolishness to me. And I continued preaching, and following after, and trusting in that righteousness whereby no flesh can be justified."

During the days of storm, Wesley tried to keep to his rigorous program but could not throw off his fear as the ship rocked and jarred "with the utmost violence." The gale died down but another struck a few days later. Again, a great wave knocked him over! He found he was unhurt yet "could but say to myself, 'How is it that thou hast no faith?' being still unwilling to die."

On the Sunday evening, with the ship so rolling that he could hardly walk the companion-ways, he went to join the twenty-six Moravians. He found them joyfully singing one of their magnificent hymns. As they sang, a great wave struck the ship, split the mainsail, and poured in between the decks. "A terrible screaming began among the English. The Germans looked up and without intermission calmly sang on. I asked one of them afterwards, 'Was you not afraid?' He answered, 'I thank God, no.' I asked, 'But were not your women and children afraid?' He replied mildly, 'No; our women and children are not afraid to die.'"

When the storm blew itself out at last, Wesley resumed his personal discipline and his pastoral work as ship's chaplain. He was particularly pleased that a Mrs. Hawkins, the young wife of a surgeon sailing to a post in Georgia, was hanging on his exhortations and renouncing her frivolous ways. Charles, however, believed she was a hypocrite. The brothers argued. "Charles perverse," noted Wesley several times in his diary.

On February 4 they saw land. When the *Simmonds* anchored in the Savannah River, Wesley was entranced by "the exceeding beautiful prospect"—the rows of pines, palms, and cedars along the shore beneath a cloudless sky. Early next morning he set foot in Georgia. Oglethorpe led them across the foreshore of an island to rising ground, where they knelt down in thanksgiving. Oglethorpe then took boat for Savannah while Wesley held a service under the myrtles and cedars, sheltered from sun and wind.

When the colonel returned after a day and night ashore, he brought with him the energetic and learned leader of the original

Moravian settlers, a man about the same age as Wesley called August Spangenberg. His cheerful demeanor and year of experience in America encouraged Wesley to ask him for advice on how to proceed, but to Wesley's surprise, Spangenberg declined to give it. He said he must first ask Wesley some questions.

"Do you know yourself?" Spangenberg asked. "Have you the witness in yourself? Does the Spirit of God bear witness with your spirit that you are a child of God?"

While Wesley recognized the text in St. John's first Epistle from which the questions derived, he hesitated to answer. Spangenberg then put a direct question, though kindly: "Do you know Jesus Christ?"

Wesley paused in some confusion, then replied lamely: "I know He is the Saviour of the world."

"True," said the German. "But do you know He has saved *you?*"

Wesley replied uncomfortably, "I hope He has died to save me."

Spangenberg did not pursue his catechism. He merely repeated the question: "Do you know yourself?"

Wesley replied, "I do." (Later he wrote, "but I fear they were vain words.") Spangenberg then offered various practical suggestions about Georgia.

His strange questions were soon forgotten by Wesley in the rush of his secretarial work for Oglethorpe and in preparing the flock for their settlement on land. Wesley had come to convert the Indians, but the Georgia trustees, while he had lain becalmed in English waters, had sent to appoint him rector of Savannah in succession to Mr. Quincy, who wanted to return north to Boston.

Wesley was encouraged, however, when an ancient Indian chief, who believed himself to be nearly 100, came on board. Dressed in English clothes such as he had worn when Oglethorpe presented him to King George II in London, Chief Tomo-chachi was accompanied by some younger relations, also in English dress, and by the king of the Savannah nation, who wore a large blanket, beads in his hair, and a scarlet feather behind one ear.

Chief Tomo-chachi made a grave speech, interpreted by an Indian woman who had married an English trader, which led Wesley to believe that the Indian nations would welcome Christianity. He was disappointed when he returned the chief's visit; the wigwams were empty. Later, Wesley often met the few braves and squaws who lived near Savannah, but Oglethorpe scotched Wesley's plans to follow distant forest tracks or the waterways in search of tribes to convert; he might be captured by the French or the Spanish and embroil the colony in war.

About a month after Wesley's arrival, the colonists crowded into the courthouse, which served as their church on Sundays, for their new parson's first service. The second Scripture lesson at the Morning Prayer that Sunday put him in mind of the motto of St. Francis of Assisi: "Naked to follow the naked Christ," which he feared was scarcely appropriate to himself because Georgia seemed a most pleasant place to live. He preached from St. Paul's chapter on Christian love. The people listened "with deep affection" without hint of future hate.

Wesley lodged with the Moravians until his predecessor left, then he moved to the parsonage, unpacked his books, and threw himself into the work of pastor to Savannah and to the scattered settlements of ex-debtors, Scottish highlanders (who had their own minister), and

Young Adventurers—the title given to young men who had come out at their own expense. Oglethorpe warned him to beware of "log house converts," but Wesley was taken in by the pretended "zeal for holiness" of a Dutch youth who was afterward revealed to be a thief and a liar and had hoped to manipulate Wesley for his own ends.

The weeks in Savannah passed in devotional exercises, pastoral duties, secretarial work for the colony—particularly burdensome on the days when Wesley fasted—and travel. He walked the forest paths in Indian shoes or traveled the waterways by canoe or skiff, sleeping nights wrapped in an Indian blanket. He was especially pleased at opportunities to be with the Moravians or to visit the Protestant refugees from Salzburg who called their place Ebenezer ("Hitherto hath the Lord helped us"). Though he could not approve their lack of a rigid framework of fasts, prayers, and liturgical services, he envied these Continental Christians their joy, their humble assurance, and their purity of heart. He began to translate the German hymns, which he loved to sing.

The colonists were somewhat amazed by their new little parson. They approved his zeal for visiting the sick, bereaved, and the few prisoners and for catechizing the children. They admired his energy and his willingness to cut down trees and help build houses. They were amused at his habit of bursting into song and puzzled at his hourly stops to say a prayer. They were not so pleased when he divided the services in the *Book of Common Prayer* to conform, he said, with the *First Prayer Book of Edward VI*, which he thought more in tune with the custom of the primitive church. Parents were worried at baptisms because he insisted on following the long forgotten rubric which enjoins the minister to dip the baby "discreetly and warily" into the water, not to sprinkle. And because John Wesley fasted, some thought him a papist in disguise.

He expected his people to fast too. He taught that the road to God was steep, that they must carry out frequent religious duties and exercises if they would be true Christians. Many rejected these extra burdens on their hard, pioneering lives.

John Wesley was happy. Charles, however, was not. While still on board the *Simmonds*, he had complained in a letter to the ladies at Stanton of spiritual unworthiness and misery. He had now gone south with Oglethorpe to set up a new settlement on the coast at Fort Frederica, where most of the passengers from the *Simmonds* had been allotted land. Charles had hoped that pastoral work would alter his soul for the better, but he contracted dysentery after sleeping on the ground because boards were too expensive. He disliked his work as Oglethorpe's secretary of Indian affairs, and instead of preaching to Indians, he was failing to cure settlers of bad habits.

He sent word to his brother that Mrs. Hawkins, Wesley's pious "convert," had come to him with a confession of adultery with Oglethorpe. She had then told Oglethorpe that the tale was slanderous gossip put about by the Wesley brothers.

Wesley promptly sailed to Frederica as soon as the winds allowed, and interrogated Mrs. Hawkins. After a week, not totally convinced of Oglethorpe's innocence or of Mrs. Hawkins' hypocrisy, he returned to Savannah.

And it was there that another woman became the cause of a train of events which, in little more than eighteen months, would lead him to flee the colony.

Sophia Christiana Hopkey, a pretty and kindhearted girl of seventeen, was the niece of Mrs. Thomas Causton, whose husband was chief magistrate of Savannah and the colony's storekeeper.

Rumor persisted that he had come to Georgia because of a disreputable past. John Wesley first met Sophy at church with her relations a few days after his arrival. When he took the unusual step of instituting public prayers in the early morning and a communion service on every Sunday and saint's day, she was always present.

He thought it his duty to speak privately with every communicant every week. Being determined "to have no intimacy with any woman in America," he was careful at first to choose times when Sophy and he were in the open air and never alone. In June, however, her aunt roundly hinted to Wesley that Sophy would make a good housewife. Through study of the Mystics and a misreading of the Early Fathers, Wesley was temporarily "persuaded that 'It was unlawful for a priest to marry,'" so in July he began to invite Sophy and another girl to the parsonage for devotional instruction after the early public prayers, rather to the disgust of young Philip Thicknesse, a boy boarding with the Caustons, who wondered why he was not asked: "Surely," he said, "my soul is as of much importance as theirs."

Wesley would come briskly to the temporary church after a dawn bath in the Savannah River with Charles, back from Frederica, and Delamotte. They chose the hour not only for coolness but "because the alligators were not stirring so soon. We heard them, indeed, snoring all around us."

Some day in July, apparently alone with Sophy in the parsonage, Wesley talked with her and then "I took her by the hand, and before we parted I kissed her. And from this time, I fear there was a mixture in my intention, though I was not soon sensible of it." Shortly afterward, by prior arrangement, she left Savannah to stay at Frederica with a family named Hurd.

Wesley was able to put her to the back of his mind, for on July 20 five Chickasaw Indian braves from up country, two of them being chiefs, were brought to him by an elderly clergyman, a Mr. Andrews. He knew their language, had been educated at Wesley's own Oxford college, and had once been a missionary among the Mohawks in New York Province. While Charles noted the conference in shorthand, Wesley eagerly asked about their beliefs.

"Do you believe there is One above who is over all things?" he asked.

One of the chiefs answered, "We believe there are four beloved things above: the clouds, the sun, the clear sky, and He that lives in the clear sky."

"Do you believe there is but One who lives in the clear sky?"

"We believe there are Two with Him, Three in all."

The conference took several sessions. Wesley convinced himself from their strange mixture of religious ideas that the red men were ripe for conversion, though most of the colonists said they were treacherous, cruel, and inclined to murder children.

Wesley wrote out an account of the conference and addressed it to the *Gentleman's Magazine* in London. Charles would take it, for he was going home. His health had broken; he was bickering with Oglethorpe and felt disappointed at failure to help the Indians. Since the brothers were anxious to summon recruits to their mission, they had decided, with Oglethorpe's consent, that Charles should return to England briefly and bring back more missionaries. Shortly after the conference the brothers left by sea for the long-established port of Charleston in South Carolina, whiling away the hours by reading devotional books, singing the hymns they had learned from the Germans, and visiting settlers on the islands.

In South Carolina, for the first time, Wesley saw black slaves in the fields, a fact which would come vividly to mind many years later. Georgia had expressly forbidden slavery, although some of the settlers used blacks, asserting that they were baptized and free.

Within a fortnight Wesley was back in Savannah and at once sailed to Frederica to rejoin Oglethorpe, who "gave me a large account of Miss Sophy and desired me to be with her as much as I could 'because she was in deep distress.'" She had been bothered by the attentions of a young man named Mellichamp. Her relations were urging her to accept him since he was well connected at home, but Wesley knew him to be a scamp, and Sophy did not want him. Wesley calmed her by reading pious books.

This August visit to Frederica proved to be a foretaste of troubles to come.

Mrs. Hawkins and her husband stirred up strife, claiming that Wesley had slandered her. She enticed him to her home, where she threatened to shoot him, then set upon him with a pair of scissors. She pushed him onto her bed and cut off one side of his long hair. She swore at him, tearing his cassock. Servants, husband, neighbors, and finally the constable rushed into the room and restrained her; and soon the story of the little parson's adventure was all over the colony. When Wesley returned to Savannah, young Thicknesse was much amused to watch Wesley preach "with his hair so long on one side, so short on the other"—those "fine long Adonis locks of auburn hair—hair which he took infinite pains to have in the most exact order which, with his benign and humble countenance, gave him a very pleasing aspect."

Wesley still had no suspicion that he would not stay permanently in Georgia. He wrote to George Whitefield in

England, urging him to come out and join him. Ingham had gone to live among the Indians on Pipe Makers Creek, four miles northwest of Savannah, so that "only Delamotte with me, till God shall stir up the hearts of some of his servants, who, putting their lives in their hands, shall come over and help us, where the harvest is great and the laborers few. What if thou art the man, Mr. Whitefield?" In a second letter he sketched the unlimited opportunities which he and Whitefield could seize: "Here are adults from the farthest parts of Europe and Asia, and the inmost Kingdoms of Africa. Add to these the known and unknown natives of this vast continent, and you will indeed have a great multitude."

Yet Wesley was no nearer the Indians. Oglethorpe refused to let him leave the colonists without a pastor, and the Indians themselves, at the end of his conference with them, had said they could not listen while surrounded by tribal enemies.

Darkness falls swiftly in Georgia; a small skiff must not be caught out at sea. Wesley, sailing from Frederica to Savannah in October 1736 with no other passenger except Sophy, landed on an uninhabited island.

He scented moral danger. Wesley and Sophy were alone, a bachelor with a young spinster, except for a white boy, Jemmy, who was his volunteer servant, and the boat's crew, respectfully keeping their distance. Wesley took refuge in the thought that he had not sought this temptation; Oglethorpe had ordered him to take Sophy in his boat. And if his resolution to stay single should waver, he had convinced himself that Sophy was now determined never to marry.

He had returned to Frederica to baptize, marry, bury, and to discipline an erring flock, who always failed to live according to the high standards of William Law's *Serious Call* unless their parson was among them. He had found Sophy unhappy yet dreading a return to Savannah where she must live with her uncle and aunt. Her violent suitor, Tom Mellichamp, had been put in prison for fraud, and Causton had virtually given her to Wesley if he would have her. At Frederica, Wesley had visited her frequently as her pastor and was careful to keep conversation on an exalted plane. Nevertheless, he could not disguise from himself that she tugged at his heart and would be a most suitable wife.

Once ashore on the uninhabited island, they made a fire and had supper. Wesley read prayers, and the crew rigged up the sail on four stakes to keep out the bitter northeast wind and the night dews. The sailors lay on one side; Sophy, Wesley, and Jemmy on the other.

The next morning they set sail in a rough sea but made small progress and were obliged to land on the south end of St. Katherine's Island. The wind held them there for three days. One afternoon Wesley took Sophy for a walk, and they sat in a little thicket by a spring, and Wesley talked learnedly about holiness. He was charmed by her puzzled attempt to understand. Next day they sailed on only to be turned back by the wind. That night as they lay awake by the fire, Wesley asked: "Miss Sophy, how far are you engaged to Mr. Mellichamp?"

"I have promised him either to marry him or to marry no one at all."

Wesley's feelings overcame his resolution. "Miss Sophy, I should think myself happy if I was to spend the rest of my life with you!"

9

"Lost, Sunk"

Sophy burst into tears. "I am very unhappy," she said between sobs. "I won't have Tommy, for he is a bad man. And I can have none else." She begged Wesley to say no more about marriage while half admitting that she loved him. She added, "We may converse on other subjects as freely as ever." Recovering himself, Wesley "ended our conversation with a psalm."

Sophy insisted that she could not live with her uncle and aunt. Back at Savannah on the day before her eighteenth birthday on November 1, 1736, Wesley secured an arrangement from the Caustons whereby Sophy should sleep at their house but breakfast at his, along with Delamotte, and spend the mornings and evenings in his care. She joined the devotions and sang the hymns. Between pastoral duties Wesley taught her French and read theology to her, being particularly taken with Ephraem Syrus, a fourth-century Syrian whose involved and repetitious writing had recently been republished in Greek. (Wesley presumably translated into English as he read.)

The arrangement continued all winter. Wesley disregarded gossip about his relations with Sophy, but, as he admitted eventually, "I find I cannot take fire into my bosom and not be burnt." He intended to stay celibate yet had fallen in love. As a celibate, he could ignore Sophy's feelings and continue to polish her soul, occasionally allowing himself a kiss. If and when he abandoned celibacy, he could still have her, for she would not marry except to him, having thrown off Mellichamp.

Early in 1737 he revisited Frederica and returned, having "beaten the air in this unhappy place." The colonists rejected the religious yoke he had placed on their shoulders. "[My] utter despair of doing good there ... made me content with the thought of seeing it no more."

Wesley was now in a dilemma. He still expected to be a celibate and itinerant missionary among the tribes. If he married Sophy, he would become a man of property (for a wife's estate belonged to the husband) and be tempted to settle in Savannah. Yet he was wavering. On February 3, impulsively, he dropped a broad hint about marriage. Had Sophy responded, he "would have made but a faint resistance," but she said it was best for both of them never to marry.

On reflection, Wesley "thought this a very narrow escape." He consulted the Moravian pastor, John Toeltschig, older than himself. Toeltschig urged him to marry. Ingham and Delamotte, however, argued strongly against the German's advice; they thought that Sophy was not holy enough for Wesley.

Wesley went away into the country to pray over his position and almost reached despair. When a pastoral duty forced him to walk back to Savannah, for an hour, "my heart was with Sophy all the time." Back in the countryside, however, he reached a new determination not to marry, and when he returned to his own house on February 14, he took Sophy into the garden. He said:

"I am resolved, Miss Sophy, if I marry at all, not to do it till I have been among the Indians." He still believed that she had no other suitor; she could be kept for his convenience.

Sophy very properly stopped coming to the parsonage, though they continued to meet in company. Twelve days later, calling at the Caustons, he found her alone. "Her words, her eyes, her air, her every motion and gesture, were full of such a softness and sweetness!" Had he touched her hand, he would have proposed and been accepted.

The next day Delamotte happened to leave them alone "and my resolution failed." Wesley took her by the hand, and once again he nearly proposed, restraining himself only because he believed she would never marry.

Young Delamotte was upset. The more he saw of Wesley's infatuation, the more he was disturbed. He knew that Wesley was in love; he doubted Sophy's sincerity, though unaware that she was seeing another man. Delamotte urged caution. When Wesley retorted that he had no intention of marrying, Delamotte replied: "You do not know your own heart."

On March 4 Wesley and Delamotte decided to settle the matter by lot. They wrote out three cards: "Marry." "Think not of it this year." "Think of it no more." They shuffled the cards and prayed. Delamotte drew a card. He turned it over. The lot was: "Think of it no more."

Wesley's first reaction was relief and submission, but within three days, while "drinking a dish of tea" at the Caustons, he realized that Sophy still held his heart. He had now heard a rumor that a young adventurer, William Williamson, of whom he disapproved, was courting her. She denied it and assured him she would take no step without his advice.

Wesley was "in the toils," as he recorded it in his diary. The more he saw Sophy, the more he loved her; he had begun to believe that his resolution to stay single would soon be overcome. On March 8, 1737 Sophy came to breakfast and stayed for prayers. That evening at the Caustons, he found Sophy and her aunt quarrelling over a letter from the rejected suitor, Tom Mellichamp. "Get out of my house!" Mrs. Causton shouted at her niece. "Mr. Wesley," she cried, "I wish you would take her. Take her away with ye!" Sophy wept. Wesley withdrew to his house in heaviness of spirit for Sophy's suffering.

But the next day when he walked through the rain and called on Mrs. Causton, he was astounded to be asked to publish the banns of marriage between Sophy and William Williamson. Wesley could hardly believe what he heard, for Sophy had directly denied the rumors of courtship. Mrs. Causton suggested he talk with Sophy. He returned home "amazed, in pain, prayed, meditated," as he wrote in his diary for the hour between 11 A.M. and noon. He half wondered whether Sophy's aim was to provoke him into proposing, but she was too sincere a girl for such artifice.

At noon they met. Wesley was in "a complication of passions and tumult," miserable at his loss and certain that Williamson would "make her very unhappy." Their conversation, then and in the afternoon, left him sure that she was marrying Williamson on an impulse to escape her uncle and aunt.

He walked up and down in his garden in shock. "Tried to pray, lost, sunk."

Sophy married Williamson four days later, without banns, at Purrysburg across the river in South Carolina. They were married by a priest who sat lightly to church law, but the irregular marriage was never challenged.

Despite his sore heart, Wesley stayed friendly with the Williamsons, although grieving that Sophy came less regularly to Holy Communion. He continued his parish ministry, hoping that time would heal the wound. In April, however, he discovered that Sophy had been dallying with Williamson for at least two weeks before their sudden engagement. Her assurances that she would remain single and her denials of the rumors which linked her with Williamson had been deceit. Wesley realized, with thanksgiving, that he had narrowly escaped marriage with an unsuitable girl.

His spirit was wounded. He was lonely: Ingham had returned to England, and Delamotte was little more than a youth. The Moravians always welcomed him, but their quiet faith and stirring hymns highlighted his sense of failure.

In June he wrote to his sister Kezia, suggesting that she come to Georgia to keep house. As soon as the letter had gone, he doubted the wisdom of his suggestion, even though he had no intention of leaving the colony nor of abandoning his hope of a mission to the Indians.

A Mrs. Brownfield now disclosed to him "a new and unexpected scene" of Sophy's dissimulation: Sophy had been in love with Tom Mellichamp while pretending that she wished to shake him off. Her tears on the uninhabited island had been another deceit. Wesley was hurt and angry. He wanted to refuse to admit her to Holy Communion. Delamotte dissuaded him, but a leading settler urged him to do so, and one month later after an unsatisfactory talk with Sophy, who was pregnant, he wrote her a letter describing "what I dislike about your past or present behavior." He thought he had written in the most mild and friendly manner, but to

Sophy it seemed abrupt and offensive. She miscarried, and her aunt blamed Wesley.

The next time Sophy came to church, he publicly repelled her from the Sacrament. Since he could not assert that she was "an open and notorious evil liver," he relied on a long-disused rubric that an intending communicant should give prior notice to the minister. Wesley himself had neglected another rubric that the minister should give private warning that he would withhold the Sacrament, so that the offender might stay away and avoid public rebuff.

Whether Sophy deserved to be excluded or not, Wesley had highlighted his misunderstanding of the Christian gospel. On that August Sunday in Savannah, he publicly, if unconsciously, demonstrated his current belief that Christ's consolations were only for the righteous; the sinner must strive to deserve them.

Sophy's humiliation infuriated her husband. Williamson secured a warrant for Wesley's arrest, claiming £1,000 damages for defamation, an immense sum in 1737. Wesley was arraigned before the bailiff and the recorder and was summoned to appear at the next court. Williamson demanded that bail should be set. The bailiff refused: "Mr. Wesley's word is sufficient."

Causton, as chief magistrate, now set about packing a grand jury who could be relied upon, after hearing the presentments, to find a true bill against Wesley, who would then go to trial. Forty-three men, a fifth of the adult males in Savannah, including a Frenchman who knew no English, sat for two days. By the beginning of September, the grand jury had found a true bill of indictment under ten heads. However, twelve of the grand jurors brought to Wesley a minority report which rejected most of the charges against him. They planned to send it to the trustees in London.

In Oglethorpe's absence to England, Causton had civil power. But most of the charges were ecclesiastical, for which he had no jurisdiction. Wesley, though sure of this, was willing to stand his trial, yet whenever he tried to present his case, the court adjourned without hearing him.

The colony was split. One faction abused Wesley; the other abused Causton and the Williamsons. By early November when Colonel William Stephens, a future governor, arrived in Georgia, he found that "the discord between Mr. Causton and the Parson was carried now to that height as to engage a great part of the town, which was so divided that Mr. Causton and Mr. Wesley drew their great attention and the partisans on both sides did not stick to throw plenty of scandal against their adversaries."

At church Stephens sorrowed "to see so thin an audience, which proceeded from a grown aversion to the preacher since this public strife sprung up." Wesley preached very acceptably on mutual forgiveness. Stephens heard both sides of the story and brought the protagonists together. He noted their mutual resentment: Causton was the more vehement, Wesley temperate but "of opinion that no reconciliation was possible."

Wesley's work was in ruins. He decided to lay his case before the trustees in England. On November 22 he pinned up a notice that he would leave the colony on December 2. Williamson pinned up another to remind the public of his pending claim for £1,000 damages. He threatened to prosecute "with utmost rigor" any who helped Wesley to escape before trial.

When December 2 came, Wesley sent to ask the court if they designed to stop him. In answer, the recorder, Mr. Christie, arrived with a "kind of bond," engaging Wesley "under penalty of fifty pounds" to appear when summoned. Wesley retorted that he had sought trial seven or eight times. He refused to give a bond.

The magistrates publicly ordered all constables and sentinels to prevent John Wesley from leaving the colony. He decided to escape. "Being now only a prisoner at large" in a place where every day would bring fresh accusations of "words I never said and actions I never did, I saw clearly that the hour was come for me to fly for my life."

After evening prayers he slipped out through the night on a favorable tide and crossed into South Carolina with a constable, a tithing man, and a barber who also wished to leave the colony. All three, according to Stephens, were of ill repute.

Landing, they made for Port Royal on foot. Their journey that followed seemed a parable of Wesley's life. Hot and thirsty by day, cold and hungry at night, losing the way in swamp and forest, they struggled along a forest path marked by blazes chipped in the bark of the trees. They came to a fork and "followed through an almost impossible thicket, the briers of which dealt but roughly both with our clothes and skin."

The blazes stopped. They were lost. "We prayed to God to direct us, and forced our way through the thicket once more, searched out the other blaze, and traced that, till it came to an end too."

Part Two

"IN MY HEART AND IN MY MOUTH"
1738–1749

10

Strangely Warmed

On January 24, 1738 aboard the *Samuel*, John Wesley was relieved to learn that he was now only 160 leagues from Land's End.

He had sailed from Charleston on Christmas Eve. He was a deserter, for he had left Georgia without permission of the trustees, though he had convinced himself that he was justified in returning to report to them the sad state of the colony. He had jumped his bail, but he reckoned that it should never have been set and that he must reach London before his accusers.

He had failed as a missionary. His future was uncertain. His carefully constructed method of living had collapsed, and when great seas during a "thorough storm" broke over the ship with a sound like the thunder in Georgia, he had found that he could not face death without fear.

His mind was "full of thought." In an attempt to clear it, he began to write: "I went to America to convert the Indians; but oh, who will convert me? Who, what is it that will deliver me from this evil heart of unbelief? I have a fair summer religion. I can talk well; nay, and believe myself, while no danger is near. But let death look me in the face, and my spirit is troubled." On page after page he continued to examine his spiritual poverty in Georgia, "Continually doubting whether I was right or wrong, and never out of perplexities and entanglements."

On Sunday, January 29, they "saw English land once more." The *Samuel* ran by the Lizard with a fair wind which veered the next day and held her back. Then it changed again and took her through the Straits of Dover and into the North Sea and a calm, until a strong north wind in the night "brought us safe into the Downs." They landed at Deal by boat while it was still dark on the morning of February 1, 1738.

Wesley discovered that the wind which had carried him in had carried George Whitefield out of the anchorage on board the *Whitaker*, eager to join John Wesley in Savannah.

Wesley must have heard in Georgia of the extraordinary religious revival which had begun in Bristol under Whitefield's preaching. He could not know that Whitefield was carrying letters for him from Charles, one of which described the astonishing scenes when Whitefield had preached his farewell sermons in London churches, helped by zealous friends: "God has poured out his Spirit upon them," wrote Charles, "so that the whole nation is in an uproar. They are already stigmatized for Methodists. We see all about us in an amazing ferment. Surely Christianity is once more lifting up its head. O that I might feel its renovating spirit." Charles did not tell Jack that Whitefield's sermons ignored the rigorous demands of the Oxford Methodists and proclaimed "free grace" for sinners.

Wesley would have liked to have greeted Whitefield and warn him about Georgia, but the outward-bound *Whitaker* might have sailed beyond reach of a small boat hired from the harbor. She might, on the other hand, meet an adverse wind and return or lie in the downs becalmed. Wesley was in a quandary: whether to wait in Deal or hurry to London. He decided to draw lots. In the inn he wrote the alternatives on pieces of paper. Then he drew a lot and read: "Let him return to London." He enclosed it in a hurried note which he left against Whitefield's possible return. He then read prayers and Scripture to a company who gathered at the inn, including fellow passengers from America and locals who had heard George Whitefield preach. Then he took the road for London.

The wind had dropped. Whitefield's ship lay in the downs. Hearing that his revered friend and mentor had arrived, he sent his servant ashore to arrange a meeting but learned to his grief that Wesley had gone. Later, he received the note and the piece of paper, "Let him return to London." He read it as referring to himself and was upset. He wrote a long letter to explain why he could not abandon his mission and return to London. His ship sailed for America next day.

Whitefield never forgot his distress that Wesley had not waited or come aboard but apparently had expected him to turn tail and follow to London. When, years later, they fell out, the lot of February 1, 1738 would influence events.

Two afternoons later Charles Wesley, lodging at the Huttons' house in Westminster, was astonished to hear that his brother was in England and could not believe it until Jack walked in that night. Charles was expecting to return to Georgia as soon as health permitted, but Wesley intended to resign his appointment.

John Wesley spent the next days meeting old friends and relations, explaining himself to Oglethorpe, and offering the trustees a lamentable report. The trustees were annoyed; several supposed that Wesley intended mischief. And when he preached in London churches which wanted news of Georgia, his sermons were not what congregations expected. He took his favorite theme, "Naked to follow the naked Christ," rather than soberly informing them about the colony. Churchwardens were irritated that he preached without notes with "so very much action" and vehement emphasis. They disliked his remarkable appearance, wearing his own hair long instead of a respectable clerical wig. At St. John's, Millbank, and elsewhere, he was told he would not be invited again.

Wesley gloried in giving offense, yet his spirit was in turbulence, striving all the harder to obtain more faith.

On Tuesday, February 7 ("a day much to be remembered"), he met a young German, Peter Böhler, newly arrived on his way to be a missionary in South Carolina. Born in Frankfurt and educated at the University of Jena, Böhler, only twenty-six, had come by a sudden experience into a clear understanding of justification by faith. He had joined the Moravian Brethren and been ordained by Count Zinzendorf. Wesley carried a letter for Zinzendorf and therefore sought out his representative in London, who introduced Böhler and two other intending missionaries. Wesley found them lodging near his own in Westminster.

He immediately struck up a warm friendship with Böhler, whose happy faith contrasted with his own. They conversed in Latin, for Böhler could not yet speak English. At one point Böhler contended that a true faith in Christ always brought two fruits: "Dominion over sin, and constant peace from a sense of forgiveness." Wesley was "quite amazed, and looked upon it as a new gospel. If this was so, it was clear I had not faith."

Wesley was not, however, prepared to accept Böhler's contention. He disputed "with all my might," arguing that forgiveness and peace must be earned by unceasing effort. He admitted that he groaned under the heavy yoke and that the more he tried to be holy, the more he sinned. Böhler replied frankly: "*Believe* and you will be saved. Believe in the Lord Jesus with all your heart, and nothing shall be impossible to you! This faith, like the salvation it brings, is the *free gift* of God. Seek and you will find."

He added strong words which echoed those of the Moravians of Georgia, and they sank into Wesley's consciousness: "Strip yourself naked of your own good words, and your own righteousness," said Böhler, "and go naked to him! For everyone that comes to him he will in no wise cast out."

The Wesleys invited Böhler to travel with them to Oxford, and as the coach labored through the Chilterns, the three men debated. Böhler liked the two brothers but concluded that both were far from a true faith. "The elder, John," he wrote to Zinzendorf, "is a good-natured man. He knew he did not believe on the Saviour, and was willing to be taught. His brother is at present very much distressed in his mind, but does not know how he shall begin to be acquainted with the Saviour."

At Oxford, since the Methodists had scattered to livings in town or country, Wesley took Böhler to meet one whose parish lay nearby. They also visited the Castle prison, where Wesley preached once again. They walked through the colleges together, and in one quadrangle Wesley was recognized, and they were mocked. Böhler assured him that he took no offense: "My brother, it does not stick to our clothes!"

At every opportunity they continued their discussion. Wesley still did not understand Böhler's drift "and least of all when he said, 'My brother, my brother, that philosophy of yours must be purged away.'"

Wesley had to return to London to meet the Georgia trustees again. He then took a coach for the West Country, intending to visit Samuel at Tiverton. At his brother-in-law's parish near Salisbury, where his mother was living with Sister Patty, an urgent message reached him that Charles was dying of pleurisy at Oxford.

He hired a horse to ride across the Wiltshire and Berkshire downs, speaking about God to people at the inn where he spent the night. Alone in his room he renewed his resolution to be serious and wholly religious, even resolving never to laugh again unless he must.

After he found Charles out of danger, Wesley resumed his friendly disputation with Böhler on the meaning of faith. Whenever Böhler pointed to a passage of Scripture that supported his thesis, Wesley construed it differently. But on Sunday, March 5, he suddenly saw that Böhler was right. The plain meaning leaped out of the Greek Testament which they were studying together: "I was clearly convinced of unbelief, of the want of that faith whereby alone we are saved."

Böhler had said, like St. Paul to the Philippian jailer, "Believe, and you will be saved." Wesley could not believe; his mind now assented but his heart refused the leap of faith.

"Immediately it struck into my mind, 'Leave off preaching. How can you preach to others, who have not faith yourself?'" He put this to Böhler. Ignoring the gap in age and experience, Wesley begged for advice whether he should stop preaching.

"By no means," said Böhler.

"But what can I preach?"

"Preach faith *till* you have it. And then, *because* you have it, you *will* preach faith."

Wesley tried, rather gingerly, in the prison next day. John Wesley, who had always zealously denied the possibility of a death-bed repentance, found himself telling a prisoner under sentence of death named Clifford that he could have "salvation by faith alone."

While Böhler returned to London, Wesley traveled to Manchester and back with one of his Oxford Methodists, Charles Kinchin, who now had a parish in Hampshire. Wesley wanted to see John Clayton in his parish and Kinchin to visit his parents and to bring back his younger brother, Stephen, to Oxford. All the way the two clergymen tried to bring strangers and wayfarers to God, "awakening, instructing, exhorting." Kinchin had been influenced already by Whitefield and rejoiced in "free grace." Wesley's exhortings, as he knew, were in his mouth but not in his heart.

Back in Oxford after ten days, he found that young Böhler had returned, to amaze him further with stories of "the holiness and happiness" which he claimed were "the fruits of living faith."

Wesley began to make a thorough study of his Greek New Testament to see whether these things were so. He was yet more amazed when he and Kinchin visited the prisoner Clifford in the condemned cell; he was to be hanged that day. They told him that he could be saved by grace, as a free gift, if he would trust Christ. They knelt in the straw. Wesley was so moved that after reciting collects, he broke with Anglican custom and prayed extempore, though he knew that his brother Samuel, if he ever heard of it, would be dismayed. Clifford had knelt down in gloom and confusion, conscious that he must shortly take an intolerable burden of sins into eternity. He rose from his knees and eagerly said, "I am now ready to die. I know Christ has taken away my sins; and there is no more condemnation for me." He stayed calm and composed when the jailer and sheriff called to take him to the gallows.

Welsey and Kinchin went in the cart with him. Wesley could not deny the calm assurance of this penitent thief as the noose was placed around his neck and the cart driven away, leaving him hanging, throttled, until he died; "in his last moments he was … enjoying a perfect peace, in confidence that he was 'accepted in the Beloved.'"

On Easter Day, April 2, 1738, Wesley preached in Lincoln College Chapel, and at two other services, on the text: "The hour cometh and now is, when the dead shall hear the voice of the Son of God, and they that hear shall live." He might preach but had sadly to record: "I see the promise; but it is far off."

Later in April the two Wesleys and Böhler were in London. Charles had resigned from the Georgia mission because of his health, though Oglethorpe was loath to release him. Neither of the brothers knew where the future might lie; Charles was now unemployed, and John was reluctant to resume his duties as an Oxford don. John and Charles lodged above James Hutton's bookshop near Temple Bar. Böhler lodged elsewhere, but the Wesleys sought him out on the evening of Saturday, April 22. In Böhler's words, they had "a right searching conversation."

By now Wesley had accepted that his sins would be forgiven, and he would be reconciled to God through the merits of Christ alone, not through his own actions, however ardent or religious. When this happened, he knew his life would change. On this evening Böhler went further. He maintained that the worst sinner, the most ungodly man, could be saved in an instant if he turned from his sins and trusted Christ alone. Charles was shocked. John was astounded: "I could not understand how this faith should be given in a moment: how a man could *at once* be turned from darkness to light, from sin and misery to righteousness and joy in the Holy Ghost."

He turned to the Acts of the Apostles. To his utter astonishment he found that almost all conversions which the Acts recorded were instantaneous: "scarce any so slow as that of St. Paul, who was three days in the pangs of the new birth." Wesley lamely took refuge in the claim that God no longer worked in that way.

Next evening, Sunday, Böhler brought three Englishmen to meet John Wesley in James Hutton's parlor. They drank tea, sang hymns, and then all four testified that God had "given them in a moment such a faith in the blood of his Son as translated them out of darkness into light, out of sin and fear into holiness and happiness." Each of them stressed that this faith was the free gift of God.

Wesley looked thunderstruck but refused to be impressed. "Four are not enough," he said. Böhler replied that he would bring eight more to testify that salvation is a gift. After more debate, Wesley cut them short and proposed that they sing a German hymn (which he had translated while in Georgia as "My Soul before Thee Prostrate Lies"). While they sang lustily, Böhler noticed that Wesley several times wiped his eyes.

When the others left, Wesley took Böhler into his own room. He confessed his disputing was over: "I can only cry out, 'Lord, help Thou my unbelief.'" He asked Böhler again whether he should stop teaching others (he had preached in three churches that Sunday). Böhler replied: "No. Do not hide in the earth the talent God has given you."

Next day Wesley rode down into Kent with a clerical friend, Thomas Broughton, to stay at Blendon, the mansion of Charles Delamotte's parents. The sugar merchant was away for a few days. Charles Wesley had already arrived.

The following evening they were all together in the house chapel. "We sang," recorded Charles in his journal, "and fell into a dispute whether conversion was gradual or instantaneous. My brother was very positive for the latter, and very shocking; mentioned some late instances of gross sinners believing in a moment. I was much offended at his worse than unedifying discourse. Mrs. Delamotte left us abruptly. I stayed, and insisted, a man need not know when first he had faith."

John would not agree. "His obstinacy," records Charles, "in favoring the contrary opinion drove me at last out of the room."

"My brother," records Wesley, "was very angry and told me I did not know what mischief I had done by talking thus." But, as both afterward realized, it was this dispute which kindled a fire in Charles.

Wesley rode back to London in the dusk and set out next day for Oxford on foot, Böhler walking with him the first hour. Three days later he returned hurriedly to London on news that Charles was seriously ill again at Huttons', where John found Charles better but "strongly averse from what he called 'the new faith.'" Deep down, however, a "spark of desire" was kindling in Charles' soul.

That night, May 1, 1738, the Wesleys, Hutton, and two or three others, advised by Böhler, formed "a little society" which should meet together weekly for mutual confession and prayer.

They hardly realized what they had begun. This first meeting was poignant, for Böhler was due to sail to South Carolina three days later. Before he sailed, he had a talk with Charles, who now began to long for the faith which could conquer sin "after ten years vain struggling."

Wesley now entered on a "dark night of the soul." For three days "I was sorrowful and very heavy, being neither able to read, nor meditate, nor sing, nor pray, nor do anything." Charles could pray, despite bodily pain, but prayer brought no sense of Christ's presence. Both brothers were still lodging above James Hutton's shop near Drury Lane, but evidently Charles' room was needed. Old Mrs. Hutton at Westminster had prepared one of her best rooms when Charles suddenly decided to go to the modest home of a brazier named Bray, "a poor ignorant mechanic, who knows nothing but Christ." Böhler had introduced him, and Charles was certain now that Bray would lead him to conversion. Charles was therefore carried in a sedan chair to Bray's home on Little Britain, the winding street near Charterhouse named after the Dukes of Brittany whose mansion and garden had once occupied the land.

Wesley called there on Saturday night. He was, records Charles, "exceeding heavy. I forced him (as he had often forced me) to sing an hymn to Christ, and almost thought he would come while we were singing."

On Sunday Wesley preached in two churches on "free salvation by the blood of Christ." The doctrine was clear to his mind yet still not in his heart. At one church he was told he would not be asked again; he supposed that the churchwardens were too religious to tolerate a faith so simple.

By the end of that week Charles again seemed to be dying "but was sure I could not die till I did believe" as he earnestly desired.

On Saturday, John Wesley gathered a few friends to spend all night in prayer for Charles, and on the morning of Whit Sunday, May 21, they went to Little Britain and stood round his bed and sang a hymn to the Holy Ghost. John then walked westward to the baroque church, twenty-one years old, of St. Mary-le-Strand. He heard "a truly Christian sermon," and since the curate fell ill during the service, he helped Dr. Heylyn, the rector, to administer Holy Communion. As they came out of church, a group of excited friends met Wesley with the news that Charles had at last believed. He was at peace with God, they said, and rejoicing and already recovering his strength. Jack walked back fast. The brothers prayed together, and Charles was disappointed that on this Day of Pentecost the Holy Spirit did not fall on Jack. Instead, Jack lapsed into misery, seeking and praying on Monday and Tuesday for "a full reliance on the blood of Christ shed for *me*; a trust in him as *my* Christ, as *my* sole justification, sanctification and redemption."

He had thought that he must become holy before he could be saved. Now he knew "that I deserve nothing but wrath." As he wrote brokenly to his Oxford friend John Gambold, who was passing through the same valley, "All my works, my righteousness, my prayers, need an atonement in themselves. So that my mouth is stopped, I have nothing to plead. God is holy; I am unholy. God is a consuming fire; I am altogether a sinner, meet to be consumed.

"Yet I hear a voice (and is it not the voice of God?) saying, 'Believe, and thou shalt be saved. He that believeth is passed from death unto life. God so loved the world that he gave his only begotten Son, that whosoever believeth on him should not perish but have everlasting life.' O thou Saviour of men, save us from trusting anything but *thee!*"

Early on Wednesday morning, May 24, 1738, Wesley opened his Greek Testament at random as was his custom. The verse which his eye lighted upon and another verse later were encouraging. That afternoon he accompanied a friend to evensong at St. Paul's Cathedral. The choir sang Purcell's anthem "Out of the Deep Have I Called unto Thee, O Lord." Every line of the singing encouraged him. The choir reached their climax: "O Israel, trust in the Lord, for with the Lord there is mercy, and with him plenteous redemption. And he shall redeem Israel from all his sins."

That evening he agreed, grudgingly, to accompany James Hutton, his host, to a little Moravian meeting in the city. They walked through mean streets and past alleys and brothels. They stepped over men and women lying drunk from cheap gin, waved away harlots, and kept an eye for pickpockets and thieves, all the very outcasts who, until lately, the Wesleys had believed could never be forgiven before prolonged penitence nor be intimate with Christ nor have power to live like him.

Hutton and Wesley reached Aldersgate Street, a few yards from Charterhouse, and turned into Nettleton Court.[1]

What followed is described in the most famous passage of John Wesley's *Journal:*

> In the evening I went very unwillingly to a society in Aldersgate Street, where one was reading Luther's preface to the Epistle to the Romans. About a quarter before nine, while he was describing the change which God works in the heart through faith in Christ, I felt my heart strangely warmed. I felt I did trust in Christ, Christ alone for salvation; and an assurance was given to me that he had taken away *my* sins, even *mine*, and saved *me* from the law of sin and death.

He began to pray at once in his heart for all who had "despitefully used me." Then he testified openly to those who were there what he now felt in his heart, "but it was not long before the enemy suggested, 'This cannot be faith; for where is thy joy?'" He then learned that faith does not depend on feeling; joy might be given or withheld. The others, rejoicing, hurried him to Charles: down Aldersgate Street, turning right shortly before it passed under Aldersgate itself, and into Little Britain. Charles was up and writing a hymn to celebrate his own conversion, "Where Shall My Wandering Soul Begin?" He records: "Towards ten my brother was brought in triumph by a troop of our friends, and declared, 'I believe.' We sang the hymn with great joy":

> *Outcasts of men, to you I call,*
> *Harlots and publicans and thieves!*
> *He spreads his arms to embrace you all;*
> *Sinners alone his grace receives;*
> *No need of him the righteous have;*
> *He came the lost to seek and save.*

Whether they picked up the words as Charles sang them verse by verse or leaned over his shoulders to read his manuscript, they sang it (to some familiar tune) right through to the ringing last lines:

> *For you the Prince of Glory died.*
> *Believe, and all your guilt's forgiven;*
> *Only believe and yours is heaven.*[2]

Charles overflowed with joy. John had no such feelings. When he had walked back to Hutton's shop and home and climbed the stairs to his room, "I was much buffeted with temptations." But at once he took his new faith to its logical conclusion and proved it. He "cried out and they fled away." Instead of strife and failure, "Now, I was always conqueror."

He went to bed. The next morning, "The moment I awaked, 'Jesus, Master,' was in my heart and in my mouth, and I found all my strength lay in keeping my eye fixed upon him."

11

Outcasts of Men

John Toeltschig, the older Moravian who had been sympathetic about Sophy in Georgia, had arrived in London on the way to Germany. Wesley sought his counsel two days after the evening in Aldersgate and confessed himself puzzled. His soul was at last in peace, resting assured that his salvation did not hang upon good works or ceremonies; it was grounded on the death of Christ, accepted by faith alone. He knew he was born again. Yet he had no joy. "What shall I do?" he asked Toeltschig. He was still buffeted by temptations.

Toeltschig answered: "You must not *fight* them as you did before. You must *flee* from them the moment they appear, and take shelter in the wounds of Jesus." Wesley left Toeltschig's lodging comforted and was further strengthened at evensong in St. Paul's by the words of the anthem. "My soul truly waiteth still upon God," sang the choir, "for of him cometh my salvation; he verily is my strength and my salvation, he is my defense, so that I shall not greatly fall."

Day after day he prayed much, on his knees and as he went about his affairs, not for his salvation as before but for his enemies and his friends. He found himself growing each day in strength "so that though I was now assaulted by many temptations, I was more than conqueror, gaining more power thereby to trust and to rejoice in God my Saviour." Yet the emotion of joy eluded him.

That first Sunday he preached twice on justification by faith. At the fashionable new church of St. George's, Bloomsbury, with its curious pyramid spire topped by a statue of George I, he was told afterward that he would not be asked again. He was told the same at a fashionable chapel near the Prince of Wales' mansion.

On Sunday evening he went to the Westminster home of James Hutton's parents, the close friends and former neighbors of Brother Samuel. Since Parson Hutton, a non-juror, was forbidden to officiate in a church, he was in the habit of reading a published sermon to a large company in his spacious study. That evening he read one from a popular series on the Sermon on the Mount by a late bishop of Exeter, Dr. Offspring Blackhall. As he ended, "Mr. John got up," so Mrs. Hutton wrote to Samuel, "and told the people that five days before he was not a Christian ... and the way for them all to be Christians was to believe, and own they were not Christians. Mr. Hutton was much surprised by this unexpected injudicious speech; but only said, 'Have a care, Mr. Wesley, how you despise the benefits received by the two Sacraments.'"

After the company left, Wesley and five or six of his friends went into the parlor for supper with the Huttons, their son and daughter, and various relations and lodgers. Mrs. Hutton had not been in the study but was horrified when Wesley made the "same wild speech" at supper in the parlor. Mrs. Hutton exclaimed: "If you was not a Christian ever since I knew you, you was a great hypocrite, for you made us all believe you was one." Thus Mrs. Hutton missed the point, though Wesley himself, years later, admitted that it might be said before Aldersgate that he had been a Christian, but with the faith of a bondservant, not of a son.

Mrs. Hutton, that Sunday, May 28, 1738, was sure that Mr. John "would do great mischief among ignorant but well-meaning Christians." She wrote to Samuel, imploring him to "convert or confine" his brother John, who "seems to be turned into a wild enthusiast or fanatic" and to be drawing their two children "into these wild notions by their great opinion of Mr. John's sanctity and judgment."

Wesley could not be silent. Christ, so long a remote component of the doctrine of the Trinity, had become a living, intimate force in his life, the center of his devotion and assurance, one whom he wanted all to know. Inwardly he was still tempted by fears and doubts, the legacy of years of introspection, yet whenever he opened his New Testament, his eye fell on promises from God which he had never noticed before, and when he claimed them, Christ drove away the tempter as he had in his own temptation in the wilderness. "And," noted Wesley, "I saw more than ever that the gospel is in truth but one great promise, from beginning to end."

He had no grandiose ideas of leading a great revival nor even of building on the work of George Whitefield, now in America. Indeed, two weeks after Aldersgate, Wesley suddenly decided to leave England. Long ago in Georgia he had formed a resolution to visit the Moravians in Germany, and now the opportunity had come to accompany Toeltschig.

He hurried down to Salisbury to say farewell to his mother. He read her his newly written account, which would become famous when published two years later in his *Journal*, of the events leading to his conversion. He understood her to approve.

Then he rode once again across the downs to preach before the University of Oxford. Wesley had already preached seven university sermons, an unusually high number for a young don, and on his return from Georgia, he had been appointed again. The date had been set far ahead: Sunday, June 11, one week before Wesley's thirty-fifth birthday. This routine appointment had become an unexpected opportunity to proclaim his gospel where it might be least expected, to set forth the message to which he would henceforth devote his life.

The vice-chancellor, the dons, and the scholars took their places in St. Mary's church (where Cranmer had given his dramatic last testimony before being burned at the stake) and heard Wesley announce his text, Ephesians 2:8—"By grace ye are saved through faith." As he warmed to his theme, Wesley emphasized that a saving faith was not merely "a speculative, rational thing, a cold, lifeless assent, a train of ideas in the head; but also a disposition of the heart. For thus saith the Scripture, 'With the heart man believeth unto righteousness.' And, 'If thou shalt confess with thy mouth the Lord Jesus, and shalt believe with thy *heart* that God hath raised him from the dead, thou shalt be saved.'"

He expounded this salvation by faith as "a salvation from sin and the consequences of sin, both often expressed in the word *justification*." Justification, he went on, implies a "deliverance from guilt and punishment by the atonement of Christ actually applied to the soul of the sinner now believing on him; and a deliverance from the power of sin, through Christ formed in his heart; so that he who is thus justified or saved by faith is indeed 'born again.' He is 'born again of the Spirit,' unto a new 'life which is that with Christ in God.'"

As the customarily long sermon unfolded, Wesley countered the objections which often were raised against justification by faith. He stressed that one who was born again would experience an urge to holiness and good works, and that "those who trust in the blood of Christ alone, use all the ordinances which he hath appointed." Later, in a passage which Wesley himself would have rejected a month before, he showed from the Acts of the Apostles that God could work this faith in men's hearts "as quick as lightning falling from heaven."

The vice-chancellor and the heads of houses may have been surprised when Wesley, who perhaps had noticed that the congregation represented town as well as gown, proclaimed: "Here is comfort, high as heaven, stronger than death! What! Mercy for all? For Zaccheus, a public robber? For Mary Magdalene, a common harlot? Methinks I hear one say, 'Then I, even I, may hope for mercy!' And so thou mayst, thou afflicted one, whom none hath comforted."

He ended the sermon with a resounding call to the Church of England to promote, once again, the doctrine which had brought about the Reformation: salvation by faith. "Nothing but this can give a check to that immorality which hath overspread the land as a flood," he said. He urged each one of his hearers to trust once again in Christ and to "march on under the great Captain of thy salvation, conquering and to conquer."

The next day he left for London and sailed for Rotterdam with Toeltschig, two Germans, Benjamin Ingham, and three Englishmen. They walked, admiring the neat Dutch countryside, then took canal boats and later sailed four days down the Rhine "through a double range of rocks and mountains, diversified with more variety than ever painter can imagine." At Marienborn, beyond Frankfurt on Main, they were received with utmost humility and graciousness by the legendary Count Zinzendorf, then aged thirty-eight but treated with veneration by his flock.

Wesley spent nearly three months with the Moravians at Marienborn and at their center, Herrnhut, in Saxony. He was impressed yet not carried away, unlike Ingham, who later left the Church of England to lead the Moravians in Yorkshire. Wesley noted Moravian practices, which he would adapt to good use, but he preserved his detachment and never wavered in loyalty to his own Church.

He returned to England in September, describing his experiences with enthusiasm. His unhappily married sister Emily was not impressed: "For God's sake tell me how a distressed woman who expects daily to have the very bed taken under her for rent can consider the state of the churches in Germany."

Wesley found that Charles had been hard at work speaking about Christ to everyone who would listen and preaching wherever he was allowed. Wesley joined him. "Though my brother and I are not permitted to preach in most of the churches of London," he wrote to his former hosts in Germany, "yet thanks be to God there are others left, wherein we have liberty to speak the truth as it is in Jesus." They were also invited to the religious societies of craftsmen, apprentices, and tradesmen, which had begun in London half a century earlier. These had declined in numbers and become little more than friendly societies within the Church of England, but their regular meetings offered the Wesleys a platform.

They moved their own "little society," founded in May above Hutton's bookshop, to a larger room on Fetter Lane, probably leasing the old Independent Chapel which had been replaced by a larger building on the opposite side of the street.[1] By October the Fetter Lane society numbered fifty-six men and eight women. They divided themselves into bands of seven, the members to support each other's faith and practice, with criticism where needed. They were to pray specially for each other and to live in unity and love. Wesley regarded this society and the others which sprang up in private homes or borrowed rooms as religious societies of the Church of England; he rejected the cry of opponents that he was forming conventicles, which should be licensed under the Toleration Act.

The societies, new and old, gave the Wesleys opportunity every weekday evening to strengthen Whitefield's converts and to "publish the word of reconciliation, sometimes to thirty, sometimes fifty or sixty, sometimes to three or four hundred." The two brothers led the singing with their strong voices. The people sang German hymns which John had translated and the new hymns which were beginning to pour from the pen of Charles. As they sang, prayed, and preached, the Wesleys sensed a new spiritual hunger in London.

On October 9 Wesley set out for Oxford on foot. When his companions had dropped off to their destinations, he passed the time, as often on a journey, in composing verses and in singing. Then he took out a new book, a description of a great awakening in a corner of New England a few years before, written by Jonathan Edwards, the pastor whose preaching had been its herald. Wesley was astonished and encouraged that the signs which they were beginning to see around them had been seen already in New England. His reading convinced him that his own land was about to experience a revival of religion, that the extraordinary scenes around George Whitefield while the Wesleys were in Georgia would be continued. God's "blessed spirit," wrote Wesley to a

Dutch friend on October 13, "has wrought so powerfully, both in London and Oxford, that there is a general awakening, and multitudes are crying out, What must we do to be saved?"

The original Oxford Methodists were not all following their former leader. Some clung to his former teaching, painfully working their methodical way toward righteousness; others were on the verge of his new "free grace." Some were puzzled, like William Law himself. Wesley had complained that Law had misled him: Law had answered lamely that his books included salvation by faith if Wesley had looked hard enough, to which he replied that Law's writings wrongly assumed that the reader had faith already.

Some of Wesley's friends vigorously opposed his new direction. His brother Samuel, from the distance of Tiverton, argued strongly against him, fearing beyond all else that Brother Jack was about to head a schism in the Church. Wesley rebutted Samuel's arguments. "By a Christian," he wrote from London on October 30, "I mean one who so believes in Christ as that sin hath no more dominion over him. And in that obvious sense of the word I was not a Christian till May 24 last past. For till then sin had the dominion over me, although I fought with it continually; but since then, from that time to this it hath not. Such is the free grace of God in Christ." He stressed the witness of the Spirit in his heart, although admitting that he still waited patiently for joy. "No settled, lasting joy," he complained in the journal he kept. "Nor have I such a peace as excludes the possibility of fear or doubt."

But the signs of a spiritual awakening were all around. The bishop of London, the learned and hardworking Dr. Gibson, received the Wesleys warily, neither stopping nor encouraging them, yet episcopal caution counted for nothing beside the widening opportunity to reach the poor and outcasts.

This was brought home to the Wesleys strongly on a raw day in November when they went very early to Newgate prison to minister to convicts who were to be hanged that noon.

Charles had already helped hardened criminals. He and Bray had once spent all night locked in the condemned cell, praying, teaching, comforting, and singing and had seen the men go to the gallows as if to a wedding. Both brothers had gone to Newgate frequently, and on November 9, "at their earnest request," they went early in the morning "to do the last good office to the condemned malefactors." After the Communion the brothers were not allowed to ride in the cart but followed in a coach down Holborn. Outside St. Giles in the Fields the procession stopped in front of the new church for the ancient custom of allowing the condemned men to drink a last stoop of ale; the Wesleys were brought a dish of tea. By the time they had reached Tyburn at the northeast corner of Hyde Park, the usual immense crowd, avid to see the condemned men swing, had poured out from the backstreets.

The Wesleys sang hymns with the men as they were made ready for death. "It was the most glorious instance I ever saw of faith triumphing over sin and death," said Wesley afterward. He asked one man who was weeping yet looking steadily upward with the rope already round his neck, "How do you feel your heart now?"

"I feel at peace," he replied calmly, "which I could not have believed to be possible. And I know it is the peace of God, which passeth understanding."

A few moments later the hangmen led the cart forward, and the man hung until he died. Then both Wesleys preached, Charles giving an impassioned sermon on repentance, faith, and the love of God which reached to the edges of the crowd.

12

Into the Fields

"**W**e are all young men—though I hope few of you are so young in spiritual, experimental knowledge, as your poor brother, *J. Wesley*." Thus Wesley concluded a letter to James Hutton from Oxford on December 1, 1738. He felt unequal to the task of evangelizing England, especially since his team was so small. Help, however, was at hand. Eleven days after writing this letter, Wesley heard that Whitefield had returned from America—younger than Wesley in years but older in experience of faith. Wesley set out on foot to London.

George Whitefield had returned to be admitted to Priest's Orders and to find recruits for Georgia and money for the orphanage in Savannah which Wesley had suggested and Whitefield hoped to open. On December 12 the two friends were reunited in London. Because Wesley had hurried foolishly from Deal in February, they had been apart for more than three years. Both felt the changed nature of their friendship. Whitefield remained a little in awe of the Oxford don, but the revival had begun through himself, not Wesley, and he was its leader. Wesley could not entirely forget that Whitefield was the junior in age and learning but freely acknowledged his spiritual maturity and the power of his ministry. Both addressed each other with humility. Whitefield was cheerful and quick to laugh whereas Wesley was graver by nature and still lacked joy.

Whitefield rejoiced that in London there seemed "to be a great pouring out of the Spirit, and many who were awakened by my preaching a year ago are now grown strong men in Christ, by the ministrations of my dear friends and fellow-laborers, John and Charles Wesley.... The old doctrine about justification by faith only, I found much revived." As letters to Georgia had missed him, he came on the scene unprepared and was all the more impressed.

They spent many hours together praying and singing and discussing in an upper room at the home of a Mrs. West and her husband, Joseph, a weaver of Spitalfields, or in Whitefield's lodgings at a Mr. Dobree's. On the last day of the year, a Sunday, Wesley preached to a packed congregation (it even seemed to him to number, impossibly, "many thousands") at St. George's, Spitalfields, where many must have been Huguenot weavers. In the afternoon Wesley preached to an even larger congregation at Whitechapel on the text "I will heal their backsliding; I will love them freely," while Whitefield, despite a heavy cold, preached at Spitalfields.

On the evening of January 1, 1739, the two Wesleys, their brother-in-law Westley Hall, Whitefield, and three other clergymen joined the sixty members of the Fetter Lane society. They held a "love feast," symbolically sharing a little bread and water. They sang and prayed. Whitefield kept awake, although his cold was heavy "and found this to be the happiest New Year's Day that I ever saw." "About three in the morning," records Wesley, "as we were continuing instant in prayer, the power of God came mightily upon us, insomuch that many cried out for exceeding joy, and many fell to the ground. As soon as we were recovered … we broke out with one voice, 'We praise thee, O God; we acknowledge thee to be the Lord.' "

A few days after this *Te Deum*, the seven clergymen met in conference at Islington, the suburb where the parson, George Stonehouse, a somewhat timid convert of Charles, was acting as his part-time curate without episcopal license. They conferred from half-past eight in the morning until 3 o'clock in the afternoon. "Seven true ministers of Jesus Christ, despised Methodists," as George Whitefield described them, "whom God has brought together from the East and the West, the North and the South. What we were in doubt about, after prayer, we determined by lot, and everything was carried on with great love, meekness and devotion."

The clergy had all been Oxford Methodists, and the nickname now stuck to their new outlook. They felt carried forward by a wave of revival but with no clear idea how it would take shape. Wesley and others urged Charles to settle at Oxford, where a parish was vacant, but he refused "without further direction from God."

Wesley's days passed in ceaseless activity—expounding in private homes, preaching in any church still open to him, "conversing" with converts and helpers, and drinking China tea.

Underneath lay uncertainties and doubts. Whitefield had written in his journal for January 4, 1739 that God's unmerited grace was making him more alive every day: "My understanding is more enlightened, my affections more inflamed, and my heart full of love towards God and man." Wesley, however, had moaned in his own journal for January 3 that he was not a Christian, whatever he had thought in May: "For a Christian is one who has the fruits of the Spirit of Christ, which (to mention no more) are love, peace, joy. But these I have not. I have not any love of God." Whitefield had passed through similar times of dryness in the months after his conversion in 1735, and the more introspective Wesley, only eight months from Aldersgate, tended to worry whether his emotions were matching his new understanding.

He did not doubt that on May 24 he had found the truth. The rector of St. Antholin's, Richard Venn, who had continued to befriend Wesley when many London clergy refused their pulpits, had now turned against the Methodists after reading Whitefield's newly published *Journal of a Voyage from London to Savannah*, an artless selection from letters which he had not intended Hutton to publish. Venn attacked Whitefield in a pamphlet. Whitefield promptly attended his church, received the Sacrament at his hands, and sought an unhurried discussion.

Whitefield brought Wesley. Venn brought John Berriman, a popular London preacher, "and some other strong opposers of the doctrine of the New Birth," as Whitefield described them. After they had eaten supper in peace and courtesy, Whitefield told them "what God had done for my soul, which made them look upon me as a madman." They debated long into a January night.

Whitefield wrote afterward: "I am fully convinced there is a fundamental difference between us and them. They believe only in an outward Christ, we further believe that he must be inwardly formed in our hearts also." Venn and his friends were proof against Whitefield's testimony and Wesley's exposition. Venn died three weeks later after a brief illness, not yet fifty. His schoolboy son, Henry, took Holy Orders after Cambridge and became "a despised

Methodist" at the age of twenty-nine, a close ally and friend of both the men whom his father had rejected.

Four days before the debate with Venn, George Whitefield had called on John Wesley early in the morning about another matter. Charles and Ingham were in the room also. They had prayers, drank tea, and read letters, and then Whitefield unburdened his mind. The previous Sunday, he told them, he had been across the Thames to preach at the parish church of Bermondsey, a suburb famous for its leatherworkers and pleasure gardens. Not only was the church full, but "I believe near a thousand people were in the churchyard, and hundreds more returned home that could not come in." The January weather was mild (in contrast to the terrible cold and snow of the next winter), and the crowds waited patiently for a sight of the famous young preacher. He could see them through the windows, but even George Whitefield's bell-like voice could not penetrate the walls to reach them. A thought had come to him that after the service he should climb on a tombstone and preach the sermon again. But he did not dare. Open-air preaching by clergymen was unknown.

Whitefield now tentatively suggested to the Wesleys that they should all break precedent and preach outdoors to reach "outcasts of men ... harlots, publicans, and thieves."

John Wesley rejected the idea "as a mad notion." It would be conduct unbecoming to a clergyman of the established church.

One of the letters which Whitefield may have shared was from a young Welshman of his own age, Howell Harris, who had seen a copy of Whitefield's *Journal* and wrote of a revival which had begun independently in Wales through himself and two clergymen. Harris, a layman, was preaching in the open air to large crowds.

The Wesleys, Whitefield, and Ingham knelt down "and prayed that nothing may be done rashly."

Early in February Whitefield left London for Bristol, scene of his earlier triumphs. On the way he called at Salisbury. Old Mrs. Wesley, who had seemed to approve the experiences and activity of her younger sons, had later accepted the hostile arguments of her eldest; she became alarmed. Whitefield reassured her and wrote to Wesley that his mother's prejudices "are entirely removed, and she only longs to be with you in your societies in London. Arguments from Tiverton, I believe, will now have but little weight." Whitefield's conclusion was premature.

Wesley was now lodging at the home of John Bray, the hospitable brazier of Little Britain who had several lodgers in a house of moderate size. Wesley could not escape the clamor of the workshop below, the unceasing noise from the street, or the tendency of family and lodgers to sing hymns at all hours.

He therefore liked to go the short distance to the Charterhouse and exercise his right as an Old Carthusian to walk on Green where he had run and played as a boy. He was amused to see how small the present generation of Carthusians looked compared with the big boys he remembered. He made friends with one of the pensioner brothers, Jonathan Aguttir (or Agutter), who must have been admitted younger than some, for he remained at Charterhouse another fifteen years. Aguttir opened his room and vacated his desk to Wesley. Sometimes Bray or others joined them, but the murmur of their extempore prayer would not have reached the gownboys.

There was much to meditate upon as Wesley walked around the Green. Opposition seemed to be slackening; the revival might spread across the Church. When the Wesleys had taken the horse ferry to Lambeth, a little above where London's second bridge was being built slowly at Westminster, they had been received with "great affection" by the archbishop of Canterbury, John Potter, who had ordained them when he was bishop of Oxford.

His cautions were wise and gentle. They recrossed the Thames to call immediately on the bishop of London in St. James's Square. He too was kind, if somewhat dismissive of their influence, and merely remarked that "G. Whitefield's *Journal* was tainted with enthusiasm, though he was himself a pious, well-meaning youth."

Societies, mostly informal, had sprung up at all social levels, including "a noble company of women" in fashionable St. James', where Wesley may have met the young Countess of Huntingdon for the first time. Two of her husband's sisters had been Whitefield's converts and recently had brought her into the revival.

This was keeping Wesley on the stretch seven days a week. On the last Sunday in February, he preached near the Tower at 10 o'clock in the morning, then walked to rural Islington for dinner and an afternoon service; the congregation was so numerous that St. Mary's church was positively hot despite the time of year. "I think I was never so much strengthened before," wrote Wesley to Whitefield, "and the fields, after service, were white with people praising God."

He walked back to the city and expounded at 5 o'clock to a society, organized by a butcher, which used a large room in the Minories, the wide street of gunsmiths near the Tower. Three hundred men and women, he estimated, were present. An hour later he drank a quick cup of tea, then went to sing with a society brought together by a watchcase maker near Bishopsgate. Next, at 8:15, he was at his own society at Fetter Lane, and at last, at 9 o'clock in the evening, he returned to the Brays for yet another meeting before supper and prayer. When Whitefield read of all this, he rejoiced "in your indefatigable zeal, and great success in the gospel of our dear Redeemer."

Before Whitefield wrote that, he had taken the "mad" step which he had proposed after Bermondsey: he had preached in the open air to coal miners as they left the forest pits in Kingswood, Bristol. These colliers (as they were usually called, rather than coal miners) were regarded as savages, and no parson ministered to them because their shacks lay on the edge of four parishes. Whitefield had been nervous when he stood on Hanham Mount to call out his text, but as he preached he saw the "white gutters made by their tears down their black cheeks." When, a few days later, a young collier called Tom Maxfield found his way shyly to Whitefield's lodgings and begged him to come again, Whitefield had exclaimed: "Blessed be God that I have broken the ice."

He now wanted Wesley's aid: "There is a glorious door opened among the colliers. You must come and water what God has enabled me to plant." Wesley could form the converts into bands more skillfully than Whitefield, who was due to return to America. "I am but a novice," Whitefield wrote on March 22. "You are acquainted with the great things of God. Come, I beseech you, come quickly. I have promised not to leave this people till you or somebody come to supply my place." He had even arranged the loan of a horse for the journey.

Wesley did not wish to leave London, partly because he believed his health was about to collapse under the pressures of his ministry and he would soon be dead; all the Scriptures which sprang up at him whenever he opened the Bible at random after prayer seemed to warn him. On March 28 he put the question to the Fetter Lane society in accord with their rule that any member who intended a journey should consult the others.

Charles could scarcely bear to hear of it. "We dissuaded my brother," he wrote in his journal, "from going to Bristol, from an unaccountable fear that it would prove fatal to him. A great power was among us. He offered himself willingly to whatsoever the Lord should appoint." Charles opened his Bible to Ezekiel 24:16 and was shaken to read: "Son of man, behold, I take away from thee the desire of thine eyes with a stroke; yet neither shalt thou mourn nor weep, neither shall thy tears run down." Charles took it as a message from God that Jack must leave them.

The others continued to demur. The more they debated, the more divided they were. Wesley at last proposed that they decide the issue by lot, "and by this it was determined I should go."

As Wesley dismounted at Marlborough on the second evening of his journey, his watch fell out of his pocket. The glass flew off but did not break, nor was the watch damaged—as if to assure its owner that the extraordinary events which lay ahead would not break him.

The horse had been lent by a kindly tradesman who was riding and leading another horse; he had overtaken Wesley a few miles back walking behind his own borrowed horse which was too tired to carry him farther. At the inn after supper, Wesley "preached the gospel to our little company," to the disgust of a well-dressed gentleman. The next day Wesley and his horse ("so tired he could scarce go a foot-pace") continued along the Bath Road. Over breakfast at Calne, Wesley rebuked a local landowner who talked in "so obscene and profane a manner as I never remember to have heard anyone do, no, not even in the streets of London." In the evening the weary horse and its rider came down from the hills into Bristol, the second city of England, and found their way to the home of Whitefield's sister, Mrs. Grevil, above her husband's grocery shop on Wine Street.

George Whitefield welcomed him with joy: "I was much refreshed with the sight of my honored friend, Mr. John Wesley, whom God's providence has sent to Bristol. 'Lord, now lettest thy servant depart in peace.'" They prayed and sang together. Wesley had taught the Methodists to sing German tunes in double-quick time, not like a Bach chorale. Then Whitefield swept him off before supper to a meeting at Weavers' Hall, where the don of Lincoln College listened happily to the former servitor of Pembroke, only twenty-four years of age.

Early on the Sunday morning, before Bristol's church time, Whitefield preached to a considerable crowd in the open air at Bowling Green with Wesley beside him. After breakfast they went among the miners of Kingswood, who were outnumbered by the thousands of city folk as Whitefield preached from Hanham Mount. In the late afternoon, against the wind, Whitefield preached his farewell sermon from Rose Mount in Kingswood to an immense crowd. Wesley guessed it as thirty thousand; his exaggeration conveys the impact of countless listeners of all ranks of society, including the rich in their coaches, others on horseback, and most on foot.

Wesley was bemused by the extraordinary scene: "I could scarce reconcile myself at first to this strange way of preaching in the fields, of which he set me an example on Sunday; having been all my life (till very lately) so tenacious of every point relating to decency and order, that I should have thought the saving of souls almost a sin, if it had not been done in a church."

In the evening while Whitefield expounded to one of the religious societies, Wesley expounded to another. He had chosen the Sermon on the Mount for his theme, and it crossed his mind that this was "a pretty remarkable precedent of field preaching."

On Monday, Whitefield left after midday dinner to ride into Wales. That afternoon Wesley went out to a brickfield at the farther end of St. Philip's plain, which had been lent to Whitefield for preaching. Wesley's name meant little as yet to Bristol, but the revival had created such sensation that the people downed tools and trades early (detaining "the Vulgar from their daily Labor," the *Gentleman's Magazine* had complained) and hastened to the brickyard.

"At four in the afternoon," Wesley afterward recorded, "I submitted to be more vile, and proclaimed in the highways the glad tidings of salvation, speaking from a little eminence in a ground adjoining to the city, to about 3,000 people. The Scripture on which I spoke was this (is it possible any should be ignorant, that it is fulfilled in every true minister of Christ?): 'The Spirit of the Lord is upon me, because he hath anointed me to preach the gospel to the poor; he hath sent me to heal the brokenhearted; to preach deliverance to the captives, and recovery of sight to the blind; to set at liberty them that are bruised, to proclaim the acceptable year of the Lord'" (Luke 4:18).

13

Signs and Wonders

John Wesley had been even "more vile" than he had intended, for he had not preached in his canonicals—they were still on the road from London. ("Dear Jemmy," he wrote to Hutton, "I want my gown and cassock every day. O how is God manifested in our brother Whitefield! I have seen none like him.") But, like Whitefield six weeks earlier, he had "broken the ice."

Bristol seemed hungry for preaching. The colliers always welcomed him. He preached at the brickfield, on the bowling green, and at a nearby suburb, always to crowds beyond counting, although his solid preaching lacked Whitefield's vivid appeal. Indoors, Wesley preached regularly in the morning at the chapel of Bristol's Newgate prison, where the jailer, Abel Dagge, had been one of the earliest converts under Whitefield in 1737. In the evening Wesley was at the religious societies. Often the press to enter the rooms was so great that he would expound from a window to the overflow in the court or the street below, and on one occasion the floor sank but did not crash into the cellar. No one was hurt, and they continued to listen. Afterward they found that an importer had just stored numerous hogsheads of tobacco to the ceiling, giving the support which prevented tragedy.

Wesley organized the converts into small bands of men and small bands of women. As in London, each band should meet privately to "confess their faults one to another and pray one for another that they may be healed." Twice a week the bands came together into their religious society. The meeting might take nearly two hours.

Charles had been writing more hymns and John a few, and they were newly published. After the expounding and the singing came the prayers. Wesley would read out requests and then pray extemporarily over each. A Dissenter from the Midlands was present one evening. He wrote: "Never did I see or hear such evident marks of fervency in the service of God. At the close of every petition a serious *amen*, like a gentle, rushing sound of waters, ran thro' the whole audience, with such a solemn air as quite distinguished it from whatever of that nature I have heard attending the responses in the church services.... If there be such a thing as heavenly music upon earth, I heard it there: If there be such an enjoyment, such an attainment, as heaven upon earth, numbers in that society seemed to possess it. As for my own part I do not remember my heart to have been so elevated in divine love and praise as it was there and then for many years past if ever; and an affecting sense and savour thereof abode in my mind many weeks after."

Converts were joining the societies every week. When Brother Samuel wrote from Tiverton protesting that God does not work instantaneously, Wesley rejected his argument: "I have seen (as far as it can be seen) very many persons changed in a moment from the spirit of horror, fear, and despair, to the spirit of hope; and from sinful desires, till then reigning over them, to a pure desire of doing the will of God. These are matters of fact, whereof I have been, and almost daily am, eye- or ear-witness.... Saw you him that was a lion till then, and is now a lamb; him that was a drunkard, but now exemplarily sober; the whoremonger that was, who now abhors the very lusts of the flesh? These are my living arguments, for what I assert, that God now, as aforetime, gives remission of sins and the gift of the Holy Ghost."

Wesley added in this letter of April 4, 1739 that he did not expect they would meet again; he had nearly finished his earthly course. Samuel thought this nonsense and referred to "your iron constitution," yet they did not meet, for later that year Samuel was taken ill and died, aged forty-eight, arguing affectionately with Wesley by letter to the last.

To Wesley's surprise, many whose consciences were convicted by his unemotional preaching showed extraordinary physical reactions. "Some of them," he wrote some months later, "drop down as dead, having no strength nor appearance of life in them. Some burst out into strong cries and tears, some exceedingly tremble and quake." Others began to sweat or struggled as if in agonies of death so that strong men might have needed to keep a woman from hurting herself. Sometimes Wesley had to stop preaching and pray. Many of the afflicted persons would suddenly cease their struggles and begin to praise God; others would "continue days or weeks in heaviness."

These manifestations had seldom accompanied Whitefield's colorful preaching in Bristol, although at his mass meetings in the open air near London a little later, Charles Wesley recorded that "the cries of the wounded were heard on every side." And swoonings and agonies were common in the New England revival led by the austere Jonathan Edwards. Wesley never consciously encouraged these physical reactions, and often crowds listened to him "with awful silence and great attention," but he did not discourage these reactions, and the rumors spread, inevitably exaggerated until even George Whitefield was worried until he learned the facts.

Whitefield had made a whirlwind tour in Wales with Howell Harris, preaching from market crosses and on the commons against much opposition and uproar. He had come preaching through Gloucestershire, had been snubbed by the vice-chancellor of Oxford, and had reached London. On Sunday, April 29, 1739, he made a dangerous decision. After hurriedly printed handbills had announced his intention, he went at sunrise with Charles Wesley and others to Moorfields, the fairground and archery grounds north of the city, where a large mob of London's poor had gathered to hear him. He knew he might unwillingly cause a riot or be arrested, but in spite of difficult moments, this first open-air preaching in London encouraged Whitefield to preach the same afternoon to an even greater crowd on Kennington Common, south of the Thames.

During the following week, all London was stirred as Whitefield preached in the open to thousands who would seldom or never enter a church. Charles Wesley remarked that the devil had gained nothing from excluding Whitefield from the churches.

Wesley, meanwhile, that same Sunday had felt compelled to preach a sermon in Bristol which caused the first cracks in the unity of the revival leaders.

Before Whitefield had left Bristol, he had warned Wesley to "enter into no disputes, least of all concerning predestination, because this people was so deeply prejudiced for it." Bristol had many Dissenters, and they had supported Whitefield, but among them were high Calvinists who put strong emphasis on St. Paul's words about predestination and ignored his equally clear words on free will. These Bristol Calvinists spoke much of Paul's teaching that God eternally decrees some to salvation and some to damnation (or "reprobation") but little about his teaching and preaching that "whosoever shall call upon the name of the Lord shall be saved" (Romans 10:13).

The roots of the controversy lay deep in the history of England since the Reformation. To Wesley, however, the overriding fact was that "the Lord is longsuffering to us—not willing that any should perish, but that all should come to repentance" (2 Peter 3:9). Those who refused to repent would perish, but when Wesley urged his hearers to be saved by faith in Christ, he was not concerned with eternal decrees before the beginning of time; he feared that men who emphasized the predestination of some to eternal death would be inhibited from offering Christ freely to all. Wesley seized on Calvin's comment in his *Institutes of the Christian Religion:* "The decree, I admit, is dreadful" (in the original Latin, *Decretum horribile*) and referred to predestination as "the horrible decree."

On Tuesday, April 24, he returned from the field and preached near Bath in pouring rain to a smaller congregation than usual. He went to Kingswood and preached to the coal miners, who took him afterward to see the hill in the middle of the forest, two miles each way from any church or school, where Whitefield had laid the foundation stone of the school they intended to build.

On Wesley's return to Wine Street, he was handed a letter. Noticing the date, he learned that it had already been circulating for at least two weeks, widely read, before being sealed and taken to his lodgings.

The letter charged Wesley with "resisting and perverting the truth as it is in Jesus by preaching against God's decree of predestination"—on which in fact he had been silent. Another letter was shown him which warned the godly to avoid him as a false teacher. He decided to say nothing, but wondered whether he should publicly declare the truth of the issue as he saw it. Early the next morning, after he and his fellow lodgers and their hosts had sung hymns and before they had breakfast, he wrote a sermon on predestination. He was not sure whether he should preach it. He consulted the young man who had come down with him from London as his assistant and scribe, John Purdy, as they walked to Newgate. Purdy advised him to preach.

On Thursday he was again at the service at Newgate, preaching on the text "He that believeth on me hath everlasting life" (John 6:36). Suddenly the prisoners and the city people who now crowded the prison chapel were startled. "I was led, I know not how," Wesley recorded, "to speak strongly and explicitly" against the doctrine that some could never be saved because they were predestined to be reprobates. The crowd heard him pray to God aloud as he preached that "if I spake not the truth of God he would stay his hand, and work no more among us." Then Wesley cried, "If this is thy truth, do not delay to confirm it by signs following."

Wesley recorded that immediately "the power of God fell among us. One, and another, and another, sunk to the earth. You might see them dropping on all sides as thunderstruck." One, Ann

Davis, cried out. Wesley went across and prayed over her, and she began to praise God.

Dagge, the jailer, was upset by the uproar in his chapel. Meanwhile, Wesley remained doubtful whether to preach formally against predestination. Purdy again urged him to do so. They therefore wrote out four cards with different courses of action on each. They drew the lot: "Preach and Print."

On Sunday, April 29, early in the morning, Wesley went to the bowling green, where several thousand were waiting, and after they had sung, he called out his text from the Epistle to the Romans: "He that spared not his own Son, but delivered him up for us all, how shall he not with him also freely give us all things?" (Romans 8:32)

"How freely does God love the world!" he began. He expounded his text briefly and exclaimed, "Verily, free grace is all in all." Then he contrasted the High Calvinist doctrine as he remembered it from a close study many years before. He touched on its varieties but concluded: "Call it therefore by whatever name you please.... It comes in the end to the same thing. The sense of all is plainly this—by virtue of an eternal, unchangeable, irresistible decree of God, one part of mankind are infallibly saved, and the rest infallibly damned." This, he contended, meant that the purpose of preaching "to save souls" was void.

Calvinists who heard him would have thought he was distorting their theology—as they had misrepresented his—but Wesley's mind was always inclined to drive a position to its bleakly logical conclusion, regardless of the illogicalities of life which may soften a theological position in practice. For him, the Calvinist interpretation destroyed all God's attributes at once. "This is the blasphemy clearly contained in the *horrible decree* of predestination!

And here I fix my foot. On this I join issue with every assertor of it. You represent God as worse than the devil; more false, more cruel, more unjust. But you say you will prove it by Scripture!"

The long sermon continued, with much satire, until he reached his peroration with a resounding reiteration of great New Testament texts of free grace for all, such as the words of Jesus himself: "If any man thirst, let him come to me and drink"; and St. Paul's: "God commandeth all men everywhere to repent." "All men, everywhere!" cried Wesley, "—every man in every place, without any exception, either of place or person."

He had the sermon printed and published in Bristol. He sent copies to London for distribution by Hutton, who seems to have queried the order as controversial, for Wesley had to remind him that "generally I speak on faith, remission of sins, and the gift of the Holy Ghost." Hutton did not hurry to publish.

Wesley continued his round of preaching and of building up converts. He brought them into societies; within these, the smaller bands were organized for mutual help. The two original Bristol religious societies which Whitefield and Wesley had taken over were now too large for their premises. They came together, gave money, and bought land at the Horsefair on which to build "the New Room," which went up fast and became Wesley's headquarters.

He preached in any church which would allow him but mostly in the meadows or on commons, in the countryside around Bristol, and out to Bath. And thus occurred the celebrated incident of June 5, 1739 with "Beau" Nash, the uncrowned king of Bath.

Richard Nash was then nearly sixty-five, and though an adventurer and philanderer who lived by gaming, he had a kind heart. For thirty-four years he had been the arbiter of affairs at Bath, making the spa famous for entertainment and elegance; even royalty and duchesses obeyed his rules at the Pump Room. He was, however, a notorious scoffer at religion.

He became annoyed that people of all ranks should flock to hear Wesley. Beau Nash let it be known that he would stop him. When Wesley arrived at Bath at half past 1:00 on the afternoon of June 5 and was at dinner at Mr. Dibble's, he was begged not to preach "because no one knew what would happen." He arrived at the meadow to find that "I had gained a larger audience than usual, including many of the rich and great" sitting in their chariots or on comfortable chairs.

Wesley's heart went out to them, and he preached that all were guilty before God—rich and poor, high and low. This doctrine surprised them, just as it would disgust his parents' old patron, the proud Duchess of Buckingham. She would remark when invited to hear Whitefield at a drawing room meeting that "it is monstrous to be told that you have a heart as sinful as the common wretches that crawl on the earth. This is highly offensive and insulting."

The fashionable audience that day at Bath was "sinking apace into seriousness, when their champion appeared."

Beau Nash always drove in a chariot drawn by six gray horses with footmen on the box who announced his coming by blowing on French horns. His arrival at the back of the crowd was thus an interruption, and the people made way when he walked ponderously, in his lace-covered coat and his enormous cream-colored beaver hat, toward Wesley as he preached in his cassock, gown, and bands.

Wesley paused. Nash demanded by what authority he was doing these things.

"By the authority," replied Wesley, "of Jesus Christ, conveyed to me by the (now) Archbishop of Canterbury, when he laid hands upon me, and said, 'Take thou authority to preach the gospel.'"

"This is contrary to Act of Parliament," said Nash. "This is a conventicle."

"Sir, the conventicles mentioned in that Act are seditious meetings; but here is no shadow of sedition; therefore it is not contrary to that Act."

"I say it is; and, beside, your preaching frightens people out of their wits!"

"Sir, did you ever hear me preach?"

"No."

"How, then, can you judge of what you never heard?"

"Sir, by common report."

"Common report is not enough," replied Wesley, as the crowd warmed to this interchange. "Give me leave, sir, to ask, is not your name Nash?"

"My name is Nash."

"Sir," said Wesley with a flash of wit which delighted his fashionable hearers, "I dare not judge of you by common report: I think it not enough to judge by."

This retort reduced Nash to silence; finally he said, "I desire to know what this people comes here for."

At that an old woman spoke up. "Sir, leave him to me: let an old woman answer him. You, Mr. Nash, take care of your body; we take care of our souls; and for the food of our souls we come here."

Nash walked away without another word.

Some days afterward Wesley hurried to London, having been warned that the Fetter Lane society was split by dissensions. Some were following a French prophetess; some were leaning toward Moravian customs, which did not sit easily in the Church of England. The system of small bands of believers keeping each other up to the mark had a tendency to sink into carping and priggery. Wesley sorted out the problems as far as he could, and believed that he left the society humbled and united.

Whitefield had been prevented from sailing to America by an embargo on outward bound shipping, for England was on the verge of war with Spain (the "War of Jenkin's Ear"). He was staying with the Delamottes at Blendon when Wesley arrived for dinner, having read, as he rode, George Whitefield's new autobiography of his early life. That evening they went to Blackheath, where a vast concourse had gathered.[1]

They had come to hear Whitefield. To Wesley's surprise Whitefield asked him to preach instead, "which I did (though nature recoiled), on my favorite subject, 'Jesus Christ, who of God is made unto us wisdom, righteousness, sanctification, and redemption.' I was greatly moved with compassion for the rich that were there. Some of them seemed to attend, while others drove away their coaches from so uncouth a preacher."

Whitefield had acted deliberately. "In the evening," he recorded, "had the pleasure of introducing my honored and revered friend, Mr. John Wesley, to preach at Blackheath. The Lord give him ten thousand times more success than he has given me!"

After that, Wesley was ready to field-preach in London. On the next Sunday, early on a June morning, he preached to a less vast crowd (he put it at six or seven thousand) at Moorfields while Whitefield preached on Kennington Common.

Among the crowd at Moorfields was a sailor's wife, Grace Murray. Wesley was unaware of the existence of this woman who was to cross his path so fatefully ten years later.

In 1739 she was unhappy: she had lost her child, her husband was at sea, her parents were far away in the North. A neighbor had spoken of the comfort received through hearing John Wesley preach. "The next Saturday," related Grace Murray, "the young woman sent to me again to tell me Mr. Wesley was come, and was to preach in the fields next morning. I slept little that night. I rose at 3:00 and about 4:00 set out, though I knew not where Moorfields was. I overtook a woman going thither, who shewed me the way.

"When Mr. W stood up and looked round on the congregation, I fixed my eyes upon him and felt an inexpressible conviction, that he was sent of God. And when he spoke those words, 'Except a man be born again, he cannot see the Kingdom of God,' they went through me like a dart and I cried out, 'Alas! What shall I do? How shall I be born again?' After the sermon, a young woman [Maria Price] seeing me all in tears asked, 'What is the matter with you?' I said, 'I don't know.' She said, 'I will tell you; the hammer of God's love is breaking your heart; only follow on, to know the Lord.' She spoke many other sweet words. I went home a mere sinner, not knowing what I wanted, an atonement for my sins."

14

*"A Horrid Thing,
a Very Horrid Thing"*

Two evenings later Wesley preached again at Bristol. Whitefield's friend Howell Harris was among the crowd on Bowling Green.

The Welsh layman—he had been refused ordination by nervous bishops—whose preaching fanned the revival in the mountains and valleys, had heard Calvinist gossip that Wesley preached a universal redemption for all mankind and not the Christian gospel.

That June night, however, shortly after sunset as they sat down to supper, Harris called at Wine Street where Wesley still lodged with Whitefield's sister and widowed mother, and he confessed that he had nearly avoided Bowling Green. Harris told Wesley, "I had not been long there before my spirit was knit to you, as it was to dear Mr. Whitefield, and before you had done I was so overpowered with joy and love that I could scarce stand, and with much difficulty got home." They talked together for two hours and through a second supper.

The visit of Harris was a much needed encouragement, for Wesley was afraid that "all our society was falling to pieces," although he had been away only eight days. Some were arguing bitterly for or against predestination; others were being swept into frenzies by the activity of "French prophets," a few men and women from among the exiled Huguenots who had settled in Bristol.

Wesley worked hard to heal divisions, blow away misunderstandings both among the men and the women, and restore peace. Far away in London, Whitefield felt that Wesley had helped to cause the trouble by the sermon on free grace. Not knowing that it was already published in Bristol, he wrote on June 25: "I hear, honored sir, you are about to print a sermon against predestination. It shocks me to think of it. What will be the consequence but controversy? If people ask me my opinion, what shall I do? I have a critical part to act. God enable me to behave aright. Silence on both sides will be best. It is noised abroad already that there is a division between you and me. Oh! my heart within me is grieved."

Whitefield sympathized with the Dissenters' doctrines although he did not yet count himself a Calvinist. He wrote again on July 2 that he was "grieved from my soul" by rumor that someone who held predestination had been excluded from the society. "If so, is it right? Would Jesus Christ have done so? Is this to act with a catholic spirit?" Before the end of his letter, he reverted again to the sermon on free grace. "Dear honored sir, if you have any regard to the peace of the Church, keep in your sermon on predestination. But you have cast a lot. Oh! my heart in the midst of my body is like melted wax. The Lord direct us all! Honored sir, indeed I wish you all the success you can wish for. May you increase though I decrease! I would willingly wash your feet.... O wrestle, wrestle, honored sir, in prayer, that not the least alienation of affections may be between you and, honored sir, your obedient son and servant in Christ, *G. W.*"

When Whitefield came to Bristol in mid-July, Wesley rebuked him for listening to rumors. They had long talks; they shared the preaching and rode together through the rain-soaked countryside as far as Gloucester for Whitefield's final farewell before America. They settled their differences. "I love you the more for reproving me," wrote Whitefield from London.

The New Room was going up fast, and the school at Kingswood only lacked a roof; Wesley preached inside it in the rain and again under a sycamore tree in the rain. His work was unremitting. Even when his horse stumbled and pitched him on to the road and he bruised his shoulder, he did not fail the waiting crowd.

All this time he was thinking about the "unusual manner" of his ministry. He had no fear that he was swerving into heresy. Soon after his conversion, he had studied the homilies which had been authorized in the reign of Edward VI to be read out in parish churches when the minister did not preach a sermon of his own; Wesley then realized that he had rediscovered the forgotten teaching of the Church of England. He had promptly published an abridged edition, and when clergy attacked Whitefield and him from pulpits or in pamphlets, he would reply by emphasizing "in very plain words the difference between the true, old Christianity, commonly called by the new name of Methodism, and the Christianity now generally taught."

He could easily rebut wild charges that he led people to rely on visions and dreams or that he stirred up strife. One London preacher had published a violent sermon branding the Methodists with "spiritual pride, enthusiasm, false doctrine, heresy, uncharitableness." He charged that they preached "crude, indigested notions of dismal consequences." Wesley wrote to him: "O Sir, how could you possibly be induced to pass such a sentence, even in your heart, till you had done us the common heathen justice of hearing us answer for ourselves?"

More serious was the charge that Wesley was disturbing the peace of the church and "stealing sheep" from the flocks of other parsons: "I do, indeed, go out into the highways and hedges to call poor sinners to Christ," he wrote to a distinguished pamphleteer, Dr. Henry Stebbing,[1] "but not 'in a tumultuous manner,' not 'to the disturbance of the public peace' or 'the prejudice of families.' Neither herein do I break any law which I know, much less 'set at naught all rule and authority.' Nor can I be said to 'intrude into the labors' of those who do not labor at all, but suffer thousands of those for whom Christ died to 'perish for lack of knowledge.'"

Field preaching inevitably involved preaching in other men's parishes, for every acre of England was in a parish. As a fellow of an Oxford college, Wesley had a general license to preach, but this implied the permission of the local incumbent, and Wesley preached whether invited or not. He told an old friend who objected to these proceedings: "God in Scripture commands me, according to my power, to instruct the ignorant, reform the wicked, confirm the virtuous. Man forbids me to do this in another's parish; that is, in effect, to do it at all; seeing that I have now no parish of my own, nor probably ever shall. Whom then shall I hear, God or man?

"Suffer me now," he went on, "to tell you *my* principles in the matter." And he coined the phrase which was to be inscribed, long after, on his memorial in Westminster Abbey: "I look upon *all the world as my parish*."

This famous phrase, which Wesley first put into writing in the spring or early summer of 1739, he defined as meaning that in whatever part of the world he was, "I judge it meet, right and my bounden duty to declare, unto all that are willing to hear, the glad tidings of salvation. This is the work which I know God has called me." He had been providentially disengaged "for all things else that I might singly attend on this very thing, 'and go about doing good.'"

He could no longer be confined to church buildings. This still shocked his eldest brother. John was unashamed. "How is it," he asked in the last letter which Samuel received a few weeks before he died, "that you can't praise God for saving so many souls from death, and covering such a multitude of sins, unless he will begin this work within 'consecrated walls'? Why should he not fill heaven and earth? You cannot, indeed you cannot, confine the Most High within temples made with hands. I do not despise them, any more than you. But I rejoice to find that God is everywhere.

"I love the rites and ceremonies of the Church. But I see, well-pleased, that our great Lord can work without them. And howsoever and wheresoever a sinner is converted from the error of his ways, and by whomsoever, I therein rejoice, yea, and will you rejoice!"

Field preaching and the physical reactions had antagonized the bishops. They now were willing to believe the worst, so that Whitefield had written to Wesley in midsummer, "I hear we shall be excommunicated soon." Excommunication was unlikely, but a bishop might formally inhibit Wesley from preaching in his diocese; if Wesley defied the ban, he could be unfrocked. He could not then lawfully officiate or preach unless he took out a license under the Toleration Act as a dissenting minister. And that would dampen the flame of revival in the Church of England. Wesley's whole being was now concentrated on the twin aims of pleading with individuals to be reconciled to God, and returning the national church to the doctrines of the Reformation.

When, therefore, he was summoned by the bishop of Bristol on August 16, 1739, he knew that his ministry had reached a crisis. Joseph Butler, the philosopher who was much celebrated for his recent book *The Analogy of Religion*, had been bishop for less than a year. In the gloomy preface to his book he had complained that it was "taken for granted by many persons that Christianity is ... discovered to be fictitious" and was a subject of mirth and ridicule. He had endeavored to prove the contrary by reasoned and original argument in a book which was already considered the greatest theological work of the age. When Wesley read it some years later, he thought it "a strong and well-wrote treatise; but, I am afraid, far too deep" for those to whom it was primarily addressed.

At forty-seven Dr. Butler was eleven years older than Wesley and comparatively young for a bishop, even of the poorest diocese in England. Wesley had already had a brief interview during the summer, and on August 16 he went to the palace, on which Butler was spending more than he could afford, at 11 o'clock in the morning. The dean of Bristol was present.

They fell at once to disputing about justification by faith. The bishop contended that Wesley made God tyrannical: if some people were justified without previous goodness, why were not all?

"Because, my lord, they resist his Spirit, because they 'will not come to him that they may have life'; because they suffer him not 'to work in them both to will and to do.' They cannot be saved because they will not believe."

"Sir, what do you mean by faith?" asked the bishop.

"My lord, by justifying faith I mean a conviction wrought in a man by the Holy Ghost that Christ hath loved *him*, and given himself for *him*, and that through Christ *his* sins are forgiven."

The bishop, missing the point, remarked that "some good men have this, but not all" and asked how Wesley proved this to be "the justifying faith taught by our Church."

Wesley quoted from the authorized Homily on Salvation. They argued over its meaning.

Then the bishop said: "Mr. Wesley, I will deal plainly with you. I once thought Mr. Whitefield and you well-meaning men. But I can't think so now. For I have heard more of you—matters of fact, sir. And Mr. Whitefield says in his *Journal*, 'There are promises still to be fulfilled in me.'

"Sir," exclaimed the bishop, in a sentence which would become famous, "the pretending to extraordinary revelations and gifts of the Holy Ghost is a horrid thing, a very horrid thing!"

"My lord, for what Mr. Whitefield says Mr. Whitefield and not I is accountable. I pretend to no extraordinary revelations and gifts of the Holy Ghost—none but what every Christian may receive, and ought to expect and pray for. But I do not wonder your lordship has heard facts asserted which, if true, would prove the contrary. Nor do I wonder that your lordship, believing them true, should alter the opinion you once had of me. A quarter of an hour I spent with your lordship before. And about an hour now. And perhaps you have never conversed one other hour with anyone who spoke in my favor. But how many with those who spoke on the other side! So that your lordship could not but think as you do."

Wesley asked for the "matters of fact." The bishop accused him of administering the Sacrament in the societies (and thus in unconsecrated buildings, which was not lawful except at a sickbed). Wesley denied it: "I never did yet, and believe I never shall"—in which he prophesied wrongly.

"I hear, too, many people fall into fits in your societies, and that you pray over them."

"I do so, my lord. When any show by strong cries and tears that their soul is in deep anguish, I frequently pray to God to deliver them from it. And our prayer is often answered in that hour."

"Very extraordinary indeed! Well, sir, since you ask my advice, I will give it you very freely. You have no business here. You are not commissioned to preach in this diocese. Therefore I advise you to go hence."

"My lord, my business on earth is to do what good I can. Wherever therefore I think I can do most good, there must I stay so long as I think so. At present I think I can do most good here. Therefore here I stay."

Wesley reminded the bishop that an ordained fellow of an Oxford college was not limited to a single parish but could preach "to any part of the Church of England." The bishop did not contest that and closed the interview.

Yet his lordship might still inhibit John Wesley by due process of ecclesiastical law. When, therefore, Wesley received a second summons two days later, he was nervous. Furthermore, he had received that morning a note from a well-wisher to warn him of two men who were resolved to murder him as he went out of town. Wesley had promptly written to each. Both had hastily denied the rumor.

Before going into the palace, Wesley attended evening prayer at the cathedral and was much comforted by words of one of the set psalms and by passages in both lessons which seemed specially apt: "Be not afraid of their terror, neither be ye troubled.... Having a good conscience, that whereas they speak evil of you, as of evildoers, they may be ashamed that falsely accuse your good conversation in Christ" (1 Peter 3:14, 16).

He went into the palace with a humbled but high heart, ready for persecution. Instead, he found the Reverend Reginald Tucker, vicar of All Saints and a future dean of Gloucester, with the bishop. Wesley had commented during their previous discussion that Tucker (who had led the clergy in shutting the Bristol pulpits to Whitefield, and thus to Wesley) had said in a sermon that original sin needs no atonement. The bishop chose to treat this complaint as a formal presentment, which Wesley denied making. The three had an amicable debate about the sermon; the bishop offered "several reasons why there must be something good in us before God could justify us, some morally good temper."

Wesley left the palace without converting either the bishop or, apparently, the future dean, although on the next Good Friday he was "much comforted by Mr. T's sermon at All Saints; as well as by the affectionate seriousness wherewith he delivered the holy bread to a very large congregation. May the good Lord fill him with all the life of love, and with 'all spiritual blessings in Christ Jesus!'"

The bishop had not inhibited John Welsey from preaching. Wesley's course was clear. He must "preach the gospel wheresoever I am in the habitable world," as he had told the bishop. The long pilgrimage through Oxford, Georgia, and Aldersgate Street to the "mad step" of preaching in the fields had brought him to his vocation. His vast theological reading, his love of worship and deep knowledge of the Bible, his self-discipline and compassion had not saved him in themselves, but they were at the service of the gospel for such years as might remain. He had reached a deep contentment, though his joy was not expressive like Whitefield's. Wesley indeed was still somewhat wary of laughter or jesting: he kept his sense of humor under strict control.

As if to set a seal on his vocation, good news awaited him at the end of the month in London, where his mother had moved from Salisbury with her daughter and son-in-law, Westley Hall. When Wesley had seen her during his brief London visit in July, she had reproached him for his account of the events leading to Aldersgate Street, which Samuel had sent her with criticisms; she had not realized that it was the same paper which Wesley had read to her a year before. But now, on September 3, she had a happy surprise for her Jack.

She told him that until a short time ago she had scarcely heard mentioned the good news that sins may be forgiven at once rather than at the final reckoning on the Last Day, nor that God's Spirit would make his presence felt in a person's heart. She quoted St. Paul's words in the Epistle to the Romans (8:16): "The Spirit itself beareth witness with our spirit, that we are the children of God" and said that she had never imagined that this was the common privilege of all true believers.

"Therefore," said Susanna Wesley, "I never dared ask for it myself. But two or three weeks ago, while my son Hall was pronouncing those words, in delivering the cup to me, 'The blood of our Lord Jesus Christ, which was given for thee,' the words struck through my heart, and I knew God for Christ's sake had forgiven *me* all *my* sins."

15

Unhappy Divisions

By mid-January 1740 all southern England had lain under snow or hard frost for several weeks. Down at Bristol John Wesley grieved for the poor, especially the day laborers in the countryside who had no work in the frozen fields and therefore no wages. He found families which were starving because several parishes were providing no relief although legally required to do so.

He took up a collection from the congregations at three services that week. Appointing helpers, he organized soup kitchens to feed about 100 and sometimes 150 daily while the severe weather continued.

The Kingswood colliers were still able to mine underground. Wesley could look around happily at their transformation thanks to Whitefield's courage and his own work: "The scene is already changed. Kingswood does not now, as a year ago, resound with cursing and blasphemy. It is no more filled with drunkenness and uncleanness, no longer full of wars and fightings, of wrath and envyings. Peace and love are there. Great numbers of the people are mild, gentle, and easy to be entreated. Hardly is their 'voice heard in the streets,' or, indeed, in their own wood, unless when they are at their usual evening diversion, singing praise unto God their Saviour."

Wesley himself returned unexpectedly to London, "called away in a manner I could not resist." A young man of good family, bad habits, and no religion named Gwillam Snowde had come to Bristol the previous year, intending to seek his fortune abroad. Apparently converted under Wesley's preaching, he and another man became assistants at the new school for the colliers' children, but after a few months they disappeared with some of the building fund. Snowde turned highwayman, was caught, and was now sentenced to death. He sent an urgent message begging Wesley to see him before he hanged. Willing to leave the crowded congregations of Bristol for the sake of one man who had betrayed his trust, Wesley set out. The stage coach could not make the hills, so he rode, a journey which took five days through that frozen countryside with a rest on Sunday at Newbury, where he preached in the parish church.

He went at once to Newgate. The man was truly penitent and so plainly ready for heaven that Wesley was not sure "whether to rejoice or grieve" when Snowde was reprieved and transported to the American colonies.

In London, the Thames was frozen over, and an ox had been roasted whole on the ice. Wesley, however, was still able to preach to crowds because the previous November he had bought cheaply from the government the derelict King's Foundery on the edge of Upper Moorfields. The Foundery had been built to recast the bronze cannon captured in the wars of Marlborough but was accidentally wrecked and the Royal Arsenal transferred to Woolwich. Methodists were now restoring the Foundery to make a roomy preaching hall with a spartan home for Wesley and Charles at the back.

The evangelical revival was spreading and coalescing; Wesley made two brief preaching tours in Wales, "where there is indeed a great awakening. God has done great things by Howell Harris." In Yorkshire and the Midlands Benjamin Ingham had become an itinerant evangelist. "The Methodists make a mighty noise in the nation," wrote Wesley's sister Emily, asking her brother for information. "Most people condemn their doctrines, yet whether out of curiosity or goodness I can't tell. Never were any preachers more followed."

Not only were numerous pamphlets being written to damn or defend them, but the Methodists began to meet violence. Twice in London that year, Wesley was surrounded by howling roughs as he got down from a coach to enter his house. He calmly faced them and spoke to them about Christ until they listened quietly. In Bristol on April 1, he was expounding at the New Room when a mob came to disrupt the service: "Not only the court and the alleys, but all the street, upwards and downwards, was filled with people shouting, cursing and swearing, and ready to swallow the ground with fierceness and rage. The mayor sent order that they should disperse. But they set him at nought. The chief constable came next in person, who was, till then, sufficiently prejudiced against us. But they insulted him also in so gross a manner, as I believe fully opened his eyes. At length the mayor sent several of his officers, who took the ringleaders into custody, and did not go till all the rest were dispersed."

At the quarter sessions next day the rioters tried to excuse themselves by complaints against Wesley, but the mayor cut them short: "What Mr. Wesley is, is nothing to you. I will keep the peace; I will have no rioting in this city."

Yet the very next day a sheriff of Bristol refused to allow Wesley to minister to two criminals who had asked to talk with him before they were hanged. This alderman's brother, who was incumbent of a Bristol church, later repelled Charles Wesley and his collier friends from Holy Communion, even when Charles exclaimed: "You can *see* I am a clergyman."

The revival, however, faced a more subtle danger—internal disputes which threatened to extinguish what violence could not destroy.

Back in the autumn of 1739 a Moravian, Philip Molther, had stopped in London on his way from Germany to America. He had visited the Fetter Lane society while the Wesleys were both away and soon had such influence that he postponed his departure to the colonies. When the Wesleys returned, they found the society in confusion with many of their best friends following Molther's new teaching. He had persuaded them that unless faith was strong, it was not faith at all—"weak faith is no faith"—and that those who lacked strong faith must not receive the Sacrament or go to church but be "still," awaiting faith. The society meetings, which once had been loud with hymns and exclamations of joy ("animal spirits," Molther had complained) were now for much of the time silent and still as the members waited for faith.

Wesley tried to turn them back to scriptural paths. He thought he had succeeded but, as Charles said six months later: "How fatal was our delay and false moderation!" For by the spring of 1740 the Wesleys were losing their friends fast: the Delamottes, Hutton, and John Bray, in whose house Charles had been converted. "I labored for peace," wrote Charles after disputing with Bray and others, "but only the Almighty can root out those cursed tares of pride, contempt and self-sufficiency with which our Moravianized brethren are overrun."

Jemmy Hutton was fast turning Moravian. Writing to Count Zinzendorf, he complained that John Wesley was too ambitious. He thought Wesley should be content "to awaken souls in preaching, but not to lead them to Christ. But he will have the glory of doing all things." Meanwhile George Stonehouse, vicar of Islington, was so influenced by the new teaching that he refused to pray with an elderly dying woman who was not yet converted or to read the Bible to her or bring her the Sacrament. He told her daughter: "These outward things must be laid aside. She has nothing to do but to be still." When John Wesley tried to reason with him, Stonehouse said he intended to sell the living of Islington when he could get his price, and leave the church: "No honest man can officiate as a minister in the Church of England," he asserted.

By midsummer, the "stillness" controversy had reached new heights. One evening Wesley was prevented from speaking at Fetter Lane, although he had sat patiently through an hour of "dumb show," as Charles called it. On another occasion Wesley recorded, "I went to Fetter Lane, and plainly told our poor, confused, shattered society where they had erred from the faith. It was as I feared: they could not receive my saying."

On June 22, "finding there was no time to delay without utterly destroying the cause of God," Wesley struck "at the root of the grand delusion." In a series of early morning expositions at the Foundery, he set forth the differences between the new doctrines, which Molther had foisted on the Moravians and on the Fetter

Lane society, and the plain teaching of Scripture. Early in July he went to the Fetter Lane meeting again, "but I found their hearts were quite estranged." Two days later he met "a little handful of them who still stand in the old paths" but were under great pressure. On July 18, certain that "the thing was now come to a crisis," he brought nineteen supporters together, including his mother, Lady Huntingdon, and Benjamin Ingham (who later joined the Moravians). He conducted a Communion service for them, and they unanimously decided to leave Fetter Lane.

On the next Sunday evening, July 20, 1740, after preaching out of doors in Moorfields, Wesley went to Fetter Lane. Some ninety men and women were there. Wesley sat silently through their silent "love feast" and their shorter vocal service. Then he rose, took the platform, and read out a brief summary of his opponents' position. He concluded: "I believe these assertions to be flatly contrary to the Word of God." He had warned them and begged them again and again, "but as I find you more and more confirmed in the error of your ways, nothing now remains but that I should give you up to God."

"You that are of the same judgment, *follow me!*"

He walked out without another word. Only eighteen or nineteen followed him. The next Wednesday "our little company met at The Foundery instead of Fetter Lane." A total of some twenty-five men and women, including Mrs. Wesley and Lady Huntingdon, became the nucleus of a new society.

Fetter Lane turned Moravian. In 1742 it was formally constituted a society of the (Moravian) Church of the United Brethren, which was later licensed in England as a dissenting body.

Wesley was to write during the following year: "My belief is that the present design of God is to visit the poor Church of England."

If he were to be part of that design, he could not allow himself or the revival to become the property of a small foreign sect previously unknown in England, however much they had helped his spiritual search. He had no alternative but separation from Fetter Lane.

Meanwhile, a more damaging dispute had blown up.

During 1740 letters were passing across the Atlantic between Wesley and Whitefield. Three months might elapse, even four, between the posting of a letter and the opening of the reply, however prompt.

Sometime in May Wesley received an affectionate letter dated Savannah, March 26. Whitefield, whose evangelism was having sensational success in the colonies, begged Wesley to "write no more to me about misrepresentations wherein we differ." He was "ten thousand times more convinced," he said, of the doctrine of election and of the final perseverence "of those that are truly in Christ." "You think otherwise," he wrote. "Why then should we dispute when there is no probability of convincing? … Let us offer salvation freely to all by the blood of Jesus."

The Wesleys indeed gloried in offering "universal redemption," by which they meant that all, however wicked, may respond to the gospel and be saved if they repent and trust Christ. Whitefield, however, lived far away from the Wesleys and depended on sometimes garbled reports.

As the year wore on, he became convinced that by "universal redemption" the Wesleys meant that all *would* be saved whether they repented or not. Wesley, for his part, was wrongly beginning to identify Whitefield with the rigorous Calvinism of men like the Bristol bigot who, until no longer admitted, had disrupted the society at the New Room by asserting vehemently to Wesley's face: "You and your brother are false prophets…. You are all wrong…. I hold that a certain number of mankind is elected from eternity, and these must and shall be saved: and all the rest of mankind must and shall be damned." This attitude, to Wesley, implied that evangelizing was superfluous, as he had trenchantly contended in his Bristol sermon against predestination.

In August two letters crossed somewhere in the Atlantic. Whitefield's letter deflected Wesley's implication: "Since," wrote Whitefield, "we know not who are the elect, and who are reprobate, we are to preach promiscuously to all." Wesley's letter implied that he and Whitefield should each go his own way: "The case is quite plain. There are bigots both for predestination and against it. God is sending a message to those on either side. But neither will receive it unless from one who is of their own opinion. Therefore for a time you are suffered to be of one opinion and I of another." He added that God would bring them to one mind eventually.

Whitefield wrote back: "I cannot bear the thought of opposing you." The Bristol sermon, however, had been republished in America. Whether this was instigated by Wesley or by an interested party cannot be determined, nor whether Wesley had personally sent a copy to one of Whitefield's chief opponents in Charleston, South Carolina, as Whitefield complained. Whitefield reluctantly composed a reply to it to be published as an open letter to Wesley.

Whitefield was fully engaged in the whirlwind preaching tour in New England which, more than any other factor, brought about the Great Awakening. He had no time to weigh every phrase of his public letter although he showed the draft to experienced Presbyterian clergy in America. He dated the letter December 24,

1740 and sent one manuscript copy to be printed in Charleston, left another at a Boston printer, and carried a third when he embarked on the *Minerva* for England to have it printed in London.

In January 1741 rumors of the letter's existence reached England, probably through one of the American clergy who had seen it in manuscript. "If," wrote Charles to Wesley in Bristol on the night of January 10, "GW has declared against the truth, GW will come to nothing. Therefore leave him. He that believeth shall not make haste."

Wesley was back in London by the end of the month. Whitefield was still at sea, and on Sunday, February 1, he went down to his cabin and wrote a private letter to Wesley to be added to the pile which he would post on arrival in England. Sorrowfully but firmly he gave the Wesleys notice that he was going into print.

He did not know that one of the men who had seen the letter in America had sent a copy ahead which a London printer pirated.

That same day, Sunday, February 1, Wesley rose at 4:30 A.M. at the Foundery, where he was now living with Charles and their mother and sister Kezzy, who died later that year, having never recovered from being jilted. After prayer and breakfast Wesley went to the preaching hall in the Foundery, where he would expound to a large congregation before going on to Communion, with many other of his Methodists, at a parish church. As he entered the hall, he learned that a pamphlet had been handed to worshipers as they approached the doors. He procured a copy and glanced at the title: "A Letter to the Reverend John Wesley" ... by the Reverend George Whitefield.

Wesley mounted the preaching platform and looked at the large congregation, the men and the women sitting separately as usual. Many held copies of the pamphlet. Without comment, Wesley led the prayers and singing and preached his prepared sermon on the subject of marriage from a text in the Sermon on the Mount.

Then, a trifle dramatically, he announced: "A private letter, wrote to me by Mr. Whitefield, has been printed without his leave or mine. I will do just what I believe Mr. Whitefield would were he here himself." He tore the letter into pieces. Everyone who had received the pamphlet did the same "so that in two minutes there was not a whole copy left."

Later in the month Wesley left London before daybreak by horse (he was therefore safe from "footpads"—robbers on foot) and came in midafternoon to Oxford, where he left the horse, which possibly he was bringing to its owner, for he continued by foot. After lingering over dinner at a household of friends, he set out with less than an hour of daylight to reach John Gambold at Stanton Harcourt rectory. "Walked, rain, dark, weary! prayed!" runs the terse entry in his diary for February 17. Behind the entry came a tale he loved to tell.

As night fell, a heavy rain drenched him. He lost his way, and even if he saw a signpost, no tinderbox could be lit in the rain. "I could not help saying in my heart (though ashamed of my want of resignation to God's will), 'Oh that thou wouldst stay the bottles of heaven; or at least give me light, or an honest guide, or some help in the manner thou knowest.'" Soon the rain stopped. The moon emerged, and he could see where he was. Then "a friendly man overtook me, who set me upon his own horse, and walked by my side, till we came to Mr. Gambold's door." Welsey rejoiced that a threefold prayer had received a threefold answer.

By foot and by horse he reached Bristol in two days more. He found the United Society split and quarreling. John Cennick, his own chief assistant, the schoolmaster of the school that Whitefield had founded at Kingswood, was leading the opposition to his theology.

John Cennick (Wesley sometimes spelled his name "Cenwick") was a young man from Reading whose grandparents were Quakers and his parents members of the Church of England. After a mildly dissolute youth, he had been overtaken by a longing for forgiveness and the knowledge of God, which he sought to achieve by rigorous acts of devotion, even contemplating crossing the seas to enter a monastery since none existed in England. On September 6, 1737, about two years after Whitefield and eight months before Wesley—and unknown to either—Cennick was transformed by a similar conversion. Wesley met him at Reading in March 1739—"a young man, strong in the faith of our Lord Jesus"—and later invited Cennick to be the schoolmaster at Kingswood and encouraged him to preach. Whitefield doubted Wesley's wisdom in allowing a layman who had never sought Holy Orders to act "in so public a manner."

Cennick was soon influenced by the Calvinist Dissenters at Bristol, then by Howell Harris and Whitefield. By the time that Wesley had returned to Bristol in March 1740, Cennick was convinced that truth, as he saw it, must not be compromised or denied.

Wesley, from an opposite angle, believed likewise; his quarrel with Cennick lay with his behavior rather than his beliefs. "You have not done right in speaking against me behind my back," said Wesley when Cennick and some twenty others came up to him in the New Room after the sermon. He tried to show that they misunderstood his teaching, but Cennick was adamant and told Wesley they would continue to attend the United Society but were already meeting by themselves to promote the doctrines which Wesley attacked.

"You should have told me this before," answered Wesley, "and not have supplanted me in my own house, stealing the hearts of the people, and by private accusations, separating very friends." Cennick denied the charge. Wesley then read aloud a copy of a letter which Cennick had written to Whitefield and circulated in Bristol imploring him to come to their rescue.

To keep tempers low, Wesley adjourned the discussion to a private room. Cennick and his friends could not agree that they had been in the wrong. Wesley had no wish to see the United Society lapse into a theological debating club when its purpose was to save and build up souls, and he believed that Cennick and his friends had been guilty of "tale-bearing, back-biting, and evil speaking, dissembling, lying and slandering." They had scoffed at the Wesleys behind their backs while expressing love and esteem to their faces.

An uncomfortable meeting of the United Society took place a few days later. Each member on the list was considered by others. "To those who were sufficiently recommended," as Wesley recorded, tickets to denote membership were given on the following day. Wesley continued to urge the recalcitrants to a better mind, for he was "still fearful of doing anything rashly, or contrary to the great law of love," but Cennick believed that he could form his own society while remaining a member of Wesley's.

On February 28 Cennick sat, as he usually did, on the platform beside Wesley and was shocked when Wesley publicly expelled him "by the consent and approbation of the band-society in Kingswood." Cennick said nothing. "I was a little surprised," he recorded in his diary, "yet I showed little of it to the souls, only they saw me weep as I went out."

Wesley's imperiousness demanded loyalty, but his affection for Cennick urged restraint. He begged Cennick to wrestle in prayer, hoping he would acknowledge his faults and be readmitted. Cennick was sure that his offense in Wesley's eyes was a belief in predestination; Wesley countered that he had not expelled him for his opinions. The final break came on Sunday, March 8, when Cennick and fifty-one others withdrew from the Kingswood society (mainly composed of converted colliers) and ninety stayed with Wesley. Thus, though Wesley and Cennick continued in friendship, two competing Methodist societies arose in Kingswood.

And Wesley was in danger of becoming isolated, for in the east of England, Joseph Humphreys of the society at Deptford, a layman whom Wesley had appointed to preach and lead classes, had gone over to the Calvinists. Charles Welsey was leaning toward the Moravians, for he dearly loved Stonehouse, Hutton, and the Delamottes. In a fit of "stillness," Charles had abruptly left off expounding at the Foundery in the middle of a series.

Wesley worked hard to hold him. The danger passed, yet when Peter Böhler returned to England a few weeks later, Wesley was so drawn toward this young missionary who more than anyone had led him to his trust in Christ that he almost longed to be a Moravian himself: "I marvel how I refrain from joining these men. I scarce see any of them but my heart burns within me. I long to be with them, yet I am kept from them."

16

Whitefield Reconciled

George Whitefield landed at Falmouth in Cornwall on March 11, 1741 and reached London on the Sunday four days later. Wesley first knew of his arrival when a letter came from Charles "in a panic about GW," urging immediate return. "George Whitefield you know is come," he wrote in cipher, adding in longhand, "His fair words are not to be trusted to; for his actions show most unfriendly."

Whitefield had arrived in time to preach to the great crowds which had gathered on Kennington Common and Moorfields to hear Charles, who, it seems, gladly gave him the open-air pulpit. Next day they met privately. George produced the manuscript of his intended open letter, but Charles refused to read it, urging George, by an apposite text, not to carry out his anti-Wesley attack. The Wesleys found themselves in deep disagreement, and they wept as they prayed. That night when Charles began his letter to John, he advised that the Wesleys should not attack Whitefield either.

Early next morning when Charles was expounding at the Foundery on "the believer's privilege: *i.e.*, power over sin," George joined him on the platform. After a while, Charles invited him to preach. George thereupon, to Charles' dismay, inveighed against some of the Wesleys' doctrines as he understood them. He thought they had been preaching *sinless* perfection and had dressed up the doctrine of election "in such horrible colors" that many of George's former friends were shunning him.

Whitefield was acting deliberately. As he wrote to his assistant in Georgia: "What is most cutting of all, I am constrained, on account of our differing principles, publicly to separate from my dear, dear old friends Messrs. John and Charles Wesley, whom I still love as my own soul."

Charles longed for peace, longed for his brother. Indeed, had John and not Charles been in London that week before Whitefield had published the open letter or preached against them, his sharper theological perception might have cleared mutual misunderstandings.

On March 25 Wesley rode out from Bristol in the dark, two hours before sunrise, and with short stops for meals and a brief night in Berkshire, reached the Foundery by early evening after nineteen hours in the saddle in two days.

Charles and Tom Maxfield, who had been Whitefield's first collier convert and afterward Wesley's assistant, told him of "Mr. Whitefield's unkind behavior since his return from Georgia." Wesley went round, with Westley Hall as witness, to Whitefield's lodgings two days later. They were frank with each other after experiencing the double-dealers of Bristol. Wesley approved Whitefield's plain speaking; as Wesley commented thirty years later, "integrity was inseparable from his whole character."

Whitefield, speaking respectfully as he always did to Wesley, insisted that he could not remain in fellowship but was resolved publicly to preach against the Wesleys because they and he "preached two different gospels."

Wesley knew that Whitefield would never put friendship before principle: "He was immovable ... wherever his conscience was concerned." Both men were distressed. Whitefield probably showed it more openly, for (as Wesley said) "he had a heart susceptible of the most generous and the most tender friendship. I have frequently thought that this, of all others, was the distinguishing part of his character. How few have we known of so kind a temper, of such large and flowing affections."

To the world they might soon appear rivals rather than friends, for Whitefield's supporters were erecting a wooden preaching hall (the Tabernacle) on the edge of Moorfields only a short distance from the Foundery.

Then Whitefield published his open letter, printed with his authority, and Wesley was annoyed. On the morning of April 4, with Westley Hall again as witness, he confronted Whitefield. For whatever reason, this next conversation took place in a coach, a location which softened the impression of an Oxford don of thirty-seven disciplining a graduate of twenty-six.

"Both love and justice," records Wesley, "required that I speak my sentiments freely." He sternly told Whitefield that the very act of publishing had given a weapon to their enemies, "who loved neither the one nor the other." If Whitefield had felt that he must publish an answer to the Bristol sermon on free grace, he should have put out a treatise "without ever calling my name in question." Thirdly, Wesley argued that the letter was "a mere burlesque upon an answer, leaving four of my arguments untouched, and handling the other four in so gentle a manner as if he were afraid they would burn his fingers."

The heart of Wesley's annoyance, however, was that Whitefield had revealed a private matter. To underline his point that the drawing of a lot ("preach and print") might be false guidance, Whitefield had told the public about Wesley's lot at Deal in February 1738: "Let him return to London." Wesley regarded the revelation as irrelevant and treacherous: it would "make an open (and probably irreparable) breach between him and me."

Even then the two friends might not have split asunder, but when Whitefield went down to Bristol, he found many matters which were not to his liking. He wrote to Wesley a letter which is lost. Urged on by his sister, Mrs. Grevil, he laid claim to the ownership of the New Room and to the Kingswood School. Wesley answered him in a long letter at the end of April, point by point. Then he reverted to their dispute over the open letter: "To proceed as you have done is so far from friendship that it is not moral honesty." He asserted that Whitefield's sermons were holding him up to ridicule, but that he would not retaliate: "This field you have all to yourself. I cannot dwell on those things which have an immediate tendency to make you odious and contemptible."

Both Wesley and Whitefield were relying on hearsay. As Whitefield said afterward: "Busybodies on both sides blew up the coals. We harkened too much to tale bearers." Both, in the privacy of their closets, poured out their distress to the same Savior, whom they both proclaimed with love and fervor; yet unless Wesley and Whitefield could heal their breach, the evangelical revival might peter out.

All through the summer of 1741 they were estranged. Whitefield toured Scotland, where he preached to great audiences and was bullied by extreme Calvinists who were affronted that he would not leave the Church of England. Wesley toured the Midlands, preached before the University of Oxford, and worked in London and Bristol. He made no move toward Whitefield.

Early in October, Wesley toured in Wales. At Abergavenny some Calvinists who were "bitter in spirit" had stirred up such prejudice that he had no audience except in the household of a widow, Mrs. James, who "received us gladly as she had done aforetime." Mrs. James was to become Mrs. George Whitefield the following month. Wesley completed his tour and returned to Bristol. He had preached at Kingswood and was about to lie down when a message came from the Calvinist Howell Harris, newly arrived from London and ready to travel into Wales before dawn. Wesley went to his lodgings, where Harris and his two companions "immediately fell upon their favorite subject." After two hours of fruitless argument, Wesley "begged we might exchange controversy for prayer. We did so, and then parted in much love, about 2 in the morning."

That prayer meeting was the dawn of reconciliation. The next day (his journey being deferred) Harris came round to see Wesley. They found themselves in much closer agreement, and Wesley at short notice joined Harris when he set out for Wales, where they met Daniel Rowlands, whose character and preaching impressed Wesley. Deeper into Wales, Harris and Rowlands took his part when two Calvinists tore into his doctrines and motives at a small meeting which had been intended "to provoke one another to love and good works." The next day Wesley went to a house where several men and women had been invited, including the two angry Calvinists. The room fell silent as he entered, but Mrs. James, the future Mrs. Whitefield ("a woman of candor and humanity"), sharply rebuked the two for criticizing Wesley behind his back and not to his face.

Then Harris came in "and God blessed the healing words which he spoke; so that we parted in much love, being all determined to let controversy alone, and to preach 'Jesus Christ and him crucified.'"

Harris wrote to Whitefield in Scotland. As Whitefield must have been courting his future wife by the mails, she may have written too. Late in October, Wesley in Bristol opened a letter from Aberdeen.[1] "Reverend and dear brother," wrote Whitefield, "I have for a long time expected that you would have sent me an answer to my last letter, but I suppose that you are afraid to correspond with me, because I revealed your secret about the lot. Though much may be said for my doing it, yet I am sorry now that any such thing dropped from my pen, and I humbly ask pardon. I find I love you as much as ever, and pray God, if it be his blessed will, that we may be all united together."

Whitefield hoped all obstacles would be removed. He held particular election, he said, "yet I offer Jesus freely to every individual soul." Whitefield did not agree with Wesley's views on sanctification, but this need not divide them. He expected to be in Bristol in three weeks. "May all disputing cease, and each of us talk of nothing but Jesus and him crucified!"

When Whitefield reached Bristol in November, having escaped a highwayman in Scotland and married Mrs. James in Caerphilly, he found Wesley recovering from a severe attack of "the ague"—malaria. ("My heart and lungs, and all that was within me, and my soul too, seemed to be in perfect uproar. But I cried unto the Lord in my trouble, and he delivered me out of my distress.")

In the garret at the New Room or, if Wesley was up, the "little room, by the school, where I speak with the people that come to me," they healed their seven-month breach. Neither left a record of their talk.

Affection returned, yet the close unity of the early days never was fully restored: the theological divisions which two centuries earlier had weakened the Reformation were dividing their minds though not their hearts, and each believed he was right. "I spent an agreeable hour with Mr. Wh.," wrote Wesley in April 1742. "I believe he is sincere in all he says concerning his desire of joining hands with all that love the Lord Jesus Christ. But if (as some would persuade me) he is not, the loss is all on his side. I am just as I was: I go on my way, whether he goes with me or stays behind."

Together they could have done even more for Britain and America—Whitefield the incomparable preacher, Wesley the patient organizer. Instead, the evangelical revival would flow in two channels, although leaders and friends would often support each other. Both Wesley and Whitefield sought a more formal unity from time to time, but their differences were not overcome. They prayed for one another and corresponded. "Yesterday," wrote Whitefield to Wesley about a year after their reconciliation, "I had your kind letter.... In answer to the first part of it I say, 'Let old things pass away, and all things become new.' I can certainly say 'Amen' to the latter part of it. 'Let the king live for ever, and controversy die.' It has died with me long ago.... God be praised for giving you such a mind.... I subscribe myself, reverend and very dear sir, your most affectionate, though younger brother, in the gospel of our glorious Emmanuel."

17

The Opening of the North

In the second week of May 1742, Wesley and Whitefield went twice together to the archbishop of Canterbury and to the bishop of London and stood their ground. On the following Monday, Wesley had planned to start early for Bristol, preaching at various places. Some trivial circumstance delayed him, and he was still at the Foundery when a letter came from the Countess of Huntingdon, who was down in Leicestershire at the family seat, Donnington Park.

Selina Huntingdon, then aged nearly thirty-five, had become a strong supporter of both evangelists and was in frequent correspondence with Wesley; he sent her the manuscript of the journal he had prepared for publication, and she thought that he ought to leave out the passage about Beau Nash.

She now wrote that a young relation, Fanny Cowper, ("my little saint"), was dying of consumption and had expressed a desire to see John or Charles before she died: "I beg you will set out as soon as may be after receiving this, as every day she has lived this past fortnight seems a fresh miracle, wrought for some

purpose not yet known." Selina had ordered a horse for one of
her servants, John Taylor, to accompany John Wesley ("he is a
sweet and humble spirit, ... honest of heart, but weak in faith")
and apparently had arranged for Lord Huntingdon's stable to
mount Wesley too.

Wesley had been thinking of Yorkshire for later that summer
and was willing to bring it forward. Instead of westward down the
Bath Road, he rode north up Watling Street, the Old Roman Road,
and turned off at the thirty-eighth milestone. After refreshment
at Newport Pagnell, he and John Taylor overtook another rider
whose sober clothes suggested a "serious man," probably a
Presbyterian Dissenter. Wesley put his book back into the saddle
bag. He always seized an opportunity on the road or in an inn
or at a forge when his horse cast a shoe, to speak about Christ.
Once, for two days, he yielded to the advice of friends to relax
and found himself treated as "a civil, good-natured gentleman,"
but his conscience smote him and thenceforth he "took up his
cross," as he put it.

The "serious man" near Newport Pagnell was eager to promote
Predestination. Wesley did not contradict. The man demanded
his views, but "I told him over and over, 'We had better keep to
practical things, lest we should be angry at one another.' And so
we did for two miles, till he caught me unawares, and dragged me
into the dispute before I knew where I was. He then grew warmer
and warmer, told me I was rotten at heart, and supposed I was
one of John Wesley's followers. I told him, 'No, I am John Wesley
himself.'"

The man shot forward like (Wesley used a Latin tag from
Virgil) "one who unawares has trodden upon a snake." But Lord
Huntingdon's horse had its uses—"being the better mounted of

the two, I kept close to his side, and endeavored to show him his heart, till we came into the street of Northampton."

Reaching Donnington Park, Wesley found Countess Selina's little saint just alive. "As soon as we came in her spirit greatly revived. For three days we rejoiced in the grace of God, whereby she was filled with a hope full of immortality; with meekness, gentleness, patience, and humble love, knowing in whom she had believed." Wesley never shunned a deathbed. As he once said, "Our people die well." The drugged departures of a much later generation were unknown; the dying were often alert until the last breath, and Wesley loved to see a man, woman, or child conscious of Christ's presence at the sickbed, strengthening eternal hope, driving away gloom and fear.

Countess Selina had another matter on her mind. She urged upon Wesley the needs of the coal miners of Newcastle upon Tyne in the far north of England. Like the Kingswood miners before Whitefield, they were illiterate, rough, and godless. "They have churches," the countess said, "but they never go to them! And ministers, but they seldom or never hear them! Perhaps they may hear you. And what if you save (under God) one soul?"

Wesley and Taylor therefore rode out for the north early on a May morning and came the next evening to Birstall in Yorkshire, which had been the original object of the journey he had planned for the summer.

At Birstall lived a young stonemason, John Nelson, whom Wesley had last met in London as they both walked back from a service in St. Paul's Cathedral.

Nelson, a skilled ornamental craftsman, already married with a growing family, had come to London to work. He had heard Whitefield preach in Moorfields: "I loved the man so that if any offered to disturb him I was ready to fight for him; but I did not understand him." Nelson studied the Bible and prayed without more than a little hope of mercy. One June day he joined the early crowd at Moorfields when Whitefield was across the river and John Wesley took his place. As Nelson records: "O that was a blessed morning for my soul! As soon as he got upon the stand he stroked back his hair and turned his face toward where I stood, and I thought he fixed his eyes on me. His countenance struck such an awful dread upon me before I heard him speak that it made my heart beat like the pendulum of a clock; and when he did speak, I thought his whole discourse was aimed at me." When Wesley finished, Nelson said to himself, "This man can tell the secrets of my heart. He hath not left me there, for he hath shown me the remedy, even the blood of Jesus."

After a while Nelson returned to Yorkshire on his own initiative as an evangelist. Unordained, uncommissioned, supporting himself by his skill as a mason, he would go out after work, with hammer and trowel struck into his apron, and give out his text.

Wesley could now see for himself why the revival spread so fast across England as men converted in London or Bristol took the message home. As he preached from the top of Birstall Hill, examined converts, and listened to Nelson's stories, he realized that he had not labored in vain: "Many of the greatest profligates in all the country were now changed." Swearers praised God, drunkards were sober. "The whole town wore a new face. Such a change did God work by the artless testimony of one plain man! And from thence his words sounded forth to Leeds, Wakefield, Halifax, and all the West Riding of Yorkshire."

Tearing himself from Birstall after one day, Wesley rode onward to the north with Taylor at his side. As they passed through

Knaresborough, they spoke to a man and gave him a printed sermon. They rode forward, but on their return journey some days later they were stopped in the street and told that this one conversation had led to several conversions and that "the sermon we gave him had traveled from one end of the town to the other."

They reached Newcastle upon Tyne at last—the great coal port which sent the "sea coal" to London. The walls of Newcastle still enclosed the town, with the Tyne on one side and the open country on the other.

Wesley was dismayed by the uncouthness of the Tynesiders: half of them appeared to be drunk; even the children swore.

About 7 o'clock on the morning of Sunday, May 30, 1742, he walked with John Taylor down Sandgate, then the poorest part of the town, and stood at the pump. They began to sing "All people that on earth do dwell" to the "Old Hundredth," a tune known to any Englishman who had ever ventured into a church. "Three or four people came out to see what was the matter." Wesley called out the text from Isaiah 53:5: "He was wounded for our transgressions, he was bruised for our iniquities: the chastisement of our peace was upon him; and with his stripes we are healed." The crowd grew until the street and every side alley was packed; people stood on the town walls or hung out of windows of houses.

"Observing the people, when I had done, to stand gaping and staring upon me, with the most profound astonishment, I told them, 'If you desire to know who I am, my name is John Wesley. At five in the evening, with God's help, I design to preach here again.'"

"At five, the hill on which I designed to preach was covered, from the top to the bottom. I never saw so large a number of people together, either at Moorfields, or at Kennington Common.

I knew it was not possible for the one half to hear, although my voice was then strong and clear; and I stood so as to have all in view, as they were ranged on the side of the hill.

"After preaching, the poor people were ready to tread me under foot, out of pure love and kindness. It was some time before I could possibly get out of the press. I then went back another way than I came; but several were got to our inn before me; by whom I was vehemently importuned to stay with them, at least a few days; or, however, one day more."

"This thing made a huge noise," recalled a young wagoner, Christopher Hopper. "The populace entertained various conjectures about him: but few, if any, could tell the motive on which he came, or the end he had in view. He made a short blaze, soon disappeared, and left us in a great consternation."

Wesley could not stay because he had promised to be back in Birstall, where John Nelson had summoned hearers from all the West Riding for Tuesday night. But he determined to make Newcastle another Bristol or Foundery, and the following winter returned to acquire land for an orphanage, a school, and a room where the Methodist society would meet. "He visited and preached in the neighborhood," adds Hopper. "His name was well known in town and country. All mouths were filled with Wesley and his followers; some for and many against them." Hopper later joined Wesley as one of his itinerant preachers, like several from the town. Newcastle became the third of Wesley's home bases.

Wesley decided to return from Newcastle and Yorkshire by Epworth, where on the Sunday morning at service time he offered his help to the curate-in-charge, John Romley, who as a local boy had been given his chance in life by old Samuel Wesley. Rowley refused to allow Samuel's son to preach or to read the prayers to the small congregation. In the afternoon the church was packed because of a rumor that John Wesley would preach; instead, the crowd and Wesley himself had to listen to the curate damning "enthusiasts."

Wesley whispered to John Taylor. Taylor slipped out after the sermon, and stood in the churchyard as the people left. He shouted: "Mr Wesley, not being permitted to preach in the church, designs to preach here at six o'clock."

Mr. Wesley found "such a congregation as I believe Epworth never saw before." He stood upon his father's high tomb outside the east end and preached.

He had intended to resume his journey but could not resist the opportunity to work again in his homeland, preaching in the hamlets and villages, visiting the sick, reaping where his father had sown without seeing a harvest. Each evening in the fine June weather Wesley returned to Epworth churchyard and used his father's tomb as pulpit. The curate did not interfere.

On a Tuesday evening, perhaps unnoticed by Wesley, his sister's widower, John Whitelamb, now rector of Wroot, stood at the back of the crowd. He sent a sad letter a few days later: "Fain would I have spoken to you, but that I am quite at a loss how to address or behave. Your way of thinking is so extraordinary that your presence creates an awe, as if you were an inhabitant of another world." Whitelamb, who had become almost a Deist, expressed doctrinal dissent but true affection and added: "I am quite forgot! None of the family ever honors me with a line! ... Dear sir, is it in my power to serve or oblige you any way? Glad I should be that you would make use of me. God open all our eyes, and lead us into truth, whatever it be."

Thus invited, Wesley preached in Wroot Church on the next Sunday morning and afternoon, "but the church could not contain the people, many of whom came from far." That evening he preached for the last time from his father's tomb.

The Epworth visit was apt; he returned to London in time to describe it to his mother, now in peace of soul after her years of struggle, and happy to see the revival of religion for which her husband had yearned.

She was failing rapidly. On the last day of that July 1742, Wesley wrote to Charles in Bristol: "Yesterday about 3 in the afternoon, as soon as intercession was ended, I went up to my mother. I found her pulse almost gone, and her fingers dead, so that it was easy to see her spirit was on the wing for eternity. After using the commendatory prayer, I sat down on her bedside, and with three or four of our sisters sung a requiem to her parting soul. She continued in just the same way as my father was, struggling and gasping for life, though (as I could judge by several signs) perfectly sensible, till near 4 o'clock. I was then going to drink a dish of tea, being faint and weary, when one called me again to the bedside. It was just 4 o'clock. She opened her eyes wide and fixed them upward for a moment. Then the lids dropped, and the soul was set at liberty, without one struggle or groan or sigh."

18

"All Round England"

For the next few years John Wesley's life had a triangular base: London, Bristol, and Newcastle. He stayed for long periods at each in succession while ranging widely in his travels between them, not without incident.

One winter morning Wesley and an assistant were riding across the Wiltshire downs on their way to Bristol: "About 10 o'clock we were met by a loaded waggon, in a deep, hollow way. There was a narrow path between the road and the bank: I stepped into this, and John Trembath followed me. When the waggon came near, my horse began to rear, and to attempt climbing up the bank. This frightened the horse which was close behind, and made him prance and throw his head to and fro, till the bit of the bridle catched hold of the cape of my great coat, and pulled me backward off my horse. I fell as exact on the path, between the waggon and the bank, as if one had taken me in his arms and laid me down there. Both our horses stood stock still, one just behind me, the other before; so, by the blessing of God, I rose unhurt, mounted again, and rode on."

At each base Wesley had far more to do than preaching. At Bristol and Newcastle he had to oversee the orphan houses, which included many foundlings picked out of the gutters or left on the doorstep. At Bristol he had full control of Kingswood school, where the boys were educated along the lines laid down by his mother for the Wesley children, thus submitting them to a discipline and course of studies which stretched the severities of eighteenth-century schooling to their limits.

He was also much engaged in relief for the poor. He was generous, passing on the income from his books, and he encouraged generosity in others. He aimed not only to relieve distress but also to help the poor help themselves. Thus, in a severe winter in London he organized weaving by women who had no means of support.

Recognizing that gin could ruin them, converts were turning to tea. But Wesley discovered that many of the poor were spending more than they could afford on tea. All tea came expensively from China and carried a heavy excise duty. And the poor liked their tea strong. He urged them to give it up. Much as he loved it, he set them an example. John too had liked his tea strong, though with sugar and cream, and suffered extraordinary withdrawal symptoms; so did Charles, who complained also that in some parts of England "tea was my beer." Instead both Wesleys began to drink sage "tea" or nettle "tea," or orange- and lemon-peel "tea" as an example for the poor to follow.

Wesley set up free clinics. He was one of the first in England to use electricity for medical purposes; he acquired a machine (still in existence) which gave electric shocks and became popular with users of the clinics. To be "electrified" twice a day was, in Wesley's eyes, a cure for many disorders.

He wrote a book titled *Primitive Physick, or an Easy and Natural Method of Curing Most Diseases*, remarking in the preface that whoever owned a copy had a "physician always in his house, and one that attends without fee or reward." Some of the cures were distinctly curious: "*For an Ague*, make six middling pills of cobwebs. Take one a little before the cold fit; *For Dry or Convulsive Asthma*: Dry and powder a toad; *For Hoarseness*: Rub the soles of the feet before the fire, with garlick and lard, well beaten together, over night. The hoarseness will be gone next day." Wesley would add the word *Tried* to all cures he had used himself. The medical profession was skeptical, but the book was popular for many years.

Wesley never allowed charity or education to become ends in themselves. He held firmly to his belief that a man or woman or a child must be remade in Christ; thus the biblical teaching and preaching came first. But the movement was spreading too widely for Wesley or Charles to conduct it without help. In London, Wesley had allowed Cennick and Joseph Humphreys to lead prayer meetings. Both had education and some training as preachers and had progressed naturally to sermons.

Tom Maxfield, the former Kingswood coal miner, had not been trained. Some years earlier, while Susanna Wesley was still living, Maxfield had begun to preach in London during Wesley's absence without his permission and had proved himself such an able expounder that Lady Huntingdon herself urged him on. When Wesley heard, he hurried back, annoyed, intending to discipline Maxfield. But Susanna had warned her son: "Take care what you do with respect to that young man, for he is as surely called of

God to preach as you are. Examine what have been the fruits of his preaching; and hear him yourself."

Wesley accepted her advice. Maxfield and two other young men asked to be allowed to help Wesley as itinerant preachers wherever he should direct. Others joined them. Wesley worried lest lay preachers might antagonize the bishops yet further, until he discovered that nearly 200 years earlier Queen Elizabeth had appointed twelve itinerant preachers and that the office still existed. The Queen's preachers were ordained men, a fact he glossed over, for most of his preachers, or "helpers" as he called them at first, were humble in origin and indifferent in education. He organized their movements round the circuits which developed as Methodist societies became established; each society was to be visited regularly.

"Be diligent," he would tell the preachers. "Never be unemployed. Never be triflingly employed. Never *while* away time, nor spend more time at any place than is strictly necessary.... You have nothing to do but to save souls. Therefore spend and be spent in this work. And go always, not only to those who want you, but to those who want you most."

Wesley puzzled how to ensure that all Methodists could be kept to the high morality and unceasing spiritual progress which are among the marks of Christ's true disciples. Finally, on February 15, 1742 he began to find his answer.

Leaders of the United Society at Bristol were discussing the debt which still burdened the New Room. A sea captain named Foy, from one of Bristol's chief mercantile families, suggested in a letter that every member should give the quite generous sum of one penny a week until the debt was paid.[1]

Somebody objected that many could not afford the penny.

"Then put eleven of the poorest with me," said Foy. "If they can give anything, well: I will call on them weekly. If they can give nothing, I will give for them as well as for myself." Wesley heard Foy urge all those present to call on eleven Methodist neighbors weekly: "Receive what they can give, and make up what is wanting."

The idea caught on. A group of twelve was named a "class" (not in the educational sense but the classical, as in "middle class"), and the man or woman who collected the contributions was called a "leader." After a while, several leaders mentioned that some in their class were not living as Christians should. Wesley saw at once that the class leader could become much more than a subscription collector; he or she could oversee faith and morals. The class became the unit of Methodist cohesion, not only in Bristol but everywhere.

Five years later a sympathetic curate reported to a hostile bishop: "A class is between 12 and 20 persons of any age or sex that live near each other, who meet together to sing and pray with their leader once or twice a week. The leader of the class examines each person with respect to the state of their soul, gives some short admonition and makes a report to the preacher of the society," who could expel them if they were unrepentant. The society in the curate's neighborhood numbered some 250 members, though three times as many might attend the twice-weekly evening meetings. On Fridays they fasted and met for intercession.

"When," continued the curate, "they have made some considerable advancement, and have, as they express it, received justifying Faith, they are united into Bands. A Band is 5 or 6 such persons of the same age and sex, which when they meet together are more unreserved, and declare, as they say, the inmost secrets of their hearts."

"The preachers are frequently removed, and I'm told Mr. Wesley goes all round England once or twice a year."

Mr. Wesley kept a sharp eye on their discipline. While rejoicing at happy and glorious ex-drunkards, ex-lechers, ex-swearers, and ex-atheists, he was not surprised if others left a society or were expelled. When he arrived at Newcastle in March 1743, he noted that the large numbers who had flocked into the society in the rapturous early days had been whittled down.

Seventy-six had withdrawn, among them:

> Fourteen (chiefly Dissenters) said they left it because otherwise their ministers would not give them the sacrament;
> Nine, because their husbands or wives were not willing they should stay in it.
> Twelve, because their parents were not willing.
> Five, because their master or mistress would not let them come.
> Seven, because their acquaintance persuaded them.
> Five, because people said such bad things of the society.
> Nine, because they would not be laughed at.
> Three, because they would not lose the poor's allowance.
> Three, because they could not spare the time to come.
> Two, because it was too far off.
> One, because she was afraid of falling into fits.
> One, because people were so rude in the street.
> Two, because Thomas Naisbit was in the society....

The number of those who were expelled was sixty-four:

> Two for cursing and swearing.
> Two for habitual Sabbath-breaking.

Seventeen for drunkenness.

Two for retailing spiritous liquors.

Three for quarreling and brawling.

One for beating his wife.

Three for habitual, willful lying.

Four for railing and evilspeaking.

One for idleness and laziness.

Nine-and-twenty for lightness and carelessness.

None had been expelled for his opinions. Wesley gloried in the absence of any doctrinal subscription, yet a strong and definite Christian theology was the bedrock of the movement, to be taught all the time by sermon, by exposition of Scripture—and by hymns.

Both the Wesleys regarded their hymns as an "exercise in practical divinity." Men and women of little education could learn Christian truth when they stood "to sing [their] dear Redeemer's praise." Charles was writing hymns full of doctrine, and John wrote several which were ascribed to his brother; they were published anonymously.

The Wesleys set the hymns to simple tunes which do not obscure the words or deflect the mind and heart. When John came upon a group of Methodists having a high time singing hymns as if they were choruses from a Handel oratorio, he stopped them. In the early days the tunes were plain, often adapted from stately German chorales and sung fast. Many stirring tunes came later, often from the north of England, to be sung to great hymns, such as "And Can It Be," "Love Divine All Loves Excelling," and "O for a Thousand Tongues to Sing."[2]

The hymns would change English worship, yet for most of Wesley's lifetime they were seldom heard in parish churches. Men and women in the thousands sang them in the market squares and on the hillsides and in the Methodist preaching houses. The revival spread by song.

It was also spreading by print. John Wesley's published sermons became the guide to his theology. He brought before the public the great Reformation doctrines. He also put forward a doctrine which would be much misunderstood.

From the earliest days of his pilgrimage, Wesley had sought to obey Christ's injunction: "Be ye perfect, even as your Father which is in heaven is perfect" (Matthew 5:48). In Oxford and Georgia he had sought perfect holiness by fasting, prayer, self-examination, and sacraments; he had drawn ideas from the Early Fathers and medieval mystics. After Aldersgate Street, he knew he was justified by trust in Christ alone, but the assurance of Christ's presence had strengthened, all the more, the desire to be holy in thought, word, and deed—not now to save himself from damnation but for the glory of God. Wesley spoke frequently of holiness or perfection, using the words almost interchangeably.

In 1741 he came across a rare and rambling book of seventeenth-century theology by Robert Gell, a former fellow of Christ's College, Cambridge, and archbishop's chaplain. Gell taught that God's grace could triumph in a human being while he yet lived; he need not wait for heaven. Love for God and love for neighbor would displace all desire to sin. Wesley became certain that this change could be effected instantaneously by the Spirit of Christ. Certainly the God of love never intended to limit the attainment of holiness to select saints, as traditional church teaching would have it. Every sinner, however humble, however recent his or her conversion, could be "changed from glory into glory, till in heaven we take our place," as Charles wrote in his famous hymn "Love

Divine." But when Charles wrote "pure and *sinless* may we be," John altered the word to *spotless*. In speech and print he always emphasized that "a man may be filled with pure love and still be liable to error."

He wrote to one of his helpers who had broken away, "I like your doctrine of *perfection*, or pure love; love excluding sin; your insisting that it is merely by *faith*; that consequently it is *instantaneous* (though preceded and followed by a gradual work), and that it may be *now*, at this instant. But I dislike your supposing a man may be as perfect as an *angel*; that he can be *absolutely* perfect; that he can be infallible, or above being *tempted*; or, that the moment he is pure in heart, he *cannot fall* from it."

The Calvinists indeed taught that whoever is predestined to salvation cannot fail but will persevere to the end even if frequently defeated in the struggle against sin. Wesley believed that any who were living a life of joyful holiness might fall away at any moment, even their last. As the burial service in the *Book of Common Prayer* put it: "Suffer us not, at our last hour, for any pains of death, to fall from thee." Often Wesley would say of some who had shown sweetness under persecution or similar signs of grace: "And shall these fail at the last?" He believed that God could keep them and that those who are perfect may grow in grace, "not only while they are in the body, but in all eternity."

Wesley's doctrine of Christian perfection ("*sinless perfection* is a phrase I never use") would provoke much debate in the next centuries, but he had recovered a strand of Christian experience in victorious living which would influence churches all over the world. He wrote: "To abandon all, to strip one's self of all, in order to seek and to follow Jesus Christ naked to Bethlehem, where he was born; naked, to the hall where he was scourged, and naked to Calvary, where he died on the cross, is so great a mercy, that neither the thing, nor the knowledge of it, is given to any, but through faith in the Son of God."

In 1743 Wesley acquired a consecrated building. West Street Chapel near Covent Garden had been erected by newly exiled Huguenots and consecrated by a bishop about 1700, twenty years after the street had been laid out on the mad Earl of Newport's estate. The Huguenots had moved elsewhere and sold it to the Church of St. Clement Danes, which had let the building for secular use to finance a charity for poor widows. "By a strange chain of providences" Wesley secured the lease. He now had a preaching house in the West End like the Foundery in the city, with the important difference that the West Street Chapel was an episcopally consecrated building.

At 10 A.M. on Trinity Sunday, May 29, 1743, with every seat filled, he said the Lord's Prayer and began the liturgy: "Almighty God, unto whom all hearts be open, all desires known and from whom no secrets are hid; cleanse the thoughts of our hearts by the inspiration of thy Holy Spirit, that we may perfectly love thee and worthily magnify thy holy name, through Christ our Lord." The resounding "Amen" in this first Communion was a hint of the strength of Methodism.

He preached on John 3:1–15: "Except a man be born again, he cannot see the Kingdom of God…. Ye must be born again"—an appropriate text, for Wesley always held that Holy Communion was a service to convert sinners as well as to confirm saints. He then "administered the Lord's Supper to some hundreds of communicants." He wrote, "I was a little afraid that my strength would not suffice, when a service of five hours (for it lasted from 10 to 3) was added to my usual employment. But God looked to that: so I must think; and they that call it enthusiasm may."

He rode across London to find "an immense congregation" of the poor and unchurched waiting in an open space in Whitechapel, the Great Gardens, where he had been hit by a stone as he preached nine months before. He took the same text as in the morning: "Ye must be born again." Then he met the local class leaders and afterward the bands, and claimed that "at 10 at night I was less weary than at 6 in the morning."

West Street Chapel attracted so many that on the next Sunday the service continued until 4 P.M., and Wesley "found it needful, for the time to come, to divide the communicants into three parts, so that we might not have above six hundred at once."

A year later he passed another milestone when he summoned helpers from many parts of the country to meet at the Foundery for five days in June 1744. The Wesleys and four parish clergymen were present, with all the lay helpers or itinerants. Lady Huntingdon invited them for a public service in her mansion, where Wesley preached on the text: "What hath God wrought."

They discussed all the many matters of discipline, doctrine, and policy which had emerged since 1738. Using a question and answer method, Wesley secured genuine debate, but he was now the undoubted leader whose will dominated the proceedings.

The conferences were henceforth held annually, but Charles felt that his brother nearly always got his way. As he complained in shorthand two years later, "I find it is utterly in vain to write to you upon anything whereon we are not already agreed. Either you set aside the whole by the short answer that I am in an ill humor, or you take no notice at all of my reasons, but plead conscience....

I have so little success in my remonstrances that I have many times resolved never to contradict your judgment as to any thing or person."

Some six weeks later Wesley preached again before the University of Oxford—for the last time.

In 1741 his turn to preach had fallen during the Long Vacation. He had wanted to discharge his soul by trenchantly condemning Oxford's lapses in doctrine and practice, and therefore wrote an English version of a Latin exercise, which he had prepared two years earlier when intending to proceed to the degree of Bachelor of Divinity (he never did so, having been called away from Oxford to his brother Samuel's deathbed). Basing the sermon on Isaiah 1:21—"How is the faithful city become an harlot!"—he had written vigorously against the hypocrisy found in a supposedly Christian university. ("How hath she departed from her Lord! How hath she denied him.") He used satire to make some of his points. He then read the English version to the Countess of Huntingdon.

She persuaded him that the sermon would enrage without convincing or converting. He laid it aside and never preached or published it but kept both English and Latin manuscripts. He preached instead on "The Almost Christian," which made his point without attacking Oxford.

Three years later he was listed to preach on St. Bartholomew's Day, August 24, 1744—again in the Long Vacation, probably by design of the university authorities, who wished to save undergraduates from the dangers of Enthusiasm, for which Wesley was now famous. Many, however, had returned for the races. One undergraduate who hurried to hear him "as a matter of great curiosity" was Benjamin Kennicott of Wadham, afterward a distinguished Hebrew scholar.

When Wesley entered the university Church of St. Mary's at 10 o'clock on the Friday morning to preach on "Scriptural Christianity," he had already been two days in Oxford preaching among the poor and in inns and private houses. Kennicott recorded: "There were present the vice-chancellor, the proctors, most of the heads of houses, a vast number of gownsmen, and a multitude of private people, with many of his followers, both brethren and sisters, who, with general faces and plain attire, came from around to attend their master and teacher.

"When he mounted the pulpit, I fixed my eyes on him and his behavior. He is neither tall nor fat; for the latter would ill become a Methodist. His black hair quite smooth, and parted very exactly, added to a peculiar composure in his countenance, showed him to be an uncommon man. His prayer was soft, short, and conformable to the rules of the university. His text, Acts 4:31—'And they were all filled with the Holy Ghost.' And now he began to exalt his voice. He spoke the text very slowly and with an agreeable emphasis."

Wesley showed first that *all* might be filled with the Holy Ghost and then briefly traced the course of Christianity from its first reception, its progress from one age to another, and (as Kennicott understood him to mean) "its final completion in the universal conversion of the world to the Christian faith."

"Under these three heads," continued Kennicott, "he expressed himself like a very good scholar, but a rigid zealot; and then he came to what he called his plain, practical conclusion."

"Here was what he had been preparing for all along; and he fired his address with so much zeal and unbounded satire as quite spoiled what otherwise might have been turned to great advantage; for as I liked some, so I disliked other parts of his discourse extremely. Having, under his third head, displayed the happiness of the world under it—complete final reformation— 'Now,' says he, 'where is this Christianity to be found? Is this a Christian nation? Is this a Christian city?'—asserting the contrary to both. I liked some of his freedom; such as calling the generality of young gownsmen "a generation of triflers," and many other just invectives. But considering how many shining lights are here that are the glory of the Christian cause, his sacred censure was much too flaming and strong, and his charity much too weak in not making large allowances."

Kennicott's definition of a "shining light" was different from Wesley's, but he was gripped by the climax of the sermon: "After having summed up the measure of our iniquities, he concluded with a lifted up eye in this most solemn form, 'It is time for thee, Lord, to lay to thine hand'—words full of such presumption and seeming imprecation, that they gave an universal shock."

Oxford's reaction was hostile. Wesley, Charles, and two Methodist friends were shunned as they walked away. Though the dean of Christ Church remarked generously, "John Wesley will always be thought a man of sound sense, though an enthusiast," the pro-vice-chancellor, Dr. John Mather, sent the beadle round to demand the script with a view to public rebuke. Wesley was pleased that many heads of houses and professors would, as he supposed, study a sermon they might otherwise quickly forget. He sealed up the notes so that the beadle should not lose a page. Dr. Mather had intended to summon "Mr. Wesly [sic] before proper persons" and was disappointed when the beadle had "found him preparing to go out of town." Dr. Mather kept the notes "in my own custody."

Four days later a young Old Carthusian and fellow of All Souls, later to be famous as the eminent jurist Sir William Blackstone, wrote to a friend: "On much deliberation it has been thought proper to punish him by a mortifying neglect."

Wesley was never allowed the university pulpit again. Whenever his turn came round, another was paid to preach in his place.

19

"Crucify Him!"

King George II liked to walk in the gardens at Kew, which lay between his favorite residence, Richmond Lodge, and Kew Palace, home of the Prince of Wales. Among the respectable neighbors to whom he gave keys was a prosperous merchant who had been an Oxford Methodist but had become a Quaker. The King enjoyed his conversation when they met on the lawns or the flower walks and politely ignored the breaches of protocol caused by the man's loyalty to the Society of Friends, such as not removing his hat in the royal presence and addressing the King by his name, not as "Your Majesty" and then "Sir."

One day the King, now a widower in his forties, asked the Quaker whether he had known the Wesleys at Oxford, adding "They make a great noise in the nation."

"I know them well, King George," the Quaker replied. "And thee may be assured that thee has not two better men in thy dominions, nor men that love thee better, than John and Charles Wesley." The Quaker described their principles and conduct, which pleased the King, for he had wondered why their preaching provoked riots.

Shortly afterward the King declared to the Duke of Newcastle, secretary of state for the Southern Department: "No man in my dominions shall be persecuted on the account of religion while I sit on my throne."[1]

The duke thereupon gave orders to Sir John Ganson, chairman of the Middlesex magistrates, and Sir John came in his coach to the Foundery. He told Wesley that if riotous mobs molested his meetings again, he should apply to him for redress.

In London the mobs were stirred up by outraged publicans and pimps, who found customers deserting them for prayer meetings, and by thieves, pickpockets and louts who had passed word that the law would not protect Methodists. Once a mob tried to pull the roof off the Foundery. On another day when Wesley was preaching outside in Charles Square north of the city, a rabble drove an ox at the attentive crowd, but the animal ran left and right and "at length broke through the midst of them clear away, leaving us calmly rejoicing and praising God."

After Wesley applied to Sir John, the disturbances slackened in London. In the provinces, however, the royal commands did not run so surely. Wesley was struck by a brick on the shoulder; a year later, a stone hit him between the eyes. (The first Methodist martyr, William Seward, a close associate of Whitefield, had been killed by a stone.)

In Wiltshire, Wesley was preaching from a table on a village green "when a rabble came furiously upon us, bringing a bull which they had been baiting."

The beast ran wildly on either side. Wesley stopped preaching and led the people, surrounded by uproar, in hymns and prayer for nearly an hour. "The poor wretches at length seized upon the bull, now weak and tired, after having been so long torn and beaten, both by dogs and men; and, by main strength, partly dragged and partly thrust him in among the people.

"When they had forced their way to the little table on which I stood, they strove several times to throw it down, by thrusting the helpless beast against it. I once or twice put aside his head with my hand, that the blood might not drop upon my clothes; intending to go on as soon as the hurry should be over. But, the table falling down, some of our friends caught me and carried me right away on their shoulders; while the rabble wreaked their vengeance on the table. We went a little way off, where I finished my discourse without any noise or interruption."

In Staffordshire, in 1743, Wesley nearly lost his life.

During November 1742 Charles had preached with effect among the coal miners near Wednesbury and its neighboring towns of Darlaston and Walsall, an area which mined the hottest burning coal in England, much favored for smithy forges up and down the land. A Methodist society numbering about a hundred had grown up by the time John Wesley came for the first time in January 1743. The vicar of Wednesbury, Edward Egginton, who had been incumbent for nearly a quarter of a century but was partial to the bottle, received him kindly and told him to come often. Wesley preached in the town hall on the Saturday and heard the vicar preach "a plain useful sermon" in the magnificent parish church on the Sunday. Then the whole congregation joined the crowd in the nearby great hollow, famous for cockfighting and bullbaiting, where Wesley preached on Ephesians 2:8—"By grace are ye saved through faith." The society grew to nearly four hundred.

In the early spring of 1743, however, one of Wesley's itinerant preachers provoked Parson Egginton. Next, Moravians from Yorkshire arrived. They caused disputes in the society and urged members to leave the church. Wesley frequently needed to repair damage done in Yorkshire and the Midlands by followers of his former German friends, and, because Moravian influence had spread in England at about the same time as Methodism, the two movements were often regarded as one. The support of the vicar of Wednesbury turned into hatred. When Wesley next came, he had to sit through a very different discourse. "I think I have never heard so wicked a sermon, and delivered with such bitterness of voice and manner, as that which Mr. E. preached in the afternoon."

Wesley tried to prepare his friends for persecution, for he had learned that Egginton, his curate at Darlaston, and the vicar of Walsall were all determined to destroy the society. They spread word among roughs and bruisers in their parishes that cockfighting, bullbaiting, and prizefights were in danger; the local magistrates were persuaded to turn a blind eye.

In May, Charles came again and was knocked about by a violent crowd. That summer, Methodists had windows broken and houses, shops, and workshops shamelessly looted. They were beaten and splattered with mud. "Some, even pregnant women, were treated in a manner that cannot be mentioned," so Wesley, in his old age, told young Henry Moore. Wesley came back briefly on his way to Newcastle and sought legal advice for his flock but was reluctant to prosecute, especially as the local bench blamed the Methodists.

Peace seemed to have returned to Wednesbury when Wesley rode in from Birmingham on October 20, 1743. At midday he mounted a horse block on the open space in the center of the town and preached "to a far larger congregation than was expected, on, 'Jesus Christ, the same yesterday, and today, and forever.' I believe everyone present felt the power of God: and no creature offered to molest us, either going or coming; but the Lord fought for us, and we held our peace."

During the afternoon Wesley was writing in the house of Francis Ward, the leader of the society, who had nearly lost an eye in the earlier violence. A number of the Methodists were in the house, their normal meeting place, waiting for Wesley to expound and pray with them. Suddenly they heard the horn which summoned the roughs. Soon an agitated Methodist cried out that a mob surrounded the house. Wesley calmly announced that they would pray. They knelt round him as he and then others prayed extempore. The howls and threats outside died down until within half an hour, when someone looked out the door, "not a man was left."

Wesley suggested he had better leave as the mob was after him rather than them, but they begged him to stay. He foresaw the result.

About five the mob was back in greater force—it came from Darlaston, where the mines were, rather than from the quieter market town of Wednesbury itself. Wesley could hear the cry, "Bring out the minister! We'll have the minister!" He told a frightened Methodist to go to the front door and bring in the ringleader "by the hand."

Those in the room were astonished by what happened next. The ringleader entered, his face contorted with rage. Wesley smiled and spoke to him quietly. "After a few sentences interchanged between us, the lion was become a lamb." Wesley told him to fetch one or two more and he brought a man and a woman, both in a rage, "but in two minutes they were as calm as he."

Wesley then went to the door, stood on a chair, and the crowd quietened. He asked what they wanted. Perhaps because word had been passed that any itinerant preacher should be captured and brought before a magistrate, they said they wanted him to come to the justice. Wesley agreed "with all my heart." He spoke a few words about the love of God, and the mob cheered. The woman ringleader cried out, "The gentleman is an honest gentleman, and we will spill our blood in his defense!"

They wanted to go at once, so Wesley set off at their head. Most of the Methodists had fled out the back door while the mob was screaming at the front, but three men and one woman, Joan Parks, kept close as an escort. William Sitch held his arm throughout. As darkness fell, a heavy downpour began, and they were all wet before they reached Bentley Hall, between Wednesbury and Darlaston, where Lane, a justice of the peace, was already in bed, or so they were told. His son asked for their complaint. Somebody replied in broad Stafford shire, "Why, an't please you, they sing psalms all day; nay, and make folks rise at five in the morning. And what would your worship advise us to do?"

"To go home," said young Lane, "and be quiet."

They then hurried Wesley to the magistrate who lived outside Walsall, but when they reached his house at 7:00, he too was diplomatically in bed. The now friendly mob, nonplussed, settled to take Wesley back to Wednesbury; some fifty acted as escort, and the rest slunk off home to Darlaston in the opposite direction.

Hardly had Wesley and his escort covered a hundred yards when a great mob roared up out of Walsall. Wesley found himself caught in the midst of gang warfare between traditional enemies. "The Darlaston mob made what defense they could; but they were weary, as well as outnumbered: so that in short time, many being knocked down, the rest ran away, and left me in their hands." The Darlaston collier woman who had sworn to defend him charged the Walsall mob "and knocked down three or four men, one after another. But many assaulting her at once, she was soon overpowered, and had probably been killed in a few minutes (three men keeping her down and beating her with all their might), had not a man called to one of them, 'Hold, Tom, hold!' "

Tom stopped beating the woman; he had recognized the voice of the champion prizefighter of Walsall, "Honest Munchin," whose real name was George Clifton. At Munchin's command Tom let the woman go, and she stumbled off home.

The screaming mob pulled Wesley, Joan Parks, and the faithful Edward Sitch, who never let go, toward Walsall down the steep and wet cobbled streets. One slip and Wesley would have gone down, and they would have pummeled him to death, but he kept his feet, with his heart at peace. Several blows with bludgeons were deflected—he knew not how except that his small size made him a difficult target in a melee. And one man who "came rushing through the press, and raising his arm to strike, on a sudden let it drop, and only stroked my head, saying, 'What soft hair he has!' "

As they hustled him along, Wesley saw a large house with an open door. He stopped and tried to enter, but a man dragged him back by his long hair and would have brought him down had not Sitch bitten the bully's arm.

The mob bore them on down the street until Wesley saw another open door at a chandler's shop. The chandler was standing in the door. He refused to let him enter, saying they would pull the shop down round his ears, but unknown to Wesley the man was the newly appointed mayor of Walsall, William Haselwood. The mob, assuming that Wesley's stop was deliberate, calmed a little.

Wesley shouted: "Will you hear me?"

"No, no! Knock his brains out! Kill him!"

"What evil have I done? Which of you have I wronged?"

He began to speak of the love of God and they listened. He spoke for a quarter of an hour, when his voice failed.

The determined mob, led by Honest Munchin, the prize-fighter, roared again: "Bring him away! Strip him!"

"You needn't do that: I will give you my clothes."

"Crucify him!"—Wesley was sure he heard the words.

His voice then recovered, and he began to pray aloud as if oblivious of anyone but Christ. Suddenly the prizefighter turned to him. "Sir, I will spend my life for you: follow me, and not one soul shall touch a hair of your head." Two or three others said likewise and closed up on him while the timorous mayor found his voice and a neighboring butcher also cried, "Shame! shame! Let him go!"

Out of respect to their own ringleader, Honest Munchin, the mob parted, and the escort took him down the slippery street toward the flooded brook at the bottom of the town, but before they could cross the footbridge at the mill dam, the mob began to bay for his blood again. "Throw him in!" cried some. The threat did not bother Wesley—he could swim.

A man hit him on the mouth and nose. The blood gushed, but Wesley felt no pain and all at once realized why the martyrs had died so calmly in the flames.

The new escort fought back, and one young man had his arm broken. Joan Parks was thrown into the water, but Munchin got Wesley and Sitch across the bridge and into the meadows where they were soon lost to their pursuers in the darkness. So at last they came back to Ward's house, where the Methodists had regathered to pray for Wesley's safety, and now rejoiced.

The next day, an apologetic, humble message came from the curate of Darlaston, who had heard of Wesley's courage and now "wished all his parish were Methodists." When Wesley rode out toward Nottingham, bruised but happy, "everyone I met expressed such cordial affection that I could scarce believe what I saw and heard." At Nottingham, Charles was waiting. "My brother came," he wrote, "delivered out of the mouth of the lion. He *looked* like a soldier of Christ. His clothes were torn to tatters."

Charles went immediately to Wednesbury (as they had planned), and the young man with the broken arm and the prizefighter, Honest Munchin, were received into the society as probationary members. "Munchin," wrote Charles, "has been constantly under the Word since he rescued my brother. I asked him what he thought of him.

" 'Think of him!' said he: 'That he is a man of God. And God was on his side, when so many of us could not kill one man.' " Munchin Clifton became a pillar of the Methodists of Wednesbury and Walsall—whose persecutions were not ended for some years—until his death, aged eighty-five, forty-six years later.

20

Cornwall

Shortly before the Wednesbury and Walsall riot, Wesley had made the first of no less than thirty-three visits to Cornwall, a land where his influence would locally be more decisive than in almost any other part of the kingdom except perhaps Yorkshire.

Cornwall, once the thriving steppingstone of traffic between France and Ireland and rich in tin and gold, had declined since the Reformation—which had swept away immemorial shrines—and the defeat of the Royalists in the Civil War when Cornishmen had passionately supported Charles I. Cornwall had numerous parish churches, but because many were on the site of Celtic shrines, far from villages, contemporaries claimed that Cornishmen were often married and buried without benefit of clergy.

The diocesan, the bishop of Exeter, lived far away; even the archdeacon's home was out of the county. There were many large estates and some well-endowed clerical livings but a gulf between rich and poor. The tin miners, farm laborers, and fishermen were rough and illiterate, famous as smugglers and wreckers and for the violence and cruelty of their pastimes. The King's peace scarcely reached the remoter parts; murders were frequent and unpunished.

Two clergymen in the north of Cornwall, George Thomson of St. Gennys, above Crackington Haven, and the elderly John Bennet of North Tamerton, had become evangelicals even before Whitefield, but their influence had been limited to their parishes. Too many of the clergy were lazy and drunken and cared little for parishioners, provided they paid their tithes.

The Wesleys sent in two itinerant preachers; then Charles came during the summer of 1743 and worked out of St. Ives, the fishing port on the north coast, where the parson opposed him, but the mayor, "an honest Presbyterian," quelled a riot against him.

At the end of that August, John Wesley rode to Cornwall after preaching to a great crowd at Exeter on the site of Rougemount Castle. This first visit to Cornwall began unpropitiously; he and his companion were overtaken by dusk on Bodmin Moor. They lost the path, only finding their way after dark by the sound of Bodmin's curfew bell, rung every night to guide lost travelers. Two of his itinerant preachers, John Nelson and John Downes, had gone ahead, sharing a horse because Downes' mount had dropped dead.

Wesley reached St. Ives on August 30. Charles had found a small religious society. He had left a Methodist society which had taken root, meeting in the house of a young fish curer, John Nance, where John Wesley, Nelson, and Downes apparently had to sleep three to one bed, a common practice of the time, both among families and travelers.

Wesley began to preach in the neighborhood but met little response except "an earnest, stupid attention," possibly because his accent mystified the Cornish, though it was nothing to the broad Yorkshire of Nelson and Downes. The Cornish "all appeared quite pleased and unconcerned.... At Trewilhen Downs he observed for the first time "a little impression on two or three of the listeners; the rest, as usual showing huge approbriation and absolute unconcern." By September 6, Wesley wrote, "I still could not find a way into the hearts of the hearers, although they were earnest to hear what they understood not."

On Sunday a change appeared. Preaching to a large congregation in the medieval amphitheater outside St. Just (after a somewhat awed sightseeing visit to the farthest rocks of Lands End), he felt that the truth had reached their hearts. Next evening in the society at St. Ives, "the dread of God fell upon us while I was speaking, so that I could hardly utter a word." Wesley began to pray aloud for Cornwall, and the people joined fervently in spirit. He continued praying, unable to stifle his longing for a movement of God, until he lost all sense of time.

Next day, having a "a great desire to go and publish the love of God our Saviour in the Isles of Scilly," he put to sea from St. Ives in a small fishing boat. When his landlubber Yorkshire companions were frightened, he led them in a rousing hymn as the boat tossed in the waves. Apart from the night on the Scillies, they slept at St. Ives. Downes fell ill of a fever. Wesley and Nelson therefore slept on the stone floor night after night. "He had my greatcoat for his pillow," records Nelson, "and I had Burkitt's *Notes on the New Testament* for mine.... One morning, about 3 o'clock, Mr. Wesley turned over, and, finding me awake, clapped me on the side saying, "Brother Nelson, let us be of good cheer: I have one whole side yet!" (The skin on his other had been rubbed bare by the hard stone.)

They both got hungry as they preached on the commons, riding from village to village. One afternoon they preached on Hilary Downs. "As we returned, Mr. Wesley stopped his horse to pick the blackberries, saying, 'Brother Nelson, we ought to be thankful that there are plenty of blackberries; for this is the best county I ever saw for getting a stomach, but the worst that I ever saw for getting food. Do the people think we can live by preaching?'" Nelson replied that one woman had given him a good meal of barley bread and honey.

Later Wesley, riding alone, stopped at a cottage where a woman was removing honeycomb from her hive. He asked for a glass of water. Alice Daniel invited him in and gave him barley bread and honey, and he seized the occasion to speak about "the judgments of the Lord ... sweeter than honey and the honeycomb." Alice fetched some neighbors to hear a parson who talked as she had never heard a parson talk before. Both Alice and her husband, John Daniel, a godless miner and smallholder, became devoted Christians and even added two rooms to their cottage so that Wesley or other itinerant preachers might lodge there.

As in Staffordshire, Wesley saw conversions and met violence. The mob of St. Ives broke into Nance's house as the Methodists met; some of Wesley's hearers were terrified and others, new converts, reverted to fisticuffs. Wesley stopped expounding and went into the melee, receiving a blow on the head before he could lead the riot leader by the hand to the desk, where Wesley exercised the extraordinary power of his eye and his words to quiet the most unruly. The next evening an alderman sat with the society to deter those who had threatened a "general assault."

The following day Wesley preached to an enormous crowd, locally reckoned at 10,000, near the most famous amphitheater in Cornwall, the Gwennap Pit near Redruth. He was to leave for Devon in the morning. When darkness fell he was still preaching, "and there was on all sides the deepest attention; none speaking, stirring or scarce looking aside. Surely here, though in a temple not made with hands, was God worshiped 'in the beauty of holiness.'"

Very early the next morning in St. Ives, he was woken by the sound of singing. A large company of tinners, afraid they might be too late to say good-bye, were serenading him a farewell, "singing and praising God." Wesley recorded that he then "preached once more on 'Believe on the Lord Jesus Christ, and thou shalt be saved.' They all devoured the Word."

While Wesley was away, nearly losing his life at Walsall, Methodism spread far and wide in Cornwall, and opposition too: "All this summer," he wrote next year, "our brethren in the west had as hot service as those in the north of England: the war against the Methodists, so called, being everywhere carried on with far more vigor than that against the Spaniards."

The very fact that England was at war with Spain, France, and Prussia (the War of the Austrian Succession) helped to explain the opposition in Cornwall. The magistrates and clergy, fearful of a Jacobite rising, believed that the Wesleys were Jesuits in disguise or French agents. One Cornishman had positively identified John Downes as the Young Pretender, Prince Charles Edward, whom he had seen in France. Another rumor affirmed that the preacher calling himself Mr. Wesley must be an imposter because "Mr. Wesley is dead" (Brother Samuel had died in the West Country).

John Wesley had come again in the spring of 1744 for a fortnight. On April 11, he had preached at Gwennap Pit itself.

Formed by the falling in of derelict workings, the amphitheater had exceptional acoustics and was "by far the finest I know in the Kingdom. It is a round, green hollow, gently shelving down, about fifty feet deep; but I suppose it is two hundred across one way, and near three hundred the other.[1]

"[I] stood on the wall in the calm still evening, with the setting sun behind me, and almost an innumerable multitude before, behind, and on either hand. Many likewise sat on the little hills, at some distance from the bulk of the congregation. But they could all hear distinctly."

On Wesley's third visit, in June 1745, a magistrate who was both a leading parish clergyman and a high government official, Dr. Borlase of Morvah, issued a warrant to press him "into the service of His Majesty."

The British Army was fighting on the continent and needed recruits. The Navy could only press seamen. Magistrates could press any able-bodied man into the Army, but no gentleman in good standing would be touched, and clergymen were exempt, as Borlase knew. Unfriendly magistrates in several counties found this an excellent way to silence a Methodist; John Nelson had already been forcibly enlisted in the Midlands. Lady Huntingdon and Charles secured Nelson's release, but most of those who were taken had to serve. Wesley received stirring letters from disciples who carried their gospel and the hymns into the violence and licentiousness of army life. After the battle of Fontenoy, he learned of Methodist courage and of desperately wounded men who died praising God.

On June 20, at Redruth in Cornwall, Wesley learned that Tom Maxfield had been seized while preaching several miles away at Crowan. Wesley and Thomson, the rector of St. Gennys, rode to his rescue but heard on the way that he had been removed. As Wesley recorded with a touch of humor: "The valiant constables who guarded him, having received timely notice that a body of five hundred Methodists were coming to take him away by force, with great precipitation carried him two miles farther, to the house of one Henry Tomkins. Here we found him, nothing terrified by his adversaries." He was to appear before the magistrates at Marazion the next day.

Borlase tricked Wesley to prevent him from entering a plea for Maxfield, who was thrown into Penzance Dungeon, then handed to the Army by Borlase himself to serve for several years as a soldier.

During the week after Maxfield's arrest, Wesley had finished preaching at St. Just when a constable seized a middle-aged, married miner (with seven children) who once had been a byword for swearing and the bottle. Wesley asked "a little gentleman at St. Just" what was the objection to this Edward Greenfield. "Why," he replied, "the man is well enough in other things; but his impudence the gentlemen cannot bear. Why, sir, he says he knows his sins are forgiven!"

"And for this cause," commented Wesley, "he is adjudged to banishment or death on the battlefields of Europe or America."

The next day as Wesley concluded his evening open-air sermon one of the local gentry walked up, and the crowd respectfully parted to let him by. "Sir," he said, "I have a warrant from Dr. Borlase, and you must go with me." They arranged a time for the next morning, but the man seemed unwilling to keep the appointment, and then rode with Wesley as slowly as he could. When he found that Dr. Borlase was not at home, he refused to detain Wesley further.

That afternoon Wesley took his assistant, Shepherd, also named in the warrant, to Gwennap. They had expected to expound in a cottage, but so many neighbors wished to hear Wesley that he spoke from the doorway. As always when preaching, he wore cassock, gown, and bands. Hardly had he announced his text when the bailiff of the local squire, Beauchamp of Pengreep, rode his horse violently into the throng. Several listeners were hustled away by the bailiff's men. Beauchamp himself, even angrier, rode up with a posse.

"Most of the people," recorded Wesley, "stood still as they were before, and began singing an hymn. Upon this Mr. B. lost his patience, and cried out with all his might, "Seize him, seize him, I say, seize the preacher for His Majesty's service." But no one stirring, he rode up and struck several of his attendants.... Perceiving still that they would not move, he leaped off his horse, swore he would do it himself, and caught hold of my cassock, crying, 'I take you to serve His Majesty.' A servant taking his horse, he took me by the arm, and we walked arm in arm for about three quarters of a mile. He entertained me all the time, with the 'wickedness of the fellows belonging to the society.'

"When he was taking breath, I said, 'Sir, be they what they will, I apprehend it will not justify you in seizing me in this manner, and violently carrying me away, as you said, to serve His Majesty.' He replied, 'I seize you? And violently carry you away? No, Sir, no. Nothing like it. I asked you to go with me to my house, and you said you was willing; and if so, you are welcome; and if not, you are welcome to go where you please.' "

Beauchamp, probably a secret Jacobite and no friend to Borlase, would have been aware that a clergyman should not have been named in the warrant. He put Wesley on a horse, mounted his own, and rode back with him through the rabble of retainers to the cottage.

The worst trial came the next day. Unknown to the Cornishmen, Prince Charles Edward was embarking from France. Rumors of Jacobite rebellion and French invasion grew louder. Wesley went to Falmouth. During the afternoon he entered the house of a sick woman who lived with her daughter, Kitty. A big rabble arrived howling, "Bring out the Canorum!"—the local term for Methodist, derived from a Cornish word connected with singing.

"No answer being given, they quickly forced open the outer door, and filled the passage. Only a wainscot-partition was between us, which was not likely to stand long. I immediately took down a large looking glass which hung against it, supposing the whole side would fall in at once. When they began their work with abundance of bitter imprecations, poor Kitty was utterly astonished, and cried out, 'O Sir, what must we do?' I said, 'We must pray.' Indeed at that time, to all appearance, our lives were not worth an hour's purchase. She asked, 'But, Sir, is it not better for you to hide yourself? To get into the closet?' I answered, 'No. It is best for me to stand just where I am.'

"Among those without were the crews of some privateers which were lately come into harbor. Some of these, being angry at the slowness of the rest, thrust them away, and, coming up all together, set their shoulders to the inner door, and cried out, 'Avast, lads, avast!' Away went all the hinges at once, and the door fell back into the room.

"I stepped forward at once into the midst of them, and said, 'Here I am. Which of you has anything to say to me? To which of you have I done any wrong? To you? Or you? Or you?' I continued speaking till I came, bareheaded as I was (for I purposely left my hat that they might all see my face), into the middle of the street, and then raising my voice, said, 'Neighbors, countrymen! Do you desire to hear me speak?' They cried vehemently, 'Yes, yes. He shall speak. He shall. Nobody shall hinder him.' But having nothing to stand on, and no advantage of ground, I could be heard by few only. However, I spoke without intermission, and, as far as the sound reached, the people were still."

One or two ringleaders swore that no one should touch Wesley. A clergyman, hearing the uproar, rebuked the mob, and two or three prominent citizens came up to escort Wesley, still speaking to the mob as they shoved and pushed about him, to the house of his Falmouth hostess, which backed on the harbor. They advised him to leave by water and sent his horse ahead.

The rabble of sailors and town roughs had been roused by word that Wesley had come to spy for the French and the Pretender. "A few of the fiercest ran along the shore, to receive me at my landing. I walked up the steep narrow passage from the sea, at the top of which the foremost man stood. I looked him in the face, and said, 'I wish you a good night.' He spake not, nor moved hand or foot till I was on horseback. Then he said, 'I wish you was in hell,' and turned back to his companions."

As Wesley rode to the next confrontation, he reflected that even at Walsall the hand of God had not been so plainly shown. "There I had many companions who were willing to die with me: here, not a friend, but one simple girl."

When Prince Charles Edward and his Highlanders took Edinburgh, then won the Battle of Prestonpans on September 20, 1745, Wesley was at Newcastle. His house stood outside the walls, and he wrote excitedly to Charles: "I have only just time to inform you that since the account is confirmed by an express to the mayor that General Cope is fled and his forces defeated (all that did not run away), the consternation of the poor people is redoubled. The townsmen are put under arms, the walls planted with cannon; and those who live without the gates are removing their goods with all speed. We stand our ground as yet, glory be to God, to the no small astonishment of our neighbors. Brethren, pray for us, that, if need be, we may 'True in the fiery trial prove, / And pay him back his dying love.'"

The Pretender was expected to march his terrifying Highlanders down the East Coast to take Newcastle. The defending Hanoverian commander sent a "surly man" to the orphanage who rudely made Wesley come to the door and ordered him to pull down his "battlements." Wesley suspected a plot to harm the Methodists and complained to the general, adding that he was willing to pull the whole house down if it would help Newcastle withstand a seige.

He was in no doubt where his loyalty lay. The previous year he had drafted a loyal and humble address to King George II from "the societies in England and Wales, in derision called Methodists," but Charles had persuaded him not to send it because "it would constitute us a sect. At least it would *seem to allow* that we are a body distinct from the National Church, whereas we are only a sound part of that Church."

Rumors of the Highlanders' advance fanned the panic at Newcastle. Wesley inspired them by word and example. He tried to stem the "open, flagrant wickedness, the drunkenness, and profaneness which so abound." He asked the mayor to complain to the general about "the continual cursing and swearing, and the wanton blasphemy of the soldiers … a torture to a sober ear." The Pretender was reported to be advancing. Churches were packed by frightened worshipers "and we cried mightily to God to send His Majesty King George help from his holy place, and to spare a sinful land yet a little longer." At the request of the vicar of St. Nicholas, Wesley preached: "The congregation was so moved that I began again and again and knew not how to conclude."

The Pretender still did not invade. Wesley rode to Sheffield and Epworth to strengthen the societies, then returned to Newcastle, finding himself somewhat a hero for his inspiring leadership. He preached as near as he could to the army camp, and on November 4, left for the South, passing riders who shouted that the Pretender had crossed the border.

Prince Charles avoided Newcastle. He advanced down the west side of England, and when the prince reached Derby on December 4, putting King and people in a panic, Wesley was writing quietly in a village north of London. He came to the Foundery and the West Street Chapel for the National Fast Day. "Such a solemnity and seriousness everywhere appeared as had not lately been seen in England." He organized a mass distribution of his tract, "An Earnest Exhortation to Serious Repentance" at every church door in London and to "the house of every householder who was not at church."

Five months after the Jacobite rebellion had ended on Culloden Moor, Wesley returned to Cornwall (in September 1746). He was never again personally assaulted in the county. Persecution of Methodists continued sporadically from clergy and magistrates, but, as Charles had written dramatically a few weeks previously:

"For one preacher they cut off, twenty spring up. Neither persuasion nor threatening, flattery nor violence, dungeons, or sufferings of various kinds, can conquer them."

The ordinary people were less inclined to riot. At Brea, a village near St. Ives, John Wesley found that "vehement opposers ... opposed no more." He went on to preach at Sithney. "Before I had done the night came on; but the moon shone bright upon us. I intended, after preaching, to meet the society; but it was hardly practicable, the poor people so eagerly crowding in upon us. So I met them all together, and exhorted them not to leave their first love."

The next day, Sunday, September 14, 1746, he waited until 8 o'clock in the evening "for the sake of those who came from afar." Many from Helston were there, including most of those who in earlier years had raised riots against him. "But the fear of God was upon them; they all stood uncovered, and calmly attended from the beginning to the end.

"About 1, I began preaching near Porkellis to a much larger congregation; and, about half an hour after 4, at Gwennap, to an immense multitude of people on 'To me to live is Christ, and to die is gain.' I was at first afraid my voice would not reach them all; but without cause, for it was so strengthened that I believe thousands more might have heard every word."

At Redruth, the town nearest Gwennap, almost the entire population except the gentry were now Methodists. In February 1747 a new bishop, George Lavington, was enthroned at Exeter. He had not yet emerged as a hater of Methodism when two magistrates in the neighborhood of St. Austell in southwest Cornwall, Birkhead and Tremayne, sent him an unintentional tribute to Wesley's strong influence in the four years since his first visit: "A set of people," they wrote, "who stile themselves Methodists have infus'd their enthusiastick notions into the minds of vast numbers of the meaner sort of people in the Western part of this County, and they are very strenuously endeavoring to propagate them all over it: several have assembled frequently within this fortnight in the Parish of Saint Ewe in which we live; and the preacher they are so very fond of, is no better than a mean illiterate Tinner, and what is more surprizing, but a boy of nineteen years old." The justices were particularly disgusted that many of the preachers, "for the most part ignorant men," had "been notoriously wicked, but now under pretence of being both reformed and inspired, they, and even women of the same stamp are adored preachers." When threatened with the Conventicle Act, the Methodists retorted that they did not differ from the Established Church and therefore were not guilty of any crime, but they spoke strongly against the wickedness of clergy. The justices asked the bishop how to deal with the matter.

The bishop's reply is not on record, but three years later Wesley would sum up the situation at St. Ewe with a neat comment: "There was much struggling here at first; but the two gentlemen who occasioned it are now removed—one to London and the other to eternity."

The struggle was already won in many parts when Wesley returned in the summer of 1747, shortly before his first preaching tour in Ireland. He walked to the parish church of St. Ives without an insult. "How strangely," he wrote, "has one year changed the scene in Cornwall! This is now a peaceable, nay honorable station. They give us good words almost in every place." John Wesley was already becoming a folk hero in Cornwall: "He was only a little man, but when he spoke the houses shook."

Methodists were building meeting places wherever the parish church stood a long way off, though they would always attend the church on Sundays. In these or in cottages, barns, or the engine houses of mines, they would go once or twice a week very early before work or late in the evening to sing and pray and hear a preacher. They could be at the mercy of self-styled "exhorters," whom Wesley on his visits would sternly examine. Several "exhorters" were hypocrites, others ignorant or swayed by heresy, and Wesley had to be rough. He was plagued by a few who taught that a man or woman, once saved, could do any wickedness because they would still go to heaven.

Inevitably, some Methodists lost their first fervor, turned coward under persecution, or were "choked with cares and riches and pleasures of this life." Most, however, were noticeable for the change in their outlook and habits. As Thomas Vivian, curate of Redruth, wrote to the new bishop of Exeter in August 1747: "They are to all appearance persons of great sanctity of life, avoiding strictly, not only gross sins but every approach to evil. They never frequent any sports, revels, diversions, etc. and sigh and grieve to see others do so; calling them the Devil's Snares whereby he entraps unwary souls. Besides that which is spent in labor and sleep they pass their time usually in walking together, talking on Religious Subjects, reading, singing hymns, and praying.

"They frequently affront people by reproving them for singing idle songs, talking of worldly matters in going or coming from church, being angry, irregularly merry etc. If they see any person drunk, swearing, or the like, they reprove him, and are apt to tell him he is in the way to Damnation. They call each other Brother and Sister, seem to be linkt together in the strictest friendship, and make it an invariable rule to tell each other if they think or suspect anything to be amiss.

"In their devotions they sometimes make use of the collects of the Church, but usually extempore prayer.... They are very constant attendants at church and the Sacrament, and when there, seem very attentive and much affected." Vivian continued to describe Methodists in great detail, assuring his bishop that whatever their mistakes "there is something very commendable about them."

The undistinguished Bishop George Lavington might have tolerated Methodists in Devon or Cornwall had he not been enraged in 1748 by a forgery of his handwriting which was circulated and then printed with a supposed extract from the bishop's first charge to his clergy. It purported to show him as not only actively sympathetic but preaching Methodist doctrine himself. Lavington scribbled on his own copy, "All above absolutely false. *G.Ex*," and accused Wesley and Whitefield of being the authors or sponsors of the forgery, but he produced no evidence; the intervention of Lady Huntingdon made him grudgingly retract.

He turned to attacking them in two anonymous pamphlets on "The Enthusiasm of Methodists and Papists Compared" in which he jumbled extracts from the published journals of Wesley to falsify his teaching and practice.

Wesley easily won the pamphlet war, but one of Lavington's stories he thought "so silly and improbable" that it needed no refutation until Wesley's friends insisted. Lavington had seized on a report from the chancellor of his diocese and the archdeacon of Barnstaple that Wesley had "attempted to debauch" a maidservant in the Plume of Feathers inn at Mitchell near Truro. When, on his next visit, Wesley confronted the publican and his wife, they changed their evidence. The maidservant indignantly denied that

Wesley had made improper advances, and she threatened to sue her employers. Wesley had no difficulty in proving his innocence.

According to legend in Cornwall, however, he had an artless habit wherever he stayed of giving a good-night kiss to any ladies who were present.

He was unaware that some years earlier, James Hutton, when smarting from Wesley's withdrawal from the Fetter Lane Society, had written in the course of a long letter to Count Zinzendorf: "J.W. and C.W., both of them, are dangerous snares to many young women; several are in love with them. I wish they were married to some good sisters, but I would not give them one of my sisters if I had many."

By 1748 Charles was engaged to be married. That year John Wesley believed that he too had found a bride.

21

The Higher Love

In August 1748 Wesley rode into Newcastle reading the tenth *Iliad* of Homer and put up at his orphan house, and during his stay, he fell sick. The mistress of the orphan house, widow Murray, moved quietly in and out of his room, catering to his needs, and the more he observed her, the more he realized that she would make an excellent wife.

The most recent conference of his preachers had recommended marriage as a suitable state for all the itinerants. John Wesley had begun to look for a wife, rather halfheartedly.

He had come to appreciate Grace Murray since the day, years before, when she had first listened on Kennington Common, then only one of several thousands of unknown faces before him. Born in Newcastle, daughter of a respectable craftsman, low in the social scale, she had gone to London and had briefly entered domestic service, being treated more as a child of the house than as a servant. Then she had married Alexander Murray, son of a small Scots laird who had been out in the Fifteen Rebellion for which he was banished from Scotland and his estate forfeited to the Crown. His son, reduced to penury, went to sea as a common seaman.

Grace had been much impressed by Whitefield's preaching on Blackheath in May 1739 soon after she had lost her baby daughter. She heard Wesley many times that summer and was converted in her own house while another young woman was reading aloud from the fifth chapter of Romans: "And in a moment all things became new. I seemed to have new eyes and a new understanding. I saw all I read in a new light. My burden dropped off. My soul was at peace. My tears were all gone."

After her husband was drowned at sea, she returned to Newcastle and later became one of Wesley's class leaders and then mistress of the new orphan house. She had traveled with Wesley around the northern societies and proved excellent at questioning and counseling the women. She had a deep if sometimes troubled faith and a sweet nature, but her brisk efficiency tended to attract the jealousy of the sisters who worked with her.

Grace was an excellent nurse. One of her former patients had been a Methodist lay preacher of her own age from Derbyshire, John Bennet. During a long illness and convalescence at Newcastle, he had fallen in love with Grace but had not declared his love before returning to Derbyshire.

During his four-day illness, Wesley watched Grace Murray with growing interest: "I esteemed and loved her more and more. And when I was little recovered I told her, sliding into it I know not how, 'If ever I marry, I think you will be the person'"—the very words he had used to Sophia Hockey in Georgia twelve years before.

As he prepared to resume his itinerant preaching, Wesley spoke more directly. Grace looked utterly amazed. "This is too great a blessing for me," she said. "I can't tell how to believe it. This is all I could have wished for under Heaven, if I had dared to wish for it."

Wesley now regarded her as engaged to marry him. The night before he was due to leave Newcastle, he said: "I am convinced God has called you to be my fellow laborer in the gospel. I will take you with me to Ireland in the spring. Now we must part for a time. But, if we meet again, I trust we shall part no more."

Grace begged that they should not part so soon. Wesley therefore allowed her to saddle her horse and ride with himself and William Mackford, a middle-aged helper, into Yorkshire. They traveled south, Wesley reading Dr. Hodge's *Account of the Plague in London*. At Halifax market cross he stilled the roaring of "an immense number of people" by the vigor of his preaching, but before he had finished a gentleman bribed some roughs to pelt him with stones. One cut him badly on the face. The crowd began to roar again until Wesley could not make himself heard. Stanching the blood from his wound, he led the way to a meadow outside the town, followed by a large part of his audience, who listened quietly and sang the hymns powerfully.

Wesley and his small party rode on across Yorkshire. Grace was "unspeakably useful both to me and the Societies." She showed no fear when a mob from Colne, incited by a clergyman, invaded the open-air service at Roughlee under the forested lower slopes of Pendle and beat Wesley to the ground. Roughs covered his close friend Parson Grimshaw of Haworth with muck and mud, dragged Mackford by the hair, and threw some local Methodists into the river. The local constable "sat well pleased close to the place, not attempting in the least to hinder them."

Wesley, Grace, and Mackford came into Derbyshire. John Bennet joined them. He had not expected Grace, and soon he burned for her. He knew nothing of Wesley's interest since Wesley, for the sake of his authority among the Methodists, gave no sign.

They reached Bennet's home at Chinley on the edge of the Peak District and stayed the night after Wesley had preached. All rode together next day to Astbury near Congleton in Cheshire. Wesley preached again while a mob howled outside the house.

Wesley was now certain that he wanted to marry Grace, but he was needed in London and had to ride posthaste. On Friday morning, September 2, 1748, he entrusted Grace to the care of John Bennet, in all innocence, "and went on my way rejoicing."

Bennet took Grace and Mackford back to Chinley to rest before their long ride back to Newcastle. In his own home the next day, John Bennet asked Grace Murray to marry him.

Grace still could not believe that Wesley had meant marriage: "It seemed too strange to be true." And she was not sure; perhaps she loved her earlier patient who was now asking for her hand. She gave no answer to Bennet.

That night, immediately on getting into bed, Bennet was puzzled by a waking dream or mental vision (for he was sure he had not yet fallen asleep) in which he saw Grace in deep distress and no less a person than Mr. Wesley coming to her tenderly and saying, "I love thee as well as I did on the day when I took thee first." But "she put him away from her with her hand."

Next morning Bennet asked Grace directly, "Is there not a contract between you and Mr. Wesley?"

"There is not," she replied.

Strictly, though not morally, she was right, for Wesley had not formally proposed, and she seems to have been confused by a growing love for Bennet and by fear of betraying Wesley's feelings to one of his helpers.

Bennet did not write to Wesley for clarification, although as a preacher he was obliged by their rules to request his permission to marry. Instead, Bennet renewed his suit. Two days later Grace accepted him.

Wesley, meanwhile, completed his business in London, which included some preaching at Lady Huntingdon's house in Chelsea, and went into Cornwall. Somewhere in the West Country he received letters and was "utterly amazed": Bennet asked his consent; Grace assured him that she believed it was the will of God. Wesley, assuming they were already married, stifled his feelings and "wrote a mild answer to both." He had told no one, not even Charles, of his intention to marry Grace. He put the matter sadly out of his mind—until a reply came from Grace. She wrote "in so affectionate a manner" that he thought her engagement to Bennet must have been broken off.

Wesley worked in London that winter while Grace remained at Newcastle and Bennet in Derbyshire. Grace was in a ferment of indecision. Whenever she had a letter from Wesley, as he learned from her afterwards, she resolved "to live and die with me and wrote to me just what she felt." If a letter came from Derbyshire, her affection for Bennet revived, and she replied to him tenderly. When, in February 1749, she received her traveling instructions from Wesley for the promised visit to Ireland in April, she begged Bennet to meet her at Sheffield, or she could not answer for the consequences. Bennet was prevented at the last moment by a death in the family. Grace waited in vain for him at Sheffield, then rode to Bristol to meet Wesley.

She told him her story, and Wesley convinced her that the engagement to him had precedence of any to Bennet. She wished she could talk it over with some woman of wisdom, but felt that any disclosure would harm Wesley.

Charles had arrived in Bristol on his way to his wedding in Wales. The three of them, with William Tucker, set out on April 3 and were caught by a storm in the Severn estuary, so that Wesley missed a preaching engagement at Newport and was "wet and weary" when he preached near Caerphilly.

As they traveled the valleys and across the mountains, he kept silent about Grace; Charles remained in ignorance that the widow who rode with them, helping with the sisters wherever they examined the societies, was his brother's intended wife. Charles regarded her as little more than a servant. At Garth near Builth Wells, John married Charles to Sarah, the twenty-two-year-old third daughter of Marmaduke Gwynne, a gentleman of ancient lineage; Sally would bring Charles lifelong happiness and many children.

The others rode on to Holyhead and crossed to Dublin for Wesley's tour of Ireland, his third. During the spring and summer months which followed, Grace accompanied Wesley as he rode through the southern counties strengthening the Methodists. She was at hand when he had a severe cold with swelling in the cheek, for which he successfully applied boiled nettles and warm treacle. She heard him preach in Protestant churches—many rectors were sympathetic—and in market houses and open fields. At Birr on the road to Limerick, the congregation was so sleepy and unconcerned by his gentle sermon that the next day he "spoke very plain and rough." The effect was dramatic, and Wesley reflected "that love will not always prevail; but there is a time for the terrors of the Lord." At Athlone he found a society ripe for revival: "I think more found peace with God in these four days than in sixteen months before."

In all this, Wesley was delighted with Grace. "I saw the work of God prosper in her hands. She lightened my burden more than can be expressed. She gave spiritual counsel to the women in the smaller societies and the believers in every place. She settled all the women bands; visited the sick; prayed with the mourners; more and more of whom received remission of sins during her conversation or prayer.

"Meantime she was to me both a servant and friend, as well as a fellow-laborer in the gospel. She provided everything I wanted. She told me with all faithfulness and freedom, if she thought anything amiss in my behavior."

Wesley was charmed by Grace's skill at rebuking him; she combined plainness of speech with deep respect, tenderness, and "exquisite modesty."

She had no letters from Bennet. Wesley had one letter in which Bennet reported on local Methodist affairs, then added that Wesley had misunderstood him about Grace; they would not have married before they could discuss the matter with him in person. Bennet warned that Grace was spiritually weak; he was a trifle rude about her qualities, and this helped to convince Wesley that the Bennet episode was over. Grace was his own, and the more they were together, "the more I loved her."

Before leaving Dublin they made a verbal contract private to themselves but valid in law as it then stood. He stated with solemn formality: "I do take thee as my wife," and she stated: "I do take thee as my husband." Until Hardwicke's Act five years later, one party to such a contract *per verba de praesenti* could be compelled by the other to go through a church marriage before witnesses, which would thus be registered as binding. On the other hand, a church marriage to a third party would

erase the contract *de praesenti*—one of the confusions in the
law of marriage which Hardwicke's Act (1753) would resolve
by laying down that henceforth no marriage was valid unless
performed after banns or by license.

Wesley landed at Bristol with Grace on July 24 believing that
she was to all intents married to him. But according to the spirit
of the rules which he had laid down, he could not complete the
contract publicly in church until he had informed all his helpers
and the societies, obtained his brother's consent, and made sure
that John Bennet as another suitor was satisfied. When Grace
begged Wesley to hurry on the marriage, he refused.

At Bristol she happened to hear unkind gossip that Wesley
had once shown familiarity to a Methodist sister named Molly
Francis. In a "sudden vehement fit of jealousy," Grace wrote and
dispatched a love letter to Bennet. The next day she repented of
her action and went to Wesley "in agony of mind." But the letter
could not be recalled.

On the evening of August 30, Wesley and Grace rode into
Epworth. Here, in Wesley's native town, John Bennet was
waiting, having ridden from Derbyshire, hot with renewed love
for Grace.

Grace, unknown to Wesley, had again been thrown into
confusion. While the Wesley brothers had been conferring with
"that loving, mild, judicious Christian Dr. Doddridge," the
Dissenter, whose famous book *The Rise and Progress of Religion
in the Soul* had been published three years earlier, Grace had
been talking with Tom Maxfield's wellborn wife (he had married
above him). Grace hinted that Wesley would marry her. Elizabeth

Maxfield scorned the very idea; they would both be miserable, and she was unworthy.

Bennet was now determined. When they met at Epworth, Wesley began to stake his prior claim to Grace, but Bennet cut him short. She had sent on to him, he said, all the letters which Wesley had written her (which apparently was a lie). Wesley left the room under a firm impression that Grace loved Bennet and that they "should marry without delay." He wrote her a note to end their own relationship, at which Grace came running to him "in an agony of tears" saying this would kill her, and adding tender expressions until Wesley was at a loss. Then Bennet walked in. "He claimed her as his right," Wesley wrote. "I was stunned and knew not what to say, still thinking, 'She loves him best.'" Wesley thought that if one of them did not withdraw she would die: "So I again determined to give her up."

Wesley and Grace set off for Newcastle together, on what must have been a painfully silent ride, for Wesley was in "an anguish of spirit from a piercing conviction of the irreparable loss I had sustained." On the road Grace fell ill and took to her bed at the inn. He visited her as a pastor, only to have her declare her love for him again, yet saying that Bennet would go mad if she refused; she waved a letter. The next day Bennet arrived at the inn with a friend, and they pleaded at her bedside until she promised her hand, yet she disclosed this the next morning to Wesley, who was "more perplexed than ever." He explained, "As I now knew she loved me, and as she was contracted to me before, I knew not whether I ought to let her go."

They resumed their journey, each unresolved, until they were approaching Newcastle when Wesley insisted that she choose. Then he heard her declare "again and again, 'I am determined by conscience, as well as inclination to live and die with *you*.'"

Wesley now decided that Bennet was using them ill. On September 7 he wrote him a long and stiff letter, going over the whole story and ending: "O that you would take Scripture and reason for your rule; instead of blind and impetuous passion! I can say no more, only this—you may tear her away by violence; but my consent I cannot, dare not give. Nor, I fear, can God give you his blessing."

He handed the letter to another preacher, "who promised to deliver it with his own hand. But it was not delivered at all." Wesley, however, sent a copy to Charles, which eventually reached him in Bristol. Amazed and horrified that Jack should want to marry a servant, Charles saddled his horse, said a hurried good-bye to his wife of five months, and rode posthaste to stop it.

Wesley took Grace on his next pastoral and preaching visit to Berwick-on-Tweed, and their love deepened. Back at Newcastle, with Grace showing great affection, he tried to discover why she was unpopular with the other women. Charles was now riding furiously north. Wesley took Grace on his next tour. They rode west through wild moors toward the Lake District with young Charles Perronet, a son of Vincent Perronet, the vicar of Shoreham, near Sevenoaks in Kent, who was one of Wesley's most valued older advisers.

Before they attempted the roughest country, they left Grace with a Methodist farming family, the Broadwoods, at Hindley Hill in Allendale. At her request Wesley and Grace solemnly renewed their contract to marry, with Christopher Hopper, the young preacher from Newcastle who lived nearby, as witness. Wesley rode on through the glorious scenery without one uneasy thought and reached the coaling port of Whitehaven, where revival had been spreading fast. He was now certain that he would be married to Grace as soon as Charles had acknowledged his letter.

In Whitehaven on Sunday he received an alarming intimation that God might have other plans for him.

Wesley had preached twice at outlying coalfields to large crowds, then hurried to attend the parish church. The first lesson happened to be from the prophet Ezekiel. Suddenly he heard words that "came as a sword to my heart, '*Son of Man, behold I take from thee the desire of thine eyes with a stroke!*' Immediately a shivering ran through me, and in a few minutes I was in a fever. But when I came home, seeing a vast congregation in the Market Place, I could not send them empty away. And while I was speaking to them, God remembered me and strengthened me both in soul and body." Almost the entire town seemed to be there, listening quietly. When a gang of sailors tried to disrupt the service by striking up sea chanties, the very newly devout colliers roughed them up and broke their fiddles.

Charles had reached Leeds and learned wrongly that Grace had been engaged already when Jack proposed; moreover, Bennet was one of Charles' close friends.

Charles reached Newcastle and swallowed gossip against Grace. He scarcely noticed that scriptural holiness and Christian perfection were perhaps in short supply among the Methodist women, and "he flew on" (as Wesley put it) across the moors and mountains, desperate to reach Jack in time to stop him from stealing another man's bride and wrecking the entire movement by the scandal. At Whitehaven he dismounted in a sweat, his horse in a lather, and was surprised to find Jack without Grace. Charles was now in such a state that he would not listen to Jack's side of the story but cried that all the preachers would desert and the societies break up if Jack married such a woman.

Jack withdrew, took paper and pen, and calmly went through the whole matter, setting out his thoughts in form of a letter.

Convinced that Grace was legally and morally his wife, subject only to the ecclesiastical ceremony, and that such a marriage would benefit the Methodist movement, Jack handed Charles the letter, directing that he show it to old Vincent Perronet in Kent. They would all abide by his arbitration.

Charles scarcely looked at the letter but argued hotly. Still convinced that Grace was stolen from Bennet, he waited until Jack had left on a pastoral call, then galloped back across the mountains, Jack having artlessly revealed where Grace was staying.

That afternoon Wesley set off by himself. He was suffering from diarrhea, his horse was "all in a sweat," but the scenery and his thoughts of God and Grace made it "a solemn and delightful ride." Both man and beast grew stronger every hour.

The next day Wesley left Keswick before dawn. Late in the afternoon he rode down into Allendale, expecting to see Grace in a few more minutes at Hindley Hill. The wife of farmer James Broadwood, Hannah, had been watching for him. She met him and said, " 'Mr. Charles left us two hours since, and carried Sister Murray behind him.' I said, 'The Lord gave and the Lord hath taken away! Blessed be the name of the Lord!' Soon James Broadwood came in. He looked at me and burst into tears. I said, 'I must go on to Newcastle.' James said, 'No, I will go, and with God's leave bring her back.' In a quarter of an hour, he took horse, and I calmly committed the cause to God!"

Wesley had reached a decisive crisis in his life.

James Broadwood had no authority over Charles, whose removal of Grace implied that he was determined to prevent the marriage. If John Wesley changed his mind and went to Newcastle, he could still win her, but he dared not influence the course of events except by prayer. With sore heart he carried out a preaching engagement at Hindley Hill, spent a day in fasting and prayer, then rode back to Whitehaven in the teeth of a violent wind. "If I had more regard for her I loved, than for the work of God, I should now have gone on straight to Newcastle, and not back to Whitehaven. I knew this was giving up all: but I knew God called."

At Whitehaven, as he went about his ministry, Wesley was "in great heaviness, my heart was sinking in me like a stone. Only, so long as I was preaching I felt ease." He was comforted by hearing the lessons at church and in taking the Sacrament. He was deeply depressed by a dream in which he saw Grace led out to be hanged, yet he would not lift a finger to force the will of God.

His assistant reminded him that he was engaged to preach at Leeds, and a letter came from George Whitefield urging him and Charles to meet him there.

On the evening of Wednesday, October 9, 1749, Wesley reached Leeds: "Here I found, not my brother, but Mr. Whitefield. I lay down by him on the bed. He told me my brother would not come till JB and GM were married. I was troubled. He perceived it. He wept and prayed over me. But I could not shed a tear. He said all that was in his power to comfort me: but it was in vain. He told me it was his judgment she was my wife and that he had said so to JB: That he would fain have persuaded them to wait, and not to marry till they had seen me: But that my brother's impetuosity prevailed and bore down all before it.

"I felt no murmuring thought, but deep distress. I accepted the just punishment of my manifold unfaithfulness and unfruitfulness and therefore could not complain. But I felt the loss both to me and the people, which I did not expect could ever be repaired. I tried to sleep: but I tried in vain; for sleep was fled from my eyes. I was in a burning fever and more and more thoughts still crowding into my mind, I perceived, if this continued long, it would affect my senses. But God took that matter into his hand; giving me a sudden, sound and quiet sleep."

George Whitefield, anxious to soften the blow, did not reveal that he had been a witness when Grace and Bennet were married the day before by special license in Newcastle.

Wesley eventually pieced together what had happened at Hindley Hill while he was riding into Allendale. Charles, he learned, had burst in on Grace, shouting, "You have broken my heart," and fell at her feet in a dead faint. Recovered, he persuaded her that she would ruin the Methodist movement by marrying his brother. He showed her a letter he had written on the road which made her believe that John Wesley had jilted her, yet when Grace rode away on a pillion, she thought Charles was taking her to John. At Newcastle, Charles and others had falsely convinced her that she could never have John Wesley and that he had behaved dishonorably: "Good God," one had cried, "what will the world say? He is tired of her, and so thrusts his whore into a corner. Sister Murray, will you consent to this!"

Only then had Grace agreed reluctantly to immediate marriage with Bennet.

When Wesley woke from distressed sleep at Leeds the next morning, a Methodist from Newcastle gave the news that they were married.

One hour later, Charles arrived. Jack, though not angry, refused to meet him. Whitefield persuaded them to come together, but Charles, still in a fury at the supposed scandal he had averted, flung at his brother, "You villain! I renounce all intercourse with you, but what I would have with an heathen man and a publican!" Jack stayed calm while Whitefield and Nelson burst into tears and cried and prayed and entreated until the brothers silently embraced.

Bennet came. In silence the two suitors kissed each other and wept. Bennet left. Then Charles at last listened quietly to Jack. Suddenly, it dawned on Charles that he had totally misunderstood the facts, had not sifted accusations and gossip, had wounded his brother irrevocably and unjustly. "He seemed utterly amazed," noted Jack. "He clearly saw I was not what he had thought, and now blamed her only."

The bride and bridegroom joined them for an emotional though almost silent confrontation. Bennet asked forgiveness for hard words. Later Grace came alone, in tears, to assure Wesley that she had never blamed him.

Wesley rode sadly back to Newcastle alone, composing a long prayer in verse which offered his "deep unutter'd grief" to God and vowed to obey him. At Newcastle when he learned more of what had happened, he strove to prevent the conflict from damaging the society and to love Bennet and Grace as brother and sister.

He found especially hard the slander that he was to blame, and when Bennet wrote three weeks later objecting to criticisms, Wesley could not refrain from plain words: "Once for all I must speak," he wrote Bennet on November 3, 1749, "for my heart is full. Although, alas! what avails it now? I loved you as my own soul. I left with you my dearest friend, one who was necessary to me as a right hand, as dear as a right eye. One whom I looked upon then (and not on slight grounds) as contracted to myself. But suppose I say only, one I loved above all on earth, and fully designed for my wife. To this woman you proposed marriage, without either my knowledge or consent.

"Was this well done? God warned you the same night that I had *took* her first (but I could not take her unless she *took* me too). You wrote me word you would take no farther step without my consent. Nevertheless, not only without my consent, but with a thousand circumstances of aggravation, you tore her from me whether I would or no—when all I desired was to refer the whole to impartial men! And all the blame lies upon me! And you have acted with a clear conscience to this day!

"I think not. I think you have done me the deepest wrong which I can receive on this side of the grave. But I spare you. 'Tis but for a little time, and I shall be where the weary are at rest.'"

Grace bore Bennet six sons before he died of jaundice ten years later, having erected his own Calvinist meeting house after leaving Wesley's societies. Grace, as a widow, rejoined them, saw Wesley occasionally, and lived to be over ninety.

Charles was never again so close to John. The breach slowly healed, affection returned, and their joint ministry absorbed them; yet their trust in each other could no longer be absolute.

John Wesley, by the renunciation at Hindley Hill when he refused to hurry after Grace, had set his course for the rest of his life. He would marry, though not for happiness. His sole aim would be to preach and teach and build up. His years would unfold as variations on a single theme.

Part Three

"THE WORLD,
MY PARISH"
1750–1791

22

Back from the Dead

"**M**ay I request one thing of you, sir? Do not speak evil of Jesus Christ. You may sometime stand in need of him. And if you should (I can say from a very little experience), you will find him the best friend in heaven or earth."

Thus Wesley wrote on October 23, 1749 after a long discussion over dinner in Calveley Hall with Richard Davenport, a Cheshire squire and a Deist who would later be a patron of Jean-Jacques Rousseau. Only two weeks earlier on his sad ride from Leeds after losing Grace Murray, Wesley had experienced afresh that Jesus Christ was indeed his "best friend." He would spend the rest of his life promoting his Friend's interest in all ways and at all times.

In 1750 he traveled widely in Ireland. He wrote to a friend in London: "I have had so hurrying a time for two or three months as I scarce ever had before—such a mixture of storms and clear sunshine, of huge applause and huge opposition." He found the Irish true to a tag he had heard: "Impetuous in their love and in their hate."

Catholic peasants in the countryside would gather in groups by the crossroads as he rode by and listen if they understood English.

The Anglo-Irish in the towns were often ready to listen in large numbers, and although he found many Protestants who hated Christianity, Methodist societies sprang up. As he had written on a previous visit to Limerick: "A few years ago, if we heard of one notorious sinner truly converted to God, it was a matter of solemn joy to all that loved or feared him; and now that multitudes of every kind and degree are daily turned from the power of darkness to God, we pass it over as a common thing! O God give us thankful hearts!"

Yet cutthroats would murder (or miss) his preachers as they rode along peaceful roads, and in Cork and elsewhere Protestant magistrates would allow violent rioting and then accuse Methodists of breaching the peace. Wesley went in danger of his life at Cork because the mayor refused to quell a mob.

Wesley loved Ireland, north and south. When Londoners complained of his long visits (forty-two in all) and the number of preachers he sent, he prophesied rightly that Ireland would repay England by the strong Christians who would emerge from the movement. One was Thomas Walsh, a young Limerick man, once a Roman Catholic. He became an effective evangelist in Irish and English and developed a grasp of the Bible in Hebrew and Greek, which amazed even Wesley; yet he remained intense and gloomy and complained that Wesley's cheerfulness was a snare: "Among three or four persons who tempt me to levity, you, sir, are one, by your witty proverbs." Walsh died at the age of twenty-nine.

One of the letters which Wesley wrote from Dublin that summer of 1750 went to Threadneedle Street in London, addressed to a forty-year-old widow, Molly Vazeille, whose husband, a London merchant of reasonable prosperity, had died three years before, leaving her well-off, with grown children. Like her late husband, she was of Huguenot descent and had become a friend of Ned Perronet, another of the vicar of Shoreham's sons; many years later he would write the famous hymn "All Hail the Power of Jesus' Name." The Perronets were Swiss in origin and moved naturally among the Huguenots.

Charles Wesley had met Molly Vazeille at Perronet's and found her "a woman of a sorrowful spirit." Charles and Sally befriended her. In May 1750 she stayed with them in Shropshire, where Sally's parents now lived; and then with Sally's brother-in-law they rode back to London, making a tourist visit to Blenheim Palace on the way. The Wesleys stayed with her in London for a week's sightseeing. By that time Charles had put a low valuation on Molly, and she had taken a dislike to Sally.

Wesley's letter to Mrs. Vazeille from Dublin was pastoral, like hundreds which he wrote to women and men alike.

Back in London that autumn he began to think of Molly Vazeille as a possible wife but kept his thoughts from Charles. She was not a member of the society, and Wesley would be free of the jealousies which had hung round Grace Murray. Molly was past the age of childbearing so that he would not waste time being a parent; Grace had agreed that any offspring of their intended marriage should be brought up at Kingswood School, and they would never have known the happy childhood of their cousins, the large family of Charles and Sally. Molly's financial independence would save Wesley from having to support her and thus restrict his giving to the poor.

Molly Vazeille impressed him. He praised her for "your indefatigable industry, your exact frugality, your uncommon neatness and cleanness both in your person, your clothes and all things round you." As so often with women, he could see no deeper.

By January 1751 Wesley had settled the question subject to the approval of Vincent Perronet, who was to have arbitrated over Bennet's claim on Grace. Perronet gave his consent on February 2. Then, honoring the letter but not the spirit of his earlier pledge that neither he nor Charles would marry without the agreement of the other, Wesley announced his intention to Charles, who was "thunderstruck ... and retired to mourn with my faithful Sally." On Saturday, February 9, John Wesley and Molly Vazeille signed a marriage settlement before four trustees as witnesses, whereby he would not touch her fortune, and she would not be responsible for his debts; without such a settlement her entire property would have become his absolutely.

He had not intended an immediate wedding but rather to leave on a preaching tour to the north on the Monday. Early on Sunday morning, however, walking to preach south of the river, he slipped on the ice on London Bridge and sprained his foot. Instead of a tour to the north, he spent a week's convalescence at the home of Mrs. Vazeille. If this was a providential opportunity to think twice about joining her in holy matrimony, he failed to take it: he spent much of the time writing a Hebrew grammar and *Lessons for Children*. Still unable to walk or stand, he announced his intended marriage at the Foundery service from a kneeling position, rather defensively. Charles said it "made us all hide our faces." On February 18 or 19 (the precise date and the church are uncertain) the marriage took place. Charles complained that he was "one of the last that heard of his unhappy marriage."

Two weeks later, still lame, Wesley rode off with Ned Perronet for a conference of the itinerant preachers in Bristol. He was disappointed that Molly, whose spelling and handwriting left much to be desired, did not write for at least "four whole days." He, however, taking pen and paper, conversed a little: "My body is stronger and stronger—and so is my love to you. God grant it may never go beyond his will! O that we may continue to love one another as Christ has loved us."

Both tried for a little, but Wesley had no intention of changing his routine or shedding responsibility. Molly resented his absences and began to show a violent temper; Wesley tried every method to soften it in vain. For a time she valiantly went with him on his travels, worked among the poor, and even shared a riot. Discomforts soon depressed her; her heart was not in his mission nor her mind on his level. Wesley expected wifely obedience and true sympathy. Instead, she resented his openhanded generosity, was jealous of his women correspondents (he had innocently encouraged her to open letters in his absence), and took a violent dislike to Sally and Charles; Charles would ironically refer to her when writing to Sally as "my best friend." By 1753 Ned Perronet called her "absolutely intractable."

Whatever Wesley's faults toward his wife, she soon became a handicap and a trial. He needed all his spiritual resources to walk toward Christian perfection while Molly was around.

By his marriage Wesley ceased to be a fellow of Lincoln College. He had been cut off from the university in all but name since the sermon which had so displeased the vice-chancellor. He had cared nothing for the stipend, and as for the license to preach in any parish of the realm, which the Oxford fellowship gave him, he had long ceased to care whether he had ecclesiastical permission; he looked upon all the world as his parish.

Marriage did not improve his health. He continued to ride round the societies and to preach outdoors wherever he went and to write his letters and books, but the rigors of the road affected his chest. At the end of October 1753, he fell ill with fever in London. He cured himself by doses of chinchona bark (quinine), although it disagreed with his constitution; but within ten days he had a relapse and became so weak that George Whitefield was deeply distressed when he visited him.

The eminent physician, John Fothergill, a Quaker about forty who was already famous for his medical skill and his botanical garden, diagnosed "galloping consumption" (advanced tuberculosis). Fothergill offered little hope. He ordered Wesley to leave London: "If anything does thee good, it must be the country air, with rest, asses' milk, and riding daily."

Wesley was too weak to ride. A generous banker, Ebenezer Blackwell, came round to the Foundery in his coach and took John and Molly down to his palatial country residence, The Limes at Lewisham, five miles southwest of London, where Mrs. Blackwell could nurse him; Wesley never forgot Molly's devoted care either.

Blackwell was one of Wesley's closest friends. They were frank with each other's spiritual needs. Wesley had warned the prosperous banker against "being ashamed, not of sin, but of holiness." Blackwell had warned the great evangelist against "popularity, a thirst of power and applause; against envy, producing a seeming contempt for the conveniences or grandeur of this life; against an affected humility," and showing off by self-denial. (Wesley replied: "I am not conscious to myself that is my case. However, the warning is always friendly.") Wesley loved The Limes, where he wrote several of his books.

He now expected to die there. On the evening of his arrival he drafted an inscription for his tombstone, to "prevent vile panegyric":

Here lieth
The body of JOHN WESLEY,
A brand plucked out of the burning,
Who died of Consumption
in the fifty-first year of his age,
And leaving, after his debts are paid,
ten pounds behind him;
Praying,
God be merciful to me,
an unprofitable servant.

Charles hurried down to Lewisham and wept when he saw his brother. Jack expressed a dying wish that Charles and Molly should be reconciled: "My brother," wrote Charles to Sally, "entreated me yesterday, and his wife, to forget all that is past, on both sides. I *sincerely* told him I would for his, as well as Christ's sake. My sister said the same."

Charles rode back and summoned the Foundery congregation to urgent prayer. A message went to Whitefield, now in Bristol, who on December 3 wrote a grief-stricken letter to Wesley on his "approaching dissolution. I pity myself and the Church," he wrote, "but not you—a radiant throne awaits you, and ere long you will enter into your Master's joy.... But I, poor I, that have been waiting for my dissolution these nineteen years, must be left behind to grovel here below!"

If prayers could detain the heavenly chariots, continued Whitefield, Wesley "shall not leave us yet. But if the decree is gone forth that you must now fall asleep in Jesus, may he kiss your soul away, and give you to die in the embraces of triumphant love! If in the land of the living, I hope to pay my respects to you next week. If not, rev and very dear sir, F-a-r-e-w-e-l-l." After a Latin tag, he ended: "My heart is too big, tears trickle down too fast, and you, I fear, too weak for me to enlarge. Underneath you may there be Christ's everlasting arms. I commend you to his never-failing mercy, and am, rev and very dear sir, your most affectionate, sympathizing, and afflicted younger brother in the gospel of our common Lord, *G. W.*"

By the time this letter reached Lewisham, Wesley was in the saddle again for short rides; Charles ascribed the recovery to the prayers at the Foundery. By January 5, 1754 Wesley was convalescing at Clifton Hot Wells near Bristol. He wrote to the Blackwells to thank his "best friends ... who have been the greatest instruments, in God's hands, of my recovery thus far." He drank the waters at Clifton and worked hard on a new book, *Notes on the New Testament*, since the doctor would not allow him to preach. By spring he was ready for the next crisis in Methodism.

23

"To Invite, To Convince, To Offer Christ"

Wesley's main aim was "to promote, as far as I am able, vital practical religion; and by the grace of God to beget, preserve and increase the life of God in the souls of men." For this purpose he aimed also (as an anonymous obituarist would put it neatly at the end of Wesley's life) "to revive the obsolete doctrines and extinguished Spirit of the Church of England."

These two aims were sometimes in conflict and produced tension between the Wesley brothers. John Wesley tended to put first the claims of evangelism; Charles, the Church. Both Wesleys saw the societies as essentially within the Church, but Methodists who were rebuffed from Holy Communion by unsympathetic clergy became impatient; they wanted to take the Lord's Supper in their own consecrated chapels, although this would effectively separate them from the Church.

Too many parish clergy were idle, ignorant, or opposed to the gospel; therefore, Wesley was forced to appoint itinerant lay preachers. Bishops refused to recognize them, but Wesley regarded his preachers as a lay order within the church rather like the Church Army captains of the far future. Although he allowed them to take out licenses from local magistrates for protection, he now held that this did not imply separation. Most of the preachers were drawn from the "lower orders" of British society. Many were deeply sincere, if ill-educated, but a few wanted to rise in the social scale by acquiring the status of ministers of religion. Since no bishop would ordain them, they would have liked to become Dissenting ministers if only Wesley would take the Methodist movement out of the Church.

Charles Wesley grumbled to Lady Huntingdon that "the preachers will destroy the work of God. What has well nigh ruined many of them is their being taken from their trades.... The tinner, barber, thatcher, forgot himself, and set up for a gentleman, and looked out for a fortune, having lost the only way of maintaining himself."

Charles wanted all preachers to support themselves by their trades and no longer receive stipends administered by his brother. He did not dare reveal one of his reasons to Jack: "It will break his power, their not depending on him for bread, and reduce his authority within due bounds, as well as guard against that rashness and credulity of his, which has kept me in continual awe and bondage for many years."

Wesley saw this letter and retorted: "In what respect do you want to 'break my power' and 'to reduce my authority within due bounds'? I am quite ready to part with the whole or any part of it. It is no pleasure to me, nor ever was."

By the summer of 1754, when he had recovered from his illness, Wesley found himself assailed from both sides; the sons of Vincent Perronet were threatening to withdraw from the movement if he did not separate from the church; Charles was threatening to withdraw if he did. The Perronets tried to force the issue by administering the Sacrament to some lay preachers.

The following year Wesley wrote a lengthy paper, "Ought We to Separate from the Church of England?" He read it to the conference of preachers in May 1755 at Leeds, and they debated for much of three days. Charles had already prepared a long letter in verse to his brother begging him not to separate. Before the conference ended, Charles hurried away, relieved that no immediate break was likely but fearful lest it come later because his brother had settled the question on expediency rather than principle. Charles therefore published his verse "Epistle to the Reverend Mr. John Wesley."

Charles underestimated his brother's attachment to the Church, but another danger arose—that Methodist clergy might be thrown out. On June 23, 1755 Wesley sent a hurried note to Charles in Bristol that the bishop of London (Sherlock had succeeded on Gibson's death) had "excommunicated" a Methodist clergyman. With a Latin tag which Charles paraphrased to Lady Huntingdon as "my turn next," Wesley wrote: "It is probable the point will now be speedily determined concerning the church. For if we must either *dissent* or *be silent, Actum est*" (it is all over).

The danger passed; no bishop dared to proceed against Wesley himself. The tension within the movement, however, remained strong. Charles Wesley gained the support of two clergymen whom his brother respected: Samuel Walker of Truro in Cornwall and William Grimshaw of Haworth in Yorkshire, one of Wesley's closest advisers and strongest supporters. When in 1760 three of the lay preachers administered the Sacrament in the Methodists' chapel at Norwich, Charles wrote to Grimshaw that "things are come to a crisis. We must now resolve either to separate from the Church or to continue in it for the rest of our lives."

Wesley was away in Ireland; he had published his twelve reasons against separation and showed little concern at aberrations. Grimshaw, however, was adamant that he must rebuke the Norwich preachers and threatened to "disown all connection with the Methodists." When Charles read Grimshaw's letter aloud at the Foundery service, the people "cried out that they would live and die in the Church."

Wesley duly rebuked the Norwich men. At the next conference he made plain that when he appointed preachers, he did not ordain them; the "people called Methodists" stayed with the Church of England. But Wesley was to find in his later years that the question "Shall we separate?" had not been answered finally—because the message and the method were for all the world.

In June 1763 Wesley reached his sixtieth birthday. He looked younger: his hair was still dark, and he was now more physically fit than he had been for years, with renewed vigor and unwearied determination "to reform the nation, and in particular the Church; to spread scriptural holiness over the land."

His life had fallen into a routine which he called "as fixed as the sun." He spent the winters in London and Bristol overseeing the societies, schools, and orphanages while in the summer "I am almost perpetually in motion." He rode throughout England in a regular rotation, sometimes accompanied by Molly. He visited Scotland twenty-two times and made his many journeys to Ireland.

Wesley was reviving the long discarded pattern of the preaching friars of the medieval church when he spoke from market crosses and on commons and hillsides, often with a lad to play an oboe for the hymns. In all his preaching he aimed "to invite; to convince; to offer Christ." His sermons included frequent anecdotes and much Scripture and were informed by the vast range of his reading of books by Christian and classical authors; yet he wore his learning so lightly that the simplest hearer could understand. His reading on the long rides enabled him to expand his knowledge continually, for he had an insatiable curiosity not only for intellectual knowledge but about the history, geography, and customs of the places he passed, which he would include in his printed *Journal* published at regular intervals.

He took a servant as valet and groom, always choosing a man from the societies. For some years he had Michael Fenwick from Newcastle, whom Wesley called "an original." Fenwick was vain (and not always truthful) and once complained that every helper was mentioned in the *Journal* except himself. Wesley then played a little joke. In the next *Journal* he included an entry: "Mon. 25. I left Epworth with great satisfaction, and about 1 o'clock preached at Clayworth. I think none was unmoved but Michael Fenwick, who fell fast asleep under an adjoining haystack."

Fenwick later got into trouble; Wesley dismissed and expelled him, "a poor wicked man." He was reinstated later and lived to old age in much sanctity, very generous to the poor and perhaps dining out on his memories.

Wherever Wesley went he would examine the bands and the classes, keeping Methodists to the mark. The societies ensured that the preaching and evangelizing would have lasting effect on a district. "My brother Wesley acted wisely," wrote Whitefield to a friend who was one of Wesley's local preachers. "The souls that were awakened under his ministry he joined in class and thus preserved the fruits of his labors. This I neglected, and my people are a rope of sand." Whitefield had no inclination or time "to weave a web," and if many of his converts joined Wesleyan classes when cold-shouldered by parish clergy, he rejoiced: "Let the name of Whitefield die, so that the cause of Jesus Christ may live." Wesley had an equal distaste for the name *Wesleyan* which was beginning to be heard but, as Whitefield commented to him, "You, I suppose, are for settling societies everywhere."

He liked especially to settle them among the poor, giving hope and dignity and purpose to the "outcasts of men" about whom Charles and he had sung on the night of his conversion. "I love the poor," he wrote in 1757. "In many of them I find pure, genuine grace, unmixed with paint, folly and affectation," a sideswipe at the Hanoverian aristocracy. "I *bear* the rich," he wrote when he was sixty-one, "and *love* the poor; therefore I spend *almost all* my time with them." He was never happier than when he visited the cellars and garrets of "the choicest part of London society. I mean the poor." Often he saw the power of the gospel replace sloth, extravagance, and the bottle with enterprise, thrift, and sobriety; Methodists were able to leave cellar or garret.

As the Industrial Revolution began to erect factories and mills on the edges of once sleepy towns, and the country people migrated to the hurriedly built terraces which soon became slums, the societies spread fast, in Yorkshire especially. Here and in London a local society would often number more than its parish church could contain, even if the parson were welcoming rather than hostile. Methodist meeting houses or chapels went up more quickly than new churches in the expanding towns, but the meetings were not to be at the time of church services, which the members were urged to attend, especially on Sacrament Sundays.

In the few parishes where the vicar or rector was evangelical, the Communion hymns of Charles Wesley, verse after verse, would be sung while the communicants moved forward to take the bread and wine.

A distinctive Methodist character was indeed beginning to reform the nation—a new spirit of enterprise and self-help, a seriousness which sharpened skills. "Be active, be diligent," Wesley would urge. "Avoid all laziness, sloth, indolence. Fly from every degree, every appearance of it; else you will never be more than half a Christian.

"Be cleanly. In this let the Methodists take pattern by the Quakers. Avoid all nastiness, dirt, slovenliness, both in your person, clothes, house, and all about you." And he added with a touch of humor, "Do not stink above ground. This is a bad fruit of laziness; use all diligence to be clean....

"Whatever clothes you have, let them be whole; no rents, no tatters, no rags. These are a scandal to either man or woman, being another fruit of vile laziness. Mend your clothes, or I shall never expect you to mend your lives. Let none ever see a ragged Methodist."

The converted trifler or drunk became a hard worker. This brought a new prosperity and with it a stronger sense of charity toward the afflicted and those who could not help themselves, since all was to be done for the glory of God and the good of mankind.

Wesley could visit most of the societies only occasionally, but he wrote scores of letters in his own hand, squeezing his sessions of writing into a crowded day. "He wrote as he spoke," recalled one correspondent who knew him well. "He literally *talks* upon paper."

"I have you before my eyes," Wesley said to another, and except when he was composing a careful reply or an instruction, his pen flew across the paper: he could be terse, but the affection and warmth which the recipient remembered would spring out of the neat lines of rather square handwriting which gave no sign of their swift composition.

Wesley kept in touch also by the *Journal* and the other books and pamphlets which continued to pour from his pen. These had an influence far beyond the membership of his societies, for his own reading was so wide that he could introduce subjects which interested all classes. He realized early the dangers arising from the intellectual movement becoming known as the Enlightenment, which taught that reason answered all human questions—that faith and revelation must give way to reason and stay on the margins of thought and experience—and that man is born good, needing growth but not redemption.

Against the Enlightenment movement, Wesley brought before the public his own books and his abridgement or summaries of Christian classics of all ages: the Christian Library. Wesley read books so fast that he occasionally missed their point. Sometimes he abridged or summarized rather shamelessly to support his own views: in one instance he reprinted an almost unknown book by Richard Baxter, the famous Puritan divine, without revealing that Baxter had later repudiated much of it. Another rather naughty abridgement was to cause Wesley much trouble.

Whatever the weaknesses of the Christian Library, Wesley's books, his sermons, letters, and personal example were forging a new synthesis between faith, holy living, and Christian knowledge, giving new life to theology and practice in Britain and beyond the seas.

24

The Chimney Sweeper

In 1761 a fresh wave of revival swept across England, strengthening the evangelical movement.

It also brought some fanaticism which in 1762 gave Wesley "more care and trouble in six months than in several years preceding." Tom Maxfield was infected. Maxfield, the excollier converted through Whitefield who had become Wesley's helper until forcibly enlisted into the Army, had surprisingly received Holy Orders after his discharge. A friendly Irish bishop ordained him at Bath "to help that good man, Mr. John Wesley, that he may not work himself to death."

Maxfield fell under the spell of an ex-corporal of the Life Guards named George Bell, who boasted that he was now sinless and that the world would end on February 28, 1763. Many nervous persons spent that night in the fields. Bell was arrested for causing a public disturbance; he lost his faith and took to radical politics. Maxfield broke from Wesley, led 200 of the society to form his own independent chapel, and became a violent opponent.

Wesley reacted mildly. As his physician and early biographer Thomas Whitehead commented, Wesley's quick temper had been "in a great measure" corrected by the influence of religion and his "habit of close thinking." If strangers persecuted or abused him, he bore it without anger or outward emotion; and when colleagues abused his confidence, his loyal friends found that he was "not easy to convince that any one intentionally deceived him." He forgave injuries. Wesley even preached for Maxfield and visited him on his deathbed. *The Gentlemen's Magazine*, a secular journal, marveled that Wesley "has been known to receive into his confidence even those who have basely injured him; they have not only subsisted on his bounty, but shared in his affection."

Much more serious than Maxfield's schism was the renewed controversy with the Calvinists.

The Calvinists dubbed Wesley an "Arminian," a label derived from the Latin name of early seventeenth-century Dutch theologian Arminius, and adopted by Archbishop Laud and many of the high Anglican divines of the reigns of Charles I and Charles II. As popularly understood, the Arminians regarded a believer's good works and growth in holiness as decisive to his salvation; this was not Wesley's position after 1738, but he accepted the label and gave an evangelical twist to the old title. However, he had no wish to form a party. He tried hard to preserve unity and could not understand why Calvinists attacked him for views which he held starkly and without compromise.

In his desire for unity he inclined to refashion his opponents' thoughts and to demolish their arguments by selective quotation. And one of his opponents remarked of Wesley's editing of books in his Christian library: "Why should poor John Bunyan be disembowled to make him look like Mr. Wesley?" Another, the gentle James Hervey, former Oxford Methodist and now a mild Calvinist, complained that "Mr. Wesley is so unfair in his quotations and so magisterial in his manner that I find it no small difficulty to preserve the decency of the gentleman and the meekness of the Christian in my intended answer." Hervey wrote eleven stiff letters to Wesley which he left unposted and unpublished at his early death in 1758.

These were printed in a garbled version without authority. Hervey's brother then corrected and reissued them in 1765. Wesley replied by preaching and printing "For the Benefit of the Poor," a sermon on the theme "The Lord Our Righteousness." He stood his ground on the matters in dispute but pleaded against bigotry: "What shall we wrangle about? ... Let us strengthen each others' hands in God."

"How dreadful," he insisted, "and how innumerable are the contests which have arisen about religion! And not only among the children of the world, ... but even among the children of God, those who had experienced 'the Kingdom of God within them,' who had tasted of 'righteousness, and peace, and joy in the Holy Ghost.' How many of these in all ages, instead of joining together against the common enemy, have turned their weapons against each other, and so not only wasted their precious time but hurt one another's spirits, weakened each other's hands, and so hindered the great work of their common Master!"

For a few years more it seemed that unity would be stronger than dispute. Wesley had written round to some fifty clergymen proposing a union not of opinions, expressions, or organization but a union of the heart, each agreeing never to speak unkindly or to hinder the work of the others. Only three replied, but several more agreed without feeling the need of a reply.

Many were temporarily more united in the evangelical gospel than divided by theology: Berridge, the jovial bachelor who was rector of Everton in Cambridgeshire; Venn, the young son of Wesley's and Whitefield's opponent of 1739; Fletcher of Madeley, an austere Swiss who was Wesley's closest younger confidant and a much loved Shropshire vicar; the Countess of Huntingdon; Howell Harris, and others. Whitefield himself was closer to the Wesleys than at any time since the early days. When he returned again from America, "Mr. Whitefield called on me," recorded Wesley on January 31, 1766. "He breathes nothing but peace and love. Bigotry cannot stand before him, but hides its head wherever he comes."

That summer Lady Huntingdon begged Wesley to hurry back from Bristol for conference with Charles and Whitefield. "Our firm union" seemed to be the result. Wesley recorded on August 17, 1766: "My brother and I conferred with him every day; and ... we resolved, by the grace of God, to go on, hand in hand, through honor and dishonor."

Wesley was convinced that each evangelical leader could complement the others. Brother Charles had been somewhat aloof. He had ceased itinerating and had settled to pastoral oversight of the main Methodist societies, first in Bristol and then in London, where he lived comfortably in the western suburb of Marylebone with his devoted wife and children, two of whom were showing musical genius. Wesley urged his brother to put his shoulder to the wheel again. In a letter from Whitehaven in Cumberland a few weeks before the conference with Whitefield, John wrote humbly, even exclaiming in their private shorthand, "I do not love God. I never did.... I am only an honest heathen.... And yet to be so employed of God and so hedged in that I can neither get forward nor backward!"

He urged Charles to continue preaching "*full* redemption, receivable by *faith alone!* consequently to be looked for *now.*" Charles had a special gift for bringing hearers to decision: "In connexion I beat you; but in strong, pointed *sentences* you beat me. Go on, in your *own way* what God has peculiarly called you to. Press the *instantaneous* blessing: then I shall have more time for my peculiar calling, enforcing the *gradual* work."

A Swedish professor, John Liden of Uppsala, recorded in his private journal his impressions of Wesley, newly returned from Ireland, as he preached to 4,000 or more in the Methodist chapel at Spitalfields east of the city of London on the text "Blessed be the Lord God of Israel, for he hath visited and redeemed his people."

"The sermon," noted the professor on October 15, 1769, "was short but eminently evangelical. He has not great oratorical gift, no outward appearance, but he speaks clear and pleasant. After the Holy Communion, which in all English churches is held with closed doors at the end of the preaching service, when none but the Communicants usually are present, and which here was celebrated very orderly and pathetic, I went forward to shake hands with Mr. Wesley, who already knew my name, and was received by him in his usual amiable and friendly way.

"He is a small, thin old man, with his own long and strait hair, and looks as the worst country curate in Sweden, but has learning as a Bishop and zeal for the glory of God which is quite extraordinary. His talk is very agreeable, and his mild face and pious manner secure him the love of all rightminded men. He is the personification of piety, and he seems to me as a living representation of the loving Apostle John. The old man Wesley is already sixty-six years, but very lively and exceedingly industrious. I also spoke with his younger brother, Mr. Charles Wesley, also a Methodist minister and a pious man, but neither in learning or activity can he be compared with the older brother."

In the afternoon the professor heard Wesley again at the Foundery, where the crush was almost unbearable as the chapel was smaller. After the service Wesley invited him, he wrote, "to attend their so-called Private Society, when only Methodists were present, furnished with tickets. First a psalm was sung, and then Mr. Wesley to their edification spoke about practical Christianity, and encouraged them to diligent prayer and celebrating the Lord's Supper as the best means to grow in grace, exhorted them to peace, unity, and love as the distinct character of a Christian. Afterwards some finance matters were attended to, and the whole was ended with prayer and song about 8 P.M.

"The song of the Methodists is the most beautiful I ever heard. Their fine psalms have exceedingly beautiful melodies composed by great masters. They sing in a proper way, with devotion, serene mind and charm. It added not a little to the harmonious charm of the song that some lines were sung by only the women, and afterwards the whole congregation joined in the chorus."

That same year of 1769 a twenty-nine-year-old Devonshire vicar named Augustus Toplady, an able Calvinist theologian, translated a sixteenth-century German's exposition of predestination in its severest form. In 1770 Wesley abridged Toplady's translation in such a way that the argument was reduced to absurdity. In Toplady's eyes, Wesley compounded his crime by adding a mock final word by "the young translator:" "The sum of all is this: One in twenty (suppose) of mankind are elected; nineteen are reprobated. The elect shall be saved, do what they will; the reprobate shall be damned, do what they can, witness my hand, A——. T——."

This witty naughtiness enraged Toplady. Toplady was popular with his Devonshire parishioners and was to write, some five years later, one of the finest hymns in the English language, "Rock of Ages." But when he turned to controversy, his devout sentiments were replaced by bile and fury, perhaps partly explained by the ill health which shortened his life.[1] He damned Wesley in thirty pages of theological odium: "Pernicious doctrines ... all the sophistry of a Jesuit and the dictatorial authority of a pope ... a lurking, sly assassin ... low serpentine cunning ... dirty subterfuges which sink a divine into the level of an oyster woman." Toplady ended: "I would no more enter in a formal controversy with such a scribbler, than I would contend, for the wall, with a chimney sweeper."

Wesley declined to read further than the title page of the "exquisite coxcomb." "Mr. Augustus Toplady I know well, but I do not fight with chimney sweepers" (who in the 1770s were small boys sent naked up the chimneys, scattering soot on the roof and in the room, and emerging black all over). "He is too dirty a writer for me to meddle with; I should only foul my fingers." Charles said he never heard from John an unkind word about Toplady.

Toplady's attack had fouled the air when Wesley's next conference of preachers met in London in August 1770. Wesley had been much concerned by the spread of the heresy of antinomianism whose adherents taught that those who are saved may behave immorally because they can never lose their salvation. Wesley's brother-in-law Westley Hall was one of the worst: he had left Patty for a mistress and then advocated polygamy.

Wesley considered that Methodists had "leaned too much towards Calvinism," which could degenerate into antinomianism. The conference drew up an antidote which appeared in the minutes so loosely worded that even Wesley had to admit afterward that they appeared to suggest that a man could be saved by good works, especially if he had never heard the name of Christ.

Lady Huntingdon read the minutes and wept. She decided that Wesley had abandoned "free justification" in favor of heresy, teaching that good works were the ground of salvation in Christ, not its consequence. Lady Huntingdon had founded a college at Trevecca, Howell Harris' birthplace in Wales, to train Methodist clergy and preachers, whether Calvinist or Arminian. Two of Wesley's nearest disciples, Fletcher and Benson, were president and headmaster. She now ordered that students and staff should "fully and absolutely disavow and renounce the doctrine contained in Mr. Wesley's minutes," or be expelled. Fletcher and Benson resigned; Fletcher then wrote a "vindication" of the minutes, which heated the controversy higher.

The two sides had broken apart again, yet friendships and cooperation were often stronger than mutual suspicions, and on Sunday, November 18, 1770, this was shown plainly. The news of Whitefield's death and burial in New England at the age of fifty-six had reached London. Whitefield had frequently expressed the desire that Wesley should preach his funeral sermon. Wesley retired to The Limes at Lewisham to write it.

On Sunday afternoon he was summoned ninety minutes early to Whitefield's huge chapel on Tottenham Court Road to find that "an immense multitude was gathered together from all corners of the town." The chapel was full two and a half hours before the advertised time and hundreds stood outside and made such a noise that "I was at first afraid that a great part of the congregation would not be able to hear; but it pleased God to strengthen my voice that even those at the door heard distinctly." All in attendance were in black; many were weeping. Wesley preached a notable and affectionate tribute.

He ended with an impassioned prayer: "Let the fire of thy love fall on every heart! And because we love thee, let us love one another with a 'love stronger than death.' Take away from us all 'anger, and wrath, and bitterness; all clamor, and evil speaking.' Let thy spirit so rest upon us that from this hour we may be 'kind to each other, tender hearted; forgiving one another, even as God for Christ's sake has forgiven us!' "

And then they sang the hymn that Charles had written for the occasion:

> *Servant of God, well done!*
> *Thy glorious warfare's past.*

"Of the two greatest and most useful ministers I ever knew," wrote John Fletcher the next year, "one is no more. The other, after amazing labors, flies still, with unwearied diligence, through the three kingdoms, calling sinners to repentance. Though oppressed with the weight of near seventy years, and the cares of near thirty thousand souls, he shames still, by his unabated zeal and immense labors, all the young ministers in England, perhaps in Christendom. He has generally blown the gospel trumpet, and rode twenty miles, before most of the professors who despise his labors, have left their downy pillows. As he begins the day, the week, the year, so he concludes them, still intent upon extensive services for the glory of the Redeemer, and the good of souls."

Controversy continued. Without it, the evangelical movement would have been stronger still. The followers of Whitefield were more to be found in vicarages and rectories—though few enough compared with those clergy who despised or hated Methodists—while Wesley's lay followers were beginning to feel closer to their Methodist preaching houses than to the parish churches, however much Wesley might urge them to support both.

Pamphlets flew back and forth. Wesley never descended to personalities or theological abuse. He brushed aside the chimney-sweeper style of several Calvinist authors. As Dr. Whitehead, recalling conversation with Wesley, could write of these chimney sweepers, "Their railing was much more violent than their reasons were cogent. Mr. Wesley kept his temper, and wrote like a Christian, a gentleman and a scholar."

Much of the argument was needless or based on misconception, as young Charles Simeon of Cambridge noted a few years later when he met the elderly Wesley.

"Sir," ventured Simeon, "I understand that you are called an Arminian; and I have been sometimes called a Calvinist; and therefore I suppose we are to draw daggers. But before I consent to begin the combat, with your permission I will ask you a few questions, not from impertinent curiosity, but for real instruction.... Pray Sir, do you feel yourself a depraved creature, so depraved that you would never have thought of turning to God if God had not first put it into your heart?"

"Yes, I do indeed," replied Wesley.

"And do you utterly despair of recommending yourself to God by anything you can do; and look for salvation solely through the blood and righteousness of Christ?"

"Yes, solely through Christ."

"But, Sir, supposing you were first saved by Christ, are you not somehow or other to save yourself afterwards by your own works?"

"No; I must be saved by Christ from first to last."

"Allowing then that you were first turned by the grace of God, are you not in some way or other to keep yourself by your own power?"

"No."

"What then, are you to be upheld every hour and every moment by God, as much as an infant in its mother's arms?"

"Yes, altogether."

"And is all your hope in the grace and mercy of God to preserve you unto his heavenly kingdom?"

"Yes, I have no hope but in him."

"Then, Sir, with your leave, I will put up my dagger again; for this is all my Calvinism; this is my election, my justification by faith, my final perseverance; it is, in substance, all that I hold, and as I hold it: and therefore, if you please, instead of searching out terms and phrases to be a ground of contention between us, we will cordially unite in those things wherein we agree."

25

The Cry of the Poor and the Slaves

On November 27, 1771 Wesley took the stagecoach from London to Norwich, arriving in the evening. He met the society early next morning and learned that many members were "in the utmost want (such a general decay of trade having hardly been known in the memory of man)." In the evening he had a larger congregation than usual. He believed that the widespread hunger was turning many to think about God: when bread was plentiful, they "never considered whether they had souls or not."

He therefore preached emphatically on Christ's words: "Seek ye first the kingdom of God and all these things shall be added to you" (Matthew 6:33). Faith came first; provision would follow. Wesley's words could be accepted by hungry people because they knew he was doing all that lay in his power to help by action and word.

Recent harvests had been disastrous, inflating the price of corn. That very week King George III, in his speech from the throne, had deplored the "distresses of the poor," and the government was bringing in a measure to allow foreign corn to enter British ports without being charged duty. Wesley knew that more fundamental change was required.

He had seen "with my own eyes," in every corner of the land, "thousands starving because out of work; who could afford only "a little coarse food every other day." He knew a woman who had picked up "stinking sprats from a dunghill" to feed her children; another who gathered bones left by dogs in the streets, "making broth of them, to prolong a wretched life." Yet the rich were "abounding with all the necessaries, the conveniences, the superfluities of life!"

Wesley wrote powerfully to the press about the wide gulf between rich and poor, as he had often done before. He suggested that bread would be cheaper if great quantities of corn were not used in distilling strong drink; meat would not be so scarce and dear if the nobility and gentry would stop the "amazing waste" allowed in their kitchens and eat less enormous meals. Wesley poured out his suggestions, some of which had been proposed by others.

Visiting the sick in London, he was surprised that they were few; he could "hardly remember so healthy a winter. So wisely does God order all things that the poor may not utterly be destroyed by hunger and sickness together." But he and his congregation at the Foundery were "greatly embarrassed by the necessities of the poor." On New Year's Eve 1771 he led strong prayers for their relief; he urged Methodists to relieve and to evangelize the poor systematically, and encouraged a young man, George Mackie, to organize a body of volunteers, thus founding a charity which continued long into the next century as "the Christian Community."

Wesley urged men and women to "gain all you can" by rightful means and hard work without harming others, to "save all you can" by avoiding extravagance and needless expense. "Having first *gained* all you can, and secondly *saved* all you can, then *give* all you can." To save did not mean to hoard. In Wesley's view, "You may as well throw your money into the sea as bury it in the earth … or in the Bank of England. Not to use, is effectually to throw it away." The money should provide "things needful for yourself and your household," and what is left over should be given away to help the poor and to extend the kingdom of God.

Most of Wesley's own income from his books went to relieve distress or support the spread of the Methodist movement. When Parliament imposed a tax on gold and silver plate and he received a pompous demand to send a prompt return of the plate that a clergyman of his eminence was sure to possess, he took some pleasure in a brisk reply: "*Sir*: I have two silver teaspoons at London and two at Bristol. This is all the plate which I have at present, and I shall not buy any more while so many around me want bread. I am, sir, your most humble servant, *John Wesley*."

Wesley was certain that the nation must change its ways if the country were not to fall under the judgement of God. On the eve of the American war, he wrote a long letter to the Earl of Dartmouth, who had become a strong evangelical Christian through Lady Huntingdon and was secretary of state for the colonies: "When I consider (to say nothing of ten thousand other vices shocking to human nature) the astonishing *luxury* of the rich and the *profaneness* of rich and poor, I doubt whether general dissoluteness of manners does not demand a general visitation. Perhaps the decree is already gone forth from the Governor of the world."

Wesley feared that England was on the verge of revolution. In this same letter written June 14, 1775, he told Dartmouth: "As I travel four or five thousand miles a year, I have an opportunity of conversing freely with more persons of every denomination than anyone else in the three kingdoms. I cannot therefore but know the general disposition of the people, English, Scots, and Irish; and I know an huge majority of them are exasperated almost to madness."

Against the background of "a general decay of trade" and an "uncommon dearness of provisions," inflammatory papers spread "with the utmost diligence in every corner of the land." The people were "ripe for open rebellion. And I assure your Lordship they want nothing but a leader."

No rebellion came, either during the years of the American war or following the French Revolution, and Wesley was afterward hailed by historians as a prime factor in saving Britain. Other scholars contested this, pointing out that Britain's Parliamentary system, even with a restricted vote, made revolution unnecessary, "screaming out for liberty while they have it in their hands," as Wesley said in 1775. Yet there were times when agitators might have set all Britain in a flame, had not multitudes already found a better hope than political anarchy. The nineteenth-century leaders of "working men," as they were called, were largely influenced by Wesleyan chapels and, therefore, abhorred violence.

Wesley and the early evangelicals had also begun the slow process of bringing the rich and powerful to a more just and compassionate approach to the problems of poverty. The change in the national conscience of Britain between the mid-eighteenth century and the Victorian Age at all social levels owed much to Wesley.

What is more, he raised his voice against the greatest evil, almost universally condoned, of the age: "that execrable sum of all villainies, commonly called the slave trade."

When he had ridden through parts of South Carolina during his time in America and had seen the slaves working in the fields, Wesley was shocked by their conditions and punishments but did not suppose slavery wrong or the slave trade a crime against humanity.

In 1758 while preaching at Liverpool, he dined with a thirty-three-year-old ex-slave trader who had been converted in a storm at sea some years earlier. John Newton, future author of "How Sweet the Name of Jesus Sounds," had continued as captain of a slave ship while a Christian, though he hated the work; afterward he said that his tender conscience would have stopped him had he realized that he was engaged in crime rather than in a lawful but unpleasant occupation. An illness forced him ashore. When Wesley met him, he was a tide surveyor and an active disciple of Whitefield rather than of Wesley.

On later visits Newton told of his difficulty in finding a bishop to ordain him (several had refused him, to Wesley's disgust, on the feeble excuse that he did not hold a degree from Oxford or Cambridge). If they discussed the slave trade, Wesley makes no mention of it in his *Journal*.

In 1764 Newton's autobiography (published anonymously in early editions, as strange as it may seem),[1] which Wesley read twice, did not attack the slave trade. Newton was beginning to have moral scruples, but Whitefield had persuaded the Georgia trustees to allow the use of slaves, hitherto banned, although he castigated planters who mistreated them.

On Wednesday, February 12, 1772, Wesley traveled from Dorking to London. On the way down he had read Sterne's *Sentimental Journey*. ("For oddity, uncouthness and unlikeness to all the world beside, I suppose the writer is without a rival.") On the way back he read a very different book, newly published: *Some Historical Account of Guinea ... with an Inquiry into the Rise and Progress of the Slave Trade, its Nature and Lamentable Effects* by Anthony Benezet, an American Quaker of French birth.

The subject was much to the fore because the benevolent Granville Sharp had just brought a suit before the Lord Chief Justice in the Court of King's Bench to stop the export back to Barbados of a runaway slave who had been recaptured in London. Lord Mansfield's famous judgment that a slave setting foot in England became free would not be given until June.

Wesley was horrified by Benezet's revelations of slavery in the British Colonies in America and the Carribbean. "I read of nothing like it in the heathen world, whether ancient or modern; and it infinitely exceeds, in every instance of barbarity, whatever Christian slaves suffer in Mahometan countries."

In 1774, recalling his own memories but following his frequent custom of abridging other men's labors, Wesley drew on Benezet to write *Thoughts on Slavery*. Wesley was thus the first voice of importance to be raised in England though Granville Sharp's successful action had been widely reported. Wesley condemned both the slave trade and slavery itself: "And this equally concerns every gentleman that has an estate in our American plantations; yea, all slave-holders, of whatever rank and degree; seeing men-buyers are exactly on a level with men-stealers."

His call was uncompromising: "Give liberty to whom liberty is due, that is, to every child of man, to every partaker of human nature. Let none serve you but by his own act and deed, by his own voluntary action. Away with all whips, all chains, all compulsion! Be gentle toward all men; and see that you invariably do with every one as you would he should do unto you."

John Newton read the pamphlet in his Buckinghamshire vicarage at Olney. Wesley's words opened Newton's eyes to the crime in which he had been engaged before and after his conversion. He grew determined to right the wrong if a way should open; eleven years later Newton was one of the chief influences on the young Member of Parliament, William Wilberforce, who as a boy had known and admired him and had turned to him at the crisis of his own conversion. The long campaign for abolition belongs to Wilberforce's story,[2] but in its early stages Wesley advised and encouraged all who were concerned. As he would write at the age of eighty-four, in a shaky handwriting, to Granville Sharp: "Ever since I heard of it first, I felt a perfect detestation of the horrid Slave Trade."

At the time that he wrote his pamphlet against the slave trade, Wesley's thoughts went much to America, not only because of the sufferings of slaves.

He deplored the dispute between the colonies and the Crown. He warned Prime Minister Lord North and Lord Dartmouth, the secretary of state, that the colonists would not be easily defeated if they rebelled, and he implored the cabinet to find a compromise which would hold the colonists to their allegiance. At first, he had sympathized with the colonists, but as they moved nearer to revolution, he contested their case and urged restraint and loyalty. He wrote "A Calm Address to Our American Colonies," which was mostly an unacknowledged paraphrase of Dr. Samuel Johnson's "Taxation No Tyranny," thus given a much wider circulation.[3]

Both the plagiarism and the change of view infuriated young Toplady, who lampooned Wesley in "An Old Fox Tarr'd and Feather'd": "Whereunto shall I liken Mr. *John Wesley?* and with what shall I compare him? I will liken him unto a *low and puny* TADPOLE *in Divinity*, which proudly seeks to disembowel *an high and mighty* WHALE *in politics.*"

Wesley left Fletcher to answer Toplady. His own concern lay with horror of rebellion, the sufferings of the wounded, and the divisions between Christians. On November 12, 1775, now aged seventy-two, he preached at St. Matthew's, Bethnal Green, a sermon which was later known by the title "Our National Sins and Miseries." In the congregation sat the representative of a provincial newspaper, the *Chester Chronicle.*

Wesley, wrote the journalist, "pathetically described the dire horrors of war, the noise of cannon, cities and villages involved with pillars of fire and smoke, garments rolled in blood, the cries of wounded and dying soldiers; the distresses of the widows and the sighs and tears of helpless orphans.

"High and low, young and old, seemed affected with Mr. Wesley's discourse; for scarce a dry eye was seen in that large assembly.

"After the sermon a good collection was made at the church doors for the support of the widows and children of those soldiers who were slain on the plains of America."

26

"To the Ends of the Earth"

On a winter's day in the time of great scarcity, John Wesley was taking a short break at the vicarage of Shoreham in Kent with his valued adviser and friend, Vincent Perronet, who had just passed his seventy-ninth birthday. The scenes of want and misery which Wesley had witnessed and the controversies which were causing him concern may have temporarily depressed him. At the end of a letter to Charles on immediate matters, he suddenly questioned the whole worth of his ministry.

"I often cry out, *Vitae me redde prior!* ["Give me back my former life," a quotation from Horace] Let me be again an Oxford Methodist! I am often in doubt whether it would not be best for me to resume all my Oxford rules, great and small. I did then walk closely with God and redeem the time. But what have I been doing these thirty years?"

Yet these moments of depression were rare. His tall, young assistant, Samuel Bradburn, who traveled with him thousands of miles and afterward became one of the most fluent of Methodist preachers, said that he "never saw him low-spirited in my life, nor could he endure to be with a melancholy person." The first time that Bradburn met Wesley he "was greatly struck with his cheerfulness and affability. From seeing him only in the pulpit, and considering his exalted station in the Church of Christ, I supposed he was very reserved and austere; but how agreeably was I disappointed when, with a pleasant smile, he took me by the hand and said, 'Beware of the fear of man, and be sure you speak flat and plain in preaching.' It is not easy to express the good effect this advice had on my mind at that time."

If Wesley had grounds for depression, one at least was the gradual breakup of his unfortunate marriage to Molly.

She stole or burned his papers, and constantly criticized him in conversation with others, including Toplady and other opponents. In 1771 she left without warning and went to live in Newcastle; within three years she came back to Wesley, but John Hampson of Manchester (father of Wesley's first biographer) once entered a room unannounced to find Molly dragging her husband across the floor by his hair.

Wesley tried to humor her and took her on his travels but never understood her troubled spirit. He assumed that her lies about his actions and character were an attempt to vindicate her own. He believed her to be a woman of true faith but poor judgment. Sometimes he wondered whether she had married him for his money derived from his books only to find that his fortune was not for his own use.

She left him finally and set up home with her son. In 1777 the Wesleys met accidentally. Molly said she was willing to return. He agreed, provided that she restored his papers and took no more.

On reflection he wrote to withdraw his offer because it would seem an admission that he had been guilty of all her accusations.

"For instance, you have said over and over that I have lived in adultery these twenty years," he told her. She had lied to others that he lay with Sarah Ryan, the housekeeper at Bristol, and that Sally, Charles' happy and devotedly faithful wife, was his mistress. He challenged Molly: "Do you believe this, or do you not? If you do, how can you think of living with such a monster?"

She may have made another approach, for in 1778 he wrote an uncompromising letter. "You have laid innumerable stumbling blocks in the way, both of the wise and the unwise. You have served the cause, and increased the number of rebels, deists, atheists; and weakened the hands of those that love and fear God.

"If you were to live a thousand years twice told, you could not undo the mischief which you have done. And until you have done all you can towards it, I bid you Farewell!"

They never met again. When she died in 1781, Wesley was not told of her death for several days nor the place and hour of her funeral. She left him a mourning ring.

The revival had now reached across Britain to an extraordinary extent. The bishops remained aloof, still shackled by the accepted opinions of past years, but the people responded.

The "select societies" of Methodists were small compared with the numbers of those who were influenced. Thus, in the fast-growing town of Manchester the society numbered some sixty persons, but when Wesley formally opened the new chapel on Oldham Street and began the service the next day, Sunday, April 1, 1781, "our country friends flocked in from all sides. At the Communion was such a sight I am persuaded was never seen at

Manchester before: eleven or twelve hundred communicants at once, and all of them fearing God."

Some months later on August 5, 1781 "at the old church in Leeds we had eighteen clergymen and about eleven hundred communicants." Again and again in the 1780s he reported over one thousand at Holy Communion, and when at Birstall "I administered the Sacrament to fifteen or sixteen hundred communicants"; his discrepancy of a hundred more or less was of no account as Wesley marveled at the eagerness of the people.

He was, however, becoming concerned lest the Methodist movement should fade away at his death. Despite growing pressure, he did not want to found a sect; Methodists might be Anglicans in England and Presbyterians in Scotland or Dissenters. "The Methodists alone," he wrote, "do not insist on your holding this or that opinion; but they think and let think. Neither do they impose any particular mode of worship. Here is our glorying; and a glorying peculiar to us; what society shares it with us?" He wanted the distinctive system to continue.

When approaching seventy, Wesley wrote to John Fletcher of Madeley, then forty-four: "What an amazing work has God wrought in these kingdoms in less than forty years! And it not only increases throughout England, Scotland and Ireland; nay, it has spread into New York, Pennsylvania, Virginia, Maryland and Carolina. But the wise men of the world say, 'When Mr. Wesley drops, then all this is at an end! And so it surely will unless, before God calls him hence, one is found to stand in his place.'"

He listed the qualities needed and then wrote: "*Thou art the man!* Come out in the name of God! Come to the help of the Lord against the mighty! Come while I am alive and capable of labor.... Come and strengthen the hands, comfort the heart, and share the labor of—Your affectionate friend and brother."

Fletcher did not feel he should leave his parish, though he was ready to help Charles should John die first. The preachers wanted Fletcher, and before long it was accepted that he was Wesley's designated successor in the event of his death. But as the years passed, Fletcher's health grew worse, forcing him to spend much time in his native Switzerland. He died prior to Wesley.

Another and younger clergyman stood at Wesley's side.

Thomas Coke was a little Welshman with a boyish but handsome face and a pleasing smile. He was energetic and able: while serving as a young curate in Somerset, he was made a Doctor of Civil Laws of Oxford and had already been bailiff or mayor of his native Brecon.

He became a Methodist and was dismissed by his vicar in 1777 at the age of thirty. By the next year he was firmly installed as Wesley's assistant. Being an ordained clergyman, he could officiate at the new chapel on City Road, which had been built (as a church rather than a preaching house) to replace the crumbling Foundery nearby.

The "little Doctor" was soon closely involved with Wesley in problems which would fundamentally influence the future.

When Wesley should die, the ownership and control of the numerous preaching houses and chapels might be disputed. And the annual conference, founded originally to advise him as he decided where to place his preachers, might degenerate into arguments between factions once his overriding personal authority had gone. Moreover, no one knew whether the conference was the master or the servant of Methodists.

While Wesley lived, the issue was scarcely relevant, but in counsel's opinion (obtained by Coke in 1783) the law would not recognize the Methodist Conference in its present state: "consequently there was no central point which might preserve the Connexion from splitting into a thousand pieces after the death of Mr. Wesley."

Wesley was physically fit. As he wrote on his next birthday: "I am as strong at eighty-one as I was at twenty-one; but abundantly more healthy, being a stranger to the head-ache, tooth-ache, and other bodily disorders which attended me in my youth. We can only say, 'The Lord reigneth!' While we live, let us live to him!'" But he could not live forever.

In February 1784 he therefore signed a declaratory deed poll, enrolled in chancery, which invested 100 named preachers as the legal members of "The Conference of the People called Methodists," with authority to carry out its specified business. Coke had wanted all the preachers to be members; Wesley decided to limit the number to what became known as the Legal Hundred. Several who were not selected were offended, and a few severed their links, while Charles Wesley saw with grief that a long step had been taken toward the eventual emergence of a new denomination, whatever his brother's strong personal love for the Church of England.

That same year of 1784 an international problem caused Wesley to take Methodists an even longer step toward the separation (after his death) which he had never intended.

In 1769 Wesley and the conference set apart two lay preachers for the American colonies; their departure involved nothing new, for they were to behave like the itinerant preachers in Britain and not to administer the Sacraments. Two years later a young itinerant from the Midlands, Francis Asbury, volunteered to join them and sailed for Philadelphia. His gifts and tireless dedication eventually made him the head of the American Methodists as general assistant, but he was a layman. Methodism spread rapidly, especially in remote parts without Anglican clergy or Presbyterian ministers. When the colonies declared independence, Asbury prevented the Methodists from breaking their connection with the conference at home.

By 1784, with the United States now a sovereign nation in equal treaty relations with its former mother country, the religious situation was grievous: scores of clergy who had kept their loyalty to King George had migrated to Canada or the West Indies or Britain. The laity wanted the Sacraments and an ordained ministry of teaching and evangelism. Whatever patriot clergy might do to elect their own bishops (having previously been legally in the diocese of London), Wesley became concerned for the spiritual welfare of Americans—those "few sheep in the wilderness," as he somewhat tactlessly called them.

He had slowly formed a plan for an independent Methodist church in America shaped like the Church of England: episcopal, not congregational, in government, though he would not call its leaders "bishops." The liturgy should be Anglican with minor variations. Coke enthusiastically supported this daring scheme.

Wesley had been persuaded by a treatise written by Lord King, Lord Chancellor in the reign of George I, that priests or presbyters belonged to the same order in the church as bishops and that therefore a presbyter might ordain in exceptional circumstances. Wesley had not exercised this power. When Charles suspected that his brother contemplated ordaining for America, he consulted Lord Chief Justice Mansfield, who had known him at Westminster and Christ Church. Lord Mansfield rejected the view of Lord King (who had been born a Presbyterian) and told Charles that "ordination is separation"—if his brother, a presbyter, ordained someone, he would effectively separate himself from the Church of England.

Wesley disagreed. He sketched his plan for the new church, prepared its liturgy, and ordained two elders for America by the laying on of hands. In September 1784 after the annual conference at Bristol, he laid hands on Thomas Coke and gave him a certificate as general superintendent of the Methodists in America.

Charles was horrified. "I can scarcely yet believe it, that in his eighty-second year my brother, my old intimate friend and companion, should have assumed the *epsicopal character*, ordained elders, consecrated a bishop, and sent him to ordain the lay preachers in America! I was then in Bristol, at his elbow; yet he never gave me the least hint of his intention. How was he surprised into so rash an action? He certainly persuaded himself that it was right."

Coke sailed for America and ordained Asbury. Both eventually assumed the title of bishop to Wesley's dismay. In 1788 he wrote to "my dear Franky" Asbury: "I study to be *little*; you study to be *great*. I *creep*; you *strut* along.... Do not seek to be *something*. Let me be nothing, and '*Christ be all in all.*'

"How can you, how dare you, suffer yourselves to be called BISHOP. I shudder, I start at the very thought! Men may call me a knave or a fool; a rascal, a scoundrel, and I am content. But they shall never, by my consent, call me *Bishop!*"

Wesley continued to believe that Methodism should be simply a society of Christians, each loyal to his own church or denomination, meeting together "to fear God and work righteousness."

But he rejoiced in the great spread of the work in America and the West Indies under Coke and Asbury and rejoiced that "the little Doctor" shared his own vision: that if Christians lived holy lives, the heathen would be unable to resist the message of Christ.

"The God of love," declared Wesley prophetically, "will then prepare his messengers and make a way into the polar regions, into the deepest recesses of America, and into the interior parts of Africa; yea, into the heart of China and Japan, with the countries adjoining to them. And 'their sound' will then 'go forth into all lands, and their voice to the ends of the earth.'"

27

The Best-Loved Man in England

In March 1788 Charles Wesley's health gave cause for anxiety. John, traveling westward, urged him to hire a carriage and "go out for at least an hour a day. I would not blame you if it were two or three. Never mind expense; I can make that up. You shall not die to save charges."

As the news worsened, a stream of advice flowed into Charles' Marylebone home, with avuncular letters to the unruly musical nephews and to Sally, the niece who was almost like a daughter to Wesley. He also ordered Sammy Bradburn, in charge at the new chapel, to summon Dr. Whitehead and to make Charles exercise at home on a "wooden horse" if he would not go out, and "I earnestly advise him to be electrified; not shocked, but only filled with electric fire."

Right to the end he urged that Charles could be raised up by prayer, but Charles died on March 29. Owing to a misdirected letter, the sad news reached John in the Midlands too late for him to travel to London for the funeral.

Three weeks later Wesley was leading the service in the Methodist preaching house at Bolton in Lancashire, which had a well-taught choir of nearly a hundred boys and girls "selected from our Sunday schools." Wesley had been touched by their singing of the first hymn. The second was listed as "Come, O Thou Traveler Unknown," Charles Wesley's great hymn on wrestling Jacob; Isaac Watts had said that hymn was "worth all the verses he himself had written," which included "When I Survey the Wondrous Cross."

As Wesley, according to custom, "lined out" the first verse of *Wrestling Jacob*, he reached the words:

> *My company before is gone,*
> *And I am left alone with thee.*

His voice faltered. He burst into tears, sat down in the pulpit, and covered his face with his hands. The congregation wept with him, and instead of song the building was rent by cries. Then he recovered himself and preached and prayed, conducting a service which none would forget.

Wesley himself passed his eighty-fifth birthday in June 1788 with a vigor, except for "some difficulty in reading a small print by candlelight," which was widely remarked upon in an age when the biblical "three score years and ten" was the normal span.

"His step was firm," recalled John Hampson, "and his appearance, till within a few years of his death, vigorous and muscular. His face, for an old man, was one of the finest we have seen. A clear smooth forehead, an aquiline nose, an eye the brightest and most piercing that can be conceived, and a freshness of complexion, scarcely ever to be found at his years, and impressive of the most perfect health, conspired to render him a venerable and interesting figure."

Wesley ascribed his good health and serenity to early rising (helped by an alarm clock which "went off with a thundering noise") and to early prayer followed by the usual preaching at 5 A.M. He loved regular exercise even in old age; he had a level temperament, and "though I am always in haste," he wrote when still in his seventies, "I am never in a hurry; because I never undertake any more work than I can go through with perfect calmness of spirit." He was also much alone, traveling in his chaise, and thus had time for reading, reflection, and more prayer. By his mid-eighties his friends sometimes felt that he preached and wrote too much, but he would not slacken.

He never fussed, for he believed that Providence ruled every event. Now that Wesley's authority was unquestioned and since his great age and fame commanded instant respect, he shed the reserve which he had imposed on himself to help maintain his leadership; the new generation could enjoy the warmhearted Wesley whereas most of his own contemporaries had only glimpsed the warmth displayed in his concern for his preachers' welfare or in little touches such as his habit of using nicknames or diminutives.

His face and manner had a "cheerfulness mingled with gravity," continued Hampson, "a sprightliness which was the natural result of an unusual flow of spirits, and was yet accompanied with every mark of the most serene tranquility.... In dress, he was a pattern of neatness and simplicity. A narrow, plaited stock, a coat with a small upright collar; no buckles at his knees, no silk or velvet in any part of his apparel; and a head as white as snow gave an idea of something primitive and apostolic: While an air of neatness and cleanliness defused over his whole person ... his manner, in private life, was the reverse of cynical or forbidding. It was sprightly and pleasant, to the last degree; and presented a beautiful contrast to the austere deportment of many of his preachers and people, who seemed to have ranked laughter among the mortal sins. It was impossible to be long in his company without partaking his hilarity."

This cheerfulness particularly impressed Alexander Knox of Londonderry, the future theological writer who, at the age of thirty-two in 1789, accompanied Wesley in Ireland. "So fine an old man I never saw!" wrote Knox. "The happiness of his mind beamed forth in his countenance: Every look shewed how fully he enjoyed 'the gay remembrance of a life well spent.'"

"Wherever he went he diffused a portion of his own felicity. Easy and affable in his demeanor, he accommodated himself to every sort of company; and shewed how happily the most finished courtesy may be blended with the most perfect peity. In his conversation we might be at a loss whether to admire most his fine classical taste, his extensive knowledge of men and things, or his overflowing goodness of heart. While the grave and serious were charmed with his wisdom, his sportive sallies of innocent mirth delighted even the young and thoughtless; and both saw in his uninterrupted cheerfulness, the excellency of true religion.... In him even old age appeared delightful, like an evening without a cloud.

He loved telling stories, grave or amusing, from his vast store of memories. His sermons were full of anecdotes which never appeared in print, and when he was in council, if the discussion was not going his way he had a slightly exasperating habit of deflecting it by anecdotes until his counselors conceded his point.

His stories were long remembered. "He was invariably an instructive and edifying guest" is the tradition at Redruth, and while he was always aware of his position and responsibility as a minister of Christ, "the smartness of his conversation and the raciness of his anecdotes would sometimes set the table 'on a roar.'"

The West Country was proof of the change which had been wrought by Methodism. On his way down on one visit in old age, he had attended a service in Exeter Cathedral and was "much pleased" by the reverent congregation and fine music. The bishop of Exeter, John Ross, invited him to dinner at the palace where Bishop Lavington had written his violent pamphlets. Wesley enjoyed the furniture ("not costly nor showy") and the meal ("plain and good but not delicate") and the "genuine, unaffected courtesy of the bishop who will be a blessing to his whole diocese." As they parted the bishop said, "Mr. Wesley, I hope I may sit at your feet in the kingdom of heaven."

On Wesley's last visit to Cornwall in August 1789, he came again to Falmouth, recalling: "The last time I was here, about forty years ago, I was taken prisoner by an immense mob, gaping and roaring like lions: but how is the tide turned! High and low now lined the street from one end of the town to the other, out of stark love and kindness, gaping and staring as if the King were going by. In the evening I preached on the smooth top of the hill, at a small distance from the sea, to the largest congregation I have ever seen in Cornwall, except in or near Redruth…. God moved wonderfully on the hearts of the people, who all seemed to know the day of their visitation."

He preached again in Gwennap Pit: "I suppose for the last time; for my voice cannot now command the still increasing multitude. It was supposed they were now more than five-and-twenty thousand. I think it scarce possible that all should hear." At Port Isaac the whole town seemed to be present. "How changed since the time" when the man who had invited him dared not ask him to stay lest the mob pull down the house. As Wesley left the county on Friday, August 28, 1789, he commented, "So there is a fair prospect in Cornwall, from Launceston to Land's End."

He continued his travels, preaching in chapels, parish churches, and in the open air and examining the Methodist classes. "He would call the name of each of the members," recalled one who was then young, "and they would leave their seat and come before him, and then he would ask them some plain, searching questions and after their answers give them some excellent advice, right to the point, and remarkable for brevity as well as adaptation.... Notwithstanding his great age he was very vigorous, for the moment he had finished his prayer he was off his knees and on his feet."

On Good Friday 1790 he dedicated his last chapel, a large building at Oldham in Lancashire. "The new house would in no wise contain the congregation but I preached to as many as it would contain." In the congregation was a small boy, John Standering, who recalled the scene in his old age: "Mr. Wesley was of small stature, aged and wrinkled and feebled in body, and yet his voice was strong. He wore a three-cornered cocked hat, gown and bands. There was an immense concourse of people. After the sermon, Mr. Wesley requested all the children to sit around the altar, and he passed around, laid his hands upon their heads, and offered a prayer for each child."

He was now beginning to fail. He preached in the open air for the last time on October 6, 1790 beneath an ash tree in the churchyard of Rye in Kent. The next week he preached in a great round meetinghouse at Colchester, one of his favorite towns. In the congregation sat Henry Crabb Robinson, then aged fifteen and afterward well-known as a diarist and literary man. Robinson recalled how Wesley "stood in the wide pulpit, and on each side of him stood a minister, and the two held him up, having their hands under his armpits. His feeble voice was barely audible; but his reverend countenance, especially his long white locks, formed a picture never to be forgotten. There was a vast crowd of lovers and admirers. It was for the most part a pantomime, but the pantomime went to the heart."

At 7 A.M. on Wednesday, February 23, 1791, John Wesley, now aged eighty-seven years and nearly nine months, set out in his two-horse chaise from the house beside the New Chapel on City Road with James Rogers, his faithful assistant, sitting beside him and Richard Summers driving.

A rich London merchant named Belson, whom he hardly knew, had lost his young wife and begged Wesley to come down to give spiritual guidance. Wesley had been ill for a few days but recovered and intended to leave in a week for Bristol and Gloucester and later to the north.

As the chaise crossed Westminister Bridge and took the Worthing road through Tooting and over Epsom downs, James Rogers read to Wesley a new book, the graphic autobiography of an African who had been kidnapped, transported, sold into slavery in Barbados, and then been educated and sent by his master to England, where he was baptized and joined the Royal Navy.

After sixteen miles they reached Kingston House in the country village of Leatherhead at the foot of North Downs. Wesley spent an hour and a half giving private comfort. Belson had meanwhile sent his servants to call in the villagers, who were sent up to the "spacious dining room, set round with fine mahogany chairs and covered with a fine carpet. The plain country people," Rogers noted, "who had come plodding through the mire, seemed rather out of their element; however they all appeared to hear with deep attention" when Wesley preached from Isaiah 55:6, "Seek ye the Lord while he may be found."

This turned out to be Wesley's last sermon. Rogers reflected on the curious fact that despite a vast acquaintance, none of Wesley's friends heard it except himself and Summers, "all the rest being entire strangers."

Wesley spent Wednesday afternoon and night at Mickleham vicarage; he wrote in his shorthand diary for the last time. On the way home next day, they stopped at a little village a few miles south of the Thames to stay with Wesley's dear friend and executor, George Wolff, another prosperous merchant, and his wife—"the lovely family at Balham."

On Thursday Wesley rose at his usual early hour and had Rogers read to him more of the African slave's autobiography. This so stirred him that he dictated a letter to young Wilberforce, in the thick of his Parliamentary fight to abolish the slave trade, to encourage "your glorious enterprise in opposing that execrable villainy which is the scandal of religion, of England, and of human nature.... O be not weary in well doing! Go on, in the name of God and in the power of his might, till even American slavery (the vilest that ever saw the sun) shall vanish away before it."

Wesley had considerable difficulty in holding the pen to sign his name. Rogers was not, however, alarmed until breakfast when

Wesley seemed ill. Rogers and Summers took him home at once with Mrs. Wolff, arriving at City Road about 11 P.M. Elizabeth Ritchie, the woman from the North Country who was now looking after him, was alarmed as she watched him step down from the chaise.

He asked to be left alone for half an hour, and then they brought him mulled wine. He threw it up and they put him to bed.

At first they thought he might recover, but soon John Wesley, who had helped so many to overcome fear of death, lay happily awaiting his departure. He said farewell to each of his "family" and focused calmly on Christ. "He is all, he is all," he murmured, and, "We have boldness to enter into the holiest by the blood of Christ."

By March 1 he was sinking, yet that morning he surprised them by starting to sing a hymn. After one verse he lay back exhausted. A little later he asked for pen and ink, but his fingers would not respond.

"Let me write for you, sir," said Elizabeth Ritchie. "Tell me what you would say."

"Nothing—but that God is with us."

If, as he lay there, Wesley's mind ranged back across his long life, he could reflect that thousands upon thousands had heard from his lips or his pen about Christ, and many had responded. All over the country and overseas his Methodist societies were strengthening Christians in their daily lives. On an even wider scale, he had helped humble believers toward holiness, and he had set in motion a profound change in the moral attitudes of England, although this would not be obvious for another half century.

He may have known, in his heart, that once he died the frigid attitude of the bishops, the ambitions of some of his followers, and the consequence of his own actions would lead Methodists to the separation he deplored. Methodism itself would then suffer splits and gradually come together again with hope of full reunion at last with the church it had left.

But the movement which he and Charles had begun under God was greater than any one church. It would touch every nation upon earth.

That afternoon of Tuesday, March 1, 1791, he decided to get up. While they were preparing his clothes, "he broke out," said Elizabeth, "in a manner which considering his extreme weakness astonished us all, in these blessed words: 'I'll praise my Maker while I've breath.'"

John Wesley sang two verses of Isaac Watts' metrical psalm.

They sat him in a chair, but soon he had to lie down again. He was able at first to speak a little and to pray and to give fervent "Amens" to the prayers of those who knelt at the bedside. Dr. Whitehead; Rogers and his wife and child; Elizabeth Ritchie; and no less than six others, including the two Sally Wesleys, Charles' widow and daughter, crowded into the little room. Once Wesley cried out in a remarkably strong voice, "The best of all is, God is with us!"

During the night he often tried to repeat Watts' psalm but could only get out, "I'll praise—I'll praise—." By Wednesday morning, March 2, 1791, the end was plainly near, "and the last word he was heard to articulate," recorded Elizabeth, "was, 'Farewell!'"

He died about 10 o'clock "without a struggle or a groan." As family and friends knelt round the bed, their loss was swallowed up by "the ineffable sweetness that filled our hearts as our beloved Pastor, Father and Friend entered his Master's joy."

They laid him in state in the City Road Chapel in an open coffin, a trace of a smile on his face. Ten thousand people (by contemporary estimate) filed by. The funeral was set for Wednesday, March 9. According to a letter written three days later by Ann ("Nancy") Bolton, one of the intimate correspondents and friends in Wesley's old age who had hurried from Witney on news of his death, his executors became worried lest a tumult of mourners should press toward the vault behind the chapel at the moment of burial. "It was agreed very late that night," wrote Nancy, "that he should be interred *early* next morning, on account of the alarming *number* thronging in. A most solemn season it was; about 20 couples (or less perhaps) of preachers, executors, etc., with Mrs. Moore, Mrs. Bradford, Miss Ritchie and myself attended the grave.... I afterwards took a very serious breakfast at Mr. Jones".

"At 10 we went to the Chapel in procession amidst such a crowd I never was witness to, though great peace and quietness by their being warded off by a vast number of constables. A most blessed sermon Doctor Whitehead preached from 2nd Samuel, 3rd chapter, 'Know ye not that a prince and a great man is fallen in Israel this day?' "

Memorial services were held in countless cities and villages throughout Great Britain and Ireland, and the presses poured out sermons and articles. In the flood of print perhaps a secular journal, which had often scorned or criticized, put John Wesley in the clearest perspective.

"Where much good is done," wrote *The Gentleman's Magazine* in a long obituary, "we should not mark every little excess. The great point in which his name and mission will be honored is this: he directed his labors towards those who had no instructor; to the highways and hedges; to the miners in Cornwall and the colliers in Kingswood.... By the humane and active endeavors of him and his brother Charles, a sense of decency, morals, and religion was introduced into the lowest classes of mankind; the ignorant were instructed; the wretched relieved; and the abandoned reclaimed....

"Though his taste was classic, and his manners elegant, he sacrificed that society in which he was particularly calculated to shine; gave up those preferments which his abilities must have obtained, and devoted a long life in practicing and enforcing the plainest duties. Instead of being 'an ornament to literature,' he was a blessing to his fellow creatures; instead of 'the genius of the age,' he was the servant of God!"

Notes

Chapter One: Plucked from the Burning

1. The name was often spelled "Westley" and plainly was pronounced with the emphasis on the first syllable. The family had originated from Westleigh, a hamlet in east Devon near Wellington, which lies just in Somerset. The ancestors of the Great Duke of Wellington, who was born Arthur Wesley, sprang from the same hamlet, but no blood connection has been proved, despite the nineteenth-century legends.

Chapter Three: The Red Notebook

1. Nehemiah Curnock, in the first volume of his *Standard Edition of Wesley's Journals* (1909), wrongly supposed "Varanese" to be Betty Kirkham, not her elder sister Sally. Other writers followed Curnock, but the discovery of a manuscript diary kept by Benjamin Ingham, which contained a key to the Wesley cipher, enabled Dr. Richard P. Heitzenrater to decipher Wesley's extant manuscript Oxford Diaries for his unpublished thesis "The Oxford Methodists" in 1972. All books published previously are inaccurate.

2. It was Dean Stanhope of Canterbury's paraphrase of à Kempis which, twenty-three years later, awakened the young slave trader John Newton, to become the famous hymn writer, preacher, and abolitionist. See the present writer's *Amazing Grace: John Newton's Story*.

Chapter Five: "Our Little Society"

1. The old packhorse trails in the Lake District and on Exmoor give some idea of early eighteenth-century roads.

2. The ellipses shown here in the letter represent six words clipped from the

original manuscript, now in the Public Library, Melbourne, Australia. See *The Works of John Wesley*, volume 25 (edited by Frank Baker, 1980), p. 346.

Chapter Seven: Oxford Deserted

1. I have told his story in *George Whitefield* (1972). In this book on Wesley I can only touch upon Whitefield's early life.

2. Queen Caroline was fifty-two in 1735, had been seriously ill the previous year, and would die two years later; Wesley may have embroidered the story.

Chapter Ten: Strangely Warmed

1. The identification of the exact location and the friend who took him have been disputed, but the best evidence suggests Nettleton Court and Hutton.

2. It is possible that the hymn he wrote on this occasion was the better known "And Can It Be that I Should Gain," but scholars consider that this was written a little later.

Chapter Eleven: Outcasts of Men

1. The precise location has never been determined.

Chapter Thirteen: Signs and Wonders

1. In his cipher diary written that day (June 14, 1739), Wesley put it at 15,000. In his published *Journal* (1740) he reduced this to "12 or 14,000." He had no way of accurately counting and almost certainly exaggerated. Later he would reckon that five persons could stand in a square yard. He estimated the size of the area and multiplied accordingly.

Chapter Fourteen: "A Horrid Thing, a Very Horrid Thing"

1. Stebbing was a royal chaplain and well-known writer who published in the summer of 1739 "A Caution against Religious Delusion. A Sermon on the New Birth: Occasioned by the Pretensions of the Methodists."

Chapter Sixteen: Whitefield Reconciled

1. The date of the letter given in Whitefield's *Works* I, p. 331, is October 10, but this must be a misreading of the manuscript, now lost.

Chapter Eighteen: "All Round England"

1. The manuscript of this letter of August 28, 1744 lies appropriately in the archives of their old school at Charterhouse, Godalming.

2. Actually "O For a Thousand Tongues to Sing" is the first line of the seventh verse of Charles Wesley's eighteen-verse hymn titled "For the Anniversary Day of One's Conversion." Modern hymn books generally print only verses seven to twelve.

Chapter Nineteen: "Crucify Him!"

1. Wesley saw George II only once at close quarters, in December 1755, when invited by a peer to attend the opening of Parliament. He wrote with some wry amusement: "I was in the robe-chamber adjoining to the House of Lords when the King put on his robes. His brow was much furrowed with age, and quite clouded with care. And is this all the world can give even to a king? A blanket of ermine round his shoulders, so heavy and cumbersome he can scarce move under it! A huge heap of borrowed hair, with a few plates of gold and glittering stones upon his head! Alas, what a bauble is human greatness! And even this will not endure."

Chapter Twenty: Cornwall

1. In the nineteenth century, Gwennap Pit was restored, on a smaller scale, as a memorial to Wesley and the early Cornish Methodists.

Chapter Twenty-four: The Chimney Sweeper

1. One of Toplady's cherished beliefs was that the entire animal creation went to heaven. He was cross when John Newton, the ex-sailor, expressed a fervent hope that there would be no fleas in heaven!

Chapter Twenty-five: The Cry of the Poor and the Slaves

1. The title page of the first edition of Newton's autobiography reads: "An Authentic Narration of Some Remarkable and Interesting Particulars in the Life of * * *, Communicated in a Series of Letters to the Rev. T. Haweis." Newton's name appeared in later editions.

2. See the present writer's *Wilberforce* (1977) and *Amazing Grace: John Newton's Story* (1981).

3. When Patty brought Wesley to dinner with Dr. Johnson (Dec. 18, 1783), and Wesley left after two hours, the doctor complained to her: "Two hours! I could talk all day, and all night too, with your brother." And to Boswell he said, "The dog enchants you with his conversation and then breaks away to go and visit some old woman!"

Two Timeless Books in One

Newton
The Liberator

JOHN POLLOCK

KINGSWAY PUBLICATIONS
EASTBOURNE

First published by Hodder & Stoughton 1981
Published in the USA by Harper & Row 1982
Published by Lion 1996
Published by Kingsway 2000
This 2-in-1 edition 2008

Cover design: PinnacleCreative.co.uk
Front cover photo © Marty141 | Dreamstime.com

ISBN 978 1 84291 387 1

Published by
KINGSWAY COMMUNICATIONS LTD
26-28 Lottbridge Drove, Eastbourne BN23 6NT, UK
books@kingsway.co.uk

Printed in Great Britain

For T.W. and Grady

Acknowledgments

Fuller details were given in the first edition, published as *Amazing Grace: The Life of John Newton*, but I would like to express again my thanks to the following for permission to use copyright material: the late Miss Catherine Bull; the Cowper-Newton Museum at Olney; Ridley Hall, Cambridge; Dr William's Library, London.

I am grateful also to the Revd Francis Dufton, the Revd Robin Leaver, the Revd John M. Preston, Dr John Wesley White, and Mrs J. E. Williams who typed my manuscript with her usual skill; also the staff of the London Library and the National Maritime Museum.

Finally I would like to mention my late father-in-law, Sir Richard Barrett-Lennard, Bt., who gave me much encouragement but died before publication. Newton's boyhood home in Essex was a tenant farm on the Belhus Estate of Sir Richard's ancestors. He lived at Belhus himself before the Second World War, and this makes a pleasant link between subject and author.

John Pollock, 2000

Amazing grace (how sweet the sound)
   That saved a wretch like me!
I once was lost, but now am found,
   Was blind, but now I see.

'Twas grace that taught my heart to fear,
   And grace my fears relieved.
How precious did that grace appear,
   The hour I first believed.

Through many dangers, toils and snares,
   I have already come;
'Tis grace hath brought me safe thus far,
   And grace will lead me home.

Contents

Prologue

Amazing grace, how sweet the sound ... The great hymn was not yet written or even in his mind, early that wild autumn evening. A strong wind was rising to a gale. John Newton struggled in the fading winter daylight from his parish church of Olney in the English Midlands towards his vicarage. He turned up the short drive, pushed open the door and threw off his cloak and sea captain's jacket.

Pausing at the parlour to blow a kiss to his dearest Polly he hurried into his study. The mid-week prayer meeting must start within a few hours at the Great House and he had not yet written a new hymn. Each week he liked to introduce a fresh one, set to a familiar tune. Some, he knew, were mere jingles of praise or teaching, but others were being sung up and down the land, in these years of the 1770s.

The little study was warm. Polly always made sure that the maid lit a fire early; Newton poked it, threw on more logs and settled at his desk. Rain beat on the windows and the wind rattled the glass as he turned the pages of his wellworn Bible, looking for a theme. He had been reading the story of King David and took it up where God promises to establish the House of David for ever;

and David, overwhelmed, turns to prayer. Newton's eye lighted on the words: 'Who am I, O Lord God, and what is my house, that thou hast brought me hitherto?'

Who am I? David, the poor shepherd boy, the exile, had become a mighty king; David the sinner had been forgiven and from his line would be born Jesus the Saviour of the world. And John Newton held the overwhelming privilege of preaching this Jesus among the people. But, *Who am I?* Who am *I?* Newton the exile, the servant of slaves; Newton the rebel and atheist, the proud, violent blasphemer.

The gale rose higher. He could hear the roar as it shook the trees in the garden. He could feel the wind which found a way through the window and under the door. Newton shivered. He moved to the easy chair near the fire, and mentally pursued the theme of the wonder of God's grace which had saved a wretch like him. He looked back at the amazing coincidences which had played their part. He recalled as equally amazing his love for a girl he could hardly expect to win, which had burned unquenched through his misfortunes and his fornications.

He closed his eyes. The howl of the wind, the splash of the rain could not fail to remind him of another gale, far out to sea in the North Atlantic, when he was a young man of twenty-two, the storm on which his entire life hinged. His mind began to recapture the memory, his heart to swell in gratitude. His ears grew deaf, his head nodded. Imperceptibly he slipped into a vivid cat-nap dream, reliving that dreadful moment when a great sea shook the *Greyhound* from stem to stern, in the early hours of 10 March 1748, and water began to flood the cabin and he heard a cry, 'We are sinking!'

'*We are sinking!*' Young Newton leapt from his bunk and without pausing to pull on thicker garments against the cold he rushed towards the companion hatch to give help on deck. The captain called down for a knife. As Newton ran back to fetch it another of the ship's company dashed up the companion ladder, and was swept overboard by a wave.

Newton found the knife and came on deck. He judged at once, from his years of experience in the merchant marine and the navy, that the ship might sink at any moment. A wave had torn away the upper timbers on one side so that she filled fast. The hull was weak after eighteen months in the tropics, and the *Greyhound* would have sunk already had she been carrying a Slave Trade cargo.

The ship tossed and rolled. Newton struggled in the darkness to one of the pumps and joined another man pumping hard, while others bailed with buckets, or tore up clothes to help staunch the leaks. When day broke and they found themselves still alive, Newton called out cheerfully above the wind as he pumped, 'In a few days this distress will serve us to talk of, over a glass of wine!'

'No!' said his mate. His tone was grave. 'It's too late now.' He was preparing to die.

Newton laughed. Hour after hour he worked at the pumps, his teeth chattering with cold despite the exertion, his strength weakening as their efforts seemed hardly to postpone the *Greyhound*'s almost inevitable foundering. At about nine, famished and exhausted as they all were, he stopped pumping, moved across deck and urged upon the captain a possible course of action.

The captain agreed. Newton turned his back towards the pumps. Spontaneously he said: 'If this will not do, the Lord have mercy on us!'

The captain was astonished to overhear such a sentiment on the lips of John Newton, this youth with scars of a naval flogging on his back, and of slave chains on his ankles, and a tongue so acid in its blasphemies that it shocked hardbitten mariners. The captain had taken him from a remote West African shore in obedience to strict instructions from England, having found him by an amazing coincidence and overborne his reluctance to come home. The captain had long wished he had never set eyes on the fellow – and now he was calling on the Lord!

Newton himself suddenly realized that he had uttered a prayer. At once he thought: 'What mercy can there be for me? What mercy for *me*? What –'

A log fell from the grate. The Reverend John Newton woke from his cat-nap with a start. The vivid dream about that dreadful day, long ago, lay strong in his newly-awake mind, with the memory of that unpremeditated prayer which he had spoken above the wind and the rush of water and the creaking of the pumps.

He could only wonder afresh at the amazing grace of God.

The way to a strong faith had been slow, hard, and was packed with adventures as the years before; but that moment on 10 March 1748 as he faced death by drowning in the North Atlantic had begun the process which had transformed him from a libertine and atheist.

Newton rose from his chair by the fire and sat at his desk. He had his hymn for the prayer meeting. Dipping his quill he wrote in his small, neat hand the first verse:

> *Amazing grace (how sweet the sound)*
> *That saved a wretch like me!*
> *I once was lost, but now am found,*
> *Was blind, but now I see.*

*   *   *

The exact circumstances of the writing of *Amazing Grace* have never been discovered; if Newton told anyone, the conversation was not noted down or the letter is lost. The only clue is the verse of Scripture with which he introduced it in *Olney Hymns*. Therefore the above account is no more than reasonable conjecture.

Of the facts behind the hymn there can be no doubt. What follows in this book may be extraordinary but it is true – the story of 'a wretch', a prodigal son, lost and 'blind', who was saved by amazing grace to become one of the best loved hymn writers of the Christian church, a preacher, evangelist and author who left his mark on his age, the one-time slaver who helped to destroy the Slave Trade.

Part One

A WRETCH LIKE ME

1

The Captain's Boy

The White Tower of the Tower of London shimmered in the sun. Tall masts and spars filled London Pool, little boats darted back and forth between the shipping. The whole scene was alive with the sights and sounds of England's commerce and pride.

Watching it from the quarter deck of a merchantman, one spring day of 1732, stood a small boy of six: John, only child of Captain John Newton, master of a vessel preparing for another Mediterranean voyage. Captain Newton liked to take his son on board whenever he checked the loading of cargo or the repairing of sails and tackle; then they would be rowed back to Wapping Stairs whence the captain, with self-conscious dignity, walked the few hundred yards home, with John following in tense silence a pace or two behind.

John lived almost in terror whenever his father returned from a voyage, for the Captain showed himself as strict a disciplinarian to his small family in their neat house in Wapping as he did to his crew. John must jump to orders like a cabin boy, stand until told to sit, keep silent unless addressed. Laughter in the presence of the Captain was insubordination unless the sea dog laughed first. He never displayed affection for his son although later on he would prove his love again and again when John's misdeeds might have forfeited it for ever.

The Captain was a curious mixture. Educated by Jesuits in Spain, where his father had gone out as a merchant or a master mariner, he remained a Protestant of strict principles, if without open religious feelings, but his habits and gait carried a flavour of Don Quixote: he walked as if he were a hidalgo with a hundred quarterings and a vast estate, instead of a quarter-deck and a small house, where the neighbours, mostly sea officer families and small merchants, thought him rather ridiculous. Yet he was a sound seaman, highly regarded by shipowners and his fellow captains.

John's mother, Elizabeth Newton, came from a Dissenter family, and her character was such a contrast to her husband's that it must have been a surprising match. She mixed little with the neighbours, she was deeply religious, and she disliked the expeditions to the anchored shipping which took her boy away from her eye. She dreaded lest his sharp memory retain sailor oaths or bawdy sailor songs, or that he catch a glimpse of a half-dead pirate hanging in chains from the gallows on Wapping mudbank, where three full tides must wash over a corpse before burial. She was more relieved than sad when the Captain once again bade a formal farewell and strutted down the street to disappear for months on another voyage.

She could then indulge her greatest delight: educating John. She lay coughing on a couch, a Spanish shawl clutched about her and a book in her hand, hearing him recite improving rhymes and the answers to Isaac Watts' catechisms for the young. John learned the multiplication table and the rudiments of Latin, which she had taught herself first, and developed a neat handwriting by copying hers.

This life appealed to John more than running around with other boys. His mother remained the only friend he wanted. For much of a year the reminders of his father were their trinkets from Spain and Venice and the Levant, and a shadowy dread of his return, but she was his to enjoy: her brown hair tied neatly under her cap, the pallid face heightened by glistening red cheeks which were the sign of the 'consumption' (tuberculosis) which was soon to carry her off. She had a merry laugh but jokes were private to themselves: the world knew her as grave, and quietly pious.

Every Sunday Mrs. Newton and John walked the short distance up the street to Prince's Square off the Radcliffe Highway, to the Dissenting chapel of Dr. David Jennings. His long prayers and sermons droned over the head of a small boy, yet the services left an indelible impression because Jennings had introduced the new hymns of Isaac Watts, whose own chapel stood a mile off within the City. The two pastors were friends and the puny head of the sickly, cheerful Watts sometimes peered over the Radcliffe Square pulpit. Whereas the parish church, where the Captain sometimes took John, sang nothing but metrical psalms, line by line after the parish clerk, the chapel sang Watts' hymns in chorus like sailors' shanties; a new concept in English hymn-singing and thrilling to a musical boy. One of Watts' hymns was famous already: *When I survey the wondrous cross*. They sang the second line as Watts originally wrote it: 'Where the young Prince of Glory died.' John sang with fervour in his high treble, right to the last line in which the young Prince of Glory 'shall have my life, my soul, my all.'

As mother and son walked home after chapel on Sunday mornings they could glimpse the shipping on the Thames. Those Sunday walks, up and back along the street, seemed to symbolize the two pulls on John's boyhood: to the pulpit, to the quarter-deck. His father planned that he should follow the family tradition and enter the Mediterranean trade, his mother that he go up to St. Andrews University in Scotland, with which David Jennings had links, and then enrol in his academy for preachers: the sea should not have her Jack.

The summer of 1732 put an end to such dreams. Elizabeth Newton's influence on her son had filtered deeper into his soul than he could realize. She had taught him that God had revealed His truth in the Bible, which must neither be doubted nor disobeyed, and that after death comes judgement. She had given him an ideal of purity and devotion which he might forget and betray but would never escape. Had she lived he might have learned her secret early in his career. Instead, though she was barely thirty years old, her cough grew worse, her face more pale and her eyes unnaturally bright.

A distant cousin and school friend, Elizabeth Churchill, who was married to a customs officer in Chatham called George Catlett, came on a visit and persuaded her to try the purer air of Kent. They boarded out John with a neighbour, under Dr. Jennings' kindly eye, and he last saw his mother enter a hackney carriage which took her and Mrs. Catlett across London Bridge, still with its houses, to their seats on the Chatham coach.

He expected her to return for his seventh birthday on 24 July 1725, but by then she was dead. They had left him behind to save him from watching her die. This was a disastrous decision. Had he gone to Chatham, and after his mother's death stayed with the Catletts for a while at least, he would have known 'Polly', their eldest child Mary, as a plump infant of three years old, becoming her adopted brother; instead, he first met her ten years later and fell hopelessly in love at an impossible time.

His life might have shaped differently, and dreams not turn to nightmares before they came true beyond all imagining.

*   *   *

Months, years could pass without news of a mariner. With his father possibly shipwrecked and drowned, or enslaved by Barbary pirates, John felt an orphan already, with no dear confidant, no pilot, no landmark at which to steer. He resolved to honour his mother's memory by growing up to be a preacher, but the young Prince of Glory seemed as remote as a planet in the sky; nor did the name of Jesus sound sweet in John Newton's ear. Then the sea blood stirred in his veins and he vowed he would sail with his father. Drifting mentally this way and that he continued through autumn and winter until the cessation of Atlantic storms allowed the Mediterranean ships to bring back their cargoes of spices and silks.

Captain Newton walked up Wapping Stairs one day in the spring of 1733 and discovered the door of his home locked and hung with faded crêpe, and his black-suited son in a house nearby. The Captain showed no emotion nor allowed his son to weep. Instead he found him a step-mother by promptly marrying again.

His bride's surname is not known (nor is that of John's mother) but she bore the unusual Christian name of Thomasin and came from Essex. The Newtons loaded their household goods on a waggon and journeyed down the Tilbury road to the parish of Aveley. Here, on a farm looking down the marshes to the Thames and the low Kentish hills beyond, they made their home with Thomasin's father, a substantial tenant grazier, who could look after them when the Captain returned to the sea.

Until the age of eleven, John Newton now suffered the fate of the unloved stepson, compounded by miserably unhappy terms away at a private school on the Essex-Middlesex border. Its headmaster was a tyrant of the cane and birch-rod. He turned John from a child who had learned much at his mother's knee into a boy who knew little except how to take a beating, until, in John's second year, a new young usher noticed that he was not the idiot he seemed, and aroused his enthusiasm for Latin. He reached the top of the class, but the usher pushed too fast and John forgot most of his Latin as soon as he left the school. His memory of the school was horrible but probably it taught him more than he allowed, for he could write a good hand, read a well argued book and, as he grew older, master the mathematics required in a sea officer.

His father, when at home during John's holidays, kept him in fear and bondage, breaking his spirit. And stopped his formal education too soon: on his eleventh birthday, 24 July 1736, John Newton boarded his father's ship at Long Reach, where the Thames runs close to Aveley, and sailed for the Mediterranean on the first of five voyages which, in the next six years, gave him a solid grounding in seamanship but no love for his father. The Captain cushioned him from the crew yet imposed a sterner discipline on his son than on a cabin boy, hardening his body and roughening his character.

Back home in Essex – for the Captain did not take his son on every voyage but left him ashore for months at a time – the young Newton ran wild with the village lads, for he was full of fun when left to himself. His half-brother William, baptized at Aveley parish church on 8 September 1736, absorbed the affections of step-mother and of the old grazier, and neither of them cared what he did away from the farmhouse. Sailor oaths and stories picked up when out of his father's eye gave him leadership in all kinds of mischief such as poaching: the great house at Aveley, an exquisite red brick mansion called Belhus, stood empty and in bad repair because the young landowner, Thomas Barrett-Lennard, afterwards Lord Dacre, lived elsewhere with an aunt. The deer in his park were targets for risky adventures; detection would lead at the very least to a sound thrashing from a gamekeeper.

These years of puberty, when Newton was neither a country boy nor a seaman but a little of both, fell into a curious oscillating pattern. Two incidents stand out.

He had free use of his step-grandfather's horses when not required and he loved to whip up speed. One day as he cantered along a lane he noticed with the corner of his eye that the hedgerows had been layered, leaving large jagged spikes of brushwood to tear out an eye or pierce a brain. At that moment the horse stumbled and threw him and he missed a spike by inches. Unhurt, he was shaken to realize that had he been thrown half a degree differently the spike would have impaled and, quite probably, projected him without warning Before Jehovah's Awful Throne, as Dr. Watts put it in The Old Hundredth. Memories flooded back: the hymn singing in chapel; the teaching of his mother, now canonized as a saint in Newton's mind; the devout intentions long since forgotten; the old certainties of heaven and hell and judgement.

He stopped swearing, kept away from rowdy youths, read religious books which he had found among his mother's belongings, and said his prayers. No one guided him between truth and error, and his new piety puffed his contempt for the earth-bound household at Aveley and the mumbling vicar. After two or three months, however, the old urges gradually pushed out the piety and he ran wild again.

The second incident had more lasting effect.

A man-of-war lay anchored in Long Reach. A waterman had promised Newton and other boys to row them out on the Sunday afternoon, for in addition to admiring the guns and holy-stoned decks, and the paintwork and rigging kept smarter than any merchantman's, a young sea dog of the merchant service could gloat over the wretched Jack Tars who lived under the rattan, the rope's end and the cat. Excited all morning, chaffing at the length of the sermon and then at the old grazier slowly eating his roast, Newton left the table at last to run and walk the two or three miles to Purfleet jetty. He arrived too late. He fumed to see the boatload of visitors, his best friend among them, nearing the man-of-war. Suddenly the boat hit an underwater hazard and turned turtle. His friend and several others drowned before his eyes.

At the funeral a chastened John Newton repented once again, this time upholding his religion for two full years of asceticism, whether on shore or at sea; yet he would still join escapades, easing his conscience by gabbling prayers in the belief that these would balance naughtiness when weighed Before Jehovah's Awful Throne.

Village lads and shipmates alike rated him peculiar, and when his father put him as a pupil with an English merchant at Alicante in Spain, and sailed away from the landlocked bay to the east, the man soon did not know what to make of a lad who daydreamed at his ledger desk and resented attempts to teach him trade; who had a merry smile and got into mischief, yet rose early to read devotional books. The merchant handed him back on the Captain's return voyage.

2

Polly

A landscape of brick houses stretched back from the quayside – the Dutch port of Middleburg, an unlikely place to alter the direction of John Newton's life.

He went ashore from his father's ship, a dreamy youth of nearly seventeen with no close friends or particular ambition except to avoid the displeasure of the captain who also was his parent. He wandered up a street where every shop had it sign which creaked above the heads of the passers by. He looked vaguely at the goods displayed, heard the apprentices shout their wares in a strange tongue, stepped into the gutter to avoid a fat burgher and, on impulse, entered a shop which sold odds and ends and books. His eye caught a title in English.

It was the second volume of the celebrated *Characteristics* by the philosopher Earl of Shaftesbury, written some thirty years before. The heading of one of the two treatises within intrigued John Newton: *The Moralists: A Philosophical Rhapsody*. He bought the book, began to read, and was at once absorbed in the argument.

They crossed the Channel after unloading their Levantine cargo and sailed up the Thames. They paid off and the Newtons rode into Essex. During long lazy hours at Aveley in the summer of 1742 John read and re-read *A Philosophical Rhapsody*, holding the book close to his face as he was short-sighted, until he almost knew by heart this charming conversation-piece. He thought it most religious because the characters spoke often of God, though never of Christ and His cross; this Lord Shaftesbury had been an early Deist, of the kind that became common in the half century following his death in 1713.

Shaftesbury's words insinuated into John Newton as he stood on the verge of manhood the idea that he must forget his dead mother's gentle insistence that goodness and wisdom grew best from obedience to God's truth revealed in the Bible. To Shaftesbury, as Newton understood him at the time, Truth was no more than an opinion and every man must form his own. If he wished to become a truly moral man he must put away childish dependence on sacred writ and cultivate virtue by following the dictates of heart and mind wherever they led.

All this put Dr. Watts' hymns out of tune, for if Shaftesbury were right, the Young Prince of Glory could be no more than a long dead moralist, a philosopher of a distant age. Years later, when John Newton, in more senses than one, had come home after his incredible adventures, he said that Shaftesbury's book had operated like a slow poison and had prepared the way for all that followed.

Certainly if Newton had not taken Shaftesbury's advice that summer, to follow the dictates of his own heart wherever they should lead, he would not have become embroiled in a chain of events the following winter, which, starting on 12 December 1742, set in motion one of the eighteenth century's most extraordinary sagas.

It began with a coincidence, the first of many which mark Newton's story.

His father, after the voyage which touched Middleburg, had retired from the sea, taken a responsible shore post with the Royal Africa Company and bought a house in London. He placed John as third mate under another Mediterranean captain, who reported on their return that this dreamy lad would never make a sailor worthy of the Newton name. Thereupon Captain Newton wrote to a Liverpool shipowner, a close friend named Joseph Manesty who had interests in slaves and sugar in Jamaica. On opening the reply the Captain summoned his son to hear good news: Manesty promised to make John's fortune; he should go to a Jamaican plantation as an overseer of slaves, with the prospect of being a planter before he was thirty. If he showed himself shrewd, hard and laborious he might return one day from the island to buy a fine estate and enter Parliament.

John liked the prospect. He would be waited on by slaves and wield power while retaining his dream world: Shaftesbury's characters in *A Rhapsody* might have been planters, for they never soiled their hands with manual labour. Newton gladly bought all he needed for a voyage to the tropics.

A few days before he was due to board the coach to Liverpool to take ship for Jamaica a letter, a rare event in itself, reached him in London. He did not recognize the hand but on breaking the seal he recognized the name from a long distant past: Elizabeth Catlett, his mother's dearest friend in whose house she had died. Mrs. Catlett had not approved Captain Newton's hasty remarriage and the two families had severed relations, but no doubt she had promised her dying friend to remember her son, since the two of them had lightly plotted that Elizabeth

Newton's John should grow up to marry Elizabeth Catlett's Mary ('Polly') who was now nearly fourteen. Mrs. Catlett's letter enquired after John's welfare and invited him to stay should ever he be near Chatham.

She had waited ten years to write. With no knowledge of his plans she had chosen the moment when he was to disappear for prolonged absence overseas. Even more of a coincidence, her invitation reached him when he was about to ride into her part of Kent, for his father had ordered him to do some small business near Maidstone. The Catletts lived half a mile off his road.

The Captain granted him leave to call on the Catletts. Yet when John reached the turn on his homeward journey on 12 December 1742 he felt indifferent, and only the prospect of a hot meal by the fire determined him to dismount at their door. He blew on his fingers and wrapped his cloak tighter in the bitter cold as he waited an answer to his knock, and looked around at a solid, not stately home, suitable to a customs officer's station in life, and the neat frostbound garden.

The door was opened, not by a serving maid but by a girl of the house, whom he knew must be Polly. Her mother, coming up behind, ran forward before he could announce himself and kissed her old friend's features which she saw in his face. She pulled him inside, gave orders for his horse to be stabled and fed, and at once made John feel at home. She told him to call her and Catlett 'uncle' and 'aunt' and to stay as long as he liked.

The family crowded round and he felt he had known them all his life. The younger daughter Elizabeth and eleven year old John treated him as a big brother who had seen the world; Sarah, aged four, and Susanna, aged two, looked on with wide eyes; George was a baby in his cradle.

Newton quickly became aware, in a very special way, of Polly. She seemed different from any girl he had met. Bashful, well grown, with a dimple and a smile, her kindness and simplicity drew him until only good breeding stopped him calling her, then and there, 'My dearest sweetest dear Polly.' She was not a great beauty. She was less intelligent than he, wrote an awkward rounded hand and could not spell. She sang sweetly and had an ear for verses; her mother and the nearby school for young ladies had taught her deportment, dancing and the household arts, and she could command the obedience and affection of the younger Catletts. Innocence and purity were self-evident, but she enjoyed a frolic and laughter. None of this explains why Newton, at seventeen, should have fallen head over heels in love within a few hours of setting eyes on Polly Catlett.

He had never been in love and did not know what afflicted him, why he was restless in her absence, tongue-tied and confused in her company. That night he hardly slept for thinking of her. Next morning he scarcely dared a glance.

Polly was unaware that she had captured this gawky sailor, that he was her prize, ready to haul down his colours and lay them at her feet as the fair captain of his destiny. Newton could not declare his love, being almost penniless and a mere youth, yet he longed to know whether she returned it. He swore to himself he would make a fortune to throw at her feet, yet he could not bear to leave her for the other side of the globe. Three days passed like a dream. A fourth went by and still Newton stayed, and the Catletts, unaware that he was bound for Jamaica, did not hurry him to saddle his horse. Love-crazed, he lingered until the West India ship must have sailed: his heart had dictated that the Atlantic should not sever him from Polly.

Thus Christmas passed at Chatham gaily; in London, his father and John's stepmother were miserable with anxiety lest he had been murdered by a highwayman or, more likely, taken by the Navy's press gang, the terror of every merchant sailor ashore. The days ticked by in silence, for John did not dare write the real reason for his absence and could not bear to concoct a false one.

He rode home after three weeks. The Captain received him in anger, but forgave quickly, having secretly regretted that his son would have left the sea. For punishment, he must sail a voyage as a common sailor. John thought it a small price for the hope of seeing Polly again within the year.

This voyage to the Levant did much to drive away his dreamy idleness. He learned to step lively to avoid punishment, to haul on the capstan singing the shanties, to eat hardtack instead of the captain's bread. He smoked a clay pipe, swore with the best, swapped bawdy stories. In the tumble of the fo'c'sle he lost his resolve to pursue virtue in the manner of Shaftesbury; even the shadowy Deity who had displaced the crucified Prince of Glory seemed more a figment of imagination. Serving before the mast stripped from John Newton most of his innocence.

He still remained a virgin. At the age of eighteen he rated fornication the ultimate profligacy, so he did not follow his friends into brothels.

And Polly held his heart. He dared to claim in middle age that none of the scenes of misery and wickedness he afterwards knew had banished her for a single hour from his thoughts. 'How wonderful,' he mused, 'that when we were both so young, an impression should be made on my mind, almost at first sight, which neither distance nor absence, nor all my sufferings, nor even all the licentiousness and folly I afterwards ran into, could obliterate!'

3

The Lost Ring

The glories of Venice, where the ship had spent several days taking in cargo, had slipped below the horizon before dusk. Young Newton, who now was homeward bound, swung his hammock and fell asleep with delicious thoughts of Polly.

He dreamed not of Polly but of Venice. He was back in the harbour at night, on watch, pacing the deck alone. A stranger appeared, in his hand a ring which glinted in the moonlight, suggesting a valuable stone. He gave the ring to Newton.

'Preserve it carefully,' said the stranger. 'While you do so, you will be happy and successful. If you lose it or part with it, you must expect nothing but trouble and misery.'

Newton slipped the ring on to his finger with expressions of gratitude. The stranger disappeared as suddenly as he had come and Newton resumed his pacing, not in the least doubting that he could preserve the ring, and glad to have future happiness in his own keeping.

A second stranger materialized. He commented on the ring, but when Newton told him its secret power, the man laughed, ridiculing such a simple belief. 'The thing is impossible,' he said, and went on to prove it by logic. 'Throw the ring away!' he urged.

Shocked, Newton argued back, until the other's blend of mockery and reasoning induced doubt. Doubt grew into certainty, mixed with shame that he had believed the first stranger's promise, until Newton impulsively pulled the ring from his finger. He dropped it over the side.

Fire burst from the distant mountains – vivid, horrifying, a judgement on his folly. The tempter, in tones of disgust, then said: 'All the mercy God had in store for you was comprised in that ring which you have wilfully thrown away. Now you must go to the burning mountain. These flames have been kindled for you!'

John Newton stood tongue-tied with terror, waiting without plea or hope to be marched to his fate. But a third person (or it might have been the ring's donor) approached him and asked why he shook in fear. Newton confessed and the dream-figure reprimanded him, then asked: 'Do you think you will be wiser if you have the ring again?'

Before Newton could answer the man jumped into the water and recovered it. As he climbed on board again the flames in the mountains went out, the tempter fled, and in joy and thanks Newton stretched out his hand for the ring.

The man withheld it. He said: 'If you were entrusted with this ring again you would very soon bring yourself into the same distress. You are unable to keep it! But I will preserve it for you. And whenever it is needed I will produce it on your behalf.'

This strange dream haunted Newton as they sailed the Adriatic and westward towards Spain, and prodded him to resume 'the orderly pursuit of virtue' for many weeks; yet before he stepped ashore at Wapping Stairs in December 1743 he had forgotten his good intentions.

Captain Newton welcomed John home. Satisfied that sentence had been served and disobedience purged, he at once procured him an officer's berth; if he did well he might be master of his own ship within a few years. John would sail very soon; Christmas leave would be brief, but his father gave him permission to visit the Catletts. He warned him, however, to be on guard against a press gang, for the rumour ran that France was about to attack England in the dispute over the Austrian Succession. The veteran reminded the boy that His Majesty's ships would be looking for merchant seamen to press into a Royal Navy expanding to a war footing: he must keep the sharpest watch, for until he joined the merchantman he could not carry the certificate of protection which compelled a press gang to leave a serving seaman alone.

The Catletts turned January into summer by their warmth of hospitality. Polly smiled at him. Newton did not declare his love, for if he now had prospects he lacked means, and no youth of eighteen in the reign of George II would presume to approach the parent of a girl even younger for permission to ask her hand. The unsuspecting Catletts treated the two as brother and sister.

Days passed too swiftly. Newton could not bear to leave Polly, a magnet stronger than the berth his father had secured. Once again, irresponsible and ungrateful, the boy wrecked his father's plans. He overstayed his leave, missed his ship and returned to an irate parent.

Newton's life story hinged on that disobedience, for had he joined his ship he would have been safe, sailing the seas, on the fatal First of March, 1744, the day on which calamity fell.

His father had nearly thrown him over but relented and again used his influence on John's behalf. Before the Captain had found him a ship the Newtons went down to the Essex farm and this proved John's undoing. Aveley being near the ferry to the Dover Road which passes Chatham, he could not resist the opportunity of riding to Polly. He forgot his father's warning that the River at the outbreak of war was dangerous to a seaman; he forgot to make enquiry before crossing to the Kentish shore, though news always spread of a naval press. He walked straight into a press gang.

They knew he was a sailor by his gait. Implacable, ignoring his plea that he had served as an officer and should not be taken into the Navy as a common seaman, they thrust him under guard into the backroom of an inn while the press looked for further prey. He was allowed to scribble a note and pay a lad to take it across the river to Aveley. If, twice before in Kent, John Newton had hidden his whereabouts, he turned desperately now to his father, whose not inconsiderable influence might save him. Hours passed; nine other wretches were thrust into the little room; at last John heard his father's voice outside, and listened to him speak urgently as one sea officer to another, and heard the young lieutenant of the press reply respectfully.

There was no hint of concession in the lieutenant's tone, and Captain Newton came sadly into the backroom to tell John that lack of a 'protection' had proved fatal. The French were already at sea and shots had been exchanged although war had not been declared (the recent southwest gale had in fact dispersed a French fleet off Dunkirk and stopped an attempt to land a Jacobite force in Kent, headed by the Young Pretender). The lieutenant would not release a well-built lad who had been excellently trained at sea by his own father.

The horrors that John knew by hearsay must be tasted to the full. He and the other nine were marched to the quay, brought downriver in the *Betsey* tender to the Nore and put on board

H.M.S. *Harwich*, a fourth rate (fifty guns) man-of-war, on Sunday 4 March. Rough hands hustled them below to a dark hole below the waterline which offered no opportunity to dive overboard before they were legally impressed, when disappearance would become desertion. In the tender and now in the ship, Newton suffered something of the airless confinement he would afterwards inflict upon African slaves. Then he was ordered to strip. Mr. Bacon the surgeon passed him fit. Soon the recruits were marched at a run to the Captain.

Philip Carteret, captain of H.M.S. *Harwich*, was related to Lord Carteret, one of the King's principal Secretaries of State, and came from a distinguished naval family. Newton was fortunate in that Carteret was a good seaman and humane. He examined each recruit about their sea experience and ordered 'John Newtown' (as the clerk entered him on the muster roll) to be impressed at the higher rate of Able Seaman, together with John Craven and James Wheeler. The other six were impressed as Ordinary Seamen.

H.M.S. *Harwich* set sail for convoy duty on 8 March, taking advantage of the freshening wind which destroyed the Jacobite's last hope of crossing the Narrows that spring. For John Newton, the voyage was a misery of pain, fatigue, fear and hunger. Spurred by the rattan cane swung expertly by the master at arms, Mr. Hedge, or the rope's end 'starter' in the hands of George Murris the bosun, or his mates, Newton and the other new men made every movement on deck at the double, and up the rigging in quick time. Driven until they would have dropped were it not for fear of worse pain, fed shamefully, although Jos Vincent, quartermaster, may have been less corrupt and inefficient than many, they were virtually slaves. The eighteenth century believed that a man-of-war's seaman would never endure the physical and mental strain of working the ship in all weathers and fighting the enemy unless first broken, and kept thereafter in dread of corporal punishment: his early training was the naval equivalent of a black slave's 'seasoning' on arrival in the West Indies.

The misery was compounded by the company which Newton had joined, three hundred men in the confined space of one of the Royal Navy's smaller fighting ships; H.M.S. *Harwich*, built two years earlier, was a hundred and forty feet long and forty feet wide. Few if any of the lower deck were volunteers. At every gaol delivery the judge would sentence a quota of convicted criminals to naval service; other youths had been handed to naval press by offended parents or outraged masters, others had ruined themselves and could see no future except enlistment; the rest had been seized by the press. Newton, familiar enough with rough ways and speech in a merchantman's crew was disgusted by naval profaneness and debauchery. The lower deck provoked in him a sense of superiority. He lessened his own profanity and attempted to live cleanly, if only to display that he was neither jailbird nor lout but a sea captain's son. And always he kept alive a slender hope: that the sea captain parent might achieve his rescue. Otherwise, nothing lay ahead beyond his nineteenth birthday except hardship.

On 3 April, after one month on the lower deck, Newton paraded with all hands to hear Captain Carteret read the Declaration of War with France. A day or two later Newton was ordered before him, and no able seaman received such a summons without fear. The Captain, however, spoke kindly. He said that a man he would gladly serve had asked him to favour the son of Captain John Newton of the Royal Africa Company and therefore he proposed to take him on the quarter-deck as a Midshipman. His father did not wish him discharged from the Royal Navy in wartime, when honour and prize money might come his way.

From being almost a slave Newton entered the comparative comfort of the gunroom, and from jumping to the command of men he despised he could lord it over former messmates. This sudden change of fortune brought out the worst in him. Midshipman Newton delighted in displaying power over Cullpack, Tarrant and the others who had shared his misery on the tender. He resented the discipline of the quarter-deck, and though skilful professionally he was sullen, and worked no harder than if he still served in the Mediterranean trade. He did not repay the kindness of Captain Carteret; which was not only ungrateful but foolish, for a man-of-war's captain is an absolute monarch. Thus he prepared for himself a fearful future which he might have foreseen had he not forgotten, in folly and pride, that power derives from duty.

Throughout May 1744 *Harwich* escorted convoys to Scotland and Norway, a dreary task leaving hours of boredom. These the gunroom dispersed by animated discussions led by the captain's clerk, James Mitchell, a man in his twenty-third or fourth year who became Newton's particular mentor and friend. Observant, well read, with an engaging manner and a touch of amusement in his voice as he demolished arguments or exposed ignorance, Mitchell noticed that Newton still had some religious views and a conscience, and at first he avoided ridicule of either. Instead, having gained Newton's confidence he disputed his interpretation of *Characteristics*, and argued that Shaftesbury sought to supplant, not support religion. A mature man, said Mitchell, had no need of devotion to a God who, if He existed, was nothing but an impersonal First Cause. Obeying such a deity did not make for happiness or success; parting with Him did not bring trouble. Newton was shocked. But like the tempter in the dream near Venice, the argument sowed doubt. Mitchell then broke his colours at the masthead, as it were, and disclosed himself as a freethinker.

He insinuated his sentiments in the most plausible way. Religion, Mitchell would suggest as they leaned over the poop idly watching the vessel's wake, is the harness by which proud teachers impose their opinions with threats of judgement or hopes of immortality. The wise man subscribes to no opinions but his own, formed by experience as broad as he can gain. Death is extinction; conscience, Mitchell would add, is merely the doubting of the immature: the grown man does as he pleases, giving the desires of body or mind free play, thus fulfilling himself in the only life he will have. If a desire exists it should be expressed: Mitchell claimed that Lord Shaftesbury's view had its echo in the well-known line from Alexander Pope, who died at Twickenham that very May: 'Whatever is, is right.'

Newton's ideas lacked substance enough to withstand such good humoured logic which, moreover, pointed him to a path he had itched to travel. His self-will and growing sensuality had long chafed at the restraints of his mother's Christian faith and morals as they lingered in his conscience. If Mitchell's teaching were right, Newton would be released, body and soul, free to indulge sexual appetites because fornication would no longer be sin to him, and free to believe any creed or none. The prospect grew daily more attractive.

Mitchell pressed his advantage. At length there came a day, somewhere off the coast of Norway that early summer of 1744, when John Newton plucked the ring of conscience and Christian faith from his finger and dropped it over the side.

No mountains burst into flame.

4

Naval Deserter

Midshipman Job Lewis was a steady youth who held to the principles he had learned in a good home. He looked up to Newton, older, and with years of sea experience; enjoyed his songs on deck, and smoked many a pipe with him in the gunroom. Lewis had noted with approval on Newton's first arrival on the quarter deck that he had a little religion and lived cleanly when they put into port.

Now Newton began to ridicule Job Lewis's religious feelings and to glory in atheism as the only creed for a man. He set out to make Job an infidel and a libertine.

They were still arguing when H.M.S. *Harwich* went into action in the North Sea, the only naval skirmish in which John Newton served. It began in the early afternoon of 30 September off the Yorkshire coast when the lookout at the masthead saw three sail to the northwest. Carteret gave chase, clearing the ship for action and ordering the men to stand to their guns. After two hours under full sail they closed on a single man-of-war which broke the French colours. At 6 p.m. *Harwich* opened fire with one of her fo'c'sle guns and kept it up as the distance narrowed, also firing a twelve-pounder out of the head door, while the enemy kept firing her stern gun without inflicting damage.

At half past six *Harwich* closed with her prey – the privateer *Solide* of Dunkirk – and gave her a destructive broadside from the upper deck and seven of the lower deck guns, while the Frenchman's broadside and hand grenades slightly damaged the rigging and wounded one man. As *Solide* fell astern, Carteret wore ship and prepared to give her another broadside when, to the cheers of the British, she struck her colours as daylight faded. Carteret sent boarders. The boats brought back her captain – one Sourbert – and Newton and his brother midshipmen and officers watched on the quarter-deck as the Frenchman surrendered his sword.

Encouraged by the prize money they would all receive they continued the dull routine of patrol and convoy, and Newton resumed his assault on the faith of Job Lewis. He succeeded, destroying it more completely than he realized until they met again nine years later, in poignant circumstances.

Yet inwardly, at first, Newton did not believe his own atheism. While accusing Job of hypocrisy he had been a hypocrite himself, hiding a gnawing anguish of conscience under big words and forced smiles. On night watch he disliked being alone with his thoughts. When off watch he would wake suddenly in the small hours, tortured by remorse, worried for the future, arguing mentally with persistent thoughts of the God he denied. The young Prince of Glory would not leave him alone.

Newton hardened himself. He had taken the freethinker's road and would not turn back. Intimations of immortality grew fainter until 'I believed my own lie.' He would say sadly in after years:

'Like an unwary sailor who quits his port just before a rising storm, I renounced the hopes and comforts of the gospel at the very time when every other comfort was about to fail me.'

This 'rising storm', this loss of all comfort, he brought on his own head. The innocent cause was Polly Catlett.

During the summer his ship had moored for several weeks in the mouth of the Medway at Sheerness, whence Newton often took boat for Chatham. Polly now boarded at a seminary for young ladies, where he pursued her in his fine uniform, daydreaming of his exquisite powers of gallantry. These never materialized in her presence: indeed her companions laughed at him as nautical and lubberly and teased Polly until she begged that if he must, he should only visit her when she went home. She knew he loved her and she instinctively, artlessly kept her guard, neither encouraging too positively nor implying an absolute refusal. He took care never to wear his new colours as a freethinker and atheist when he sailed in Polly's waters. More than once he overstayed his leave, to the annoyance of Captain Carteret; prudence went overboard with Polly in the offing.

Soon after the action against the privateer Newton learned that *Harwich* might leave home waters for a year in the Mediterranean. On his next visit to Chatham he promised Polly to return with prize money and promotion. He dared not ask her hand formally, for fear of rebuff, but implored her to remember him when she came out into Chatham society and men better skilled in the arts and niceties of the polite world proposed to her. She must suspend her answer for a year for the sake of the absent suitor whose affection, and desire to make her happy, far exceeded that of any other.

At Christmas time 1744 *Harwich* lay in the Downs, the great sea anchorage off Deal, north of the straits of Dover. To

Newton's dismay and distress he discovered that the squadron's destination had been changed. As soon as the wind veered into a favourable quarter they would sail, not for the Mediterranean but the Cape of Good Hope and the far East Indies: instead of one year he would be away five. If he survived to return at all he would be twenty-four and Polly nineteen and almost certainly in another man's arms.

He must see her once more. He asked Captain Carteret for leave. The ship rode at single anchor, ready to sail at short notice, and Carteret, though disposed to be friendly despite Newton's disobedience, could grant only twenty-four hours. Yet Chatham lay a hard day's ride from Deal. Even if Newton spent a bare hour with Polly and rode back through the night, and if the winter roads were not too muddy, and his hired hack showed the spirit of a thoroughbred, he could not be back on board in time.

His motto at this time was 'Never Deliberate'. On landing from the liberty boat he went to the livery stables and took horse for the Canterbury road, following the dictates of his passion.

At Chatham, instead of blowing hasty kisses and remounting after a hasty meal he stayed several days. Though he was still filled with silly confusion in Polly's presence, their gloom at the prospect of five years' absence betrayed the seriousness of their feelings, which previously her parents had dismissed as children's affection.

The Catletts knew by now that the lad had twice thrown away his future for Polly. This tokened a disastrous match. 'Uncle' Catlett ordered him out of the house: he must never see Polly again until Catlett gave him formal permission. The 'Aunt', Mrs. Catlett, showed more tenderness. She spoke to John as if to her own child, and promised that she would not object to an engagement in a better future; until then he must not call if Polly were at home, unless either he abandoned his suit or brought his father's written permission to continue it. She also forbade him to write, but Polly and he managed to make a secret arrangement for letters, possibly through a friendly maiden aunt who lived nearby.

Throughout the visit Newton had suffered dread of Captain Carteret, and this intensified as he cantered into Deal on the evening of 1 January 1745. He managed to see George Derby, the First Lieutenant, and to soften his heart by the true tale of love so that Derby prevailed on an angry Captain not to punish too harshly. However, Newton lost Carteret's favour, never to regain it. The storm gathered nearer.

The squadron lay in the Downs all January. Newton on night watches solaced his loneliness by holding imaginary conversations with Polly, and later one night wrote her a long letter which reached her by their secret route. She kept it all her life and it survives, the earliest Newton manuscript, signed with his monogram of J superimposed on N. He wrote gloomily of disappointments, his fear of losing her to a local swain, his belief that the voyage ahead would ruin or make him. He hoped for prize money, not merely on his own account, 'for I shall not value riches but for the opportunity of laying them at your feet.'

At last, a brave show of canvas and pennants to landsmen watching from the white cliffs of Dover or Beachy Head, the squadron sailed down Channel. Throughout February, at anchor in Spithead, Newton's fear of losing Polly while he sweated and fought in some distant clime preyed on his mind. On 23 February *Harwich* sailed with a fleet under Commodore George Pocock, flying his flag in H.M.S. *Sutherland*, and a convoy of Indiamen and Guinea ships. After three days the wind veered south westerly and forced fleet and convoy into Torbay. Then it changed again almost immediately and the Commodore led them out again, with disastrous consequences; several merchantmen and men-of-war went aground on Start Point.

Pocock ignored his losses and kept course westward until at nightfall on 28 February the fleet rounded the Lizard and met a violent gale blowing towards the Cornish coast. The fearful confusion of that roaring, moonless night, with too many vessels trying to avoid each other and a rocky lee shore, kept the whole ship's company working as Carteret's superb seamanship saved *Harwich* in several close calls. Morning revealed battered vessels on all quarters and the Commodore himself in a sorry plight with his mainmast and bowsprit gone. He ordered the fleet into Plymouth Sound.

March 1745 passed in repairing damage. The unexpected delay unsettled the crew. Stephen Forty and William Ramsey deserted, then Edward Armstrong and a trickle of other seamen, to Captain Carteret's annoyance. As for Newton, to be still in the same country as Polly Catlett quite maddened him, especially when he looked at the Guinea ships and knew that their men would be home within a year. Towards the end of the month he learned that his father was nearby at Dartmouth to inspect the damage sustained by the Africa Company. Surely, thought Newton, his father would find a way of exchanging his son out of the Navy into the Guinea service if only he could implore him face to face. But Carteret refused leave to go to Dartmouth: a midshipman who had abused his kindness could expect no favours.

On one of the first days of April the Captain ordered him to take a longboat party to fetch vegetables, fresh water and other supplies waiting on Plymouth quay. Since eleven men had run already and these shore trips gave the best opportunity, Carteret sharply reminded Newton to take utmost care that none of the people deserted.

As the longboat crew rowed him ashore, Newton suddenly decided to throw caution and duty to the winds, true to his maxim Never Deliberate. When they had made fast and the men's attention was absorbed in loading the casks he slipped aside and walked out of the Royal Navy for ever – or so he thought.

He adopted a deliberately jaunty air as he climbed westward from the town, checking his road to Dartmouth once he was far enough from the shipping. He walked on through the glory which is early spring in South Devon, and slept rough that night, not at an inn, for fear of meeting a suspicious naval person.

Next day he had passed through Morleigh and beneath the Roman encampments near Halwell and could see the high road from Totnes winding down towards the signpost where he must be less than two hours' walk from Dartmouth, his father, and freedom. Then, too late, he noticed a party of marines searching for deserters from ships wrecked in the storm. He could not avoid them. Nor, footsore, travelstained, lacking horse or carriage or written orders from his captain could he bluff them that he was either on duty or on leave. They arrested him, and marched him back the twenty-five weary miles to Plymouth, one of a motley set of absconded rascals taken on the run.

Shame at the stares of Plymouth citizens, who saw him hustled like a felon, gave way to indignation when he was kept two days in the guard house on shore. These emotions were nothing to the cold fear which crept upon him. Death was the penalty for desertion. If the Captain sent him to court-martial, Newton might be hanged from the yard arm, or awarded perhaps up to a hundred lashes with the cat o' nine tails: punishments were not as heavy as in the later part of the century. If Carteret dealt with the case summarily as absence without leave, not as desertion, a midshipman did not usually suffer more than a caning.

Newton at last found himself back on board, confined below in irons which manacled wrists and ankles. He lay raging at fate, dreading punishment, whilst unknown to him his father interceded through Admiral Medley for an exchange to a merchantman. Not surprisingly, Captain Carteret refused to grant what Newton had deserted to obtain. The boy had betrayed his trust and the Captain was implacable in resentment; but the humane Carteret did not have him court-martialled.

Newton in his autobiography passes over in six words what happened: 'I was publicly stripped and whipped.' All hands paraded on deck to witness punishment. As Carteret did not enter it in his log, and his punishment book does not survive, no evidence remains as to the severity, although by regulation no captain might award summarily more than a dozen lashes. This limit was seldom observed. Yet Carteret's character and Newton's youth alike point to the probability that two dozen would have been the very most. Twenty-four hard strokes on his bare back with a nine-tailed whip of knotted ropes, inflicted rather slowly with a roll of the drum between each, must have been exceedingly painful, though not crippling. For Newton, however, the physical agony was little to the searing disgrace as men he had bossed and abused could gloat to see him stripped and bloody. The proud freethinking disputant of the gunroom hung tied up like an animal. And it was a bosun's mate whom he had despised, on being promoted over his head, who now wielded the cat with all his strength.

The second part of Newton's punishment began when he was cut down from the gratings, sent below to the surgeon and ordered back to duty at the earliest moment that two hundred weals allowed. He returned, not as a midshipman but at the lowest rank of ordinary seaman; as he put it, 'brought down to the level of the lowest and exposed to the insults of all.' Those to whom he had been haughty and vain were not slow to get their own back, while former messmates of the gunroom who had watched his flogging with embarrassment and pity tried at first to shield him a little. They cooled quickly, not so much because of strict orders against softening the disgrace – ways could have been found without too much risk – but because Newton snarled like a wounded cur at the slightest touch of friendship.

Six years later Newton wrote that he had been 'degraded and punished as I well deserved'. When, however, he sailed from Plymouth for the Indies on 9 April 1745 he was filled with rage and injured pride, and with a sense that he had been grossly ill-used. The Captain took opportunities to display his continued resentment. Newton furiously meditated revenge, even to the limit of murder. 'My breast was filled with the most excruciating passions, eager desire, bitter rage and black despair. Every hour exposed me to some new insult or hardship, with no hope of relief or mitigation, no friend to take my part or to listen to my complaint.'

Worst of all, to his inflamed mind, was the loss of Polly. He felt he had been torn from her forcibly. He would be absent five years and unlikely to see her again; if he did, it was improbable that he would return in a condition to claim her hand.

As *Harwich* sailed past the Lizard peninsula which gave a last sight of England for the westbound fleet, Newton, off-watch, placed himself by the gunwale. With inexpressible wistfulness and regret he gazed on the English shore. His thoughts were dismal; life offered nothing but darkness and misery. Death, to his atheist mind, would at least be extinction.

He kept his eyes on the receding coastline. When he could see it no longer, he would have flung himself into the sea. 'But the secret hand of God restrained me.'

5

The Slave Coast

The May sun beat down on the varied shipping in Funchal roads, the chief anchorage of Madeira. In shallow water H.M.S. *Harwich* lay heeled half over while the crew greased the starboard side with tallow. Next day she was heeled again to grease the larboard side. Ordinary Seaman Newton might tire at this fatigue in the heat but he dared now show it: the bosun and his mates made sure that his sore back felt the touch of a 'starter' if he slacked. Even worse was the labour of blacking the bends and painting the sides with tar.

No misery, thought Newton as he splashed the hot tar, could have been greater than his during the eighteen-day passage from Plymouth. The quarter-deck mistrusted him, the fo'c'sle despised him. Hated for the arrogance he had displayed as a midshipman, he was driven exceptionally hard by the petty officers. He had again contemplated suicide. He wanted to murder Carteret too if a way offered to effect murder and suicide together. One ray of hope made him pause: that though the voyage would last five years, he might see Polly again. Newton's love for her was the single restraint left; he feared not God nor regarded man, yet he could not bear that *she* should think meanly of him when he was dead.

The labour seemed unending. Time was short because the fleet was under orders to sail for the Cape on 10 May. The fatigue of taking on fresh water in heavy casks, and all manner of stores, consumed the hours of daylight and heat until the sailors wished they were dead. That night Newton slung his hammock and fell asleep in an instant and at first light next morning, Thursday 9 May 1745, he slept right through the bosun's whistle and the bustle as the rest of the watch stowed hammocks. One of the midshipmen made his rounds. He shook Newton awake, mingling jest with his order since they had been special friends in happier days in the gun-room. But when Newton insolently took time he drew out his dirk and cut down the hammock; that back still tender from the lashes hit the floor. Newton did not dare show his anger. Furious, he dressed, stowed hammock and went on deck.

The roads, with their backcloth of the mountain, looked busy enough. Among the men of war preparing for sea rode a few ships of the Guinea trade. Small boats plied between, or back and forth to the jetties. Then Newton saw a boat bobbing at *Harwich*'s ladder; one of his messmates, preparing to embark, had already dropped down his bundle. Newton asked where he was bound. The man replied that the Captain had pressed two skilled hands from the Guinea ship lying nearest, and the Commodore had ordered *Harwich* to supply two in their places: presumably the merchant captain, who had no legal right to refuse the naval press, had complained he would be undermanned.

Newton's heart instantly burned like fire. Here was his one hope. He begged that the boat be detained a few minutes and ran to the lieutenants and intreated them to intercede with the Captain that he be the other seaman dismissed from the ship. His motto, 'Never Deliberate,' had not changed, for reflection might have cautioned him not to expect good will from either lieutenants, since he had frequently angered both. However they had secretly pitied his flogging and expulsion from the quarter-deck and went to Captain Carteret. Carteret, perhaps glad to be rid of a bad lot, at once agreed to the exchange.

In little more than half an hour from being asleep John Newton was out of the Royal Navy. His determination at Plymouth, 'I will *not* go to India; I *will* go to Guinea,' was fulfilled. Had the midshipman made his rounds a few minutes later, had the Guinea ship's pressed men come aboard a few minutes earlier, the opportunity would have missed him. It was the second of the extraordinary coincidences – or providences as he would later term them – which shaped Newton's life.

It freed him from disgrace and the bondage of naval discipline. It lost him the officer who had made him an atheist and also, as he supposed, the midshipman whose religious faith Newton in his turn had destroyed. This man, Job Lewis, would reappear in his life but he never saw the ship again: H.M.S. *Harwich* served another fifteen years until wrecked off Cuba in 1760. Captain Carteret died in 1748.

Newton's brief crossing from man-of-war to Guinea ship was his Rubicon. He had joined H.M.S. *Harwich* a rather steady and studious youth, and pride had kept him above the habits of the herd. Neither conversion to atheism nor the degradation from the quarter-deck had snapped his resolution and when the whores of Funchal swarmed aboard he kept in check the animal passions which were all the stronger since the infliction of the corporal punishment. But now he would be among strangers who never knew the chaste youth he had once been. He need disguise no longer the man he had become. Years later he could distinctly recall, 'that while I was passing from the one ship to the other, this was one reason why I rejoiced in the exchange, viz., "that I now might be as abandoned as I pleased, without any control".' He was a few weeks short of his twentieth birthday.

The captain of the Guinea ship on questioning Newton exclaimed that he knew his father. He offered friendship and protection. The future looked assured, for this ship was engaged in the triangular Slave Trade which carried Sheffield goods, cloth, fire-arms and trinkets down the Windward coast of Africa to barter for slaves; shipped the slaves by the Middle Passage to the West Indies; then ran for home before the trade winds with a cargo of sugar and rum. Any captain or mate who survived the fevers long enough could rely on a good livelihood, while a landsman who superintended a 'factory' could make his fortune, like their passenger, Mr. Clow, the ship's part-owner who was returning from England. He had first landed on the coast as poor as Newton.

Thus Newton became a slaver. For the next six months of 1745 he sailed from river mouth to river mouth, down the coast and back, while Clow and the captain bargained with chiefs and factors for the slaves they had collected in their warehouses.

The crew always received slaves on board as enemies who would attempt to regain liberty. The blacks, after being duly bought, were branded and, as soon as ten or fifteen had been shipped, were put in irons. During the coastwise voyage the number of slaves increased, and the captain lost seamen by death or sickness, while others were absent in boats; thus he might have only ten men to watch over two hundred slaves and to work the ship. Therefore the crew confined the slaves below at night. In daytime, in fine weather, they brought them up by pairs, put a chain through a ring on their irons and locked this to ringbolts fastened at intervals on the deck. Insubordination or mutiny met instant and violent punishment.

Newton shared in the brutality against his fellow creatures. If naval life had been brutal it was for a high cause. The Slave Trade was for gain, and in 1745 not a pen nor a tongue had questioned or condemned it. In old age John Newton revealed what it had done to his character as a young man when he told a Committee of the Privy Council, from his own experience, that he knew no method of getting money which had so direct a tendency to efface the moral sense, to rob the heart of every gentle and humane disposition and to harden it like steel.

About a third of the cargo was female. As black women and girls came on board, naked, trembling, terrified, almost exhausted with cold, fatigue and hunger, they were exposed to the wanton rudeness of the crew. The poor creatures could not understand English, but looks and manner were sufficiently intelligible as in imagination the prey was divided upon the spot for future use.

John Newton let lust run unchecked. His heart lay with Polly but his body refused to be denied. Since the women were kept on deck at liberty in daytime, a seaman's opportunity came easily and he need ask no consent, since resistance or refusal would be in vain. Sometimes, he might take one at night while on duty, for owing to the heat and filth the crew went naked in the holds where the women lay, equally naked, and discipline could not restrain desire, especially before the holds grew crowded. Any consequence would be born far away in the sugar islands, perhaps adding to the profit of the voyage. It is a curious fact that there may be American or Caribbean blacks in whose veins runs the blood of John Newton.

Newton later referred to a Scripture verse which he said aptly described his activities at this time' *2 Peter 2: 14.* It begins, 'Having eyes full of adultery, and that cannot cease from sin.' He was a lecher. Yet his wickedness, as he later saw it, was not of the flesh only. In his mind and soul he was a militant atheist, and the verse continues: '*beguiling unstable souls.*' John Newton ridiculed faith and morals and took special delight in destroying any vestiges of religion which he detected in crew members.

Nine years later, in the earliest account of his Christian conversion (a letter to Dr. Jennings) he wrote an uninhibited pen portrait of himself at this time: 'That I was a slave to every customary vice was perhaps the lightest part of my character. My obstinate contempt of the glorious gospel, and the horrid effrontery with which I treated it, distinguished me even amongst freethinkers themselves before I had reached the age of 20; and so industrious was I in propagating my tenets that I believe for some years I never was an hour in any company without attempting to corrupt them.

'Methinks I had rather borne the infamous character of a thief, then I could perhaps have made restitution; but now, however wonderfully the Divine forgiveness may be vouchsafed to me, I fear there are too many will have lasting reason to bewail the day in which they first become acquainted with me.'

One of these was the captain of the slaver. He was not at all religious and did not dislike wickedness except where it damaged his own interests but he much regretted on personal and professional grounds the exchange he had made at Madeira. Newton had grown careless, disobedient, even mutinous at times, stirring other members of the crew to dangerous escapades.

The captain's temper flared hot and so did Newton's. They flew into furious arguments. Worse, Newton made fun of him.

In revenge for some imagined slight Newton applied his wit, and a skill at turning verses, to the making of a song which, without naming names, ridiculed the captain, in his ship, his plans and his person. Newton could sing well. He taught the song to the whole ship's company, and thus he repaid kindness and protection. Only respect for the boy's father stayed the captain's hand from punishing such insubordination; he had the legal right and the power to make life very unpleasant for an object of his anger.

The mate of the ship also hated Newton, who tasted his temper and quarrelled with him. At the turn of the year 1745–46, when the holds were crammed with slave cargo and the ship lay in the Rio Nuna, the usual northerly boundary of the Trade, preparing for the Middle Passage, the captain died. The mate succeeded to the command.

Newton at once realized his danger. The new captain cared nothing for the father whom the dead man had respected, and as soon as the ship reached the West Indies he would take the first opportunity of putting Newton on board a man-of-war, and 'this, from what I knew already was more dreadful to me than death.'

Newton resolved to quit and to try his fortune in Africa. He asked Clow, who was about to land and continue his trading, for permission to enter his service. Clow agreed; Newton dreamed such golden dreams that he did not take the precaution of asking for a contract. The new captain consented and for six months' wages gave a bill on the owners in England, a worthless scrap of paper as it proved, since they went bankrupt.

6

Captivity

Clow had determined to develop a fresh factory. He took Newton to the largest of three small sandy in-shore islands covered with coconut palms and plantains (banana trees) and known to traders as the Plantains. The islands lay some twenty leagues south of a river mouth guarded by a mountainous peninsula which gave the river its name: Sierra Leone, Lion Mountain.

The Plantains were uninhabited. Clow judged that their location might afford him a prime market. Using slaves bought at the factory a few leagues away on the Benanoes, he and Newton made themselves a commodious place. The buildings, of coconut logs thatched with banana leaves, included a central homestead for living rooms, smaller huts for sleeping and kitchen, and shelters for the merchandise, whether deadstock such as knives, guns, rum and other imports, or the livestock – the slaves which they would export as native chiefs made their way in for trade. John Newton determined to retrieve lost time and be diligent, and the new factory thrived; it worried him not at all that his traffic was in human flesh. He laid aside his contentiousness as an atheist, for Clow had long abandoned pretensions to religion and thus offered no scope for argument or ridicule.

When the Plantains had become thoroughly habitable Clow left Newton in charge and sailed away several hundred miles north to collect his woman. Newton had learned already that she was a princess of her tribe and that Clow's early success in trade, and his wealth, owed much to having won her favour. No parson or witchdoctor had joined them together in matrimony but she had learned European ways and when she arrived on the island Clow expected everyone to treat her as the mistress of the house. Her name sounded like Pee-eye, or P.I. pronounced as separate letters.

Unfortunately for Newton, Princess P.I. showed herself prejudiced against him from the first, whether because she feared the influence of another white man or resented his share of profits. She soon had opportunity to do him harm. Shortly before Clow had planned to take him in the shallop (a small, masted boat for river and in-shore work) up the coast to trade, Newton fell sick, and into that misery which a tropical fever can generate in the strongest man, his throat fiery, brow throbbing, body prostrated by lassitude.

Clow gave orders for his comfort but refused to delay departure, and at daybreak Newton awoke to see the shallop sail pass rapidly out of sight behind the palms along the shore. Once Clow had gone, the black princess made herself queen of all his goods and people. Expressing annoyance and contempt for a white man's sickness, though it was common enough, she soon countermanded the orders for Newton's comfort because he did not recover quickly. She had him moved from his comfortable hut to an empty slave shelter in the lines, where his bed was a mat spread on a chest and his pillow a palm log. He could scarcely obtain water when burning with the fever, for the household slaves followed their mistress's lead and openly displayed scorn, mixed a little with pity but not enough to disobey her orders to neglect him.

She hoped he would die. The fever, however, took its course and receded, until Newton, now hungry, longed to attend the loaded table in the homestead but was too weak to go. She allowed him nothing but a ration of boiled rice, hardly enough to sustain life. Then came a day when the princess of the Plantains felt in high good humour and after dinner sent across her own dirty plate piled with half-chewed scraps and her leavings of European-style food. So humbled lay Newton's pride that he received it eagerly with thanks, like a beggar accepting alms.

A few days later she summoned him, though he could still hardly walk the short distance to where she had dined. Newton's eyes glistened at the dishes of good food left on the table. With a contemptuous gesture the princess handed him her plate with its bounty of scraps: a half finished fish, the ruins of her pile of rice and a few plantains which, for a near-starving convalescent looked a meal indeed. In his weakness 'I dropped the plate. Those who live in plenty hardly conceive how this loss touched me; but she had the cruelty to laugh at my disappointment,' and refused him another helping from the inviting dishes. She ordered him to be taken away.

That night he dragged himself to a field behind the slave lines and pulled up roots. He did not dare carry them back for fear of discovery, when she would have had him whipped as a thief, but ate them raw on the spot. His hunger left him; then he vomited as if he had taken the strongest emetic. He returned in misery to his bed with empty stomach. Such results almost always followed his nocturnal gnawing of unboiled roots yet he could not resist the urge.

Sometimes native visitors brought food, as if excusing their curiosity about P.I.'s white captive, and occasionally he heard the clink of chains: slaves awaiting export were bringing part of their own poor ration, secretly.

One day the princess paid a visit escorted by her house slaves, to insult him in broken English. She called him worthless and indolent. She ordered him to walk. Since in Clow's absence the woman held absolute power, Newton tried to stagger down the path. She spoke rapidly in her native tongue to her escort, and they began to mimic him, and to laugh and clap, and even to pelt him with limes. He learned to dread these visits of state, not only because of the physical hurt when the escort threw stones instead of limes, without any rebuke, but because scorn from a black, whom any white man in that age despised, was nearly as hard to bear as hunger.

Hunger, contempt, pain, loneliness – in that far country where John Newton had taken his journey, these were the 'husks that the swine did eat: and no man gave unto him.' Unlike the Prodigal Son, Newton did not come to himself. By his own choice, no sweet name of Jesus soothed his sorrows, healed his wounds or drove away his fear.

Clow returned. Newton, stupidly, complained to him in front of P.I. and he did not believe the tale. The awful want ended and strength returned quickly in the usual life of the homestead, but Clow now mistrusted Newton as a liar and when they sailed away together in the shallop on the next venture Newton's miseries had only begun.

At first all went well. Clow knew where to trade, Newton learned fast how to bargain and between them they doubled the profit, so that when Clow's former partner appeared on the river he found the market less attractive. Traders on the Windward Coast felt little mutual love beneath an outward affability, for success by one partnership spelt failure to a rival. This may explain what happened.

One afternoon Newton worked on board the shallop, sorting, checking and making up lots: on this journey they did not ship any slaves they bought. Clow was on shore, drinking with his crony. He returned at dusk in a fury and accused Newton of cheating him by stealing foods at night or when he was away; his old associate had warned him. Newton indignantly denied defrauding him in the smallest matter: 'This was the one vice I could not be justly charged with.' He might be a lecher, with the virility of a young body, and a swearer who could blaspheme with the conviction of an infidel; but the only remnant of a good education that he could boast of was honesty. In whatever he had been trusted he had stayed true, although P.I.'s treatment would have been excuse enough for getting a little back.

Clow refused to listen, refused to produce evidence. He condemned Newton unheard and threw him out of the cabin. Next morning, after a hard night on the deck planks, Newton might have expected his master to listen to reason. Instead, Clow locked him to the deck by a long ankle chain as if he were a slave. Putting in reach a pint of rice for the day's ration, Clow padlocked the cabin, took the two blacks of the crew ashore and began to trade in partnership with his old associate, who thus easily had disposed of a young rival.

All day Newton endured the sun and the burning refraction from the deck as best he could until Clow returned that night with the blacks. Soon the smell of fowls roasting on the spit in the galley encouraged his famished stomach, but he was to be disappointed:

a black, on Clow's orders, brought out one unplucked wing and the entrails, and a small portion of rice for Newton to boil at the deck brazier. The entrails revolted him. Then he considered that they could be bait for fish and he put them aside. After another night on deck, with never a word from Clow who appeared to have sent him to Coventry, Newton's morning repeated the pattern of his first day as a convict in chains: a pint of rice; the departure of master and crew; solitary captivity.

At the slack water when the tide changed in the estuary Newton baited a line with the entrails and fished, and when he saw a fish on the hook it gave him unbounded joy. He broiled, or rather half-burnt it at the re-lit brazier and though without sauce, salt or bread the fish tasted delicious.

The rainy season was near and that afternoon a storm burst on the unsheltered deck. Newton wore only cotton shirt and trousers, with a handkerchief round his head, and had a two foot length of cotton for outer garment. The tropical downpour quickly soaked him to the skin, and though the hot sun returned, another storm at sunset left him in drenched clothes for the night. Clow stayed on shore, dry and well fed while Newton shivered, and starved until the tide turned again and he caught another fish.

Sometimes in those weeks of floating captivity in the river mouths and island lagoons, his jailer stayed away two days and nights and never left more than one day's meagre ration of rice. If Newton caught nothing with the line he tried to sleep until the next tide in an attempt to forget his stomach cramps.

And the rains had come. Newton in middle age ascribed his twinges of lumbago and rheumatism to this dreadful period when, in thin cotton he was 'exposed for twenty, thirty, perhaps near forty hours together in incessant rains, accompanied with strong gales of wind, without the least shelter, when my master was on shore.' If Clow returned he unlocked him in bad weather, so that he could join the blacks in their cabin, but when a tornado struck at night in their absence Newton had to endure the horror alone, crouching against the gunwale through heavy rain, thunder and lightning. Perhaps Clow hoped the boy would die of fright or exposure and thus cancel any obligation of payment for his services.

By the end of two months, when the shallop tied up once more at the Plantains, the excessive cold and wet which he had suffered so soon after recovery from long sickness, had weakened Newton's physique and broken his spirits. But at least he expected release and re-instatement.

Instead Clow took him to the forge. To Newton's distress, shame and helpless misery the blacksmith, while Clow watched, put him in ankle irons. Henceforth he must clank and shuffle with two fetters linked by a chain, as if he were a slave.

7

Servant of Slaves

The head slave put Newton to planting a lime grove. The plants were small as gooseberry shoots, to be placed in lines by the hundred, a backbreaking job. Like the slaves, he was made to work nearly naked and the sun burned his body: perhaps the overseer wanted to make him a black. Inwardly too he burned – with shame that he worked under the orders of a slave, that he should be 'a servant of slaves in Africa', to quote his phrase of after years; and, what to his mind was worse, the object of their pity. Occasionally a house slave risked the wrath of Clow by bringing across left-overs from the homestead; the ill-fed Newton's gratitude was mixed with wretchedness that he should be beholden to the pity of a black.

The friendly house slave helped in a way even more important. He smuggled writing materials whenever a ship from Europe appeared off shore to respond to Clow's smoke signals for trade. Newton was convinced that a letter home to his father was the one hope of rescue. If the ship's boat approached the island, shame drove him to hide in the woods from strangers, for it was useless to appeal to some unknown officer for redress; the man would have accepted Clow's retort that his young assistant was being punished for misbehaviour by a spell of hard labour in chains. The trader's word, not English common law, counted on the Coast.

Newton wrote two or three times to his father, the slave putting the letter secretly in Clow's bag before it was sealed to be taken on board according to the custom of the trade. Newton described his condition and begged help, saying, in sincerity, that he would not return to England unless his father sent a message promising he would receive him and forgive. He wrote also to Polly; at his lowest ebb he retained a hope of seeing again the girl whom he loved passionately through all his distress.

Unless a ship were wrecked letters would be delivered after many months, first crossing to the West Indies. That kept his hope alive. Meanwhile Newton kept his sanity. He did it in a manner which afterwards struck him as curious. On first coming ashore he had put in his bundle one book only: Barrow's edition of Euclid's Elements of Geometry, which he had bought at Plymouth. This he used to take in the brief cool evening hour to remote corners of the island, to draw the diagrams with a long stick on the sand. Without other assistance he mastered the first six books of Euclid. Concentration on mathematics made him forget his misery until, all too soon, the sun dropped into the sea and the swift darkness ended the lesson. He stripped off his shirt and washed it upon the rocks and put it on wet, to dry on his back as he slept. Pensive and solitary he would creep back to the hut.

John Newton was brought low, 'depressed to a degree beyond common wretchedness,' as he puts it. 'I lost all resolution, almost all reflection. I had lost the fierceness which fired me when on board the *Harwich* and which made me capable of the most desperate attempts.' About half a century later, in his old age, Newton on one of his birthdays took down from his shelves a specially interleaved edition of his own book, *Letters to a Wife*, and wrote: 'The troubles and miseries I for a time endured were my own. I brought them upon myself, by forsaking Thy good and pleasant paths and choosing the Way of Transgressors which I found very hard; they led to slavery, contempt, famine and despair.' But not to repentance.

*   *   *

One day Clow came strolling into the lime grove, the black princess on his arm. They stopped to watch Newton at his labour. After a long silence Clow said, in tones of biting sarcasm: 'Who knows, but by the time these trees grow up and bear, you may go home to England, obtain the command of a ship, and return to reap the fruit of your labours? We see strange things happen sometimes!'

Clow and the princess laughed at the absurdity. And little did Newton think at that moment of ridicule that indeed he would revisit the place just when the lime trees were ready to bear fruit their first season; and that he would come in a condition of prosperity which excited the envy of those who once scorned to let him sit at their table.

The first change in his fortunes occurred quite soon after Clow's unconscious prophecy.

Another trader had set up home on their island, which he left frequently to attend to his factories up and down the coast. He had prospered more than Clow and employed several white assistants. He had offered to take Newton and persisted in the face of Clow's refusal, either deploring the waste of a white or because he had caught glimpses of Newton at his Euclid on the shore and sensed he could be useful. At length, late in 1746, Clow agreed. Perhaps he had wearied of Newton's dying yet was ashamed to keep him in servitude another year, and could not believe, after his own behaviour towards him, that Newton would serve him fairly if restored to a position of trust.

Newton was at once decently clothed, well fed, treated as a companion. The trader entrusted him with the care of all the domestic effects, to the amount of some thousand pounds, on next going away, and the 'sport and scorn of slaves' became virtually master of several until his new master, his new friend returned, to find him restored in body and spirits and his own affairs in good order. Sensing his embarrassment at living on a small island as neighbour to Clow and the princess, the trader appointed him to share with another Englishman the management of a factory more than a hundred miles away, in the Kittam district on the Sherbro river's southern branch.

This river actually debouches into the Atlantic not far from the Benanoes but its peculiar course flows for the last hundred miles parallel to the shoreline like a sound, never more than a mile or two inland from the sea. This strange fact would have the strongest bearing on Newton's future.

Newton became fast friends with his fellow manager. Business flourished, their employer was satisfied. They traded in the usual way of the English on the Coast. They did not think of it as dishonesty but not an article was delivered to the blacks in a genuine or entire condition: spirits were diluted by water; false heads were put into gunpowder kegs so that though the keg appeared large, there was no more powder in it than in one much smaller. Linen and cotton cloths were opened, and two or three yards according to the length of the piece were cut off in the middle, where it was not so readily noticed. They cheated in the number, weight, measure and quality of what the natives purchased, in every possible way, and the natives in their turn, particularly when trading with the English, had become jealous, shifty and revengeful.

The English and the Africans considered each other villains. A black on clearing himself of unfairness or dishonesty would answer Newton with an air of disdain: 'What! do you think I am a white man?'

Yet Newton found them at heart a gentle people with a simple morality, good laws and patriarchal government. Except for the hazard of fevers which took off strong men in a few hours, his treks upcountry brought little danger. He often slept in their towns in a house filled with goods for trade, with no one in the house but himself and no other door than a mat, enjoying a security which no sensible man would have relied upon in the England, and especially the London of 1746, without taking the precaution of strong doors, strongly locked and bolted.

Newton had begun to take his pleasures again on any slave girl he fancied, but as the weeks passed he inclined to women of the local tribe, according to trader custom. Occasionally he grew wistful at the thought of Polly Catlett, or felt remorse for the father he had wronged; or his imagination strayed to the scents and sounds of an English summer in the fields of Aveley. But he no longer pined to return. He believed that Polly would never accept him, and he could more easily bear the disappointment in Africa where he lived and moved like a king, than in England.

The local manners and customs grew on him. The throb of drums, the wild dances of the women in their voodoo worship, the sacrifices of a chicken to ward off evil or secure the favour of the gods of field and river, even the sacrifice of a newborn infant in upcountry villages, began to exercise their fascination.

Newton had noticed already that white men long on the Coast would often put more trust in charms, necromancies, amulets and divinations than did the wiser sort among the natives. In the phrase frequently used when a white became assimilated, Newton was 'growing black'. Some three months after release from Clow's captivity he renounced all idea of return to England. He thought himself happy.

Had anyone sung 'Solid joys and lasting treasure None but Zion's children know', it would have been John Newton who would have sat in the seat of the scorner to 'deride and pity' those who 'glory in Thy Name'.

*   *   *

Far away in London Captain John Newton of the Africa Company received his son's pathetic appeal, written in captivity many months before. The Captain at once wrote to his great friend Joseph Manesty, the Liverpool shipowner who years earlier had promised John the place in Jamaica which he lost by overstaying his leave after falling in love with Polly.

Manesty had a ship the *Greyhound*, not a slaver, about to sail for the Windward Coast where John was marooned. He ordered the captain to enquire all down the Coast and to fetch him home. In due course the *Greyhound* put into Sierra Leone river and asked for one John Newton, in vain. Her next port of call was the Benanoes, where men reported vaguely that Newton was a great distance up country. The captain made no further search in that quarter, and Newton might never have heard of the *Greyhound* before she sailed out of reach, had he been still on the Plantain islands. Instead, he was a hundred miles south at Kittam on the narrow strip between the Sherbro river and the sea.

Early in February 1747 he planned a trading journey far inland, and would have left already had not he and his fellow manager discovered that their assortment lacked some goods which might make the difference between moderate profit and considerable gain when bartered for slaves. They decided that Newton should wait a couple of days in case a ship passed by.

This was unlikely. The two men used sometimes to go to the beach in hope of seeing a vessel but at that period the place was seldom touched by ships seeking trade; many passed in the night, others kept a considerable distance from the shore. Newton could not recall one that had stopped.

On the third morning the other Englishman walked down to the beach, taking some of the blacks: if he did not sight a ship Newton was to march late in the afternoon in order to halt the caravan far enough from the porters' homes that night for an early start on the morrow.

As the man reached the beach he saw the sails of a Guineaman. She had already passed down wind but sailed near enough inshore to be worth a smoke signal, always the token for trade. He lit a fire and waited until, to his joy, he saw her come to and drop anchor. He embarked in a canoe and boarded.

She was the *Greyhound*.

Her master and captain said he had almost ignored the smoke, the wind being fair; if Newton's friend had not seen the ship for another fifteen minutes she would have sailed beyond recall. The captain then asked, to the other's astonishment, if he knew a young man called John Newton. When the captain heard th   at his quarry lived at that very place he came on shore at once.

They were introduced on the porch of Newton's house in Kittam with his black household around him and the porters waiting at the warehouse nearby. The captain gave his news that he had come to take home the long-lost son of his owner's friend. When he heard that Newton would have disappeared upcountry within a few hours he quite dropped his usual phlegm, as he thought how narrow had been the line between success and failure in his search, how amazing the coincidence.

Newton heard him out with indifference. The invitation would have been as life from the dead to a starving captive at the Plantains; but now, free and prosperous, settled for life as a trader, his father's forgiveness appeared a trifle. Home was where he stood.

He thanked the captain shortly and refused the offer.

The captain, unwilling to lose him, spun a yarn, a very plausible account of how at Liverpoool he had missed a large packet of letters and papers for Newton which he should have brought out. 'But I am sure of this,' he said, 'because I heard it from your father's own mouth as well as from my employer, Mr. Manesty, that a person lately dead has left you £400 per annum. And if you are in any way embarrassed in your circumstances I have express orders to redeem you, though it should cost one half of my cargo!'

It was a pack of lies. Newton himself did not believe the bit about the handsome estate, though some modest expectations from an aged relative made him think it might be true in part.

He was about to turn away when a thought of Polly stole into his mind. It awoke a spark of hope – that she might be won after all. Mature deliberation would have reckoned the odds too great but the captain's offer looked a way to her hand.

The captain was pouring out promises: 'You shall lodge in my cabin! You shall dine at my table! You shall be my constant companion without my expecting any service from you.'

Newton did not listen. His mind was made up. He would chuck his hope of fortune, chuck his mistress, his semi-royal status, his libertine life. On the spur of the moment he decided to return home and win Polly.

In after years he marvelled at the touch-and-go 'upon which my deliverance from Africa depended! Had the ship passed one quarter of an hour sooner, I had died there a wretch as I had lived.' Yet without the hope of Polly he would have stayed where he was. He once said to her: 'If I had not known you, perhaps I should never have seen the coast of Guinea. But it seems more certain that if I had not known you, I should never have returned from it!'

8

Atheist at Bay

Nearly twenty years later, when Newton was reflecting on his meekness in captivity, he wrote: 'I was no further changed than a tiger who has been tamed by hunger. Remove the occasion and he will be as wild as ever.'

The *Greyhound* proved it. In Kittam, following his near-starvation when 'a servant of slaves' on the Plantains, Newton wanted to succeed and grow rich as a trader. This aim concentrated his mind and bettered his character. But once the coast of Kittam had fallen astern the effect of idleness was calamitous.

The *Greyhound* traded for gold and ivory; for camwood, which was an ingredient for dyes; and beeswax. The camwood and beeswax would save their lives when the crisis came.

A cargo of this sort took much longer to collect than slaves, and she worked southwards down the African coast for more than a year before turning home. Newton, though a passenger who shared the captain's cabin and table and, as promised, had no duties, could have made himself useful as a supercargo to manage the trading, or, with a little refurbishing of his nautical skills, he might have assisted the sailing of the vessel. A small company of some fifteen or twenty souls, subject to the fevers and mishaps of the Coast, would welcome help and the *Greyhound's* owner would receive a good report which might prompt him, as family friend, to offer Newton a command.

Instead Newton idled, except for occasionally amusing himself with mathematics. And he fouled the ship by his presence: 'My whole life when awake was a course of most horrid impiety and profaneness; I know not I have ever since met so daring a blasphemer.' Not content with common oaths he invented new ones, so that he was often rebuked by the captain, who though a quick tempered man with the usual strong language of the sea, felt bound, as magistrate to his ship's company, to reprove his passenger's blatant breaking of Parliament's recent Profane Oaths Act. Newton also broke the earlier Blasphemy Act, by deriding the Saviour's name and denying the existence of God. And he tore at such shreds of Christian belief as remained in any member of the crew. He ridiculed and parodied the events described in the Gospels.

Newton seemed his own worst enemy. Towards the end of 1747 his wildness nearly cost him his life. The ship lay in the broad Gabon river on the Equator, nearly a thousand miles south of his place of slavery under Clow. Newton suggested and paid for a drinking bout, to pass the hot steamy hours of darkness. Normally he did not take liquor; his father had often said, when exasperated by his conduct, that while he avoided drunkenness he might still be reclaimed; but it amused John Newton to make others drunk.

Four or five of them sat with him on the deck with a large sea-shell for glass, to win a wager as to who could hold out longest, drinking alternately geneva spirits (that is, gin) and rum. Newton proposed a toast: A curse on the man who should drink first. Then they drew lots. It fell on him and he downed a shellful. He had a weak head for liquor and as the shell made its rounds he rose and danced about the deck like a madman in a blend of voodoo dance and hornpipe, much diverting the others. His hat blew overboard. In the moonlight, to Newton's drunken state, the ship's boat looked close enough for a drop from the deck, with a quick rescue of the hat to follow, and he was half over the side when somebody caught at his clothes and pulled him back.

That boat lay at least twenty feet off, and he would have fallen into the water and drowned in the strong tide, for like many sailors in that period he could not swim and the others on deck were too drunk to have saved him, and the rest of the ship's company slept.

The significance of this 'and many other deliverances', from accident, folly, and serious fevers too, 'were all at that time entirely lost on me'. Conscience lay stifled and silent.

At length the *Greyhound* had filled her holds and could turn homeward. She sailed westwards from Cape Lopez to the Spanish island of Annabona, some two hundred and fifty miles from the African coast, where they laid in provisions, especially grain for bread; poultry, milking cows; pigs and sheep which they would kill for meat; and casks of fresh water for the whole voyage. Her captain intended to make the British Isles without touching at an intermediate port, a very long navigation of more than seven thousand miles, including the circuit imposed by the trade winds.

They set sail early in January 1748. They ran westward across the Atlantic to the north-eastern tip of Brazil with normal variations of wind and weather; then northward, far out in the ocean from the sugar islands and the coast of America, until they reached the Newfoundland Banks, wrapping themselves against the cold of late February, all the harsher after their long sojourn in the tropics. Newton had passed the time in his usual amusements, studying Euclid; writing or singing witty verses; composing new blasphemies. He also read the few books on board.

One happened to be Stanhope's *The Christian's Pattern*, a late seventeenth-century paraphrase of the mediaeval classic by Thomas à Kempis, *The Imitation of Christ*. Newton read Kempis with detachment as if a romance, helped by Dean Stanhope's flowing English: 'While Jesus is present by His Grace and Comfort, nothing is hard to do, nothing grievous to suffer; but Happiness and perfect Peace dwell and reign in my breast. But the Moment He withdraws His cheering Presence, all my Supports are lost and gone, all my Faculties disabled, and every Difficulty insuperable. ...' Newton did not stop to consider whether this were so. Again: 'So all-sufficient, so delightful, so heavenly sweet is the Friendship and Company of Jesus ... Consider then how miserable thou makest thyself by placing thy Confidence or thy joy in any other.' Newton scoffed at the invitation.

From 1 March a hard westerly gale pushed the *Greyhound* fast towards home, day after day. The vessel, however, had suffered from the length of this voyage and the hot climate; timbers, sails and cordage were worn out and unfit to support stormy weather.

On the evening of 9 March, sitting with others in the forecabin, Newton picked up Thomas à; Kempis again to pass the time: 'Since Life is of short and uncertain Continuence, it highly concerns you to look about you, and take good heed how you employ it. Today the Man is vigorous, and gay, and flourishing, and tomorrow he is cut down, withered and gone ... Ah, wretched Guilty Creature! Ah, stupid Unthinking Sinner! How wilt thou appear at the Tribunal, or what plea canst thou urge at the Bar of Sentence, to Him who needs no Evidence, but is Himself privy to thy most concealed Impieties? Dost thou know this, and yet go on unconcerned, how shalt thou escape the Terrors of that Dreadful Day?'

A thought, unbidden, flitted through Newton's mind: 'What if these things should be true?'

Such an idea had not been near him for years: 'What if these things should be *true*?' His long forgotten conscience stirred uneasily. But he could not bear the inference, and rejected it. Whether true or false, 'I must abide by the consequences of my own choice.'

He put an abrupt end to uncomfortable reflections by shutting the book and joining in the chat around. When he went to bed they were clean out of his mind. Newton slept soundly.

Suddenly the force of a violent sea striking the ship flung him awake. Water poured into the cabin, his bunk lay awash, and he heard a cry from the deck: 'The ship is sinking!'

He rushed towards the companion ladder to give help on deck but the captain shouted down to him to fetch a knife. Newton turned to obey. Another man ran up the ladder and reached the deck as a second great wave, which would have caught Newton had he not gone for the knife, came in and swept the fellow overboard.

They had no leisure to lament him, nor expected to survive him long. Dark as it was, Newton could see that the upper timbers on one side had been shattered. Sails blew in shreds, the deck looked a tangle of cordage; the ship had become a wreck in a few minutes and to the seamen it was astonishing, almost miraculous, that she had not foundered in those first terrifying minutes.

The man overboard left only twelve of them, following losses in Guinea, to work the stricken ship. Some bailed with buckets and pails; others, including Newton, worked the pumps in pairs. Despite their exertions the *Greyhound* was filling. Had she carried a cargo more usual for the North Atlantic, such as cotton bales, sugar and rum, furs, or tobacco, she would have gone down: the beeswax and light woods of Africa kept her buoyant while the crew battled to empty the water. The wave which had smashed her had struck in the later part of the night, near enough to dawn to give hope that they would see the worst leaks in time. And at dawn the gale dropped a little, though the wind still blew hard, and they realized thankfully that the disaster had come at the crisis of the storm, not in its earlier hours when each successive gust would have blown more violent, whipping up higher seas which surely would have sunk them.

Daylight showed that the rotting of the timbers in the tropics had caused them to start in more places than could be counted. Men not at the pumps gathered clothes and bedding to stop the leaks. Everybody stripped off warm outer clothing despite the severe cold, and over this wadding they nailed pieces of boards.

Newton looked on it all as rather an adventure. As he pumped he tried to keep up the courage of the others, and shouted at his companion, 'In a few days this disaster will serve us to talk of, over a glass of wine!'

The other shook his head: 'No!' he said, and began to weep, and Newton caught the words: 'It is too late now.' Being a less hardened sinner the other had been thinking, What will it be like to die?

By nine o'clock in the morning four hours of relentless pumping in cold and hunger had left Newton nearly exhausted, his courage seeping as he looked around at the wreckage and the slopping of the sea water. He stopped and went to the captain, busy in another part of the ship, to offer some suggestion, which the captain accepted.

Newton turned away. As he did so, he said without the least reflection: 'If this will not do, the Lord have mercy on us!'

Instantly he was struck by his words, 'The Lord have mercy on us.' Unpremeditated, this was the first desire for mercy that he had breathed 'for the space of many years'. At once it occurred to him: '*What mercy can there be for me?*' – the ship's chief blasphemer, the loudest swearer, the man who mocked the Lord's existence – *What mercy can there be for me?*

Newton stumbled back to his pump. Again and again icy waves drenched them, until with chattering teeth the two men lashed themselves to the pump itself to stop being washed away.

Scriptures learned by heart and long forgotten welled up from the bottom of his mind. The creaking of the pump arms, alternately pushed and released, pushed and released, seemed to merge into a terrible antiphony from the Book of Proverbs, taught at his mother's knee:

> Because I have called,
> > *And ye refused;*
> I have stretched out my hand,
> > *And no man regarded;*
> But ye have set at nought all my counsel,
> > *And would none of my reproof:*
> I also will laugh at your calamity;
> > *I will mock when your fear cometh* …

The next wave poured over Newton's head, leaving sparkles of ice on his beard and his waterlogged clothing. The Book of Proverbs engulfed him too: 'I will mock when your fear cometh,' he recalled involuntarily from the depths of memory. 'When your fear cometh as desolation, and your destruction cometh as a whirlwind, when distress and anguish come upon you.'

They resumed pumping and the awful antiphony would not leave Newton alone as that first chapter of Proverbs drove into his mind:

> Then shall they call upon me,
>> *But I will not answer;*
> They shall seek me early,
>> *But they shall not find me:*
> For that they hated knowledge,
>> *And did not choose the fear of the Lord:*
> They would none of my counsel:
>> *They despised all my reproof.*

9

The Hour I First Believed

On that unforgettable 10 March, a day which, for the rest of his life, he never allowed to pass without recalling the year 1748, Newton continued to pump with waning energy until nearly noon.

He would see an immense body of water about to overwhelm their stern; if he looked forward, a chasm, equally dangerous, yawned ahead. The ship plunged. In a twinkling of an eye she crested the other side before the watery mountain behind could catch her. Newton had suffered storms often enough, though never in the North Atlantic, and knew that a vessel in good trim would run over these watery hills and dales for days or even weeks in a gale. But the *Greyhound* was broken and awash; every time she dropped into the next valley he feared she could rise no more and they would all go to the bottom.

He now dreaded death, for he thought at the time that 'if the Christian religion was true I could not be forgiven.' Almost he wished that the end would come so that he could know the worst. Yet he remained only half-convinced that the Scriptures were true. His mood alternated between impatience and despair.

At noon he could pump no more. He went below and lay exhausted on his bunk for an hour until ordered on deck again. When the captain saw that he was useless for pumping he told him to take the helm. For eleven hours until midnight, with one break for food, John Newton steered the ship.

The comparative calm and isolation of the half-shattered wheelhouse gave ample time for reflection. The past floated before him and it was not a pretty memory. He recalled his earnest religiousness in youth, the amazing interventions, coincidences and rescues; his lechery and abandon, and above all, 'my unparalleled effrontery in making the Gospel history (which I could not now be sure was false, though I was not yet assured it was true) the constant subject of profane ridicule.'

If true it was, if Christ had really lived, and had risen from the dead, 'then I thought there never was, nor could be, such a sinner as myself.' Recollection of the spiritual advantages he had contemptuously thrown away forced on Newton the conclusion that his sins were too great to be forgiven. Scripture passages again emerged from unsuspected depths of memory to appal him, such as Hebrews, 6: 4–6: 'It is impossible for those who were once enlightened … and have tasted the good word of God and the powers of the world to come, if they shall fall away, to renew them again unto repentance; seeing they crucify to themselves the son of God afresh and put him to open shame.' Such words so exactly described his character that he concluded his doom to be inevitable.

At about six in the evening, when the last daylight had gone in those northern seas, he heard that the ship was free of water. Therefore, against all probability, they might survive. He thought he saw the hand of God displayed in their favour, and there arose a gleam of hope: perhaps he, John Newton, could find the way of forgiveness after all.

He began to pray. He could not pray in faith. 'My prayer was like the cry of the ravens, which the Lord does not disdain to hear' – the instinctive cry to the Creator from one of His creatures. It was not the prayer of a Christian who draws near to a reconciled God and calls him Father, beseeching His loving protection and forgiveness, because Newton faintly perceived that the God to whom he wanted to pray was holy and utterly just. Newton had broken His laws, ridiculed His goodness, spurned His long-suffering and mercy. How could a holy Judge forgive 'a wretch like me'? – unless a way could be found whereby the load of John Newton's sin be lifted from his shoulders and placed elsewhere; perhaps then he could be forgiven.

Standing at the wheel, looking out at that dreadful sea, he began to think of Jesus, whom he had so often derided. He recalled the particulars of His life and His death, the 'wond'rous cross, On which the young Prince of Glory died,' as they had sung so long ago in Dr. Jennings' chapel. He recollected the teaching he had heard there, that Christ's death was a death for sins, but not His own: Jesus had died, 'as I remembered, for the sake of those who, in their distress, should put their trust in Him.' If it were *true* –

A slight change of wind distracted Newton's attention. Although the gale and seas declined with every hour of darkness the ruin of the rigging and the dangerous state of the timbers made *Greyhound* difficult to steer, and when he returned to his thoughts it was to find an enormous scepticism driving out his hopes. The principles of free-thinking, of atheism, had been rivetted to his soul as deeply as the iron nails which held the timbers to the frame of *Greyhound's* hull. Having lived so long in arrogant assumption that the New

Testament story was false, he could not tear unbelief away at a word and throw it overboard. When, at midnight, he was at last relieved at the helm and went below and threw himself on his bunk, he *wished* rather than believed that these things were true.

He yearned to discover 'how I should gain an assurance that the Scriptures were of divine inspiration, and a sufficient warrant for the exercise of trust and hope in God.' Was there truly a God? Could He be known and relied upon?

Newton dropped into an exhausted sleep.

The morning showed that they had survived the gale, which had slackened, and the tremendous seas, only to face starvation. Fighting the storm and the leaks and the water had given no time before darkness fell to survey the extent of the disaster, but now they found that all remaining livestock had been swept overboard – pigs, sheep, beef cattle, milking cows, poultry – and the sea water had floated the movables in the hold, so that every provision cask had been beaten in pieces by the violent motion of the ship. Except for some cod they had caught for amusement on the Banks, and a little of the pulse used to feed the hogs, they had no more than a week's supplies if rationed severely.

The sails had mostly blown away, allowing only the slowest progress although the wind blew fair from the right quarter. They believed that their position lay about a hundred leagues west of Ireland though in fact they were much farther off. They thought they had ample fresh water because the water casks, unlike the provision casks, appeared to be undamaged. Buoyed by hope, most of the crew forgot the storm and looked forward to being home after all.

Newton watched them behave as he had done himself on a dozen occasions of danger and relief, not showing the slightest sense of gratitude to God. As for him, the divine intervention looked obvious, and amazing. Yet he was the most unlikely person on the ship to receive such an impression. 'I can see no reason why the Lord singled me out for mercy ... unless it was to show, by one astonishing instance, that with Him "nothing is impossible".'

He spent all off-duty hours carefully examining the New Testament which they had on board, in an effort to discover whether he could trust it; he realized that to profess faith in Jesus Christ when he did not really believe His history to be true was no better than a mockery of God. As he read he came across Luke 11: 13: 'If ye, being evil, know how to give good gifts unto your children: how much more shall your heavenly Father give the Holy Spirit to them that ask him?'

This gave him an idea. If this book is true, he reflected, the promise in this passage is true, that God will give the Holy Spirit to those who ask. And this is the Spirit through whom the whole Bible was written, as Newton had been taught in childhood. To understand the new Testament he needed the inner guidance of the Spirit. He must therefore pray for this, and if the book were really God's He would make good His promise.

Newton was encouraged further when he reached Christ's words in John 7: 17: 'If any man will do his will, he shall know of the doctrine, whether it be of God or whether I speak of myself.' Newton did indeed now want to do God's will, and could therefore claim this promise, 'he shall know.' Since he could not really believe that every event that the gospels described, including the resurrection, had actually happened, he decided to take it all temporarily for granted.

In after years Newton wrote and talked often about his spiritual search on the *Greyhound*. Although, at the time, he could not put it clearly in words the movement of his mind may be recaptured, as this profligate sailor struggled with his newly awakened conscience, and with his past, and his hopes and fears; and with all that he read in the New Testament. The sodden, battered cabin, where he could not resist the sense that the living God dealt faithfully with him, became a place of conversion as real as that of St. Paul on the Damascus Road.

Paraphrased from his own writings in various forms his conclusions went like this: 'The more I looked at what Jesus had done on the cross, the more He met my case exactly. I needed someone or something to stand between a righteous God and my sinful self: between a God who must punish sins and blasphemies, and myself, who had wallowed in both to the neck. I needed an Almighty Saviour who should step in and take my sins away, and I found such a one in the New Testament. It told me that Jesus Christ was "God manifest in the flesh, reconciling the world to himself". I saw that because of the obedience and sufferings of Jesus, God might declare His justice, in punishing my sin, and declare His mercy also, in taking that punishment on Himself on the cross, so that I might be pardoned.'

Once he understood, however dimly, John Newton believed, and renounced his past.

Immediately he found himself freed of his ingrained habit of swearing and casual blasphemies. It did not return, even in the backslidings and uncertainties he went through before he reached Christian maturity. Newton never swore again.

*   *   *

In the early morning of the fifth day after the storm a loud joyful cry from the watch, '*Land Ahoy!*' brought everyone up on deck in a rush. They saw an uncommonly beautiful dawn, just light enough to reveal a mountainous coast about twenty miles to the eastward, terminating in a cape and two or three small islands. The sailors hugged and slapped one another, for the landfall contours and position were right for the western extremity of Ireland; if the wind stayed fair, all should be safety and plenty next day. The captain ordered, 'Splice the mainbrace!' Though little more than a pint of brandy remained for sharing among twelve, 'We shall soon have brandy enough,' he said. They ate up the rest of the bread in joy and felt like men reprieved.

The mate, however, stared at the horizon as the light grew. He spoke in grave tones: 'I wish it may prove land at last!'

Had a common sailor spoken like that the rest would have fallen upon him and beaten him for such an unreasonable doubt. Since it was an officer, they fell instead to arguing warmly whether it were land or no. Then one of their islands grew red, the sun rose beneath it, the cape broke up and faded. Within half an hour the entire 'landfall' had evaporated into blue sky – a common experience at sea.

The ship's company kept up courage by telling themselves that land, though not yet visible, could not be far, and their wind continued fair. But that very afternoon this fair wind dropped and they were becalmed. Worse, the next day a south-east gale blew up against them and they could not tack into it because the ship was so wrecked that the captain must keep the wind always on the broken side when it blew strong, or the *Greyhound* would be awash again. Day after day, therefore, she was driven farther off course, away to the north of Ireland and westward of the Hebrides, into seas where no other ship would stray at that season.

Hope faded. They had finished the brandy and bread too soon. One twelfth of half a salted cod was a day's ration for each man. They had plenty of fresh water (as they thought) but not a drop of liquor, no bread, scanty clothing in very cold weather, and incessant labour at the pumps to keep the ship afloat. One man died under the hardship. Yet sufferings were nothing to fears: the cod would not last much longer, the south east gale showed no sign of abating, and the crew would soon face a terrible choice: starve to death or turn cannibals.

The captain, now thoroughly soured, knew why they had met misfortune. He blamed it all on John Newton; it was retribution for the wickedness of his ways and speech. 'I've got a Jonah on board,' he would lament, hour after hour. 'A curse attends you, Newton, wherever you go ... All our troubles are due to my having taken you on board ... To my great grief I have a Jonah!'

This frequent mention of Jonah made Newton very uneasy, for he knew the Old Testament story where the storm tossed mariners say to Jonah: 'What shall we do unto thee that the sea may be calm unto us? for the sea wrought, and was tempestuous. And he said unto them, Take me up, and cast me forth into the sea; so shall the sea be calm unto you! for I know that for my sake this great tempest is upon you ... so they took up Jonah, and cast him forth into the sea: and the sea ceased from her raging.' Jonah I: 11–12, 15.

And indeed the captain said openly to Newton: 'If I throw you overboard we shall be preserved from death, and not otherwise'!

Newton's conscience underlined the captain's words: he was probably quite right, that 'all that had befallen us was on my account. I was at last found out by the powerful hand of God, and condemned in my own breast.' He did not believe the captain would actually throw him overboard. But a more horrible fear assailed him as the south easterly continued into a second week, driving them ever northward and farther from land, drawing starvation daily nearer.

If, in desperation, the crew decided to kill and eat one of their number, to save the rest alive, would not Newton be their choice?

Part Two

DANGERS, TOILS
AND SNARES

10

'Your Most Ardent Admirer'

On the fourteenth day of the adverse south-easterly Newton was again at the wheel.

Whenever off duty he had crept to his cabin, terrified of a contrived 'accident', from which it would be a short step to the cookpot of a starving crew. He had spent his time reading the New Testament, and à; Kempis, and a bishop's book of sermons he had found on board: a sermon on the cross moved him much. He was struggling to pray, not simply for rescue from their terrible predicament but for faith and understanding. 'How faint and wavering were my first returns to Thee.' He had been heartened especially by the story of the Prodigal Son, which seemed to parallel his own; he clung, as an illustration of God's attitude to returning sinners, to the father's goodness in running to meet such a son.

Newton could expect neither sympathy nor guidance from man. All on board would have laughed and sworn, assuming his questions some new trick in blasphemy, although they must have noticed that he swore no longer himself. They shared the hunger, cold, weariness and fears of sinking or starving, but the bitterness of heart was peculiarly Newton's own because no one else saw the hand of God in their past deliverance or hoped for Him in their present danger. Yet as he stood at the wheel on the fourteenth day he knew that for him, hope had become stronger than the despair to which all the others had abandoned themselves. Prayer came more easily. He had dared to believe that God had a particular purpose in saving his soul and therefore would save the body too, and his companions. God had saved the Apostle Paul to display him before the world as a trophy of His grace; perhaps God planned to do the same with John Newton.

It was then that he noticed a slight shift in the compass. As he watched, the strong wind came round to the very point they needed to suit the battered part of the ship which must be kept out of the water. The wind dropped. And when, hoping almost against hope, they set more canvas on their masts, it blew just gently enough for the few remaining sails to bear.

Late March was an unsettled time of year in these seas, yet this gentle, favourable wind continued all the next week without observable alteration or increase and they knew the *Greyhound* headed for Ireland again, though they must husband strictly the dwindling provisions. At last, on the twenty-seventh day since their disaster, the deck heard once again the shout, 'Land Ahoy!' This time it was land indeed, the island of Tory off Donegal. Next day they rounded Dunree Head and limped up Lough Swilly on 8 April 1748. Their very last victuals were boiling in the pot as they anchored beneath Buncrana castle.

Two hours later the wind got up and blew violently. If the *Greyhound* had been out at sea in her shattered, feeble state, they must surely have gone to the bottom.

Thankfully they began to disembark. Then a shout brought some of them running down to the hold. The mate had made a horrifying discovery: the five still untapped fresh water butts, which had relieved the crew's misery by encouraging all to drink plentifully when so short of food, and that food salted fish, were in fact empty. Their backs had been stove in by the storm.

Had the crew realized all along how little fresh water remained, they would have rationed it, and the necessarily short ration would have increased the distress. Unknowingly they had drunk their last drop as they anchored in harbour.

To John Newton the entire episode, from the first storm until the change of wind which brought them to port in the nick of time, looked nothing less than an act of God: 'Thou didst preserve me from sinking and starving.' He determined to make a solemn dedication of himself to his Deliverer.

He moved to comfortable lodgings in Londonderry, the walled city a short distance from Lough Swilly where the *Greyhound* lay under repair, and with Irish food and smiling Irish kindness his health and strength returned. He attended morning and evening prayers at a Londonderry church. The clergyman showed no interest in this mariner back from a watery grave, and when a sacrament Sunday drew near, and Newton, having studied the Book of Common Prayer, formally gave notice of his intention to take it, the clergyman smiled and said that the rubric enjoining such notice had long fallen into disuse. Newton had expected the clergyman to examine him, according to the rubric, as to whether he were 'an open and notorious evil liver', and he would have then declared himself 'to have truly repented and amended his former naughty life.'

However, when the day came he arose very early, and in his room and throughout the service in church 'was very particular and earnest in my private devotion and, with the greatest solemnity, engaged myself to be the Lord's for ever, and only His. This was not a formal but a sincere surrender under a warm sense of mercies recently received.' A deep peace but no ecstasy or thrills of joy accompanied the surrender. Newton used to say that he never experienced the 'first love', the honeymoon feelings sometimes associated with Christian conversion. And his understanding of the faith remained shallow, for he assumed that the terms on which God had prolonged his life were those of a galley slave – an interval for labouring at his duty before being called to account at the throne of judgement.

One duty lay clear: to write to his father for forgiveness.

His father replied affectionately. He had mourned his boy as drowned, the *Greyhound* being long overdue, and now rejoiced both for John's survival and for his turn from evil. The old Captain had been appointed Governor of Fort York in Hudson's Bay and would soon sail from the Nore, while the step-mother and their three children would remain at Rotherhithe on the Thames near London; he promised to take John as assistant if he reached the Nore in time. But John felt an obligation to his benefactor and rescuer, Mr. Manesty the owner of the *Greyhound*, not to leave Ireland until he could sail in her to Liverpool. Two or three affectionate letters passed between the Newtons but ship repairs took long and when the *Greyhound* reached Liverpool at last, late in May 1748, a further letter from his father broke the news that he sailed from the Nore about that very day; his forgiveness in person must wait until after the three-year term as Governor.

Those years would be strenuous, perhaps dangerous – as indeed they proved – for an elderly man; and when John Newton the younger called on his benefactor, Mr. Manesty, he learned to his surprise that they could be strenuous and dangerous for himself too.

There must have been some quality in Newton which commanded the instant respect of a stranger; this, with the report which the *Greyhound*'s captain had doubtless given of Newton's new reliability and his seamanship, together with the strength of old friendship for his father, prompted Manesty, on first setting eyes on the young man who had caused him past disappointment and trouble, to offer him the immediate command of one of his slavers, the *Brownlow*.

It would have been a prize to lay at Polly's feet, should she permit him to approach her, yet Newton hesitated and asked for time to decide. When he waited upon Manesty again he thanked him from the heart but declined. 'Until now,' he said, 'I have been unsettled and careless. I think I had better make another voyage first and learn to obey. And also gain a further insight and experience in the business of slave trading before I venture to take such a charge.' Mr. Manesty, who was treating Newton almost as a son, understood and approved. He appointed the *Greyhound*'s mate to be master of the *Brownlow* and engaged Newton as her mate or first officer.

All this time Newton had been in depths of gloom. He had not dared approach Polly. His fornications in Africa had forfeited all claim to this pure girl of his dreams, who would now be twenty years of age. He could not believe she would accept the hand of such a wretch. From Ireland therefore he had sent a letter to her aunt, possibly their previous intermediary when the Catletts had forbidden the young midshipman to write, and had begged her to discover whether Polly would allow him to pay court. He asked for a reply to Liverpool; on his arrival he had found none.

His father, when announcing immediate departure for Hudson's Bay, had told John of visiting the Catletts at Chatham on his way down river and that they gave their blessing to the match, as did he; John now had to obtain only one person's consent. But still no letter. John Newton despaired. He had nothing on which to marry (this was before Manesty's offer) and he concluded he must break it off.

He wept. Nearing his twenty-third birthday, hardened by years of adventure, he wept as he wrote to the aunt that until his affairs prospered he was determined for Polly's sake to divert his thoughts from her 'as much as possible; and though I do not expect to be ever able wholly to conquer my passion, I will endeavour to keep it within my own breast, and never to trouble either her or you any more with it.'

Then came Manesty's offer of the *Brownlow*. Soon afterwards he received from the aunt, crossing his gloomy letter, the news that the Catlett family were temporarily in London and that nothing hindered John Newton paying his respects to parents and daughter. Dipping deep into his slender resources Newton took a place in the London coach. Three or four days later the Catletts welcomed him.

He found Polly a young woman of poise and charm and good nature, with the same simplicity which had captured his heart long ago. She might not be beautiful as the world accounted beauty, but she exceeded all that he had dreamed during the terrible past four years.

But his heart quite failed to loosen his lips. John Newton stood tongue tied, scarcely making small talk as Polly's mother prattled away with harmless questions about an Africa which, fortunately, she could scarcely imagine. The man who had carelessly and heartlessly taken slave women on the Coast, who had kept a native mistress, behaved in Polly's presence like a callow youth.

And she, though polite and kindly as to a long-lost cousin returned from the sea, gave cold encouragement. He grew certain she had no other suitor, for it was not in her nature to deceive, but the passion hammering his heart evoked no echo in hers. As he left, he stammered a request to be allowed to write. She did not formally forbid him.

He returned to his stepmother's house and tried to express in a letter the love which he had failed to declare in Polly's presence. Recalling the many times he had written from the Navy and from Africa he moaned that no one had ever pursued a love affair so long without a crumb in return. In high flown language he begged 'a little of your charity, one morsel for God's sake, before I am quite starved.' The slightest encouragement, he wrote, would afford him intense pleasure without compromising her freedom to accept or reject him. He pleaded that she bestow an occasional thought on him, 'and not too precipitously put it out of my power to show to all the world what I have often repeated to you, I mean that I am with the most inviolable regard Dear Polly Your most faithful and ardent admirer and servant, *J. Newton.*'

Money did not run to a return to Liverpool by coach or even by stage waggon. He walked, day after day alone in heat, dust and fatigue; short of money, without friends. He built castles in the air, persuading himself that he had seen so much generosity in Polly's behaviour that he could hope. However, he decided as he walked that if her reply contained an absolute refusal he would try to conquer or at least to smother his passion for ever.

Her letter came within a day or two of his reaching Liverpool. He kept it for some time before he dared break the seal. When he did, O joy! She was kind. She wrote in most cautious terms but it was much in his favour that she wrote at all, and had not sent through her mother a formal rejection of his advances. She knew that he would take her letter like this. He was sure she was too honourable and good to trifle with him after he had placed the affair in a serious light.

Solemnly he resolved to be worthy of her in character and in fortune, and so serve God too. On that high note he set sail in the *Brownlow*. Little did he know what the Slave Trade would do to his resolves.

11

'The Dreadful Effects of the Trade'

The lamps of the anchored *Brownlow* cast their reflection on the dark waters of a West African estuary north of Sierra Leone. Leaning on the gunwale her mate, John Newton, could see the fires of the native village whence he had brought back a batch of women slaves: he had bargained successfully with the local chief and they were now stretched out in the holds which already began to fill nicely with males and females.

Distant drumbeats stirred his blood as they had stirred it on the Sherbro before his return to England. He fought against his feelings, but not too hard. All the way from Liverpool he had slipped little by little from the Christianity he had embraced. Everyone would expect, he once wrote, that after 'such a wonderful unhoped-for deliverance', and after his eyes had been to some extent opened, he would 'immediately cleave to the Lord and His ways ... But alas! It was far otherwise with me'.

On the outward voyage he slackened in prayer, forgot to read his Bible, cooled his gratitude for past mercies, until by the time the *Brownlow* arrived on the Coast 'I was almost as bad as before', except that his lips were free of swearing, blasphemy and 'contempt of God's word and commandment', as the Anglican litany puts it. He had lacked any human support in his pilgrimage. No brother Christian served on board, for in 1748 they were rare birds indeed among seamen. His short sojourn in Liverpool had brought him no pastor, for in those early days of the Evangelical Revival true pastors too were rare. Above all he suffered from what he himself would afterwards describe in his evidence before the Privy Council as 'the dreadful effects of the Slave Trade on the minds of those who engage in it'.

When he had shipped the slaves that afternoon he had seen the salacious eyes which the seamen cast over the naked bodies of the black girls at the inspection, and knew that each man had chosen his fancy. Newton had stifled his lust then, but now the native drums ashore were beating a quickening tempo which maddened him with desire. He fought it feebly, then hurried down to the hold and raped a girl.

Thereafter he 'followed a course of evil of which, a few months before, I should not have supposed myself any longer capable. I was fast bound in chains, I had little desire and no power at all to recover myself.' Whenever his conscience smote him, temptation proved the stronger. As in most slavers, the *Brownlow*'s captain allowed officers and men unlimited licence. Provided they carried out properly the ship's business of sailing and trading, they might do as they pleased with the women cargo, although he knew that these excesses contributed to the loss of seamen by infecting them, or weakening them against fevers until lewdness ended in death.

And so it nearly was with John Newton.

About a month after arrival in Guinea the captain sent him in the longboat to sail from place to place to buy slaves. At length he reached the Plantain islands and revisited, 'in easy circumstances' just as Clow had predicted in sarcasm, the scene of his captivity, pain and disgrace. Clow received his former slave with respect; Princess P.I. and others who had despised him were now his flatterers; the limes he had planted when in chains had grown tall and promised fruit for the following year when he might be back in command of a ship.

Newton took it all for granted, with no thought of amazing grace or memory of the storm. He lorded it with exquisite politeness over Princess P.I., treated Clow with familiarity, and the blacks, who had pitied him in his extremity, with disdain.

Clow provided him with a black girl for his pleasure, for this was a normal hospitality on the Coast. And so it might have gone on, with John Newton lost to history, had he not suddenly fallen ill of a violent fever, 'which broke the fatal chain and once more brought me to myself.' He lay wracked, throbbing, thirsty in the very room where he had watched Clow sail away at the start of the ill-treatment at P.I.'s hands. Death now summoned him, as he thought, and when he faced the prospect his heart smote him as he recalled the dangers and deliverances of the past, his earnest prayers in the time of trouble, his solemn vows before the Lord at that Holy Communion service in Ireland, and his subsequent ingratitude for all God's goodness. He began to wish that he had been allowed to drown when he first found mercy: perhaps the *Greyhound*'s captain should have thrown him overboard after all.

Despair overwhelmed him. He had crucified the Son of God afresh and thus had shut and locked the door of hope. Then he remembered that his Judge was a Father of infinite mercy and tenderness.

Weak, almost delirious, Newton rose from bed and crept to a remote corner of the island. Between the palm trees and the sea he knelt upon the shore and found a new liberty to pray. He dared not make any more resolves but cast himself before his Lord, who should do with him as He pleased. No particular text or shaft of spiritual light flooded his mind but he was able to hope and believe in a crucified Saviour. The burden fell from his conscience. Peace returned, and from that hour his health improved so fast that when he returned to the ship two days later he was well.

This was a turning point as decisive as the storm of the previous spring.

Never again did he fall right away. Prayer became a habit. And the memory of that black time reminded him often in after years 'What a poor creature I am in myself, incapable of standing a single hour without continual fresh supplies of strength and grace from the fountain-head.'

During the next six or seven months Newton commanded the long boat which sought out black cargo in creeks and shores, and villages up river, wherever a factor or a chieftain had a body or two to sell.

Sometimes he must venture in a little canoe through mountainous seas, sometimes travel through the bush, in danger from wild beasts and much oftener from the more wild inhabitants, who, not surprisingly, seemed to the slave traders to be cruel, treacherous and watching opportunities for mischief. Scorched by the sun in daytime and chilled by dews at night, since an open boat allows no proper shelter, he and his crew would be five or six days together without a dry thread about them, sleeping or waking. Even in the fair season brief storms of wind, thunder and heavy rain were frequent, while in March 1749 Newton wrote to Polly: 'Every day the weather grows worse: violent squalls of wind and prodigious thunder and lightning are bringing in by degrees the heavy rains which last almost incessantly from about the end of this month until August.'

Newton told her: 'Providence has preserved me safe through a variety of these scenes since I saw you last and I hope will continue so to do.' He wrote without irony when he ascribed his preservation to Providence, for if, in 1749, thoughtful men of God had not yet realized the iniquity of the Slave Trade, a sailor making his first stumbling steps in the Christian life could hardly be expected to think of himself as engaged in crime. And certainly there seemed to be several occasions when an unseen Hand interposed on his behalf.

One occurred when the *Brownlow* lay in the Rio Cesters, getting ready to sail for the West Indies with its cargo of blacks. Newton was bringing in wood and water daily by the longboat. He would go up river in the afternoon with the sea breeze, supervise the loading, sleep on shore and return with the land wind next morning. The old longboat, however, was now almost unfit for use. One day when the task was nearly completed he had dined on board and taken his place in the boat. They were about to let go the ropes when the captain came up from the cabin and called down that Newton should return on board. He expected further orders, but the captain said: 'I have taken it into my head that you shall remain today in the ship,' and ordered another to go.

Surprised, Newton asked why, for the longboat never went without him. The captain could give no reason except that he had taken it into his head.

Next morning a native canoe brought news that the longboat had sunk that night in the river: the substitute was drowned. Newton was much struck by this Providence, and the captain, a man of no religion, could not help being affected. 'I had no other reason for countermanding you,' he said with awe, 'but that it came suddenly into my mind to detain you!'

Again, far out in the South Atlantic during the Middle Passage, Newton might have lost his life, for one morning the male slaves rose against their captors when brought up for air and exercise. Those purchased early in the voyage down the Coast had been cooped on board for much of a year and were desperate.

One unguarded minute was enough to give them their opportunity. For the next violent quarter of an hour the *Brownlow* endured a scene frequently enacted on slavers: the helmsman killed by a blow from a marlin spike which had been smuggled below; the gong sounding the alarm; several of the crew, seizing muskets, ran up the rigging, which manacled slaves could not attempt, and fired into the tumultuous mass of blacks. Three or four slaves were killed before the rest, unarmed, gave up the unequal struggle.

Then followed retribution. In the course of his time in the Trade Newton saw slaves sentenced to unmerciful whippings, continued until hardly a sign of life remained. He saw them 'agonizing for hours, I believe for days together, under the torture of the thumb-screws; a dreadful engine, if the screw be turned by an unrelenting hand it can give intolerable anguish.'

The Atlantic passage resumed its peaceful course. Newton used his leisure hours to re-learn Latin by a tedious method which at least gave him some understanding of the beauties of Horace, and a spice of classical enthusiasm, before he reached Antigua.

Here the owner's Agent gave orders not to land the slaves but to sail on to Charleston in South Carolina. This proved a loss: the men slaves who had been so long on board began to drop fast, their patience worn out, and all told the *Brownlow* lost sixty-two out of two hundred and eighteen souls. At Charleston, so Newton told Polly, he was glad when the survivors left for the slave market, since he felt 'shut up with almost as many unclean creatures as Noah was and in a much smaller Ark.'

12

The Hand of Polly Catlett

John Newton was now an earnest but ignorant pilgrim wandering in a spiritual fog with little to light his way but good intentions.

During the weeks spent in South Carolina while they fumigated and aired the *Brownlow* and then loaded tobacco and other cargo for England, he had plenty of leisure. He wanted to know God better but 'my views of Christian truth', he would tell his friends in after years, 'were very imperfect and my conduct inconsistent. Spiritually I chiefly depended on myself: I knew I had been very bad, I had a desire to be better, and thought I should in time make myself so.'

He supposed all who attended public worship to be good Christians and that whatever came from the pulpit must be good. The sermons of the minister of the Independent congregation, Joseph Smith, helped best but Newton could not understand him clearly. Smith had been George Whitefield's strongest ally during his Charleston visits and would have gladly unfolded mysteries and introduced ardent Christians but Newton, bold enough on shipboard or in the African bush, shied from accosting a clergyman.

Instead, he would slip away alone almost every day into the woods and fields behind the town: throughout his subsequent life secluded woodlands were his favourite places of prayer. Here he began 'to taste the sweets of communion with God', praying and praising aloud. In the evenings he would join the captain's cronies in the taverns or the theatres, according to the custom of sailors ashore, although his relish for amusements had weakened 'and I was rather a spectator than a sharer in their pleasures.' He had to battle with himself when they headed towards the brothels but next day he would be back in the woods, sincerely seeking nearness to God. His thoughts ran also to Polly, and ran all the faster when the voyage resumed and they neared Liverpool, which the *Brownlow* reached before Christmas 1749.

Manesty immediately offered Newton a command of his own for the next African slaving season. On the strength of this promise Newton wrote to Polly. Receiving a kind though non-committal reply he hurried south. At Rotherhithe he found that his stepmother had a friendly invitation from the Catletts to accompany him; she was unwell but sent his young half-brother Billy along as a mark of her approval.

It was seven years since John Newton had fallen in love with Polly Catlett and now he was back at Chatham. Her family tactfully left him alone to press his suit.

His love had not abated. In Polly he saw innocence and gentleness in a world which, for him as a slave trader, was filled with deceit and violence. She was pure; only for Polly could he conquer lust. Her love would be his calm harbour where his restless, homeless spirit could anchor, to enjoy again the sunshine which had gone out of his life when his mother died.

Polly was not very literate. Her few letters which survive are too stilted to reveal much of her character. Newton speaks of her as easy and accomplished in the domestic arts and social graces and much esteemed by her genteel friends; her one portrait shows a cheerful, rounded face with laughing eyes. Yet she remains a shadowy character; posterity cannot well fathom what Newton saw in her on that winter day as he faced her awkwardly, after all those years apart, to ask her to marry him.

And Polly said, 'No.' Moreover, she said he must not raise the matter again, and she said this with so grave a face that he nearly took her refusal as final.

He withdrew to a wood nearby and walked up and down a leafy ride. Sure that no one was within hearing he spoke his thoughts aloud, considering how he might best deserve and return Polly's love and praying for her welfare. In the days to follow he had many tender soliloquies in the wood and often repeated her name, just to hear it returned by the echo from the trees.

Her kindly aunt who lived near, and had been the first channel of his love, encouraged him to persist. The whole Catlett family smiled on his efforts. One day her mother, probably as deliberate encouragement, let slip that Polly had remarked, '*If* we should be married, we should do well together.'

After that, John Newton decided to brook no denial, strengthened by his conviction that Polly was too generous to send him empty away.

At evening he touched again the subject on which she had told him to be silent. Again she refused, but he thought she did not speak in so peremptory a manner. He persisted. In a little time she heard without interrupting him, and then proceeded to argue and object in a cool, conversational way. She told him he pressed her to a life in which, as Mrs. John Newton, she would often look back with regret to 'happy Polly Catlett'. He tried to persuade her that she would not lose her pleasures, only change them.

Remembering a line from a play, 'The woman that deliberates is *gained*,' he began to urge his point more closely, until she yielded! She gave her hand in token of consent. And John, who had been for so long begging for it, could only take it in trembling and surprise, thinking he must be dreaming. He sat stupid and speechless, minute after minute, until she showed her embarrassment. His heart fluttered to such a degree that he could not get a word out.

That night he fell asleep in perfect contentment, aware as never before how strongly he loved her.

They were married on 1 February 1750. Reaction set in at once. He wondered whether he had made a mistake. Eager for heights of emotion yet diffident and awkward, while Polly was so cautious and reserved that she seemed hardly the Polly of his dreams, John Newton passed some uncomfortable weeks. Then, as he put it afterwards to Polly, 'the prospect cleared up and by quick stages I attained to that consciousness of your affection which I would not exchange for empire and the riches of the whole globe.'

The both fell deeply and irrecoverably in love. Her constant endearments loosened his tongue. 'Love cannot be ardent and intense until it becomes reciprocal,' he would say. John and Polly, still living under her parents' roof, became wrapped up in one another all day long, and when John lay in her arms at night he would silently reflect how different this was 'from the vice the libertine would disguise under the name of love', which he had tasted too often on the Coast.

They were so happy together that he began to lose his ambition to serve God. Had this matrimonial bliss continued he might have sunk without trace as a Christian. To paraphrase his comments:

'Any spiritual light I had was like the first faint streaks of early dawn; and I believe it was not yet day-break for my dear wife. She was not lacking in polite religion but knew nothing of a pilgrimage of faith. We were like two inexperienced people on the edge of a wild wilderness, without a guide, ignorant of the way they should take, entirely unaware of the difficulties they might encounter. My faint sense of dependence on God was wearing away and I was too much a coward to dare pray aloud with Polly. Christ had begun to knock at the door of my heart; if he had not mercifully determined to take no denial, my idolatrous attachment to her would I believe have barred and bolted him out.

'He designed a separation which, though very grievous to me, proved the means of drawing us both to himself.'

The African sailing season approached. Newton had been disappointed in his expectation of some family income soon after his marriage, which would have enabled him to abandon the sea and set up in a landsman's calling. With no other support for Polly he must take up his command. 'The prospect of the separation was as terrible to me as death.' In a bid to prevent it he began to gamble: he bought tickets in the Lottery. He spent more than he could afford, all the while attempting to bribe God by promising to give away a good slice of any prize. But winnings never came. All his tickets proved blanks; he ended seventy pounds in debt.

On 18 May 1750 he rode away from Chatham. The Newtons' hearts were too full to say much at parting. John had a good horse, a good road and wanted no company except the charm of happy memories. He would try to cheer himself with the thought of reunion at last, though the voyage might last a year or more.

In the event, reunion came soon. Manesty said he had no ship good enough yet for Newton and kept him on hand at Liverpool, then sent him to London on business and allowed him a week's leave afterwards. The delight of being with Polly again ended in their second parting. And this might have been the last, and Polly a widow, for on the final day of his return ride he was within a few miles of Liverpool at dusk. His horse was tired and thirsty. Newton saw what he thought was a pond a few feet below the roadside and made for it – whereupon horse and rider plunged head over heels into a marlpit. Both escaped unhurt but he heard afterwards that three people had been killed that way. Once again he saw the hand of God.

But all these deliverances were negative. As yet, he had done nothing beautiful for God. He had been saved from sinking and starving on the *Greyhound* by Divine intervention, as he was sure. He had been saved from wild animals and violent Africans; he had been saved from drowning on several occasions when landing or embarking in native canoes which the surf overturned.

And during these years he had been saved, morally, from ensnaring himself beyond hope of reclaim.

He was now nearly twenty-five years of age. It was time to be up and doing if only he could discover the way. He wrote to his mother's old pastor, Dr. Jennings, the friend of long ago. Jennings replied that he hoped to be in Liverpool but Newton sailed first – back to the Slave Trade in the line of duty, and in his first command, the *Duke of Argyle*.

No bystander watching him embark would have prophesied that one day he would be renowned as evangelist, pastor and hymn writer. And had some seen that future, they would have been hard put to guess by what route and through what adventures this uncertain Christian, Captain John Newton the younger, would make his spiritual landfall.

13

Slaver Captain

Even before he had reached Africa John Newton's ship proved a disappointment. The *Duke of Argyle* was a two masted 'snow' (somewhat similar to a brig) of a hundred and forty tons, an old and crazy vessel which he reckoned hardly fit to lie in a dock or make a river passage. Her state added to the dangers of a Guinea voyage, which Newton described as 'a complicated precarious affair'.

The crew of thirty were the usual 'set of wretches'; Newton wrote that he could 'hardly go on board a vessel but I am told, there never was such a set of wretches ... Debauchery, profaneness and insensibility dreadfully abound in every ship.' He knew the need to keep strict discipline, 'as absolute in my small dominion, except for power of life and death, as any potentate in Europe'. In port there would be a 'mighty bustle of attendance' when he left the ship and a strict watch kept lest he return unawares and not be received in due form. No one might sleep until he was back on board, so he was careful not to stay late on shore without good cause. This was unusual tact in a ship's master but Newton kept in mind what his situation had been on board H.M.S. *Harwich*, and that in Africa he had been 'a servant of slaves'.

He sought to do his duty by the common sailors 'without oppression, ill language or abuse', though his was a turbulent crew. His mate, Bridson, supported him well. Down the coast of Guinea Bridson commanded the longboat, searching out slaves for sale (as Newton had searched when mate of the *Brownlow*) with much gain to the business of the ship until he died of fever. The second mate was a good man and the surgeon, Robert Arthur, became a dear friend, but the bosun had to be put in irons on occasion to teach him a lesson.

One of the worst of the sailors was a fellow named William Lees; combating his insolence and wildness undoubtedly helped to form John Newton's character.

Lees first came to notice at the Sierra Leone river. He refused to keep his watch one night and threatened to strike the bosun who ordered him to his duty. Newton gave Lees a warning. Next day Lees was one of three who rowed a work party ashore but instead of returning on board went without leave to a French schooner and got drunk, liquor being easily obtainable because rum was a principal item in barter for slaves. After their drinking spree the three absconders landed to have a fight with their French friends. When tired of that they attempted to come off against the ebb tide but were too drunk to pull well. They grounded among the rocks and obliged Newton to borrow another captain's boat and send the second mate to their rescue. The mate got them off the rocks but could not shift the boat in time for Newton to go ashore to inspect slaves on offer: the other captain bought the five worth choosing.

Newton ordered each of Lee's partners in crime, Tom Creed and Tom True, to strip to the waist and lie across a gun. He gave them a good caning. Lees was put in irons, since he was already in the punishment book for his insolence the night before. This experience did not reform him: when the *Duke of Argyle* reached the Plantain islands and Newton, not forgetting to look for the limes now growing on the trees he had planted in his misery, paid a state visit to his old master and mistress, Lees gave yet more trouble. Newton had bought a boy and a girl and was about to embark with them for the ship when he discovered that Lees had attempted to desert by hiding on the island. Found, he was drunk and very abusive. Newton had to pay Princess P.I.'s blacks a gallon of brandy to secure him in irons and put him on the boat.

Two days later Clow and his Princess visited the *Duke of Argyle*. One of their blacks who had helped secure Lees came too near as he sat on the windlass and Lees struck at him with the carpenter's maul but just missed his head, grazing his chest, an attack which might have had a very dangerous consequence for the voyage had he struck a mainland chief's servant. However, the Princess permitted the gift of a lace hat to the injured and offended black, which made up the matter.

Newton determined to be rid of Lees. He put him in irons and stapled him to the deck like a recalcitrant slave. At this his two friends of the Sierra Leone drinking spree, Creed and True, became mutinous. Newton decided to discharge all three into a man of war, the fate he had himself avoided by taking service with Clow after being too insolent for the mate who had assumed command on their captain's death, that first voyage on the Coast.

H.M.S. *Surprise* lay in the Sierra Leone estuary. The very next day, running through a high wind, hard rain and a strong sea, Newton took Lees, in irons, by boat to Sierra Leone and delivered him to Captain Baird, who obligingly sailed *Surprise* to the

Plantains, with Newton as passenger, and anchored beyond the *Duke of Argyle*. Baird relieved Newton of his mutineers by pressing them into the Navy, giving three of his naval crew in exchange, to their unconcealed delight. Thus Newton, in the pursuit of good order, condemned his troublemakers to the terrors of naval discipline from which he himself had escaped five years before.

Sternness saved Newton from a mutiny on that occasion but on another it was an outbreak of sickness among the crew, which frustrated a conspiracy on the eve of its execution because, in delirium, one of those involved revealed the plans. Newton arrested the ringleader, who had boasted that the ship's company would rise at his word, that he would kill the first mate and the surgeon, then presumably the captain, and sail the ship to a port where they were unknown, to sell the slaves for their own profit.

The voyage of the *Duke of Argyle* did not prove particularly profitable to Newton, who found that his black cargo could be gathered only slowly. According to the custom of the Coast he worked mostly through middlemen who traded with native chiefs for slaves, just as Newton himself had traded before the *Greyhound* had found him. These traders, whether whites or mulattoes, all tried to cheat him except for Clow, whom Newton despised and resented but was obliged often to depend upon, and a mulatto who had been in England and Portugal, fat Harry Tucker; Newton secured his best purchases, whether men, women or children, through Tucker and found his word more dependable than that of any white man on the Coast: he never deceived. Tucker had acquired a great fortune in silver and slaves and lived in state, and the natives feared him because they all owed him money. He had a numerous offspring from half a dozen wives, two of whom Newton took as passengers for four days with their female attendants through a tornado, and soon heartily tired of their company but had dared not decline the honour, as he wanted further trade with their lord and master.

Tucker's son sold him an excellent lot, eighteen slaves, bought from pirates who had cut off a French slaver two nights earlier, murdering six of the crew and driving three others overboard. Tucker had redeemed the French captain. Though Newton was sorry to profit from another captain's misfortune, no man on the Coast would have expected him to have given back stolen slaves whom he had bought for good barter.

As the living cargo increased, so did the menace to the captain and crew of a slaver such as the *Duke of Argyle*. Fortunately for Newton the captives did not attempt to rise when the ship lay on the Coast, trading, with seven or eight of the best men away in the longboat searching for more. But when at last, in May 1751, the *Duke of Argyle* weighed anchor and lost sight of Africa, and ran well before a strong wind, a young slave who had not been in irons because of a large ulcer and his good behaviour, smuggled down a large marlin spike through the gratings.

A seaman noticed a suspicious action, but before the crew missed the marlin spike and searched for it among the slaves, twenty of them had sawn through their fetters; if they had been left alone another hour they would have risen and brought trouble and damage. As it was, twenty slaves were loose, and the wind blowing into a tornado. Newton could not secure them but kept men at the hatch behind a gun primed and loaded with shot which could work terrible effect in the hold. After a tense night and early morning the wind abated and by afternoon every man was back in irons.

Then Newton paraded the ringleaders, strongly built men who would sell well. He clamped them in iron collars which press upon the neck, jaws and shoulders, and gave them a taste of the thumbscrews, yet not more than to make them scream a little. After only one hour's punishment, merciful by standards of the time, he released them to join the rest below.

These slaves who had tried to regain their freedom were villains in Newton's eyes. Although he now regarded himself as a Christian, and held divine service for his crew on Sundays, an unheard of eccentricity for a slaver captain, he was unaware that he engaged in iniquity. The Slave Trade was universally regarded as a genteel occupation.

And Newton's religious light was still so dim that it was the faraway Polly and not awareness of God which kept him from adultery with the women slaves. More than forty years later he wrote in a private meditation that his affection for Polly formed 'an effectual barrier at a time when superior motives had little influence with me. Though, when upon the Coast, I was always encompassed with women over whom I had absolute power, the thought of the dear woman I had left at home had such possession of my heart that I was no less indifferent to the rest of the sex than a child of three years of age. Perhaps the faint perceptions I then had of [God's] greatness and goodness would not have been sufficient to have restrained me from many evils, which seemed to be easily checked by my attachment to her.' (Other 'African' captains, boasting of their conquests and their prostitutes, had teased him mightily, saying he was a slave to one woman. Newton teased back that they were slaves to a hundred.)

Nevertheless, though unaware that morally he was engaged in a crime against humanity, he was storing up a knowledge of the Slave Trade which would be of incalculable value when the campaign for its Abolition began more than thirty years later. Alone of the

Abolitionists John Newton had seen it from the inside, and could recall those days on the *Duke of Argyle* and his later ship: how he had put the slaves below in rows, one above the other, each side of the vessel, like books on a shelf, though he did not have them laid as close as some captains did.

Fettered hand and feet in pairs, it was difficult for them to turn or move, to attempt to rise or lie down, without hurting themselves, and the ship's motion added to the discomfort.

The *Duke of Argyle* sailed on through cloudy dark weather, which was incredibly cold considering the tropical sun, so that Newton had to keep the slaves battened down. When they were brought up to be washed with fresh water they complained so much of cold that he sent them down again once the rooms were cleaned. Soon the weather prevented their being brought up on deck, and the rooms cleaned, every day; the heat and smell would have been unbearable to a person not used to it.

Newton recorded in the Log: 'They still look very gloomy and sullen and have doubtless mischief in their heads if they could find opportunity to vent it. But I hope (by the Divine Assistance) we are fully able to over-awe them now.' He had no further trouble, and no disease on board: he buried at sea only half a dozen slaves, a small loss, before making landfall at the British island of Antigua in the West Indies. Squally weather gave him three nearly sleepless nights before he anchored in St. John's roads at sunset on 3 July 1751.

By then the crew had shaved all the men slaves and freed them from their fetters. Joy at this liberty from shackles and from the terror of the ocean was short-lived. Once landed and sold, the hardships and suffering they had already endured would, for most of them, only end in excessive toil, hunger and the tortures of the cartwhip.

Newton never forgot how Mr. Manesty's Antigua agent, who was himself a planter, remarked as they sat at dinner in his mansion at St. John's, that calculations had been made as to whether it were more economical to give slaves moderate work, good food, and treatment such as might enable them to live to old age; or, 'By rigorously straining their strength to the utmost, with hard fare and hard usage, to wear them out before they became useless; and then buy new ones.'

Most planters declared the latter mode cheaper; the agent knew of estates in Antigua where few slaves lived more than nine years.

14

Chains, Bolts and Shackles

Among the letters waiting at Antigua, which included loving missives from Polly in her laboured hand, lay one with news of old Captain Newton's death. The Governor of Fort York had gone bathing; seized with cramp he was drowned only a few days before the arrival of the ship that was to have brought him home from Hudson's Bay. Newton grieved for a father whose gruff affection and constant care had withstood his son's rebellion, and who had not lived to enjoy his reformation.

After five weeks in Antigua the voyage home with a cargo of rum and sugar was saddened further by the death of the ship's surgeon. Surgeon Arthur had been Newton's one true friend on board, with whom he could talk about Polly without feeling he degraded her: the common sailors were unworthy to hear her name. Arthur had caught a fever at St. John's but believing himself convalescent had rejected Newton's suggestion that he say behind.

The homeward passage in the hurricane season was the most risky part of the voyage as the *Duke of Argyle,* now in a dangerous state, ran before strong westerlies, through cold and storm and high seas.

Newton 'trusted to that Providence which has never failed me', and came at last to Polly's arms after fourteen months, in a reunion so sweet that it refreshed him to recall when next under the African sun.

They were at Chatham from the late autumn of 1751 to the spring of 1752. Newton read Christian books, including the classic *Life of God in the Soul of Man* by Henry Scougal, which had been the means of the conversion of George Whitefield, a name which as yet meant nothing to him though Whitefield's and Wesley's revivals had begun to change the land. 'As to preaching, I heard none but of the common sort, and hardly had an idea of any better.' He lacked a guide for his reading, found no Christian friends and, scared lest neighbours and acquaintances think him too pious, never uttered those expressions of zeal and love for Jesus 'which seem so suitable to the case of one who has had much forgiven'. In the phrases of the famous hymn he would one day write about Jesus, he enjoyed 'the music of Thy name', but did not 'Thy love proclaim with every fleeting breath'; or indeed with one.

When the time came to part again, Polly startled him by proposing that he pray aloud. Though he himself could not live without prayer he had been too cowardly to suggest praying with her. They knelt down in their bedroom in the Catletts' home, and as he prayed, Newton 'felt like a person committing his dearest treasure to his dearest Friend', and then went downstairs with a mixture of peace and grief; 'not as one violently torn away, but willingly surrendering her for a time that I might deserve her better.' He expected a long absence; but trust in God cleared away his cares and fears.

At Liverpool he saw his new command, the *African*, still on the stocks at Fisher's Yard, and reckoned it would be one of the best and strongest of vessels, although when launched it turned out to be an indifferent sailor.

This second voyage as a Slave Trade captain took Newton away from England for one year, one month and twenty-nine days. Before embarking he followed the practice (used by Nelson a generation later) of putting up a notice in the churches to interest the prayers of all good people, and to Polly he wrote of God in his first letter after leaving home waters, as 'an ever-present and an all-sufficient Helper'. During the outward voyage a captain's duties were light in a ship well made, officered and victualled. In the old *Duke of Argyle* he had spent his leisure studying Latin classics; But in the *African* he preferred the Bible. On both ships he spent hours writing to Polly the letters which eventually formed the material for his celebrated *Letters to a Wife*. He used to say that this regular writing taught him style and laid his foundations of authorship.

The months of slave trading on the Coast brought the usual hazards. The outstanding incident was his preservation from an extraordinary attempt to kidnap him. In February 1753 he was doing trade with a white man named Bryan and wished to sail onwards while still owed four slaves to the value of a hundred pounds. Bryan had agreed to hand them over on the beach near his home but produced only two and seemed in a huff. He grudgingly promised to deliver the other two at the same place four days later.

On the night before Newton should go ashore to collect them he had a disturbing dream which seemed a warning of an unpleasant and dangerous experience, with a promise that he would suffer no harm. At first light he took a boat, bringing with him another captain, Jennings, who happened to be his passenger. The surf ran high. Newton had landed in worse, yet he felt a strong inward reluctance to venture ashore. For half an hour he hesitated outside the breakers, then returned to the ship, the only occasion throughout his time in the Slave Trade that he did not keep an appointment. To Jennings he blamed the high surf, but the true reason was a strong sense of a different danger. Jennings made no comment.

That evening the missing slaves arrived on board, together with a letter from trader Bryan couched in violent terms, accusing Newton of misbehaviour with one of Bryan's mistresses, Harry Tucker's sister: the woman had confessed her adultery and was now in chains and Newton had forfeited all further friendship with Bryan.

Newton was astonished, the more so when his mate and his passenger both admitted that they had heard Bryan 'talking with such a mixture of grief and resentment that he must believe it; he had too much sense and spirit, too much honesty, to frame the charge himself just to avoid paying a debt. Besides, he was rich; he could not grudge the slaves he owed.' The charge was ridiculous, for Newton had never spoken with the woman, let alone taken her, and it was hard to think who had poisoned Bryan's ear or how the woman could have been induced to accuse herself of a falsehood which exposed her to his rage and a variety of punishment. Newton discovered that Bryan had plotted to seize him the moment he landed that morning, and would have detained him forcibly, possibly killed him. The charge, Newton says, 'greatly threatened my honour and interest both in Africa and England'. It was aimed to destroy his life or his character and would probably have ruined his voyage, had he not turned back in the surf.

At it was, he signed a declaration of innocence and on his next voyage the accusation was publicly acknowledged to be a malicious calumny.

His escape seemed to Newton further evidence of the guiding hand of God, whom he still thought of as a beneficent Providence and a merciful judge rather than as Father and Saviour; the Holy Spirit remained a mystery. Newton did not doubt that the death of Christ was the ground of his salvation, nor deny Christ's resurrection, yet between the truth he accepted and the daily life he must lead lay a fog: he saw through a glass, darkly.

Increasingly he loved to think on these things, to pray and meditate. In daytime the heat of the sun, the smoke of the furnace where they branded and fettered new-bought slaves, and the hurry of trade, were troublesome except when thoughts of Polly interposed. But when the sun set, the fires were out, the slaves battened in the hold, and all but the watch asleep, he enjoyed himself without disturbance. Sometimes he would look back on past mercies, sometimes forward in hope. He would reflect how God in His Providence had been pleased to set him apart, not only from the crowds whose miseries and sufferings were obvious but from most of those who supposed themselves happy. Though removed by a third of the globe from his only treasure, Polly, and though enduring a time of trial, God had highly distinguished him in the three greatest blessings: religion, liberty and love.

Once, on Bence Island, he had leisure for a solitary ramble on a fine and serene moonlit night, when he could pray and think aloud without fear of being overheard. The ship lay in sight at a short distance, which led Newton to recall 'the many interventions of a kind preserving Providence and encouraged me to ask the same gracious protection for the rest of the voyage'. He prayed for Polly, faithful and patient in the prolonged separations imposed by his profession as a sea captain, venturing her first uncertain steps of Christian pilgrimage; he felt that were he master of the whole coast of Africa he would part with it gladly to procure for her the peace he himself possessed, and true comfort from Religion. He prayed that soon they would love God even more than they loved each other. He prayed too for the blacks in their passions, darkness, superstition and loss of liberty.

Again, on Sundays during the Middle Passage, when he would arrange the ship's affairs to make it as much as possible a day of rest for the crew, and lead them in divine service, he would enjoy meditation on the quarter deck or in his cabin. It has been said by writers who dismiss as hypocrisy the subsequent Christian campaign for the Abolition of the Slave Trade, that Newton wrote his famous hymn, *How Sweet the Name of Jesus Sounds*, on the quarter deck of his ship while the slaves languished in their chains below, and that this at least shows his power of detachment. The legend is without substance: the hymn cannot be precisely dated but certainly was written at Olney. He still held too weak a grasp of Christian truth to have written it when at sea.

Yet he would not have seen any incongruity: 'During the time I was engaged in the Slave Trade I never had the least scruple as to its lawfulness.'

This second voyage had not proved profitable because slaves were scarce upon the Coast through over-trading, and the ship's purchases were a violent, liberty-loving lot, probably warriors from an up country tribe who had been captured in war and sold to coastal chiefs. The *African*'s crew was 'much menaced by our cargo'. The slaves' almost desperate attempts at insurrection continually alarmed Newton, and when quiet they were always watching for opportunity. At sea he surprised two of the slaves attempting to get off their irons, and three boys were caught with chisels. Newton fettered these in irons and put them slightly in the thumbscrews which soon produced a full confession. This led to further search and the discovery of knives, stones, shot and a cold chisel.

A month earlier another Liverpool ship had lost the chief mate, three or four white seamen and nineteen black slaves before an insurrection was quelled; Newton, punishing the ringleaders quite mercifully, considered he had been delivered by the favour of Divine Providence.

Two days later he was overtaken by a fast roomy London vessel, well manned and not designed for slaves. Newton boarded her and after much persuasion her captain agreed to take half a dozen of the ringleaders and keep them unfettered, which Newton in his small ship could not. He reckoned that the improvement to their physique would attract a higher price which would cover the cost of their freight.

After this, wrote Newton, 'all the slaves changed their mood, and behaved more like children in one family than slaves in chains and irons, and really were more obliging and considerate than white people.'

Newton had received instructions to land his slaves at St. Kitt's instead of Antigua, and was distraught to find no letters from Polly. He made himself ill with worry, convinced in his ignorance, that God was punishing him at the tenderest spot by removing Polly from this earth, because of his spiritual unfaithfulness, 'especially my backwardness in speaking of spiritual things, which I could hardly attempt even to her'. He thought she might have died in childbirth, for an early letter received on the Coast had hinted of pregnancy. But Polly never bore any children; quite possibly her barrenness may have been a consequence of John's former promiscuous behaviour.

Letters arrived; none from Polly. Newton lost appetite and sleep and expected to die of a broken heart. The owner's agent, Francis Guichard, and his wife showed much concern: good news for their guest was the constant toast after dinner and supper, and a thousand contrivances were set on foot to divert him. If he mentioned anything he wanted, the whole country was ransacked.

At last it crossed his mind to send the longboat to Antigua. A day or two later the boat returned, just as he had sealed his letters, including one to Polly which he had written in a valiant attempt to persuade himself that she still lived to read it. He added in a postscript: 'I gladly break open yours to tell that the boat I sent to Antigua has brought me (Oh, how kind and careful is my dear!) six letters from you, besides several others from friends which, though very acceptable, are of less importance to my peace.' All had arisen from a casual mistake: the owner's change of orders had not been passed to the letter office.

Newton recovered at once, and sent Polly sweetmeats, and a pineapple which was a present from his hostess. He followed them three weeks later, having warned her that his ship was rather of the slow sort, like her captain.

Then Polly and he had seven weeks together in the early autumn of 1753, the happiest of his life to date, for the Newtons lived at Liverpool in lodgings instead of at Chatham, where they had grudged her family's natural claims. They enjoyed evening walks in the Lancashire countryside, when the setting sun, the trees, the birds and the views contributed to enrich the scene, and as they sat together, facing another parting, their thoughts rose faster than words until the tears stole down their cheeks.

When he sailed again in the *African* on 21 October for a shorter voyage he was growing weary of separations, and had

begun to hate being a captain in the Slave Trade. He had not
woken yet to moral disgust at what he would afterwards call 'this
vile traffic'. Later Newton would confess he wondered 'how I
did not start with horror at my own employment'. But no one
except little-read philosophers had called in question a Trade
which had flourished for centuries; not until six years later did
the Philadelphian Quaker, Anthony Benezet, write his famous
pamphlet against it and several more years went by before the
first stirrings of the early Abolition movement could be detected
in England. Universal custom, the attitudes of the day, and
Newton's professional interest combined to keep him blinded to
the Trade's enormity.

'I am sure,' he would say more than thirty years later, 'that
had I thought of the Slave Trade then as I have thought of it
since, no considerations would have induced me to continue.
Though my religious views were not very clear my conscience
was very tender and I dared not have displeased God by acting
against the light of my mind. The numerous and continual
dangers to which a slave ship is exposed had thrown me into an
uncommon dependence on the Providence of God; this gave me
a confidence which must have failed in a moment, and I would
have been overwhelmed in distress and terror, if I had known or
even suspected that I was acting wrongly.'

He had begun to feel that the business was disagreeable. He disliked
being a gaoler and was 'sometimes shocked with an employment
that was perpetually conversant with chains, bolts and shackles'. He
looked on it as the line of life which God had allotted him, and
thought himself bound only to treat the slaves gently and to consult
their ease and convenience so far as was consistent with the safety of
the ship and its whole family, white and black. Yet he was praying

that God would soon fix him in a more humane calling, where he could enjoy regular Christian ministrations, and be with Polly.

His prayer would be answered. This third voyage would be the last. It would also change his life.

Its early stages, however, were unpleasant – because his past caught up with him in the shape of Job Lewis.

15

Grace My Fears Relieved

Job Lewis was the clean-living and high-principled mid-shipman in H.M.S. *Harwich* whom the young John Newton had turned into an atheist and a libertine. Lewis later left the Navy to become master of the *Lamb* in the New England trade out of Liverpool; when they next met their ships were stormbound in company for two weeks off the Isle of Man at the start of Newton's first command.

In the autumn of 1753 Newton again found Lewis at Liverpool, about to sail as master of a Guinea ship, and glad of advice on the skills and perils of the Slave Trade. As in old times they also joked, yarned and discussed books. Newton discovered that the once sober youth of H.M.S. *Harwich* was now a hardened sinner. Confronted, after all these years, with the grievous success of 'my unhappy attempts to infect him with libertine principles', Newton tried to repair the damage. 'I gave him a plain account of the manner and reason of my change and used every argument to persuade him to relinquish his infidel schemes.' Lewis stayed obdurate. When Newton 'pressed him so close that he had no other reply to make, he would remind me that I was the very first person who had given him an idea of his liberty.'

Apart from other factors, Newton's failure to convince Lewis sprang from his own uncertain grasp of Christian truth. 'I once was blind, but now I see'; yet he could not explain the why or the how. He did not abandon the attempt; and when Job's shipowner went bankrupt and threw him on the beach before he had sailed, Newton offered him a berth on the *African* as 'Volunteer and Captain's Commander'. This would provide a knowledge of the Coast, and Manesty promised him a ship of his own on their return; but Newton's object was less to serve Job's professional interest than to gain further time to win him back, hoping that 'my arguments, example and prayers' in the course of the voyage might have good effect.

Once at sea Newton had frequent reason to regret this well intended impulse. Job Lewis was 'exceedingly profane and grew worse and worse; I saw in him a lively picture of what I had once been, but it was very inconvenient to have it always before my eyes. Besides, he was not only deaf to my remonstrances but laboured all he could to counteract my influence.'

As an officer he was so bad tempered and imperious that it required all Newton's prudence and authority to restrain him, especially as the *African* had an almost new crew, mostly of seasoned lags: on the outward passage the ship's cooper and a foremast man broached a cask of ale and filled it up with water, a common trick on the Coast, and stole snuff from the cargo, and were caught. Newton ordered the seaman a dozen lashes of the cat o' nine tails, and the cooper, as a petty officer, a dozen and a half, but in mercy spared each the last lash. When the *African* reached the Coast the carpenter refused orders, grossly abused the second mate, and behaved very mutinously on shore: he got two dozen lashes at the gangway.

With a turbulent crew, and a slow start to the slaving season, Newton longed to be free of Lewis, 'a sharp thorn in my side'.

At the end of December the *African* sailed into the Sherbro river. Newton spied among the shipping a small snow, the *Racehorse*, lying in her moorings empty: she had been recovered from the natives after her British captain and crew had been cut off and killed. The *Racehorse* offered the solution to two problems at once: Manesty's orders were to sail for St. Kitts in April, yet as Newton had warned him, slaves were hard to come by that year, and three or four months gave too little time to barter all the remaining goods from England, which could not be taken onward without spoiling nor be stored on the Coast; he had bought so few slaves that his voyage faced ruin for owner and captain alike. But if he could transfer the surplus cargo to the *Racehorse*, Captain Lewis could take charge of her and continue to purchase slaves and camwood on the *African*'s account when Newton left the Coast. And he would be free of the man.

After two days of sale bargaining, Newton could give Lewis a written appointment to command the *Racehorse*, and a crew, and fit her out with a well assorted cargo. On the night of 18 January 1754 Newton came on board for a last farewell. He repeated and emphasized his best advice, both as to trade and especially as to matters of the soul. Lewis seemed truly affected, for his friendship and regard for Newton were 'as great as could be expected where principles were so diametrically opposite'. He sailed away in good spirits and high hopes.

As soon as he was free of Newton's eye, Lewis put his lust and every appetite on a loose rein. Native women, hard drinking, violent rages, and the treacherous climate, combined to deprive him of resistance when fever attacked about a month later. Newton first heard of Job's illness when the *African*'s longboat returned, shortly after a tornado, with a cargo of camwood and slaves: one of these had been acquired by Lewis, who sent word that he had bought ten more.

Three days later Newton ran the *African* to the point where he had ordered Lewis to rendezvous, and soon sighted her consort. As the *Racehorse* drew near she began to fire minute guns and he noticed her colours at half-mast, a signal that her master must be dead. The officer whom Newton had appointed first mate, Taylor, came on board with the news that Captain Lewis had died of fever four days previously and had been buried at sea. Taylor's account of Job's last days was dreadful. As the fever took hold his rage and despair struck the small crew with horror. He was going to hell, he cried, yet gave no sign that he either hoped or asked for mercy. 'He died convinced,' mused Newton in his sorrow and remorse, 'but not changed;' in the hour of extremity his atheism fell away yet he went to God's judgement seat without repentance. Newton stood all the more amazed at God's goodness to himself, a wretch who might have gone the same way.

A few weeks later Newton nearly died. He had left the *Racehorse* under command of his first mate and set out in the *African* across the Atlantic when he fell desperately ill. For eight or ten days he lay prostrated by high fever, without pains or delirium but on several occasions believing, and the surgeon too, that he was dying. He found himself facing eternity composed and tranquil, his hopes stronger than his fears. 'My trust, though weak in degree, was alone fixed upon the blood and righteousness of Jesus.' The New Testament's promise, 'He is able to save to the uttermost them that come into God by Him,' gave him great relief: he was not afraid of God's wrath. But a peculiar fear greatly troubled him, that amid all the myriads continually entering the unseen world he would be lost or overlooked. 'Perhaps,' he feared, 'the Lord will take no notice of me.' At length a verse of Scripture put his mind to rest: 'The Lord knoweth them that are His.' The Lord might seem far away, despite all Newton's prayers and studies, yet He would recognize the wretch He had saved.

The fever receded. While he convalesced before complete recovery Newton's prayers were dominated by two petitions: that he might understand the faith better so that he could rescue men like Job Lewis, whom he had failed; and that he might be free of his distasteful calling.

Both prayers would be answered.

The *African* had a quick, trouble free run to St. Kitts. Owing to the failure of trade on the Coast Newton carried only eighty-seven slaves instead of the two hundred and twenty intended, which allowed him to give them more space and to achieve the remarkable record of a passage without a single death: his entire voyage passed without a mortality, black or white, since Job Lewis had died when no longer on the ship's books.

For the last time, though he did not know it, John Newton delivered his blacks to the owner's agent, and thus to the slave market. Then he had much leisure while preparing for homeward passage.

The planters, merchants and other gentry of Basse Terre, the town of St. Kitts, kept up a lively social life to which they invited visiting captains. John Newton, with his good singing voice, his sense of humour and his skill in turning verses was a popular guest in their gracious drawing rooms where house slaves served and picaninnies pulled the fans and the hospitality derived from the sweat of field hands, toiling in the living death of the cane fields under threat of the cartwhip.

At one such party Newton met a lively, cheerful sea captain in his late thirties, and thus about ten years older than himself, named Alexander Clunie, who was not engaged in the Slave Trade. Some 'casual expressions in mixed company' revealed to both Clunie and Newton that they, alone among their hosts and fellow guests, loved God. They walked back to the quayside together and soon became inseparable companions whenever the business of their ships would permit.

Alex Clunie, a Scot, belonged to an Independent congregation in Stepney, near Newton's riverside birthplace and London Pool. His minister was Samuel Brewer, a friend of Dr. Jennings and of the late Dr. Watts the hymnwriter, who had died six years before. Clunie could impart the things of God clearly to a fellow sailor. 'I was all ears,' writes Newton, 'and what was better, he not only informed my understanding but his discourses inflamed my heart.' After their meeting Newton lost appetite for evening parties. Instead, during nearly four weeks in May and June 1754 the two spent every evening on board each other's ship alternately, often prolonging their visits to daybreak. Sometimes on a Sunday, after being together most of the day, they could hardly bear to part at midnight.

Until he met Clunie, Newton had lacked a Christian friend who spoke in a way he could follow. He had learned something of the evil of his heart; he had read through the Bible again and again, and books, and letters from Dr. Jennings, so that he had a general idea of the truth of the Christian gospel; but his ideas were confused. And he was troubled by a fear of relapsing into his old apostasy. But under Alex Clunie he grasped the Christian's security, that he could expect to be preserved, 'not by my own power and holiness but by the mighty power and promise of God through faith in an unchangeable Saviour'. He realized it at last: since he, through grace, belonged to Zion's City, none could shake his sure repose; with salvation's walls surrounded, he could smile at all his foes.

God had given His Son to be the Saviour of the world; amazing grace had saved a wretch and His providence had since interposed again and again in answer to prayer. But Newton had thought of God as a distant potentate whom he must obey. Now he discovered that God could be very near and His love be warmer than Newton had dreamed. Poring with Clunie over the Scriptures in the captain's cabin of the *African*, under Polly's smiling portrait, with the harbour sounds of Basse Terre wafting in, Newton learned that a Christian may claim the Risen Christ's promise to His first disciples: 'Lo, I am with you always.'

Newton began to find (to adapt words he afterwards wrote) that 'the union of a believer with Christ is so intimate, so unalterable, so rich in privilege, so powerful in influence that it cannot be fully represented by any earthly simile. The Lord, by His Spirit, showed and confirmed His love and made Himself known as He met me at the throne of Grace. He opened and applied His precious promises and enabled me to understand the wonder of redemption; He enabled me to cry in prayer to the Father ... Wonderful are the effects when a crucified, glorious Saviour is presented by the power of the Spirit, in the light of the Word, to the eye of faith. This sight destroys the love of sin, heals the wounds of guilt, softens the hard heart and fills the souls with peace, love and joy; and makes obedience practical, desirable and pleasant. The knowledge of His love to me produced a return of love to Him. I now adored Him and admired Him.'

Newton made an unreserved surrender of heart to Jesus, 'my Lord, my Life, my way, my end'.

Clunie encouraged Newton to pray aloud, taught the advantage of meeting other Christians and urged him to speak for God, whether among the genteel families on the islands or his hardened crew. Until then Newton had never spoken of God, apart from reading the liturgy and lessons on Sundays on board, but had tried to be cheerful always, so that if any among the ship's company realized that their captain was truly religious he would not discourage their pursuit of piety by 'undue severity or supercilious sourness'.

Before they parted, Clunie described to Newton the state of religion in England, with an account of the errors and controversies of the times ('things to which I had been entirely a stranger') and gave him addresses in London where he might gain further instruction. On 20 June 1754 the two friends parted when Newton sailed from St. Kitts, to enjoy a happy, leisured seven weeks' homeward voyage of spiritual and actual sunshine, digesting all he had learned, before the *African* ran into a dangerous, prolonged storm in the Western Approaches.

After almost a week of sleepless nights John Newton anchored safely in the Mersey. He never left English shores again.

Part Three

HOW SWEET THE SOUND

16

With Every Fleeting Breath

Newton prayed the more fervently that he might change his employment. No answer came: he looked set in the Slave Trade for years. Manesty did not hold against him the failure of the last voyage but agreed the *African* was a poor sailor and promised him a ship almost complete on the stocks; he might even select her name. She would be ready to sail in six weeks.

Newton chose the name *Bee*, and hurried off to Chatham for a month, returning afterwards with Polly. The *Bee*, however, was slow to take wing. October dragged into November. Every day's delay weighed heavier on Newton, like the bolts and shackles of his distasteful work as a gaoler of men and women whose offence was to be black, and captured by their slave-raiding fellow blacks, then sold and resold between blacks and whites until herded into the holds of the *Bee*. He did not doubt it an honourable employment and accepted that the Trade was an economic necessity to England, for all men said so; yet he hated it, and wanted more than ever to be with Polly to teach her how sweet the name of Jesus sounds, and to sit with her at the feet of the saints.

Medical symptoms in the eighteenth century cannot easily be matched with their actual cause, but in view of what happened it is hard not to believe that psychological tensions built up as the day of sailing drew closer, though Newton appeared in excellent health.

At last he had fitted out the *Bee*, chosen his crew, taken on his cargo. The *Bee* rode at anchor in the Mersey and in two days they would sail. He left the first mate on board and returned to his lodgings in the afternoon. Polly and he sat drinking tea and talking over past events.

Suddenly Newton fell insensible at her feet. He lay inert, 'deprived of all sense and motion', and she believed he was dead or dying. She kept herself rigidly under control. At her shout for help their landlady rushed in, the maid hurried to the physician, all was bustle and alarm. After about an hour John Newton opened his eyes and they helped him to a sofa.

He regained his senses but the seizure left him dizzy, with a headache and other symptoms which caused the doctors to forbid him to sail. He resigned his command. The *Bee* sailed under another captain for a voyage which turned out calamitous. Newton's substitute died, and most of the officers and many of the crew. The circumstances suggested that whoever had been master of the *Bee* on that voyage would have suffered their fate; Newton's sudden illness had saved him.

Polly and John returned to Chatham to recover his strength, and remained there through the winter and into the spring of 1755. But as Polly's fears subsided she slipped into delayed shock, and while he grew stronger she grew worse, suffering a disorder which no physician could define and no medicine remove. Her husband's concern and her mother's nursing were equally ineffective; and to his further distress Polly still showed no Christian awareness, though she loved her John dearly.

Newton used his sick leave to improve his Latin, French and Mathematics, with an hour before breakfast for devotions. When spring came he took his Bible into the fields and woods and Kentish hills, where the delightful weather and 'the music of birds in the great temple of nature, which the Lord has built for His own honour', helped him concentrate thoughts and prayers and refrain from worry, either about Polly or their future.

He sought out preachers on Sundays but the condition of the parishes around made him wonder, he wrote, whether he had not better stay at home than be present when the glorious gospel was deprecated by those appointed (and paid) to preach.

In June he visited London – and found a new hero. Newton had walked to Gravesend and taken a river boat for cheapness, for unlike many captains in the Slave Trade he had not made a fortune, and savings sank fast during unemployment. The passage up the River Thames would have been agreeable had it not been for the vile company: Newton was obliged to pace the deck for six hours because he could not go below without stopping his ears. He landed near Stepney and called on Samuel Brewer, Alex Clunie's pastor, who told him that George Whitefield had lately returned from America. Brewer wrote an introduction and sent Newton happily onward.

Clunie had already explained all about George Whitefield and John Wesley, how these two Church of England clergymen preached the gospel to great crowds in the fields and the market places, bringing a new breath of vital religion to Britain (and Whitefield to the American colonies) although nicknamed 'Methodists' and attacked by bishops for 'Enthusiasm'. Clunie had described their theological differences and pamphlet warfares, and how the two evangelists were friends again after a period of coolness. Newton had since read Whitefield's published journals and letters, and Wesley's too, and had adored the grace of God in them, but he accounted himself follower of neither.

He hastened into London with his letter of introduction. Whitefield, a florid, middle-aged man in rather untidy clerical dress, with a warm smile and hearty laugh, received Newton most kindly. Busy finishing letters to go to Carolina by a vessel that sailed that afternoon, he could not invite him to linger, so gave him a ticket which would ensure a seat at the Sunday preaching.

Newton rose at four a.m. and after prayer went to Whitefield's Tabernacle, a great shed on Moorfields, where about a thousand people of different denominations worshipped with one heart and soul. Whitefield used the Church of England service, inserting occasional exhortations and encouragements and many little intervals for the singing of hymns, until the spirit and assurance of faith which shone in the evangelist's face and preaching seemed diffused over the whole assembly. They were at it about three hours and Newton went away rejoicing. In the evening a 'prodigious multitude' came; hundreds stayed outside in the yard and many hundreds were forced to go away although the place was supposed to hold five thousand. As Whitefield preached that night a glorious vista of faith and power opened to Newton; Christ was transfigured before him until the young sea captain yearned to love and serve Him to the uttermost.

Back at Chatham he found Polly so weak that she could hardly bear anyone to walk across her room. By midsummer he feared she was dying. He went for long walks in the Medway countryside to pray for her: when faith felt strong he was partly resigned, but often his heart rebelled and he found it hard either to trust God for her recovery, or to submit to His will should she be about to die.

He prayed too about future employment, and in this 'I found it easier to trust the Lord'. The slave coast being overworked that year Manesty would not fit him out another ship until the *Bee* returned, and when she limped home and he viewed his loss he did not hurry into an appointment. Manesty knew that Newton longed to be quit of the sea. An obvious alternative was a post in the Customs and Excise but these, as Crown appointments, needed the interest of a powerful patron. Manesty obligingly tried to secure Newton one such place but missed it owing to an error.

Then came an extraordinary affair which Newton knew nothing about until it was over and a place was his.

Manesty had heard a report that a Tide Surveyor in the Customs, who had just lost his father, had been obliged by family duties to resign. Manesty immediately wrote a request that John Newton be appointed instead and sent it by hand across the Mersey into Cheshire, to old Mr. Salusbury, the innkeeper's son who had married an heiress and for many years had been one of the two Members of Parliament for Liverpool. While the messenger rode towards Shotwick Park, where Salusbury lived, Manesty learnt that the report was false: the Tide Surveyor had no intention of resigning. But the Member of Parliament did not know this when he wrote back promising to name Newton should a vacancy occur. The very day that Manesty received that promise, the Surveyor was found dead in his bed, though he had been seen in perfect health the night before. So the messenger who brought the Member's letter hurried back to Shotwick Park with news of the vacancy and Salusbury, true to his word, wrote at once to the Secretary of State nominating Newton. One hour later the Mayor of Liverpool, a far more important constituent than Joseph Manesty, applied on behalf of a nephew. He was too late: the letter had gone to London and Newton was appointed shortly before his thirtieth birthday.

Newton comments: 'These circumstances appear to me extraordinary, though of a piece with many other parts of my singular history.'

The news reached him when Polly had suffered a relapse. He had to go to London for the formalities and to pay the fees which would secure his place, and took her, with her mother and brother, to seek better medical advice. They all stayed with her aunt. On 6 August she lay in agony with bilious cholic while Newton made his round of government officials, his heart fixed at her bedside in anguish and grief that he must desert her for Liverpool, to take up a post which would be a burden without her, even if she did not love the name of Jesus.

On the second day of his journey north, while the Liverpool coach changed horses at Towcester in Northamptonshire, he wrote from the inn to Polly: 'Before this reaches you your brother will have told you how easy and composed he left me. Indeed I wonder at myself. But the Lord has been very gracious to me and fulfils His promise of giving me strength according to my day. My mind is not distressed. My companions in the coach are civil and agreeable in their way. But I would rather have been alone; for to commune with God and my own heart would be much more pleasing than the empty, amusing chit-chat I am engaged in at present.'

On reaching Liverpool he found that he had charge of fifty or sixty people and was thus a man of substance in the civic community. The Customs and Excise department provided a good office with fire and candles, and a handsome six-oared boat with a coxswain to row him about in style. The two Tide Surveyors alternated weekly between the docks and the river. Inspecting ships in dock seemed virtually a sinecure but Newton's river week could be hard – especially when the Jamaica fleet came in – and the hours dependent on the tides. He must board ships as they arrived in the Mersey, assess excise dues and search for smuggled goods; occasionally he seized some, and after their condemnation in a court of law he received half their value. In summer he might go down river and enjoy himself on the nearby hills while waiting for a vessel to make the tide. Another tide might oblige him to sit in his office until the small hours, reading or writing by his fire until the time came to embark.

A month after Newton settled in, George Whitefield came to Liverpool for the first time. The visit fell in Newton's slack week and he attended the open-air sermon, preached to a considerable but unresponsive crowd. Newton made himself known to Whitefield and next day went to his lodgings for a long talk and heard him preach twice. Then Newton had supper with him and stayed late, for Whitefield warmed to the young Tide Surveyor, saying he had never been in a place where he had so little encouragement, and that Liverpool was the most spiritually unconcerned town, for its size, in the kingdom; which perhaps is not surprising because it was busy growing fat on the Slave Trade.

Newton invited his landlady, an obliging and respectful female, to hear Whitefield preach. The idea so disgusted her that she barely gave a civil answer. However, curiosity or a better motive prevailed and she went the second day and returned very well disposed and borrowed a volume of his printed sermons. On hearing him again she became his great admirer and suggested that Newton ask him to Sunday dinner. He invited four or five Christian friends to meet him. The landlady provided a handsome meal and tried to refuse extra payment, and Whitefield's manners and discourse at table confirmed her respect, so that soon the neighbours called her a Methodist. She bore their reproach and laughter very well, Newton told Polly.

Newton too was chaffed by his acquaintance: they nick-named him 'Young Whitefield' because of his constant attendance (not, as legend has it, because he was a fiery preacher himself; his own mouth stayed shut as yet). He had more share of Whitefield's company than would have come to him in London in a year. He heard him preach nine times, supped with him three times and they dined together once at a neighbour's, in addition to the landlady's Sunday dinner.

Newton was in a seventh heaven. Whitefield stirred his soul and confirmed his faith, kindling a deep desire to know Christ better and proclaim His love, if a tongue-tied ex-sailor might discover the way. At the least, by testimony and conversation, he could reap where Whitefield sowed by his glorious voice. Liverpool had begun to respond. After Newton's dinner party they all went to St. Thomas's Square and an immense concourse, reckoned at four thousand people, listened that afternoon. 'The prospect is promising,' commented Whitefield.

On the Monday Newton accompanied him on foot with a small crowd a little way out of town until the chaise overtook them. Whitefield hugged him. The driver cracked his whip and with a last wave from the window the evangelist bowled away in a cloud of dust down the Bolton road.

In the days that followed, many of the poor would accost Newton in the street and ask with tears for news of Whitefield and when he would return. Even some of the fashionable folk had heard him before the end.

Newton wrote a long description to Polly on her bed of sickness in Chatham, longing that the girl who had borne such loneliness and suffering for her loyalty to him should share the comfort of his faith. Not long afterwards he was overjoyed to receive a letter in her own hand. She said she was better. What is more – and Newton could not contain his joy but unashamedly cried praises to God – Polly wrote that she had prayed from the heart for the first time. She had called upon God and He had delivered her. Newton seized paper and a quill, barely pausing to trim it, and wrote back at length. 'Be not afraid, only believe,' he told her. 'The Lord Jesus whom you need and seek invites you, and has declared, "Whosoever cometh I will in no wise cast out …" Go on, my dearest. I trust you are in the right way: wait patiently upon the Lord …'

Soon Polly was up and about. At the end of September she went to her aunt in London to convalesce and on Sunday slipped away secretly to Methodist preaching – almost certainly the Moorfields Tabernacle. After listening to an evangelistic sermon she remarked to one of Newton's friends, who passed it on, that hearing about the Great Physician had 'done her more good than other medicines'. Newton wrote delightedly to her, 'Well, go on. I hope you will leave London soon or you will be thought as singular as your husband!'

Her aunt despised Methodists but Polly proved scornproof. She was a little afraid that at Liverpool she would be expected to keep company with washerwomen; but he assured her that the few like-minded Christians in a godless town who would be their intimate friends ranked socially above themselves, 'though they do not aim at the top of the polite taste'.

Polly complained that her heart was hard and she would be a hypocrite. John wrote back: 'If you are really afraid of being a hypocrite, it is a good sign that you are not.' To this her reply was charming, and brings her right out of the shadows to take her place at his side as a character in her own right. She wrote: 'I delight, admire, and hang upon every sentence and every action of my dearest John, and yet how wanting, and how cold am I to the gracious Author of all our mercies to whom we owe each other, our happy affection, and all the satisfaction that flows from it!'

This heartwarming correspondence made John and Polly Newton all the more eager to be together again. At last Polly's doctor pronounced her strong enough for the long journey north. In mid-October 1755 she took a seat on the Liverpool coach and John took a seat on the London coach and at Stone in Staffordshire, a hundred and forty miles from London, sixty-five from Liverpool, they fell into each other's arms.

In the past eighteen months, between May 1754 and October 1755, John Newton had passed from seafaring in the Slave Trade to a landsman's post in the Customs; from struggling to be religious to knowing Christ with joy; from lonely pilgrimage to the strength of double harness with a wife who believed. As the Newtons lay in the Bell and Bear inn at Stone they recalled how often they had been restored to each other after long and dangerous separations. They resolved together to declare God's goodness, not merely in secret or to each other but by the whole course of their lives; to love Him more than they loved each other; to commit to Him their dearest concerns and, in every trouble, go to Him who had so often heard their prayers and done them good.

17

'I Will Not Give Up'

One day in January 1756 Newton sat down at his desk in the pleasant house which they had taken in Edmund Street and wrote a long letter to George Whitefield imploring him to return to Liverpool: 'Here are 40,000 people who in matters religious hardly know their right hand from their left.' But Whitefield could not come.

The Newtons felt inadequate as Christians in a godless town. Both of them were still unstable in faith; Polly learned fast but sometimes the way seemed miry, dark and heavy, and themselves spiritually shrivelled and useless, though they tried to put at God's service the civic influence of a senior place in the Customs.

They made their home a centre of hospitality and joy, though Newton rather restrained his sallies of wit and the turning of impromptu rhymes because the applause of the company fed his vanity. Like all evangelicals of the day they banished dancing, cards and theatre-going, and thus were called Methodists, enthusiasts, and mad; then he picked up a book by John Wesley on broken oaths, which condemned the almost universal habit among officials of accepting bribes or inducements which they had sworn, on entering office, to refuse. Newton thereupon stopped taking gratuities from captains and owners. The Collector of Customs laughed at this new scruple, saying such perquisites were allowed for, and the oath a mere form of words. The polite world of Liverpool rated Newton all the more mad, and the considerable loss of income embarrassed him for a while, especially as the Newtons loved to relieve the poor.

Liverpool considered him equally odd when their Tide Surveyor went into print and sent to the local clergy and dissenting ministers a short paper entitled *Thoughts on Religious Associations*, suggesting ways of improving the religious life of the town. He wrote for a civic society another paper on the subject which was better received and distributed widely by its officials: thus Newton was becoming well known – or notorious – to his fellow townsmen.

In August 1756, a year after Newton joined the Customs and Excise, the Seven Years War broke out. Hostilities at sea reduced the flow of commerce and thus the work of a tide surveyor. Newton used his generous leave to take Polly into Yorkshire, where the evangelical revival had spread in marked contrast to Liverpool. In particular he developed admiration and affection for one of the most unusual characters of the early revival, William Grimshaw, parson of Haworth, the isolated parish on the fells which became even more celebrated in the next century as the home of the Brontes.

Grimshaw had tamed a wild crew in a wild country. The people were more afraid of the parson than of a justice; his reproof was so stern, yet so mild and friendly, that the stoutest sinner could not stand before him and the people loved him. Crowds from far and near thronged his church, yet he often cheerfully walked miles in winter, in storms of wind, rain or snow, upon lonely unsheltered moors, to preach to small companies of aged decrepit people in cottages.

Grimshaw's sense of the evil of sin, of the worth of souls, and the nearness of eternity, fired Newton's heart, and Polly's. And Grimshaw's quarter-deck manner helped awaken in Newton a slumbering hope that one day he too might be captain of a parish or pastorate. He had never forgotten his mother's wish. He meditated on the Apostle Paul's words about the early disciples: 'They heard that he which persecuted us in times past, now preacheth the faith which he once destroyed. And they glorified God in me ...' Newton saw these words as peculiarly apt for himself and longed for a similar public opportunity. He reckoned that he was more fit than most to be set forth, like Paul, as an example of sinners whom Christ Jesus came into the world to save, and that he had obtained mercy for that purpose.

However, Newton had been too often tongue-tied, both privately, as at Chatham one day when he had tried to say something about Christ to Polly's mother at tea; and publicly, as when he had gone to a meeting in Spitalfields where people might testify. He had silently criticized the style and delivery of those who spoke before him yet when he stood up himself he did much worse. And as with many future clergy his first attempt from a pulpit was a disaster; by 1756 he had concluded that God had not called him to the honour and privilege of being a preacher of the amazing grace of God.

But in Yorkshire he was frequently asked to tell his story, at Haworth and its hamlets and wherever he travelled, among churchmen and dissenters alike. He began to lose his shyness in public. He told his tale so artlessly, with many a whimsical touch and graphic scene, that the people hung on his words. Each visit made him a more acceptable speaker, especially as he passed from mere autobiography, however dramatic, to exposition of the gospel behind the conversion, until early in 1758 some of his Yorkshire friends startled him by proposing that he take holy orders.

He had continued to educate himself despite concluding that he was too tongue-tied to be a minister. He mastered the Greek of the New Testament and the Septuagint; he read the best writers in divinity he could lay hands on in English and Latin, and some in French, for he had picked up French in his seafaring. He had just begun to teach himself Hebrew, a massive task for a mariner whose formal education had stopped at his eleventh birthday; he found it dry and tedious to learn.

When the Yorkshiremen proposed ordination Newton resolved to make Hebrew a test: he would not consider the question until he could read a chapter in the Hebrew Bible with tolerable ease.

By the end of June he could read the historical books and Psalms, although the prophets drove him to lexicons. He therefore bought a notebook in which to jot down over the next few weeks his thoughts on the great proposal. His thirty-third birthday fell on 4 August 1758 (by the New Style calendar. Since 1752 Newton had accepted the logic of the 'lost Eleven Days' and kept 4 August instead of 24 July, just as 'the Fourth of June' became famous as the birthday of George III, born 24 May 1739 when Britain still observed the Julian calendar.) Newton set 4 August apart to close all deliberations on whether to offer for the Christian ministry. From six in the morning he fasted and prayed. Around five in the evening he reached assurance. He would be ordained. From that time on he waited only for clear direction as to where and when; inwardly he regarded himself as already 'torn from the world and worldly concerns and appointed for sanctuary service'.

He rather assumed that his vocation would lie with the Independent Dissenters among whom his mother had brought him up – the people of Dr. Jennings and Samuel Brewer and the late Isaac Watts. But a romantic episode, quite in keeping with the extraordinary twists of his story, changed his direction.

A girl named Kitty, a close friend of the Newtons in Liverpool, had been bereaved of her brother, a Christian like herself, who had died young. Kitty was in love with a rich young man of Hunslet in Yorkshire. Her father forbade the match because the suitor was a 'Methodist', but on the first anniversary of his son's death he relented and begged Newton to escort her to the wedding which he refused to attend himself. Newton left for Hunslet in a hurry, without his boots or his superior's leave, and duly delivered the bride.

While staying at Hunslet vicarage for Kitty's wedding he had much talk with his host, Harry Crook, a friend of Wesley and of Whitefield. Crook not only overcame Newton's scruples about the Church of England but offered a title to holy orders as his curate. Newton returned to Liverpool to consult Polly.

His stipend would be a quarter of his present earnings. After thought and prayer, and Polly's cheerful acceptance of the sacrifices, he wrote accepting. He told Harry Crook that all religious persuasions had their faults and that the Established Church was the best route to reach the people, most of whom were ignorant of the great truths of the gospel.

Newton now needed character testimonials from three clergymen. The first three he approached in Liverpool refused to give them to 'a man who mixed with Methodists'. He found others and in December 1758 left Polly for Leeds, received his title from Crook and took coach to London where he should find the bishop of his own diocese, Chester, attending the House of Lords. He sought hospitality with a family where, to mutual surprise, he met Polly's father. Old Mr. Catlett had heard of his son-in-law turning preacher and was grieved, because he thought it must be among the Independents; both of them were uneasy all evening while in company, but once they were alone and John could explain, Catlett brightened and offered a Rochester acquaintance, Dr. Soan, rector of three livings and headmaster of the grammar school, who was said to be seeking a curate and could pay more than Crook.

Then came utter disappointment. The Bishop of Chester, the rich and proud Dr. Keene, who by law might ordain one of his own flock if he wished, refused to do more than countersign the testimonials. He sent Newton to the Archbishop of York, Mr. Crook's diocesan, the elderly, idle Dr. Gilbert, who was also in London.

The Archbishop declined to receive John Newton, let alone ordain him. 'His Grace,' said the secretary in softest tones, 'was inflexible in supporting the rules and canons of the church' – and one rule, broken by no means rarely, was that a man could not be admitted to holy orders unless holding a degree from Oxford or Cambridge.

The absurdity of this excuse by the Archbishop was well put by John Wesley after he dined with the Newtons in Liverpool some little while later. Wesley knew that the standards for an Oxford or Cambridge degree were then notoriously low, and he wrote in the next volume of his published journal: 'I had a good deal of conversation with Mr. N – – – –n. His case is very peculiar: our Church requires that clergymen should be men of learning, and to this end have a university education: but how many have a university education and yet no learning at all: Yet these men are ordained! Meantime one of eminent learning as well as unblameable behaviour, cannot be ordained, "because he was not at the university"! What a mere farce is this? Who would believe that any Christian Bishop would stoop to so poor an evasion?'

Newton did not doubt that the real reason was his fervent evangelical message and activity. He was suspected of Enthusiasm and rejected as an improper if not a dangerous person, charged with designing to create a disturbance in the Church, 'though it would have been my aim to unite rather than divide'.

Nevertheless he felt humiliated, especially after he had pursued the matter right up to the Archbishop of Canterbury. In Liverpool much excitement had been caused by the Tide Surveyor leaving to become a curate; and the further news that he had been refused holy orders provoked such resounding gossip that Newton could scarcely see three people talking in a street but he assumed they discussed him.

A Yorkshire Independent offered ordination. Newton declined. Wesley offered to make him one of his itinerant lay preachers, but a constitution broken by Africa would not have stood thirty mile rides in the rain; moreover the pittance and the absences would put Polly in want and loneliness. And he disliked the sourness and gloominess of some of Wesley's preachers, though he loved 'the people called Methodist'. He continued as Tide Surveyor. One day he escaped with his life when some business on shore detained him until he reached the boat late, to his vexation and the surprise of the crew, who knew of his strict punctuality at all times. They rowed him out to inspect a ship. As they neared her she blew up with loss of all hands; a few minutes earlier and he would have died with them.

Customs business grew so slack at the height of the war that the Collector gave Newton three months' leave in 1760 to accept temporary charge of an Independent meeting house at Cow Lane in Warwick. He left Polly at Chatham for a short visit, heard Whitefield preach in London, breakfasted with him and found him delighted that Newton wanted to engage 'in the good work' some way or other. He boarded the stage coach for Warwick and went back along the Liverpool road which Polly and he had travelled by chaise a few days earlier. Even early nineteenth-century travellers, in the heyday of stage coaches after the Telford and Macadam improvements, had little idea how tedious were the rough, steep, twisting, main roads which Newton, the Wesleys and Whitefield endured, not least in the Home Counties around London. The quite adventurous journey to Warwick emphasized his loneliness. He would recall how at this bank his dear Polly got off to walk down the hill, at this gate she mounted again – here she laughed, here she cried, 'Oh dear, I shall be down!' He found he was like a child in all concerning her, missing her more than on an African voyage.

At Warwick he settled to his little charge with great expectations. 'Fear not, Paul,' he read as he wandered in the open fields at his devotions, 'I have much people in this city;' this promise in Acts of the Apostles must be claimed as his own. But he soon discovered, as he put it quaintly, 'that Paul was not John and Corinth was not Warwick!' Nevertheless at the end of the three months the congregation urged him to resign from the Customs and become their permanent minister.

The Newtons were undecided. John returned to Liverpool while Polly used the opportunity for another visit to her parents, and he wrote to her 'in a good deal of anxiety and suspense about our Warwick affair, and I have nowhere to unburden myself, or if I had a thousand friends, they would signify little without you.' Her brother Jack, a rising lawyer in London, urged him angrily not to become a despised and impecunious dissenting minister: John's religion, he said, made him behave with the madness of a man blinded by passion; he should consider whether vanity and pride were not the real motives.

John and Polly after much deliberation and prayer sent the Warwick Dissenters a refusal. Church of England orders would have incomparably wider influence in a land where that Church alone was Established by law and held the allegiance of the bulk of the people. 'As to laying aside all thoughts of the ministry,' Newton wrote to Captain Clunie in the summer of 1762, 'it is quite out of my power. I cannot, I will not give up the desire, though I hope I shall not "run before I am sent".'

Yet he nearly did so. Yorkshire friends urged him to open an Independents (Dissenting) Chapel of his own in Liverpool, where he already held small informal services in the Edmund Street house on Sunday evenings with plenty of hymn singing. Sick of hiding his light under a bushel as a layman, he leant strongly towards this idea, with Yorkshire help promised for the first months. But Polly knew better. She saw it as a rash step which he would soon regret. She employed all her love and womanly arts to stop him. He remained adamant. She persevered. And she won. Thirty years afterwards he admitted that no arguments but hers could have dissuaded him. She 'kept me quiet until the Lord's time came when I should have the desire of my heart. The Lord's time is like the time of the tide, which no human power can either accelerate or retard. Though it tarry, wait for it.'

As a sea captain Newton knew how imperceptible is the actual turn of the tide. During a visit to Oxford he met a young Cornishman, a curate named Thomas Haweis. Soon afterwards the curate lost his episcopal licence for being too evangelical and moved to London. They corresponded. By his letters Haweis became the friend Newton lacked in Liverpool – a man of intellect and spirit to whom he could open his heart, his doubts and difficulties. Haweis directed his studies in Hebrew, Greek and church history.

It happened that at the end of 1762 Haweis was staying at Sandwich on the Kentish coast and met another friend of Newton's, a Dissenting minister named Fawcett, who showed him letters which Newton had written the previous summer with some description of his adventures and miseries in Africa, and of the way in which amazing grace had saved 'a wretch like me'. Intrigued, Haweis wrote at once for a fuller account. In January 1763 Newton replied with the first of fourteen letters each filling both sides of a quarto sheet written close, and written in haste as letters between friends, with no thought of publication. Haweis took them to the Earl of Dartmouth, the rich young nobleman who a few years before, through the friendship of the Countess of Huntingdon, had become an ardent Christian. He was almost the only evangelical peer and already a man of influence; later he was George III's Secretary of State for the colonies at the outbreak of the American revolution. By Haweis' action Lord Dartmouth came to know John Newton's story, his qualities, and his desire to be a clergyman.

One year later, in January 1764, Newton consulted Haweis concerning ordination to a Presbyterian church in Yorkshire; despairing of holy orders in the Church of England Newton had decided to accept but the elders set awkward conditions on which he needed advice. At that very moment Lord Dartmouth offered Haweis the parish of Olney in Buckinghamshire, a living in his gift. It would be a curacy to an absentee incumbent; the curate would be entirely his own master though with smaller stipend.

Haweis needed a living himself, yet urged Dartmouth to offer this curacy to Newton, and told Newton what he had done. Newton did not hesitate a moment between a parish and a Presbyterian chapel. On 26 February 1764 he wrote accepting Olney. Once again Newton's life story had turned on the narrowest coincidence. Had the proposal been deferred one week longer it would have been too late: he would have become a Presbyterian.

On 4 March, in the parlour in Edmund Street, Newton broke open a seal carrying the Earl of Dartmouth's arms and read the official offer of Olney in his own hand. Within it lay a note from Haweis urging him to drop everything and come to London at once for ordination. Polly was not afraid to stay by herself and their maids in Liverpool, for she was overjoyed that her John would not be buried away as a Dissenting pastor in Yorkshire.

Arrived in London Newton stayed with Haweis and went with him on the Sunday to the chapel near Hyde Park Corner where he assisted. After the service Lord Dartmouth came round to the pew where Newton sat and carried him off to dinner. Events appeared to move fast. The Bishop of Lincoln, in whose diocese Olney lay, sent word to Lord Dartmouth that the new Archbishop of York would be holding a private ordination next day: if Newton wished to be among those to be ordained he must at once be examined by the Archbishop's chaplain.

Newton received the note an hour after he should have been there, and ran almost the whole way, nearly a mile and a half – only to be kept waiting two hours, and then to suffer a bitter shock. The Archbishop's secretary hummed and hawed and at length said, 'Sir, not to mince the matter, you know you were formerly disappointed. His Grace has heard of it and desires to be excused.' The Bishop of Lincoln could do as he pleased.

Newton, disconcerted, ran back to St. James's Square, arriving in time not to interrupt Lord Dartmouth's dinner, and returned to the Archbishop, whose political interests would lean him towards doing Dartmouth a favour, with a letter from the Earl which opened the way to the Archbishop himself. Archbishop Hay Drummond was a warm-hearted, rather convivial prelate, and though he still made his excuses he was sure the Bishop of Lincoln would ordain. But Newton, hungry and weary, feared York's refusal would stop the whole affair; and it gave Thomas Haweis such a fit of the vapours that he could hardly eat his supper or speak another word that evening. Newton described all these happenings in great detail to Polly.

Lord Dartmouth paid a call on him next day, an act of condescension from a great magnate to a mere tide surveyor which showed Christian humility and love. He brought encouragement from the Bishop of Lincoln. Newton was not wholly free from anxiety, but the Bishop, though he had gone into print against Whitefield, treated Newton with honesty and gentleness, discussed at length his few remaining scruples about the Church, and promised to ordain him.

On 29 April 1764, in the Chapel of the Bishop of Lincoln's great palace at Buckden near Huntingdon, John Newton became a Clerk in Holy Orders of the Church of England. He wrote to Polly: 'Oh what zeal, faith, patience, watchfulness and courage will be needful for my support and guidance! My only hope is in the name and power of Jesus. May that precious name be as ointment poured forth to your soul and mine. May that power be triumphantly manifested in our weakness!'

He rode across country (could it be then that *How Sweet the Name* took shape?) for a peep at Olney and its people. He returned to Liverpool to settle his affairs and collect Polly. And Liverpool, which had despised and objected to its evangelistic tide surveyor, turned round and gave him a great send-off by inviting him to preach in the parish church before the mayor and corporation.

As he looked at the great congregation of friends and neighbours high and low his heart was overwhelmed with praise to God 'for putting me into the ministry. No one could be more *unworthy*, for I had been long a persecutor and blasphemer and a profligate. And considering my situation, connections and habits of life, no one could be more *unlikely!*'

18

The Music of Thy Name

Above the fireplace of his study in Olney vicarage John Newton put an inscription, painted in clear letters so that he could not ignore it whenever he entered the room.

Formed from two texts of Scripture, one from Isaiah, the other from Deuteronomy, it read:

> *Since thou wast precious in my sight thou hast been honourable. But thou shalt remember that thou wast a bondman in Egypt, and the Lord thy God redeemed thee.*

Through forty-three years of ordained ministry Newton always did remember. 'Never,' he wrote, 'was there a more clearly demonstrated proof of the freeness and efficacy of divine grace – powerful to change the most hardened offender, and merciful to forgive the most aggravated offences.'

The present book is the story of that 'amazing grace' rather than a full biography of Newton, but some description of his ministry in Olney, and later in London, must round it off.

John and Polly Newton took up residence in their parish on 26 May 1764. Olney was then a small market town with one long main street beside a stream, which so frequently flooded that the folk had built a raised causeway in the centre of the road. At the south end of the town flowed the Ouse, which also overflowed its banks. The coach road crossed the river and water meadows by a long bridge of irregular arches. The immediate countryside was flat and dreary with frequent mists and fogs. Olney men worked the fields and the women pored for ten or twelve hours a day making pillow lace in their thatched cottages, where the confined air tended to give them lung trouble and sometimes affected their minds. Most of the inhabitants lived from hand to mouth. Newton's heart stretched out to them, and when, almost immediately, he received through a friend of Polly's father the offer of a more lucrative living near London, he refused it.

In addition to Sunday services he had already started a less formal weeknight 'lecture' in the old church with its tower topped by a spire. Each Thursday he borrowed a room in Lord Dartmouth's disused Great House, an old manor fallen into a neglected and rather filthy state, for a children's meeting, an innovation which anticipated Robert Raikes' famous Sunday school movement by fifteen years. Eighty-nine children came the first time, almost more than the room could contain, and his aim was to 'talk, preach, and reason with them, and explain the Scriptures to them in their own little way'. He taught them plenty of hymns; he shrewdly instituted a system of rewards for knowledge and good behaviour; but it was his manner and affection, and not least his sea stories which drew them.

Newton quickly won his parishioners' love. Unlike many rural clergy of the day he visited them frequently in their sickness and their health and regarded himself as their servant. Here was no coldly distant scholar or idle sprig of the gentry but a jolly sea captain turned parson; deeply serious in teaching and aims, something of the quarter-deck about him, but larding his sermons with anecdotes and nautical allusions, and his conversation with quaint sayings and touches of fun. He seldom wore clerical dress on weekdays, preferring to visit in his old sea jacket, whereas neighbouring clergy wore clerical dress when riding to hounds or shooting with their squires.

The people flocked to hear him. 'Neither short days, uncertain weather or dirty roads,' he wrote to Alex Clunie that first winter, 'make any considerable diminution in our assemblies, and their attention and seriousness give me hope that they do not all come in vain.' Within a year he had to add a gallery to the church.

He was not a polished preacher. He preached extempore, and did not always prepare as he should. Articulation was poor and gestures ungraceful, yet he held his hearers by the strength and passion of his convictions and the love which shone through his words. He used to say that the point in all his preaching was 'to break a hard heart and to heal a broken heart'. He did not preach too long, aware that an overlong sermon competes in the listener's mind with the pudding overboiling at home, but the sermon formed the centre of the service, always expounding Scripture.

Newton did not overrate his early success, built as it was on a foundation laid by his predecessor; and if ever he felt proud he would take a dash of 'Plantain sauce' by recalling his African days of sin and starvation. Not that Olney brought wealth. He had been earning much more at Liverpool; the expenses of moving and settling ate into reserves; and within a few months his small savings disappeared when Manesty the ship-owner went bankrupt, ruined by the strangulation of trade in the Seven Years' War, and soon afterwards died.

But, 'When one spring dries up, the Lord opens another.' Thomas Haweis and Alex Clunie, who now held a post in the Customs and Excise in London, had persuaded Newton to publish the letters in which he had told the extraordinary story of his adventures and conversion. Haweis provided a preface, Clunie arranged the printing, and in August 1764 an immediate bestseller appeared, at first anonymously: *An Authentic Narrative of Some Remarkable and Interesting Particulars in the Life of***, communicated, in a Series of Letters, to the Rev. T. Haweis*. The sums due to the author arrived at a critical time, especially as the Newtons dipped into their pockets to relieve parish distress.

An Authentic Narrative reached all classes. At Olney, little groups would gather in the cottages and a 'scholard' would read it aloud to illiterate neighbours. Everybody knew the letters had been written by their parson. 'The people stare at me,' Newton told Clunie, 'and well they may. I am indeed a wonder to many, a wonder to myself; especially I wonder that I wonder no more.' In cold print, the grace that saved him looked even more amazing, yet he had not given half the detail of 'my wickedness, misery and hair-breadth escapes as my memory would have furnished'.

Newton quickly recognized that his book placed the marvel of God's grace before many who would not listen to Whitefield or Wesley. It brought correspondence and visits from seekers and learners in the faith. It strengthened friendships. One in particular did good to Olney. Newton had already met the richest merchant in England, John Thornton, who was Whitefield's convert and Lord Dartmouth's friend. After reading *An Authentic Narrative* and visiting Olney Thornton asked Newton to accept an annual sum of two hundred pounds: 'Be hospitable and keep an open house ... Help the poor and needy,' and draw on him for more whenever there was occasion. Newton reckoned that when he left Olney after fifteen years the then very considerable sum of three thousand pounds had passed through his hands from Thornton.

An Authentic Narrative played a part in bringing to Olney the man whose name will always be associated with Newton's: William Cowper, then aged thirty-two and not yet the most celebrated poet of his age.

The frail, nervous Cowper had already recovered from two periods of insanity and three attempts at suicide. His family had placed him in the care of a kindly physician of St. Albans, Nathaniel Cotton. In the same summer, 1764, that the Newtons went to Olney, William Cowper recovered his sanity after coming into evangelical faith through the influence of his cousin, Martin Madan (to whom Thomas Haweis had been curate) and Cotton's gentle teaching and care.

In the summer of 1767 Cowper was living as 'a sort of adopted son' with a clerical family, Morley and Mary Unwin, at Huntingdon, the county town close to the bishop's palace where Newton had been ordained deacon and priest. The Unwins showed Cowper Newton's book. After reading it he wrote a manuscript of his own conversion for strictly private circulation, and was therefore delighted when he heard that a mutual friend had suggested the Newtons visit the Unwins to meet Cowper, on their way home from a tour among old acquaintance in Lancashire and Yorkshire.

The Newtons arrived in July to find a stricken household: Morley Unwin had been killed by a fall from his horse three days before. The widow, with her unmarried daughter and Cowper, wished to leave Huntingdon as soon as possible and asked Newton among others to look around. By 18 July Cowper was writing to his aunt, Mrs. Madan: 'Mr. Newton seems to have conceived a great desire to have us for neighbours, and I am sure we shall think ourselves highly favoured to be committed to the care of such a pastor.' In August they visited Olney and settled on a house of somewhat severe appearance and bad repair on the south side of the market place, called Orchard Side. While it was being made ready they stayed with the Newtons for nearly five months.

Newton and Cowper became close friends at once. Besides a common faith they shared a love of poetry and of the countryside and were hard walkers. Both of them had a great sense of humour, though Cowper's melancholy was never far away. He was an enthusiastic gardener and so was Polly, doting on their gardens, which were separated by a single field; the two households paid the owner for a right of way to allow them to visit each other's homes and gardens without going round by road. The townsfolk called their new neighbour 'Sir Cowper' or Squire Cowper, for he was cousin to an earl. He loved to visit the poor and sit with the children at the Great House and to walk through rain or snow to the prayer meeting at Molly Mole's cottage, which Newton jocularly dubbed the Mole hill.

While Cowper was still a guest under the Newton's roof, before daybreak on 9 December 1767, when reading the passage in Genesis, 'Enoch walked with God,' he began to compose one of his loveliest hymns, *Oh for a closer walk with God, A calm and Heavenly frame*. After two lines he fell asleep. 'When I awaked again the third and fourth were whispered to my heart in a way which I have often experienced.' He wrote down:

> *A Light to shine upon the Road*
> *That leads me to the Lamb!*

The entire hymn of six verses followed.

He probably read it out at the breakfast table. Within a few months he had written *Hark my Soul! It is the Lord*. Soon Cowper and Newton were stimulating each other to hymnwriting. Together they made Olney famous for its hymns, sending them anonymously to magazines or collections, but later conceiving the plan of producing their own hymnbook.

In the cold spring of 1769 Newton secured Dartmouth's permission to transfer the parish prayer meeting to the Great House's 'great room', which he described as 'a noble place with a parlour behind it, and holds one hundred and thirty people conveniently'; the prayer meeting had outgrown Molly Mole's cottage. The great room needed cleaning and refurbishing. For the formal opening Cowper and Newton each wrote a hymn. Newton wrote *O Lord! our languid souls inspire*, but it is Cowper's *Jesus, where'er Thy people meet* which has become part of earth's Christian heritage. After this Newton, though composition did not come easily, usually turned out one hymn a week to expound and teach at the Great House, and others for the lacemakers to sing in the 'Lace Tellings'. To sing hymns in the parish church itself, except for metrical psalms, still seemed a little daring.

Cowper had written *There is a fountain filled with blood* by 1772, but the actual date of Newton's *How Sweet the Name of Jesus sounds* remains obscure. In the later part of 1772 tragedy struck the partnership. 'Sir Cowper' showed signs of renewed mental derangement, fearing once again that he was eternally damned. Attacks grew more frequent, until madness struck him down early on Sunday 24 January 1773. The Newtons were sent for in haste at four in the morning. Newton stayed until eight, when Cowper seemed calmer, and Polly stayed at his side all day. But Cowper, as he wrote long after, had 'plunged into a melancholy that made me almost an infant'.

The myth that the supposed severity of Newton's ministrations or theology were primarily responsible cannot stand up to the evidence. The Newtons worked hard to save their friend's mind from fear of damnation, to make him laugh at quaint sayings or comic verses or funny stories, to help him feel loved: they even put up with Cowper and Mrs Unwin as uninvited guests for more than a year in the vicarage because he felt happier than in his own Orchard Side.

By October 1773 Cowper seemed more stable, though never smiling or writing or making intelligent conversation, and the Newtons therefore ventured on their annual preaching visit to Warwick and on to Northampton. Here they received an agitated letter from Mrs. Unwin imploring their return: Cowper, convinced that God demanded a human sacrifice, had tried to hang himself. They hurried back. Newton still did not lose 'hope for a happy issue'. It is said, though without firm evidence, that after this suicide attempt Cowper wrote one of the best known of all his hymns, *God moves in a mysterious way*, which was published in 1774.

Cowper's mental illness dried up Newton's hymnwriting. 'My grief and disappointment were great; I hung my harp upon the willows, and for some time thought myself determined to proceed no farther without him.'

At length in April 1774 Cowper smiled again at a little joke. In May he and Mrs. Unwin left the vicarage. His recovery proceeded rapidly, though he never lost a sense of despair, of banishment from God's presence. Newton began to write hymns again, adding another almost weekly. Cowper wrote no more, though his greatest poetry lay ahead.

In 1779 Newton published *Olney Hymns*, 348 pieces by two authors, of which 282 were by Newton. Many of these hardly survived their own day or were too autobiographical for wide acceptance but two or three dozen achieved lasting fame.

Thus the ex-slave trader and ex-sea captain, the one-time blasphemer and writer of scurrilous rhymes, enriched the world's worship by hymns that will never die, sung in countless translations as well as in their original English; hymns such as *How Sweet the name of Jesus sounds, Glorious things of thee are spoken, May the Grace of Christ our Saviour, Be still my heart! these anxious cares.* And *Amazing Grace.*

19

'A Little Odd-looking Man'

'At the archdeacon's visitation at Long Stratford appeared as minister of Olney one Mr. Newton, a little odd looking man of the methodistical order, and without any clerical habit. He said he was Mr. Browne's curate.' So wrote William Cole, rector of Bletchley, whom posterity celebrates as antiquary rather than as parson. Newton may have been twisting the lion's tail unnecessarily in attending the archdeacon's visitation in his sea jacket but Cole's tone reflects the distaste of neighbouring clergy for Newton as an 'enthusiast'.

He annoyed them further by loving Dissenters, a side of him which did not quite please Polly, always the churchwoman. When the local association of Baptist ministers met at Olney in 1768 he attended their meetings and they his lecture in the parish church. Newton was ahead of his time in this, and stood for peace in an age of theological wrangles, even within the evangelical camp. 'I am sick of the spirit of party of all parties,' he once wrote from Olney. 'I wish to be able to throw some water upon the fire of contention. I feel desire of publishing two small pamphlets – one upon the comparative insignificance of forms and modes of worship – the other to show the wrong principles and bad effects of the dispute between the Calvinists and Arminians.'

His closest ministerial friend in the neighbourhood was an Independent named William Bull, who had begun at the next town up river, Newport Pagnell, a few months after Newton's arrival. A man of intelligence, imagination and wide reading, and a great talker, Bull was then aged twenty-six but it was not for some seven years that the two became warmly attached. Newton found Bull to be Christlike and a deep thinker; Polly liked him and he would come to dinner and to preach at their prayer meetings, the parish church being barred by law to a Dissenter. 'We only want to hear those who can tell us about Jesus and stir us up to live to Him,' he wrote to Bull, and at another time: 'When you are with the King, and getting good for yourself, speak a word for me and mine. I have reason to think you see Him oftener and have nearer access to Him than myself. ...'

One day they were in Bull's booklined library puffing at their long 'churchwarden' pipes, discussing Scripture as they often did, when a Dissenting minister from Northampton knocked to tell them that the author of *Rock of Ages*, Augustus Toplady, was resting at the Swan: 'He is on his way to London and will not live long.' They hastened to the inn and found an emaciated, disease-stricken clergyman, alert enough to talk. They were interrupted, however, by a noise in the street and were disgusted to see a bull-baiting pass by. Mr. Toplady, distressed at the cruelty to the bull, pronounced the sight unbearable were it not that all these poor suffering animals would be compensated in heaven.

'I certainly hope that all *bulls* will go to heaven,' punned William Bull, 'but will *all* the animal creation?'

'Yes, certainly,' said Toplady with great emphasis, for this was one of his pet beliefs. 'All, all!'

'What,' exclaimed Newton jokingly, recalling shipboard discomfort, 'Do you suppose, sir, there will be *fleas* in heaven? I have a special aversion to fleas!'

Toplady looked hurt, though he held his peace. But when Newton begged him to stay at Olney should he come that way again, the author of *Rock of Ages* replied quite rudely (for he was a trifle cantankerous even in health) to the author of *How Sweet the Name* who wanted no fleas in heaven.

Newton's nearest clerical neighbour in later years at Olney, the curate of the next village to the west, held him in contempt and derision. This was a young clergyman of rough country background, self-educated, named Thomas Scott. He was more interested in teaching himself Hebrew than in the people of his parish but was ashamed when he learned that Newton had several times visited two dying parishioners of Scott's, a man and wife, whom he had neglected himself because 'not sent for'. He went to their cottage, found one already dead, and with much remorse attempted to do his pastoral duty by the other.

Scott scarcely believed in Christ's divinity. At the next archdeacon's visitation (to stifle his bad conscience about the dead cottagers) he tried angrily to argue the point with Newton, who declined to be drawn. They began a correspondence. Scott attempted to stir up controversy and 'filled my letters with definitions, enquiries, arguments, objections ... He, on the other hand, shunned everything controversial as much as possible and filled his letters with the most useful and least offensive instructions,' only dropping occasional hints of the necessity of faith and how it could be found. This annoyed Scott and he dropped the correspondence and shunned Newton's company – until a time of discouragement led him to call at Olney vicarage, where he found help.

Mutual affection grew; Scott attended Newton's weekday lectures; at length, nearly four years after the incident of the cottagers, Scott 'began to perceive our Lord's meaning when he says, "Except ye receive the kingdom of heaven as a little child, ye shall in no wise enter therein." ' Scott's story of his conversion, *The Force of Truth*, is a classic of spiritual autobiography. A monumental biblical commentary and many other books made him in after years one of the most influential evangelicals of his day.

Newton was already influential by his books, far beyond Olney. Long ago he had begun an Ecclesiastical History 'to trace the gospel spirit, its abuses and the oppositions to it, through the several ages of the Church', and worked at it off and on for years. It had got no further than the close of the Acts of the Apostles when published in 1770, but Joseph Milner of Hull took up the theme and gave the world his celebrated history. Newton had expected to do most good in print by literary works but from *An Authentic Narrative* onwards it was the publication of letters which made him well known, 'letters which I wrote without study, or any public design. But the Lord said, "You shall be most useful by *them*," and I learned to say, "Thy will be done! Use me as thou pleasest, only *make* me useful." '

Letter writing became one of his chief ministries; by the end of his life he had written thousands in his neat, small handwriting, to scores of correspondents. His habit was to write once a quarter ('my quarterly budget') to his friends and his disciples, unless some anniversary or occasion or problem required more frequent communication. Since his circle enlarged continually, and he was unstinting in replies to strangers, he spent hours every week at his desk. He wrote from the heart and the letters reached the heart, for his own past and his learning, and his experience with souls, gave him profound insight into what he called 'the study of the human heart, with its workings and counterworkings, as it is differently affected in a state of nature and of grace.' Whenever he borrowed back a few and published them the books became favourites with the public, especially *Cardiphonia*, the 'sound of the heart', a title suggested by Cowper. *Cardiphonia* was soon republished in America and translated into French and Dutch.

Newton's private or published letters brought a stream of guests to Olney vicarage, a cheerful house with plenty of laughter and welcome. Since the Newtons had no children yet were fond of them they gladly adopted Polly's orphaned nieces Betsy Catlett and Elizabeth Cunningham; Eliza died in childhood after showing a beautiful faith and character which Newton described feelingly in a pamphlet The household always stayed united, with master and mistress treating their maids, Sally and Molly, almost as members of the family; Newton made a point of friendship with servants, and often wrote quaint letters of simple spiritual advice to the servants of houses where he had stayed.

As their own guests could not fail to realize, Newton and Polly remained much in love. When she was away looking after her aged father they wrote frequent letters, his flowing with ideas and encouragements, hers brief and stilted but none the less deep; and, as she once put it, 'I write sheets in my mind.' His would begin, 'My dearest charming Polly,' or 'My dearest Charmer,' or 'My dearest sweetest, dear Polly, alias Mary'; and hers 'My own precious dear'. They still felt intensely any separation: as Newton wrote to her while staying with Thornton at Clapham, 'I am always a little awkward without you, and every room where you are not present looks unfurnished.' They kept touch by prayer. Almost every hour each would bring the other to the mind's eye and shape prayers according to probable whereabouts and activity. This was easier for Polly because Newton regulated his Olney days by shipboard precision.

Polly had been a somewhat nervous creature ever since the shock of his sudden collapse at Liverpool in '55. She would be thrown into agitation if she thought her absent John in trouble or danger, as during the great blizzard of January 1776 when he had planned to join her in London, to bring her back with her father. He begged her 'not to give way to fears on my account, or to calculate the depth of the snow at present or of the floods when the snow shall melt. Since you have had an interest in me the Lord has preserved me from innumerable dangers of which you could form no idea. We may safely trust Him. His arm is not weary nor is He at any time afar off. He is always near and providence always watches over them that fear Him. But I know I cannot reason you out of your apprehensions – therefore I would turn my thoughts upwards and say, Lord do Thou keep her heart stayed upon Thee, and maintain Thy peace in her, and give her a power of trusting all in Thy hand and submitting all to Thy will.'

On the other hand a delayed letter from Polly meant agitation for John, but joy when the stage coach brought it. 'I waited about the street yesterday,' he wrote from Olney, 'until it was time to go to Orchard Side, and then deputed Molly to supply my place. At half-past four the horn sounded and my heart went pit-a-pat. But I soon saw Molly pass the window, and by her looks and speed I guessed she had a letter. I snatched it from her and read it, and was presently well.'

Newton had intended to remain at Olney until he died. He had refused a country living, with its increased stipend and status, which was in the gift of Thornton. He had been tempted when he thought he might be offered Halifax, a rising industrial town in Yorkshire, but glad when he was not. Later he refused Lord Dartmouth's offer of the presidency of the college in Savannah, Georgia, which Whitefield, now dead, had founded. Yet towards the end of the 1770s his ministry in Olney was losing momentum. It was not because Newton, like Grimshaw who had ruled Haworth with an iron rod, tried too hard to discipline the parish. He could be fierce when he chose, as on the day when local lads hooted at a funeral procession; but the trouble lay quite the other way. He made himself too cheap and he lacked discrimination. William Bull put it well, in Cowper's hearing, some two years after Newton had left Olney. 'Mr. Newton,' said Bull, 'trod a path which no man but himself could have used so long as he did, and he wore it out long before he went from Olney. Too much familiarity and condescension cost him the estimation of his people. He thought he should insure their love, to which he had the best possible title, and by those very means he lost it.'

They no longer listened as of old. A hard core of incorrigibles resisted the gospel. Divisions sprang up between those who attended the parish church on Sundays only and those who came also to the lectures and the Great House. The local clergy, by now, accepted him as a benevolent and industrious minister even when they deplored his evangelical doctrines, and the whole neighbourhood loved him for his help to the sufferers when a dreadful fire destroyed part of Olney in October 1777; yet this very disaster led to an incident which shook Newton profoundly.

Since most of the town dwellings were thatched, Newton sensibly suggested after the fire that the inhabitants should forego their customary riotous, drunken bonfire orgy on 5 November,

Guy Fawkes Day, when with all England they celebrated the national deliverance long ago from gunpowder, treason and plot. The celebration committee agreed and asked him to give notice in church. 'I really understood it to be the general sense of the town.'

On the evening of 5 November 1777 a 'wild and lawless mob', enraged by the prohibition, paraded down the long street breaking windows and demanding money with menaces. A cottager rushed to warn the Newtons that the rioters were yelling that they were on the way to the vicarage to smash every window. Polly's nerve gave way. Terrified, with a knocking growing louder inside her head, she clung to John.

The queller of mutineers prepared to face the rioters. He believed that singly they could have been reasoned with, 'but in a body, and when influenced with drink, they are terrible creatures', yet no worse than violent slaves determined to regain liberty.

At ten o'clock that night a friend hammered on the door. He warned Newton that forty or fifty, 'full of fury and liquor' were about to assault the house: their yelling could be heard through the closed windows. Polly could stand it no longer. She implored John to bribe them to go away.

As he told Thornton, 'I was forced to send an embassy and beg peace. A soft message, and a shilling to the captain of the mob, secured his protection and we slept in safety.

'Alas, "tell it not in Gath!" I am ashamed of the story.'

20

Killing the Slave Trade

In the city of London, in Lombard Street which was famous for its wealthy bankers, stood an unusual, monumental church designed by Hawksmoor: St. Mary Woolnoth. John Thornton had acquired the presentation and when the incumbent died in 1779 he offered the living to Newton.

'London is the last situation I should have chosen for myself,' commented Newton. 'I love woods and fields and streams and trees – to hear the bird sing and the sheep bleat.' But he accepted, recognizing that while usefulness at Olney decreased, Thornton's offer would make him an evangelical incumbent in London; and among all the city churches there was only one other at that decisive time in the affairs of church and state. Another City magnate then disputed the right of presentation, which involved Thornton in litigation and Newton in suspense. He had quipped to Bull: 'I am about to form a connection for life with one Mary Woolnoth, a reputed London saint in Lombard Street.' Now he had to write: 'Molly Woolnoth and I are not yet married. I told you someone forbid the banns, and the prohibition is not yet taken off, but

I believe we shall soon hasten *into the midst of things.*' To wed Molly, he said, would be pleasing, but to be divorced from Olney would be painful.

The House of Lords found in Thornton's favour. In December 1779 Newton preached his first sermon at St. Mary Woolnoth, but did not preach his farewell at Olney until January 1780, Polly following him to London in March. Cowper's distress at the loss of the Newtons was well expressed in his remark about the arrival to the pulpit and the vicarage of one Benjamin Page: 'If he is not spotless, his spots will be seen, and the plainer, because he comes after Mr. Newton.' Page soon resigned in favour of Thomas Scott. In the eyes of many, none could replace John Newton: 'You were greatly loved at Olney,' Cowper told him.

Newton, now in his middle fifties, quickly established a unique position in London. A rector or vicar in the eighteenth century had a prestige above any Dissenter, above any Church of England curate, lecturer or minister of a proprietary chapel. The parish of St. Mary Woolnoth was small but important, for it included the Mansion House, so that the Lord Mayor for each year was a parishioner, a matter of awe to Newton: 'That one of the most ignorant, the most miserable and the most abandoned of slaves should be plucked from his forlorn state of exile on the coast of Africa and at length be appointed minister of the parish of the first magistrate of the first city in the world – that he should there not only testify of such grace but stand up as a singular instance and monument of it, is a fact I can contemplate with admiration, but never sufficiently estimate.'

His testifying of grace soon brought a large congregation to his church though he neither expected nor drew the vast audiences which hung on Wesley's lips. One of his best series of sermons was provoked by the Handel Commemoration sung in Westminster Abbey, for though Newton enjoyed Handel he disapproved of Scripture being made into musical entertainment, as he regarded it. To improve the occasion he preached at St. Mary Woolnoth fifty sermons in the course of two years, expounding the Scriptures which form the libretto of Handel's *Messiah*. They were afterwards published. Newton was mildly a Calvinist but in that age of fierce theological disputation he tried to 'keep all shibboleths, and forms and terms of distinction out of sight, as we keep knives and razors out of the way of children, and if my hearers had not other means of information I think they would not know from me that there are such creatures as Arminians and Calvinists in the world. But we talk a good deal about Christ.'

Many of Newton's hearers came from a distance, often after reading one of his books. His influence never ceased to amaze him. He had, he mused, 'longed for an opportunity of preaching the gospel in some remote corner, and looked no farther. Could I expect that God should appoint me in a very public post, give me that liberty and acceptance with which I have been since favoured, and enable me to write, what has made my worthless name known to His people far and near?'

Success never induced pride; he knew his heart. This was beautifully and quaintly described in a letter he had written at Olney when a lion came to the Cherry Fair: 'The lion was wonderfully tame: as familiar with his keeper, as docile and obedient as a spaniel; yet the man told me he had his surly fits, when he durst not touch him. No looking-glass could express my face more justly than this lion did my heart. I could trace every feature. As wild and fierce by nature, yea, much more so; but grace has in some measure tamed me. I know and love my Keeper and sometimes watch His looks that I may learn His will. But oh! I have my surly fits too – seasons when I relapse into the savage again – as though I had forgotten all. I got a hymn out of this lion …'

In London the ministry was centred as much on Newton's home as in his church. St. Mary Woolnoth had no rectory. The Newtons lived two miles away in Charles Square, Hoxton, then a pleasant suburb; to their delight they could see green fields and cows, 'so that it has some little resemblance to the country'. They kept open house. The poor would receive relief at the door (the less genuine finding Newton a little too easy a touch) while the afflicted and tempted, after confidential counsel in his study, went away strengthened with sympathy or advice. As a pastor he gave himself unstintingly at home and away. He described his life amusingly to Cowper: 'My time is divided between running about to look on other people, and sitting at home like a tame elephant or a monkey for other people to come and look at me!'

Ministers and lay friends of all denominations, especially young men who were starting or intending a lifetime of Christian service, flocked to his breakfast parties. These began with family prayers. He read a chapter, added a few pithy remarks and then prayed: 'the prayer was never long, but remarkably suitable and simple.'

After breakfast he would take any male guests who were free to remain, and settle to his chair in the study, draw at his long pipe, and puffing away he would converse, recalls William Jay, a Dissenter from Bath, 'in a manner the most easy and free and varied and edifying. There was nothing about him dull or gloomy or puritanical, according to the common meaning of the term. As he had much good nature, so he had much pleasantry, and frequently emitted sparks of lively wit, or rather humour.' Richard Cecil, a fellow clergyman who was afterwards his biographer, said Newton's conversation and habits among friends 'were more peculiar, amusing and instructive than any I ever witnessed.'

Once a fly perched on Newton's nose, making him sneeze. He remarked, 'If this fly keeps a diary, he'll write: "To-day a terrible earthquake!" ' Or he would tell of an old woman whose death bed he attended, who said that despite her guilt and unworthiness she was persuaded that 'my Lord Jesus will save me from all my sins and sorrows and bring me home to Himself. And if He does, *He'll never hear the last of it!*' Jay was with him when Newton received a letter from a man in Bath whom Jay knew to be a scoundrel. 'But,' remarked Newton, 'he writes now like a penitent.'

'If he is,' replied Jay, 'I'll never despair of the conversion of anyone again.'

'Oh,' exclaimed Newton. 'I never did, since God saved me.'

One subject he brought up more and more frequently: the iniquity of the Slave Trade.

'My heart shudders that I was ever engaged in it,' he would say. His awakening had been slow. In 1763–64 when he wrote and published *An Authentic Narrative* he had begun to doubt the moral lawfulness of the Slave Trade he had left ten years earlier but he did not attack it. While he was at Olney, reading widely and in touch with John Wesley, who condemned it in a pamphlet in 1774, he became aware of the growing swell of adverse opinion which made the Trade to stink but as something that could not be abolished without disaster to a nation's economy.

By the time Newton came to London he was appalled by it. He grew intense in his opposition, bewailing this crime against humanity at every opportunity. He became something of an 'Ancient Mariner', buttonholing any who would listen to his stories of the horrors, and his dreadful concern that he should have continued in it when a Christian. He longed to make amends. When the University of New Jersey sent word that they had made him an honorary Doctor of Divinity, he refused to call himself D.D., saying that 'the dreary coast of Africa had been his university and he would never accept any diploma 'except from the poor blacks'.

The Slave Trade would not vanish because an ex-slave trader repented of his past. Only an Act of Parliament could bring in Abolition, and no one could expect a majority in either Commons or Lords to put a stop to the British trade while other nations continued with theirs. In the earlier 1780s Newton could see no prospect of success.

Then one day in December 1785, among the requests received at his vestry for interviews, lay a note signed by a name which made his heart leap: William Wilberforce.

The world knew William Wilberforce as the brilliant, amusing young man of fashion and Member of Parliament who had won Yorkshire for the Prime Minister, William Pitt, his bosom friend and contemporary. Newton knew him as the nephew of his dear friend Hannah Wilberforce, John Thornton's sister. When Wilberforce was eight years old he had lost his father, a rich merchant in Hull, and gone to live with his uncle and aunt in Wimbledon. Newton, up from Olney, had met him there and at Thornton's, and the older Wilberforces had brought him sometimes to Olney. The boy became John Newton's ardent disciple, listening wide eyed to his sea stories, laughing at his jokes, joining in his songs – and coming, as it seemed, to share his faith. Wilberforce revered John Newton almost as a parent. But the boy's mother in Hull became alarmed that he was turning into a little 'methodist'. She removed him from the Wimbledon household and thus from Newton's influence, and weaned him, over the years, from his faith. In 1781, when Wilberforce was twenty-three and already a Member of Parliament, Newton writing to Cowper about another child referred to his lost disciple: 'I am aware religious appearances in so young a subject are to be regarded with caution. The strongest and most promising views of this sort I ever met with were in the case of Mr. Wilberforce when he was a boy – but they seem now entirely worn off, not a trace left behind, except a deportment comparatively decent and moral in a young man of large fortune.'

Four years later in December 1785 Newton received the note at his church begging for a strictly secret interview. Because Wilberforce was an important man, and evangelicals were despised and derided by his friends in the world of fashion, he took almost absurd measures to cover his tracks when he went, by appointment, to Newton's house in Charles Square.

Here he unfolded a story of two journeys across France with Isaac Milner, a Yorkshireman who (unknown to Wilberforce) had become an evangelical, and how they had started to read, almost by chance, Philip Doddridge's *Rise and Progress of Religion in the Soul*. This book, and the Bible, had brought him to a spiritual crisis and anguish of soul, for once he had understood the implications of the Christian gospel he could not bring himself to surrender to Christ, fearing loss of position and popularity. By the time he talked to Newton he was willing to yield, indeed had done so, but his naturally joyous personality lay clouded by doubt and dismay and he felt he must confide in a counsellor or go out of his mind. Thus he had turned to his boyhood hero. He told Newton that he wished to resign his seat in Parliament and become a clergyman.

Newton helped him to unburden his conscience; and persuaded him not to disappear into holy orders: God might have raised him up to serve Him in the councils of state, for the good of church and nation.

Wilberforce did not resign from Parliament. By Easter 1786, with the help of Newton and others, he had come to assurance; Newton wrote to Cowper: 'I judge he is now decidedly on the right track ... I hope the Lord will make him a blessing both as a Christian and a statesman. How seldom do these characters coincide!! But they are not incompatible.'

The old ex-slave trader and the young statesman became firm friends, and whenever they were together Newton used to harp on his shame about the Trade. He was undoubtedly one of the several influences which led Wilberforce to take up Abolition and agree to lay the subject before Parliament.

The details of the long struggle which ended in the Abolition of the Slave Trade twenty one years later belong to Wilberforce's story, but Newton, until he grew too aged, was in the inner circle of Abolitionists.

And he helped to bring to deep Christian faith in 1787 one of the most effective among them – Hannah More, the celebrated playwright and wit, renowned as one of the Nine Muses of Great Britain in a famous print. She had several evangelical friends. Contrasting their ways with hers she became dissatisfied in soul and found her way to St. Mary Woolnoth. John Newton showed Hannah More how to place her faith in Christ and her pen at Christ's disposal. Her fame and popularity presented many opportunities in the world of fashion and wealth where she had long moved at ease, and later she devoted herself to the poor of her native West Country and to writings which brought the

Christian message to all ranks of British society; and she worked hard with Wilberforce in the cause of Abolition.

When battle was fully joined, Newton produced a devastating pamphlet, as the only Abolitionist leader with first hand experience. 'Silence at such a time,' he wrote in its first pages 'and on such an occasion would, in me, be criminal. If my testimony should not be necessary or serviceable, yet perhaps I am bound in conscience to take shame to myself by a public confession which, however, sincere, comes too late to prevent or repair the misery and mischief to which I have formerly been accessory.'

It did not come too late.

Newton was now in his sixty-third year, venerable in appearance and regarded with awe for his past history and present influence. In 1788 the Prime Minister placed the whole subject of the Slave Trade before a committee of the Privy Council with instructions to investigate thoroughly. One of the witnesses summoned by the committee was John Newton. The wheel had come full circle as the ex-slave trader took coach to St. James's Palace.

He mounted the stairs, somewhat painfully because of a bad leg and other aches and pains, and waited in a long corridor beneath portraits of monarchs and princes, until he heard his name called as usher to usher echoed: '*The Reverend John Newton!*'

He walked towards the open door of the committee chamber. As he turned to enter he saw, awaiting him, the Prime Minister himself: Mr. Pitt bowed. The Privy Councillors and all in the room rose to their feet.

The once flogged sailor, the former lecher and blasphemer, the slave trader who had been redeemed from slavery, found himself escorted to his seat by the King's chief minister.

'Oh, Lord, it is all Thy doings, to Thee be also the praise. To me belongs the shame and confusion of face, for I am a poor vile creature to this hour!'

Epilogue

Polly had never fully recovered from the shock of thinking John dead before her eyes in 1754. As the Newtons reached old age, still deeply in love, she suffered nervous or physical disorders with increasing frequency, without losing her cheerful spirit.

Newton's extreme and undisguised attachment used to puzzle some of his friends 'as she seemed to have few or any attractions'. They were obvious enough to him, for she was a dream wife and he had never woken from the dream.

In the autumn of 1788 new pains troubled Polly. She consulted an eminent surgeon. He diagnosed cancer. She begged him to operate when her husband should be away from home so that he would know nothing until it was over, but the surgeon warned her that an operation (without anaesthetics) might be fatal. She did not break the news until the following day that she would probably be the first to die, within two years at most. A shocked Newton tried to face the prospect in submission to the will of God, but 'strongly felt I was more likely to toss like a wild bull in a net'.

They had now moved into the City, to a house in Coleman's Buildings. She seldom appeared downstairs. In the fifteen months remaining she spent much time studying and marking her Bible and her copy of the Olney hymns, and such hours as he could spare from his duties he spent in her room, the old ardour unquenched on either side. In private, he carefully prepared his spirit for the break.

Near the end she appeared to abandon her faith and to turn against her John. Newton was thrown into agony of spirit, yet he showed himself ahead of his time in dealing with this, for he steadfastly refused to believe it to be caused by anything but a turn in her physical condition. After a fortnight her love to God and to John returned in full measure and continued unabated despite much suffering until, in the last days of 1790, after nearly forty years of marriage, the end came.

He described it to a friend a few months later: 'From about the month of August we were constrained to give up all hopes of her recovery. The Lord wonderfully preserved her from very severe pain – but she was in many respects a great sufferer though she would not readily own it, for she was favoured with exemplary and extraordinary patience. On 15th December the Lord released her from all her sorrows. I was watching over her with a candle in my hand and saw her draw her last breath.'

He insisted on preaching the next Sunday, saying, 'Dr. Pulpit is my best physician.' And he preached at her funeral, from a text, Habakkuk 3:17, 18, which he had reserved, unused, for the day of his greatest affliction, should he outlive her: 'Although the fig-tree shall not blossom, neither shall fruit be in the vine: the labour of the olive shall fail, and the fields shall yield no meat: the flock shall be cut off from the fold, and there shall be no herd in the stalls: yet I will rejoice in the Lord, I will joy in the God of my salvation.'*

---

* Cowper had turned this text into the last verse of one of the loveliest of his Olney hymns, *Sometimes a light surprises*.

When he came to speak of his wife, with a voice rather tremulous at first, he said he would like to mention candidly a few of her faults. 'He then spoke,' records one of the congregation, 'of her excessive attachment to himself – of her judging and estimating others with regard to himself, etc., which had the effect (though in the simplicity of his character he meant it not so) of leading his hearers to think and ask, "If these were her chief faults, what were her excellences?" '

He published an artless account of her last days, and on the next 15 December, and for the four years following, he sent his friends an Anniversary poem and then ceased, saying that 'the Lord had healed the wound He made'. 'He has so indeed,' he told Wilberforce in 1797. 'I can say from my heart, He has done all things well. But the *scar* remains. She is still almost continuously present to my waking thoughts ... But the Lord is good. And tho' I have often foolishly thought that if the Desire of my eyes should be taken from me, the sun would shine, *to me*, in vain, I believe taking all things together I have been more comfortable since she left me than I was before.'

He survived Polly seventeen years, almost to the day. During this time he helped to found the London Missionary Society and the equally worldwide Church Missionary Society, thankful that they would take the gospel to those parts of Africa where he had committed his crimes, as he now saw them, of enslaving God's children and carrying them to misery and death in distant lands. He was also a founder of the British and Foreign Bible Society, progenitor of countless Bible societies around the world.

Polly's niece, their adopted daughter Betsy Catlett, kept house for him until 1801, when he was in his seventy-sixth year. Then she went mad and had to be confined in Bedlam. Newton was almost overwhelmed. His eyesight was failing, so each day a maidservant or friend would lead him to Bethlehem Hospital (Bedlam's proper name) and he would stand outside her window until told that she had waved her handkerchief; he walked slowly back, content that she knew his love for her did not fail. After a year Betsy recovered, married an optician and the three lived together at Coleman's Buildings: Betsy read to him, guided him when he walked, cut up his food and watched his every need.

He grew deaf and almost wholly blind as his eightieth year approached but he went on preaching. If he had been too inclined, when younger and over-busy, to think up his sermon between his house and his church, the increase of infirmity made his sermons even more discursive and ill planned. Yet his extraordinary perception of Scripture and of spiritual truth allowed his hearers to forget the defects. 'A most touching sermon,' wrote Elizabeth Fry's sister Catherine after attending 'old Newton's church' when in spiritual trouble. 'I can never forget the enjoyment and encouragement of that evening, and the delight of the whole church service on that occasion. It was what I wanted.'

His friends grew concerned at his increasing physical weakness and lapses of memory, the occasional bouts of depression which Newton attributed purely to old age, and his confusions in the pulpit. Richard Cecil ventured to suggest that perhaps he had better stop preaching. 'What!' exclaimed blind Newton when the suggestion penetrated his deafness. Raising his voice he shouted, 'Shall the old African blasphemer stop while he can speak?'

His Olney friend William Bull heard him ramble for fifty minutes on the words of Jesus: 'I, if I be lifted up from the earth will draw all men unto me.' Newton's understanding was in ruins, Bull reported, 'yet its ruins are precious, and the bits you pick up retain their intrinsic value, beauty and richness.'

In October 1806, when the nation celebrated the first anniversary of the Battle of Trafalgar, John Newton, aged eighty-one, was led to his pulpit to preach at a charity service to raise funds for the widows and wounded. The former midshipman sailed gallantly into action, all blindness and deafness ignored, but after a while he forgot what he was supposed to be preaching about, and paused. His curate had to mount the pulpit steps to remind him.

After that, he preached no more. Five months later in March 1807 Wilberforce's hard, long campaign achieved victory when Parliament abolished the British slave trade. For Newton it was yet another amazing grace that he should live to see Abolition; just as Wilberforce, twenty-six years afterwards, heard on his death-bed that slavery itself had been abolished throughout the British Empire.

Newton lingered until four days before Christmas 1807, 'packed and sealed,' as he quipped, 'and waiting for the post.'

He was hardly able to speak. William Jay leaned over the bed to catch his last words.

Newton whispered: 'My memory is nearly gone. But I remember two things: That I am a great sinner ...'

He paused for breath. '... And that Christ – *is a great Saviour!*'

Sources

MANUSCRIPTS

Bull MSS: letters, diaries etc. of John Newton and his wife in
the possession of Miss Catherine Bull of Newport Pagnell,
Buckinghamshire, a descendant of Newton's friend and
executor, the Rev. William Bull.

Olney MSS: Newton letters etc. and especially the manuscript
pages in his specially bound interleaved copy of *Letters to a
Wife*, at the Cowper-Newton Museum, Olney.

Public Record Office MSS: Logs and Muster Book of
H.M.S. *Harwich*.

Ridley Hall, Cambridge MSS: Newton's letters to John
Thornton.

William's Library MSS: Newton's letters to Dr. David
Jennings, at Dr. Williams's Library, Gordon Square, London
W.C.1.

PRINTED WORKS BY JOHN NEWTON (*not* a complete list)
An Authentic Narrative 1764
Olney Hymns (and preface) 1779
Cardiphonia 1781

Thoughts upon the Slave Trade 1788

The Christian Correspondent: letters to Captain Alexander
Clunie 1790

Letters to A Wife 1793

Memoirs of the Rev. W. Grimshaw 1797

Journal of A Slave Trader 1750–1754, edited, with an introduction, by Bernard Martin and Mark Spurrell 1962

OTHER WORKS

Bull, Josiah, *John Newton*: An Autobiography and Narrative,
with unpublished diary extracts 1868

Bull, Josiah, *Memorials of the Rev. William Bull* 1864

Cecil, Richard, *Memoirs of the Rev. John Newton* 1808
(includes autobiographical fragment by Newton)

Jay, William, *Autobiography* 1854

King, James, and Ryskamp, Charles (eds.) *The Letters and
Prose Writings of William Cowper*, Vol. I, 1750–1781 1979

Leaver, Robin A., *Olney Hymns 1779*, two articles in *Churchman*, 1979 (4) and 1980 (1)

Martin, Bernard, *John Newton*, 1950 (revised paperback edition, *An Ancient Mariner* 1960)

Stanhope, George, *The Christian's Pattern* 1708 (a translation
of Thomas à Kempis, *De Imitatione Christi*)

Shaftesbury, 3rd Earl of, *Characteristicks* 1711

Wright, Thomas, *The Life of William Cowper* 2nd edition,
1921

The Correspondence of William Cowper 4 vols. 1904